Germany and 'the West'

Germany and 'the West'
The History of a Modern Concept

Edited by
Riccardo Bavaj & Martina Steber

berghahn
NEW YORK · OXFORD
www.berghahnbooks.com

First published in 2015 by
Berghahn Books
www.berghahnbooks.com

© 2015, 2017 Riccardo Bavaj and Martina Steber
First paperback edition published in 2017

All rights reserved. Except for the quotation of short passages
for the purposes of criticism and review, no part of this book
may be reproduced in any form or by any means, electronic or
mechanical, including photocopying, recording, or any information
storage and retrieval system now known or to be invented,
without written permission of the publisher.

Library of Congress Cataloging-in-Publication Data
Germany and 'The West' : the history of a modern concept /
edited by Riccardo Bavaj & Martina Steber.
Includes bibliographical references and index.
ISBN 978-1-78238-597-4 (hardback : alk. paper) — ISBN 978-1-78533-504-4 (paperback) — ISBN 978-1-78238-598-1 (ebook)
1. Germany--Intellectual life--19th century. 2. Germany--Intellectual life--20th century. 3. Germany--Relations--Western countries. 4. Western countries--Relations--Germany. I. Bavaj, Riccardo, 1976- II. Steber, Martina.
DD67.G49 2015
909'.09821--dc23

2014033526

British Library Cataloguing in Publication Data
A catalogue record for this book is available from the British Library

ISBN 978-1-78238-597-4 (hardback)
ISBN 978-1-78533-504-4 (paperback)
ISBN 978-1-78238-598-1 (ebook)

Contents

Preface   viii

Introduction
     Germany and 'the West': The Vagaries of a Modern Relationship   1
     Riccardo Bavaj and Martina Steber

Part 1: Rises and Silences of 'the West'

Chapter 1   41
     In Search of 'the West': The Language of Political, Social and
     Cultural Spaces in the *Sattelzeit*, from about 1770 to the 1830s
     Bernhard Struck

Chapter 2   55
     The *Kaiserreich* and the *Kulturländer*: Conceptions of the
     West in Wilhelmine Germany, 1890–1914
     Mark Hewitson

Chapter 3   69
     The First World War and the Invention of 'Western Democracy'
     Marcus Llanque

Chapter 4   81
     Perceptions of the West in Twentieth-Century Germany
     Anselm Doering-Manteuffel

Part 2: East–West Entanglements

Chapter 5   97
     Russian and German Ideas of the West in the Long
     Nineteenth Century: Entanglements of Spatial Identities
     Denis Sdvižkov

Chapter 6 — 111
'Orient' and 'Occident', 'East' and 'West' in the Discourse of German Orientalists, 1790–1930
Douglas T. McGetchin

Chapter 7 — 124
German Jews and the West: Identification, Dissimilation and Marginalization around the Turn of the Century
Stefan Vogt

Part 3: Liberal Ambiguities and Strategies of 'Westernization'

Chapter 8 — 139
Between 'East' and 'West'? A Liberal Dilemma, 1830–1848/49
Benjamin Schröder

Chapter 9 — 152
Before 'the West': Rudolf von Gneist's English Utopia
Frank Lorenz Müller

Chapter 10 — 167
Weimar and 'the West': Liberal Social Thought in Germany, 1914–1933
Austin Harrington

Chapter 11 — 183
Germany and 'Western Democracies': The Spatialization of Ernst Fraenkel's Political Thought
Riccardo Bavaj

Part 4: Nationalist Self-Centredness and Conservative Adaptations

Chapter 12 — 201
'The West' in German Cultural Criticism during the Long Nineteenth Century
Thomas Rohkrämer

Chapter 13 — 216
No Place for 'the West': National Socialism and the 'Defence of Europe'
Philipp Gassert

Chapter 14 — 230
'The West', Tocqueville and West German Conservatism from the 1950s to the 1970s
Martina Steber

Part 5: Socialists between 'East' and 'West'

Chapter 15 249
'The West' as a Paradox in German Social Democratic
Thought: Britain as Counterfoil and Model, 1871–1945
Stefan Berger

Chapter 16 262
Bridge over Troubled Water: German Left-Wing
Intellectuals between 'East' and 'West', 1945–1949
Dominik Geppert

Chapter 17 277
Antipathy and Attraction to the West and Western
Consumerism in the German Democratic Republic
Katherine Pence

Selected Bibliography 293

List of Contributors 301

Index 307

Preface

This preface is written at the height of the Crimean crisis. Russia's annexation of Crimea challenges not only Ukraine's revolutionary government but also the European Union and the United States of America. In some respects, the constellation is reminiscent of pre-1989 frontlines and it is no wonder that many commentators draw analogies between the present situation and the Cold War. The omnipresence of Cold War semantics is hard to ignore: particularly fitting, of course, for a country that etymologically translates as 'borderland' (*Ukrajina*), the Crimean conflict is framed in terms of 'East' versus 'West'. Historians, however, may be reminded of a context that goes further back in time. After all, between 1853 and 1856, Crimea had already been at the centre of international power politics. When attacking the Ottoman Empire, Russia faced a coalition of France, Britain and Sardinia who, while harbouring their own ambitions, all supported the 'sick man of Europe'. Commentators in Europe and beyond interpreted the conflict in terms of both a geopolitical and a cultural East–West divide: an opposition between autocracy and freedom, backwardness and progress. This was also true for the German public at the time. While the German lands, notably Prussia and Austria-Hungary, remained neutral, their ideological position was fiercely contested. Should the German lands side with the 'Western powers' or were they supposed to pursue a 'middle path' between 'East' and 'West'? What was Germany's place on mental maps of Europe (and the world) in the mid-nineteenth century? Whilst East–West semantics were used more prominently than ever before, these questions evoked very different answers. Germany's relationship to 'the West' was deeply contested and would remain so for decades to come.

Obviously, this is not the case any more. Germany is an integral part of the Western alliance. The Federal Republic's close alignment with 'the

West' has been a key component of its founding consensus. The semantics of East and West not only framed the history of divided Germany but still exert power over the ways in which politics is conceived and national identity is constructed. An ideologized East–West terminology, however, gained purchase well before 1949. Contrary to what is commonly believed, it also emerged before 1914 when a global conflict was framed in terms of a culture war between Germany and 'the West'. As the example of the Crimean War suggests, the German concept of the West has a much longer history. Its socio-political usage can be traced back to the post-Napoleonic era. Against this background we believe that an exploration of the shifting meanings, political usages and transnational circulations of 'the West' can shed light on German history not merely of the twentieth but also of the nineteenth century.

This volume is the fruit of a long engagement with the history of Germany and 'the West' which started with a workshop at the German Historical Institute London (GHIL) in July 2009, co-organized by the GHIL and the University of St Andrews. Some of the papers given at that workshop are published in this volume, complemented by others which have been exclusively written for it (bibliographical references have been updated to September 2013). Without the patient, friendly and engaging cooperation of all the contributors over the years, this volume would have never seen the light of the day. Our sincerest thanks go to them.

The German Historical Institute London and the University of St Andrews supported the project both financially and intellectually. It has profited enormously from the valuable comments and ideas of Professor Andreas Gestrich (GHIL) and Dr Bernhard Struck (St Andrews), and we are grateful to both of them. Particular thanks go to our copy editor, Jon Ashby (Winchester), to Elisabeth Heistinger (Institut für Zeitgeschichte) for preparing the index, as well as to the anonymous referees at Berghahn Books.

Munich and St Andrews, March 2014

Riccardo Bavaj
University of St Andrews

Martina Steber
Institut für Zeitgeschichte München-Berlin

Introduction

GERMANY AND 'THE WEST'
The Vagaries of a Modern Relationship

Riccardo Bavaj and Martina Steber

'The West' is a central concept in German public discourse.[1] Typically the term refers to a political and cultural space constituted by parliamentary democracy, the rule of law, human rights, capitalism and mass consumerism. While its geographical scope is often only vaguely defined, 'the West' is usually understood as a political grouping led by the United States, militarily organized through NATO and institutionalized in a multitude of governmental and non-governmental organizations; as such, it is most certainly conceived as including Germany. As a cultural or civilizational entity, 'the West', though sometimes defined in terms of a common (Judeo-Christian or Latin) heritage, has even more amorphous boundaries, but to many commentators it is beyond question that Germany has culturally been part of 'the West' all along. However, despite these mental mappings, it has also been argued that Germany has stood somehow apart; that, for many decades, it has had a rather troubled relationship with 'the West', travelling on a *Sonderweg* (special path) that diverged from the 'Western' trajectory. According to this argument it was only during the second half of the twentieth century that Germans joined 'the West' – and some sooner than others.

This volume does not seek to settle the question about Germany's 'actual' relationship to the West. Its principal aim is to historicize this question. When have Germans – politicians, scholars, writers and intellectuals – talked about 'the West'? What have they meant by it? Why have they referred to it in the first place? It is the intricate history of German discourses on 'the West' that is the subject of this book.

Master Narratives and Germany's 'Arrival in the West'

Today, rhetorical registers upholding 'the West' are far from unchallenged. In academic discourse, particularly, deployment of 'the West' as an analytical category has lost much of its intellectual plausibility (as has the concept of a German *Sonderweg*). In the wider public sphere, however, 'the West' is still a prominent point of reference. It is only now, moreover, that a German scholar-cum-intellectual has published a *History of the West*.[2] While the English-speaking book market has been liberally supplied with histories of the West for more than a century, Heinrich August Winkler has been the first to write one for a German audience. A multi-thousand-page trilogy, with a fourth volume in the making, this work is a performative act hard to ignore. It makes a statement no German is supposed to miss when browsing in the bookshop: Germans should care about the West because they belong to it. This theme was already the thrust of his bestseller *Germany's Long Road West*, which was published ten years after German reunification and quickly gained the status of a master narrative for the Berlin Republic. After centuries of fateful deviation from the Western norm, climaxing in Nazism's 'revolt against the political ideas of the West', Germans were to be congratulated on finally arriving in the Western haven.[3]

Winkler follows in a tradition of previous German Westernizers. His master narrative is itself part of the history of Germany's relationship with 'the West'. He has become for the 'Berlin Republic' what political scientists such as Karl Dietrich Bracher, Kurt Sontheimer and Alexander Schwan represented in the 'Bonn Republic'.[4] His scholarship and intellectual commitment reflect the legacy of a whole tradition of 'Western' missionaries: Ernst Fraenkel, Richard Löwenthal and Ralf Dahrendorf, to name but a few.[5] In contemporary Germany, Winkler has been backed up by further enthusiastic Westernizers. Udo Di Fabio, for instance, a legal scholar and former judge of Germany's Constitutional Court, has issued a fervent plea for a reappropriation of such 'Western values' as individual freedom, practical reason, civic virtue and the Weberian work ethic, reflecting at length upon 'Western culture', a 'Western value system' and the West's 'cultural self-endangerment'.[6]

The latter aspect is nothing new, as 'Westerners' have worried about the cultural cohesion and inner strength of their 'civilization', or 'community', for more than a century. Samuel Huntington's hotly debated *Clash of Civilizations* (1996) and the 9/11 terrorist attacks (2001), however, have given the subject of the 'inner fitness' and cultural self-awareness of 'Westerners' a new urgency. Political differences over the Iraq Wars (2003–2011), moreover, have sparked discussions about a hiatus within the 'Atlantic Community', an unbridgeable gap between the European Continent and what some commentators have called 'the Anglosphere'. Two 'Wests', they argue, are one too many, and may indicate that none exists at all.[7] Thus, while some commentators have been pointing to Germany's 'arrival in the West' with the establishment of the Berlin Republic,[8] it has seemed to others as though the longed-for point of perspective has vanished – not merely in relative terms because Germany has reached it, but because of a decline of 'the West' itself. Did Germans arrive in 'the West' only as its 'twilight' fell?[9]

Indeed, the new German wave of embracing 'the West' has come at a time when 'the West's' existence appears in several ways precarious. It may, of course, be argued that militant Islamism is replacing Soviet communism to provide a new alterity robust enough to keep 'the West' alive (paradoxical as this may sound). Yet commentators emphasize 'the West's' inner dividedness, as expressed in the catchy phrase 'Americans are from Mars and Europeans are from Venus',[10] or they complain about the 'pusillanimity' of 'Westerners'. Beset by nagging self-doubts and losing old certainties to a relativism in values instilled by postmodern, postcolonial questioning of 'Western paradigms', 'Westerners' are deemed unfit for the political and economic challenges of the present day. As the U.S. stands to be economically outpaced by China, the British historian, political adviser and media star Niall Ferguson urges 'Westerners' to 'reboot' the programme of 'Western civilization'.[11] Like Winkler's *History of the West* but geared towards a transatlantic readership, Ferguson's book is an attempt to boost 'Western' confidence and self-assurance. Both works are part of an extensive literature committed to stabilizing 'Western identity' in a time when 'the West' has been challenged as a political actor, economic leader, cultural entity and (to quote Arnold Toynbee's famous dictum) 'intelligible unit of historical study'.[12] The 'Western Civilization' curricula that have been taught in U.S. universities for almost a century have long lost the moral power they once exuded in the heydays of the Cold War. The 'Western Civ' narrative was an integral part of the 'liberal consensus' that crystallized in the 1940s, providing U.S. citizens with a sense of who they were, and legitimizing the United States' position as the spearhead of 'Western progress'.[13]

Approaching the West Conceptually: A Historiographical Tour d'Horizon

The present edited volume, alas, has little 'Western' morale-boosting to offer. Instead of attempting to strengthen Germany's 'Western identity', this book makes the very process of 'Western' identity-shaping a subject of investigation. When, why and for whom did 'the West' offer a central point of reference in German history? How did Germans locate their nation on mental maps permeated by the presence of 'the West'? Did they seek to anchor Germany firmly in the realm of a 'Western value community', or did they try to shape German identities in opposition to an alien, if not inimical, 'West'? In what ways did references to 'the West' serve as a means of negotiating moral values, fighting for political agendas, mobilizing people, envisioning world orders and imagining national futures? Is 'the West' a concept of the twentieth century, as has often been assumed, or is there a need to trace it through a much longer period to explore the depth of its layers of meaning? These and other questions are at the heart of this book, which offers a first, pioneering attempt at historicizing the relationship between Germany and this elusive 'West'.

For a long time, historians who have dealt with Germany's relationship to 'the West' have worked largely from the notion of a 'Western' container space – circumscribed by timeless boundaries and unaffected by what has happened within it.[14] The historicization of the *Sonderweg* thesis has done little to induce a historicization of its flip side, German concepts of what 'the West' might be;[15] and the *Geschichtliche Grundbegriffe*, generally thin on spatial concepts, have nothing to offer in this regard either.[16] There are, however, notable examples of research, on which this volume can draw.

First, the groundbreaking works of Heinz Gollwitzer and Dieter Groh, published some decades ago, offer invaluable information on German notions of the West.[17] Secondly, numerous studies have shed light on the 'ideas of 1914' and the polemical opposition between 'German culture' and 'Western civilization' which characterized the First World War as a 'war of ideas'. This dichotomy, closely related to the emerging distinction between 'Western democracy' and a German *Volksstaat* or *Volksgemeinschaft* ('people's state' or 'people's community'), fuelled notions of German exceptionalism and shaped a consciousness of the nation having its own positive *Sonderweg*.[18] Thirdly, historians have analysed conservative notions of a 'Christian *Abendland*' and socialist visions of 'Europe' as a 'third force', prevalent in West Germany's political culture following the end of the Second World War. Directed against the 'Western' model of liberal democracy, both concepts were imbued with anti-'Western' meanings but were in accordance with the West's stance against Bolshevism.[19] Fourthly, Patrick Jackson has published a study on West Germany's incorporation into NATO, which investigates the legitimating use of what he calls the 'rhetorical commonplace' of 'Western civilization' during the political formation of the 'Atlantic Community'.[20] Lastly, the Tübingen-based 'Westernization' project, carried out in the 1990s, offers another vital stimulus to the analysis of West Germany's relationship with 'the West'. It examines intellectual transfers that helped ideas of a pluralist democracy and market economy take root in the political culture of the Federal Republic of Germany (FRG). Specifically intended to account for West Germany's intellectual transformation between 1945 and 1970, the analytical tool of 'Westernization' assumes the emergence of an 'Atlantic value community' grounded in ideas of 'consensus liberalism' and 'consensus capitalism'.[21]

Some of the most vibrant fields of research focussing on 'the West', however, are those that go beyond the scope of German history. First of all, Russian history offers one of the richest hunting grounds for finding ways in which 'the West' has been imagined. Indeed, to trace its conceptual evolution, one must of necessity look to the east, for Russia emerged as the antonym that in many ways shaped the contrasting identity of what lay outside 'the West'.[22] On the other side of the fence, French and British Russophobia was a major constituting factor in the crystallization of this concept.[23] Recently, the historiographical focus on nineteenth-century Russia and Western European Russophobia has been complemented by studies on conceptions of 'the West' in East Central Europe and the Soviet Union. For communist societies, 'the West' often stood both as 'the gold standard for advanced development' and as 'a hostile order soon to be, if not in many ways already, surpassed', in the words of Michael David-Fox.[24]

A second fruitful field of research is centred on U.S. America. Almost concomitantly with the emerging historicization of representations of 'the West' in the 'Eastern Bloc', scholars have begun to examine the production and dissemination of notions of an 'Atlantic Community' that fed on ideas of 'Western civilization' and, in turn, influenced them. Such notions have been developed on both sides of the Atlantic. Since the First World War, the U.S. has been both a prominent subject and a main producer of conceptualizations of 'the West'. It was only with reluctance, however, that U.S. Americans abandoned the exceptionalist notion of their country as the self-sufficient 'city upon a hill', enjoying 'free security' because of the great Atlantic divide, and came to adopt anti-isolationist ideas of American embeddedness in the imagined community of an Atlantic 'West'. (American exceptionalism has, of course, remained part of U.S. political culture.) Scholars have placed great emphasis on Cold War strategies of empowerment, domination and securitization pursued by transnational agencies such as the Congress for Cultural Freedom, which sought to create an intellectual Atlantic Community by spreading the gospel of an overtly anti-communist 'West'.[25]

In a third relevant field, Anglo-American scholarship has turned to late nineteenth- and early twentieth-century Britain to trace the emergence of 'the West' as a prominent socio-political concept there. While the literary critic Christopher GoGwilt has shown that, between the 1880s and the 1920s, the concept of the West eclipsed the concept of Europe as the pivotal ideological term in the register of British imperialist rhetoric,[26] the geographer Alastair Bonnett argues that the idea of the West came to displace the idea of whiteness in academic and political discourse. Since it avoided untenable assumptions about racial homogeneity without precluding racist overtones, the notion 'Western' trumped the idea of 'white civilization'. Of course, as Bonnett concedes, the suggested correlation in rhetorical patterns between 'white decay' and 'the rise of the West' is far from clear-cut and requires further investigation. Yet his approach, relating 'the West' to other identities and accounting for rhetorical innovations as problem-solving devices, is promising: it helps to explain what people were doing when they employed the concept of the West and why they started using it so extensively in the first place.[27]

Lastly, there is a growing literature on representations of the West beyond Europe and America. Often informed by theoretical and thematic concerns about postcolonialism and inspired by Edward Said's pioneering, if controversial, work *Orientalism* (1978), several studies have shed light on what 'Western civilization' was conceived to be amongst people in India, China, Japan and the Muslim world from the mid nineteenth century onward. A term with multiple meanings,[28] 'Occidentalism' has become the watchword of this blossoming field of research.[29] Research on Occidentalism counteracts the Eurocentric perspective of a 'world revolution of Westernization'[30] and focuses on processes of non-Western self-assertion.[31] It shows the deployment of conceptions of the West to shape national identities in non-Western regions that have become increasingly incorporated into the 'communicative networks' of Europe and America.[32] Too little is known, however, about the entanglement of European concepts of the West with the notions of 'Westernization' and 'the Occident' discussed in India, Japan, China and the Muslim world. The context of globalization, imperialism and non-Western self-assertion around the turn of the twentieth century most certainly furthered the evolution and circulation of powerful notions of Western civilization.[33] But the role of, say, Western European orientalists as mediators who disseminated these notions at home yet remains to be explored – and a comparison is needed (especially) between British, French and German oriental experts.[34]

In fact, historians are still in the dark about many facets of the discursive construction of the West – despite the fruitful discussions on 'metageography' and 'mental maps' informed by the 'spatial turn'.[35] Considering the gaps in historical scholarship, this volume is no more than a first attempt to tackle Germany's relationship with 'the West' during the course of modern history. Its general approach is to trace German notions of the West through an analysis of the communicative contexts, semantic fields and discursive networks in which the various deployments of the concept have been embedded.

Informed by the methodology of historical semantics, this volume examines 'the West' as a spatial category manifest in its discursive constructions. It focuses on the lexical manifestations of the West (*der Westen, westlich, westlerisch* and so on), including their relations to neighbouring concepts such as *Abendland* and *Okzident*. While both these 'Occidental' concepts reach back to antiquity, 'the West' is a modern concept. As the work of Reinhart Koselleck has shown, the vocabulary of German political languages acquired its modern meanings in the period between 1750 and 1850, a period he calls *Sattelzeit* (saddle period). Koselleck identifies four dimensions of conceptual change: democratization, temporalization, ideologization (*Ideologisierbarkeit*) and politicization. This analytical framework has been adopted and modified by younger conceptual historians such as Jörn Leonhard and Willibald Steinmetz, whose works provide valuable insights into the study of historical semantics.[36] Inspired by these insights, this volume is based on several assumptions about the transformation of the directional concept 'the west' into the socio-political concept 'the West'.[37]

First, historical actors started using the concept in a general, abstract sense, referring to a group of countries, a civilization or a way of life. Use of the concept helped to register, process and articulate historical experiences; it homogenized space, reduced complexity and created orientation. Second, people started using the concept in a dynamic sense, referring to the past, present and future of a more or less well-defined area, as distinct from other parts of the world. Against the background of an increasing acceleration of developments, they temporalized 'the West', rendered it a concept of the future (*Zukunftsbegriff*) and endowed it with diverse horizons of expectation: notions of progress and modernity. A geographical direction thus became temporalized space, as 'the West' was placed in the temporal continuum of philosophies of history, with distinct orders of temporality attached to it. 'The West', in other words, metamorphosed into 'TimeSpace',[38] the dynamic quality of which became most evident in neologisms such as 'Westernizers' and 'Westernization'. Third, historical actors started using the concept in a political sense, referring to notions of reason, liberty, democracy, constitutional government, the rule of law, the middle class, private property, individuality and so on. They employed the concept as an effective tool in political debates, used it to advance political agendas and fought over its 'correct' meaning. Political languages became spatialized, and previously universal concepts became enclosed in a space called 'the West' (which, however, might still have referred in a Hegelian fashion to a state of universal progress attainable in principle by every part of the world). A relational concept from its inception, 'the West' acquired a decisive polemical thrust and a clear ideological edge through the polarized opposition to distinct antonyms such as 'Eastern barbarism', 'Oriental despotism' or the 'Asiatic mode of production'. These 'asymmetrical counter-concepts' became constitutive of 'the West'.[39]

A New World Order? The Birth of 'the West'

The socio-political concept of the West is a child of the post-Napoleonic era. It found its way into German political languages against the background of a general spatialization of political thought and a reconfiguration of global mental maps that took place between 1780 and 1830.[40] It was especially in the period from the 1820s to the 1850s that the concept of the West crystallized, developing those layers of meaning that provided the semantic pool future generations would draw from. 'The West' was integrated into a spatial coordinate system, which, by and large, has remained stable until the present day. Not only was the German concept of the West not born in the twentieth century (as many scholars have tended to believe); its twentieth-century meanings were in no small measure defined by its origins in the preceding century: in particular, its association with notions of progress, liberty, civilization and modernity; a corresponding relationship between cultural traits and political values and institutions; and a geographical anchoring of normative assumptions in the past, present and future of, above all, France, the United States and Britain. The history of the German concept of the West, however, is anything but straightforward. Though fairly well established in German political discourse by the middle of the nineteenth century, it was more or less forgotten by its end. It was resurrected in 1914 to represent everything that was considered 'un-German', but was eventually reinstated and emphatically embraced by the politicians and political commentators of the FRG.

Against the background of an emerging liberal–conservative divide in post-Napoleonic Europe and the gradual ascendancy of Russia and the

United States, European political thinkers increasingly distinguished between the constitutional states of 'the West' and the 'Eastern powers' of the Holy Alliance.[41] The political reasoning about the current and future international order was the first of three significant discursive spaces in which 'the West' – as a new concept distinct from both the *Okzident* and the *Abendland* – entered political discourse.[42] With 'the West' increasingly associated with 'revolution' and liberal constitutionalism, moreover, and with the U.S. being geographically located westward from European shores, it was no wonder that America became incorporated into European mental maps of 'the West'. Following Alexis de Tocqueville's prognosis of a global East–West conflict, the Hessian councillor Ludwig von Meseritz, writing in the *Jahrbücher der Geschichte und Staatskunst* in 1836, used the terms 'Eastern Empire' for Russia and 'Western Free State' for the U.S., the former representing 'aristocracy' and the latter 'democracy'.[43] This spatio-political terminology had become fairly common in the discourse on the new world order. The once directional concept 'the west' had been transformed into an abstract category that homogenized space and conveyed political values.

The idea of a 'West' consisting of the liberal states of Europe with the U.S. would not have gained credence, however, without a strong historical-philosophical idea supporting it. This emerged from the second discursive space in which the concept of the West was shaped – one concerned with a historical-philosophical model of progress. This discursive space was decisive for the temporalization of the concept. It became endowed with horizons of expectation and increasingly encapsulated notions of progress and promises of the future. The development of human history was seen as starting in the east and progressing to the west – an idea rooted in medieval Christian theology.[44]

In the early nineteenth century, this notion lost its theological meaning and became embedded in a secular philosophy of history.[45] As its most important appropriator, Georg Wilhelm Friedrich Hegel merged it with the idea of progress: 'World history', he asserted, 'travels from east to west; for Europe is the absolute end of history, just as Asia is the beginning'. Hegel claimed that human history began in Asia but would end in 'the West'.[46] The 'East' figured as a counter-model to an enlightened 'West': in character it was static, without history, its people unaware of their individuality. It was fettered to patriarchal structures and ruled by theocratic regimes; its societies were governed by violence. Hegel's 'West', to be sure, meant contemporary Europe. For him, the U.S. was nothing but a European offshoot with no independent worth.[47]

While Hegel's historical philosophy of the West was very influential – one may think of Karl Marx's theory of material progress, which disparaged the 'Asiatic mode of production' and was no less Eurocentric[48] – not everybody thought that the westward march of history would stop at Europe. German authors of the 1820s who were disappointed with the political situation in Europe advocated an alternative model of development, if equally grounded in historical-philosophical notions of East–West progress. August Graf von Platen, Nikolaus Lenau and Adelbert von Chamisso, for example, all believed progress to have moved out of Europe to America, which had become part of 'the West' as a civilizational idea.[49] Furthermore, Hegel's concept of a Eurocentric 'West' and an oppositional 'East' was an explicit counter-model to the Romanticist understanding of the 'Orient' prevalent in some literary and orientalist circles at the time.[50] Some German Romanticists believed they could find in 'the East' what had (allegedly) been lost to 'the West': spirituality, transcendence, harmony and eternity. For them 'the Orient', and not 'the West', figured as an ideal place of longing.[51] Douglas McGetchin shows in this volume, however, that a more complex view of the Orient was fostered by Romantic philologists who made Indian, Asian and Arabic texts accessible to the German public.

The third discursive space in which the concept of the West emerged consisted of debates about the place Europeans assigned to Russia on the mental map of Europe. Up until the early nineteenth century, Europe had been thought of as having a clear North–South divide, with Russia firmly in the North. From the 1820s, this conception changed: Russia came to be seen more as an 'Eastern' power.[52] The notion of a backward Russia at the head of 'Eastern Europe' formed a counterfoil to 'Western Europe's' association with 'revolution' and reflected contemporary political experiences in the era of bourgeois revolution. Bernhard Struck's analysis of German travelogues, giving an account of travels to regions in what is today known as East Central Europe, confirms this view. From the 1820s onward, German travellers, greatly influenced by the 1830 revolutions, began to replace the traditional North–South mapping of Europe with a perceived East–West division, mirroring the division between authoritarian and liberal forms of government. With the Crimean War this process of moving Russia from the North to the East on western European mental maps was finalized. And in these new maps, 'the West' had more definite outlines – clearly shaped by asymmetrical counter-concepts such as 'Russia', 'Eastern Europe' and 'the East'.

From the late 1820s, the spatio-political categories that emerged from this process of remapping and recoding were taken up in Russian political discourse itself. Impassioned debates on Russia's identity were intimately linked to discussions about 'Westernization'. These started with Pëtr Chaadaev's *First Philosophical Letter* (1829/36), a reaction to the authoritarian regime of Nicholas I after his crushing of the Decembrist uprising of 1825. They continued in the discourses of the 'Slavophiles', who coined the term 'Westernizers' (*zapadniki*) as a derogatory expression; and belief in an East–West dichotomy hardened among pan-Slavists like Nikolaĭ Danilevskiĭ, who propagated an aggressive Russian expansionism and constructed a clear-cut distinction between a Romano-Germanic Europe doomed to decline and a Slavic 'historico-cultural type' destined to prevail.[53] The pan-Slavist critique of 'Western' values was to be embraced with enthusiasm in early twentieth-century Germany and was to leave a far-reaching mark on how Germans conceived 'the West'. The degree to which German and Russian discourses on 'the West' were intertwined in the long nineteenth century is brought out by Denis Sdvižkov. In fact, German notions of the West cannot be understood without due consideration of German-Russian entanglements.

'The West' as it emerged in German political discourse between the 1820s and the 1850s was a multifaceted concept. It could relate (1) to an entity comprising Europe and the U.S.; (2) to European countries with a liberal constitution that stood in opposition to the Holy Alliance; (3) to the United States and France, as the countries representing 'revolution'; and (4) to the Romano-Germanic civilization. This ambiguity made it difficult for German commentators to situate the German lands on the newly emerging mental maps of Europe and the world. However, 'the West' usually derived its meanings from an oppositional positioning against 'the East' and an association with civility and progress. The concept underwent processes typical of the *Sattelzeit*: it acquired abstract meanings, which made it an attractive tool to reduce complexity; it was temporalized, as 'the West' transformed into a 'TimeSpace' embedded in philosophies of history; and it was politicized, as it was increasingly used to convey notions of freedom, democracy and individuality. These would become the key themes which in many ways would characterize the German concept of the West to this day. Its power to shape national and political identities has varied over time, but it was by no means confined to the twentieth century.

Liberal Ambivalence and Conservative Negations: Conceptions of 'East' and 'West' in the Mid Nineteenth Century

During the 1840s and 1850s, the discourse on a new world order and the remapping of Europe filtered into discussions on Germany's own political future. In the German lands, the mental mapping of the world was inextricably intertwined with a concept of international relations as alignments informed by ideological considerations. Thinking about world politics in terms of freedom versus servility, enlightened reason versus irrationality and progress versus stagnation was especially prevalent among liberals who frequently expressed their thoughts in East–West terminology (which they applied to Europe as well as to the wider world).[54] Consequently, 'the West' acquired an essentially liberal colouring. However, the liberal embrace of 'the West' was not unequivocal. Adoption of the notion by the various strands of liberal thought at the time tended to mirror the wide range of liberal ideas about European politics in general and the German place within this arena in particular.

The most enthusiastic supporters of 'the West' were situated on the liberal Left. The poet Ferdinand Freiligrath, for example, emphatically embraced the notion of a free 'West',[55] as did his like-minded contemporary, the Young Hegelian Arnold Ruge.[56] As Benjamin Schröder shows in this volume, however, *Vormärz* liberals in the Prussian Rhineland barely availed themselves of the concept of the West as a significant tool in political debates, even if, between the revolutions of 1830 and 1848–1849, they did temporalize the newly emerging East–West divide in terms of a backward 'East' and a 'civilized West'. The inner-Prussian antagonism between eastern and western provinces lent further credence to this framework. That they rarely donned the vestments of avowed Westerners reflected their ambiguous self-positioning in Europe's 'centre', between a French 'West' and a Russian 'East'. It was, above all, their Russophobia that allowed them to escape their perplexing dilemma: namely, to feel attached to the 'civilized peoples of Europe' and the 'liberal ideas' of France, but to belong to a state – Prussia – which they felt was politically backward. To circumvent this dilemma, the Rhenish liberals favoured talk about a German 'middle position' between 'East' and 'West'.

This dilemma of Rhenish *Vormärz* liberals emanated from a general ambivalence German liberals felt towards the concept of the West as it had evolved from the 1820s. On the one hand, these liberals were longing for the blessings of 'the West': civil liberties, constitutionalism, parliamentarianism and the rule of law. On the other, due to the increasing dominance of nationalism in liberal thought, it became ever more difficult to imagine Germany as part of a 'West' so closely identified with France and America. Moreover, these two countries were viewed rather differently among the various groups of liberals, whose appraisals ranged from affirmation to outright rejection. Hence, their positioning vis-à-vis 'the West' became a marker of difference between liberals themselves.

The range of attitudes in German liberalism becomes clear when the political thought of Rudolf von Gneist is considered. Unlike the Rhenish

Vormärz liberals, this Prussian legal scholar, who belonged with the mainstream German liberals of the post-1851 period, did not use the concept of the West at all. As Frank Lorenz Müller demonstrates, Gneist was a typical advocate of moderate national liberalism. He condemned the French and American Revolutions and championed a form of government purportedly achieved in post-1688 England. It was the combination of Francophobia and Anglophilia, accompanied by a lack of interest in the United States, that prevented him from deploying the concept of the West – a concept that was, after all, closely related to revolutionary change.

For many liberals, however, the Crimean War reaffirmed the notion of an East–West divide along the lines of freedom versus despotism. While in the 1840s the opposition between a civilized 'West' and a barbaric 'East' had gained common currency and had been further promoted by the 1848/49 revolution, the years of the Crimean War saw the climax of political East–West semantics in the nineteenth century.[57] In the case of Gustav Diezel, a leading national-liberal thinker on international relations, the Crimean War even prompted a recoding of the mental map. Previously convinced that a united Germany could only be realized 'in a battle against East and West',[58] Diezel now argued that Germany was part of a 'West' – a 'Romano-Germanic West' – that was fighting against the 'Slavic East'.[59] In reaction to Russia's advance to the west and the overriding concern it caused, Germany's location had shifted on national-liberal mental maps. The writings of the liberal orientalist Jakob Philipp Fallmerayer, who warned against a Russian threat to 'the West', provide another example, which shows that, once again, an antagonistic stance towards Russia helped assuage the general ambivalence felt towards 'the West'.[60] However, this ambivalence did not disappear: anti-French feeling remained a defining element in liberal thought for decades to come.[61]

While liberal reasoning about Germany and 'the West' was marked by ambiguities, conservatives did not face the problem of reconciling conflicting poles on their mental maps. Friedrich Schlegel, writing in the early 1820s, rejected the idea of East–West progress in human history and discredited the often apocalyptic prophesies of future American or Slavic world orders. Instead he reaffirmed the vitality and singularity of Christian Europe.[62] Equally negative towards the liberal association of political ideology and East–West mapping then current was the Prussian Conservative Christian Adolf Friedrich Widmann. In 1854, at the height of the Crimean War, he made the very process of conceptual transformation, and particularly the politicization of geographical categories, an object of his criticism.[63]

To ignore or repudiate the new terminology altogether was one possible reaction for German conservatives faced with the remapping of Europe. Another option was to appropriate it, but in a critical way. Such was Joseph Edmund Jörg's strategy. Analysing the global situation at the time of the Crimean War, this leading Catholic publicist eloquently advanced a Catholic Conservative notion of the West. He championed Christian Europe – Catholic of course – which he pitted against Protestant America and Orthodox Russia, an individualistic 'West' and a barbarian 'East'.[64] The German powers, meanwhile, had been put into a 'quandary' by the divisions of the Crimean War: they could ally themselves neither with 'the West' nor with 'the East'. So they were bound to pursue their own way, collectively forming a 'truly conservative German third power in the centre' (*deutscher Dritter in der Mitte*) – strong, united and embedded in a Catholic-dominated Central Europe.[65] Jörg was part of a prominent, if multifaceted strand of thought which posited a German middle position between 'East' and 'West' and which, decades later, would rise to particular prominence.[66]

The Marginalization of 'the West' in the Second Half of the Nineteenth Century

During the second half of the nineteenth century, following the end of the Crimean War, German conservatives no longer shared in the global outlook and critical appropriation of the ideological East-versus-West idea once prevalent. Typically they were caught up in nation-centred patterns of perception, as Thomas Rohkrämer shows for key exponents of German cultural criticism. Like Jörg, they argued for a strong, united German state but, unlike him, they wished it to be based on a common Germanic identity – not on the tradition of the Catholic Church. This emphasis on Germandom gained special momentum with the spread of racial lines of thought from the mid nineteenth century onwards. To be sure, this racial logic was primarily employed to bring out alleged essential differences between a 'Slavic East' and a 'Romano-Germanic West'; but it also undermined the notion of 'Western' commonalities and gave pseudoscientific evidence to the German-French antagonism. The stress on racial factors in international relations, including those within the western part of Europe, increased the doubts Germans felt about their place vis-à-vis 'the West', doubts that had beset liberal circles from the 1830s. With the racialization of the German-French antagonism, these doubts seemed to be resolved: French liberal models could not apply to Germany. This line of argument would eventually prove effective enough to call the whole idea of a progressive liberal unity of 'the West' into question. Moreover, the pan-ideologies of the nineteenth century that were rooted in ethnic convictions – pan-Germanism, pan-Romanism, pan-Anglo-Saxonism – presented compelling alternatives to the concept of the West.

A powerful exception, however, was to be found in German perceptions of pan-Slavism, which merged with racial concepts of the East. Mark Hewitson calls attention to the anti-Russian consensus in Wilhelmine Germany which transported well-known stereotypes about 'the East' into the twentieth century and invested them with racial thought. The 'Slavic East' appeared as an inferior civilization and functioned as the absolute 'Other' against which German identity was constructed.[67] The racial categorization applied to 'the Slavs' was also applied to another group from 'the East' – Jewish immigrants who had left Russia to settle in Germany. In this case both anti-Semitic and anti-Eastern stereotypes combined in a toxic mixture. Above all, the *Ostjuden* presented a challenge to the Jewish communities already established in Germany, among whom a discourse about 'the West' and 'the East' developed, which Stefan Vogt introduces here.[68]

The racialization of how the East was perceived was one reason why it remained a defining element in Imperial Germany's mental mapping.[69] Thus the concept of the West was continually used in contexts relating to Russia during the German *Kaiserreich*,[70] and significantly so during the Russo-Japanese War of 1904–1905.[71] But in the wider discursive context, the concept of the West did not reemerge in full use until 1914. It had largely lost its temporal qualities and was bereft of the horizons of expectation previously ascribed to it. For most Germans, 'the West' was neither a spectre nor a beacon of promise; it had ceased to be a concept of the future, good or bad.

In addition to an increasing racialization of political thought, new bonds of loyalty to the ascendant nation state undermined civilizational concepts such as 'the West'. The European state system changed profoundly in the 1860s, and even more so with the unification of Germany in the next decade. While the idea of a European order based on a multilateral contract system had guided international politics between the Congress of Vienna and the Crimean War, the period from 1870 to the end of the Second World War was characterized by autonomous nation states each pursuing their individual power politics, not letting their sovereignty be curtailed by multilateral commitments.[72] Discussion about international relations increasingly centred on the power politics of nation states, their alliances and ententes, and it largely abstained from reflections on supranational commonalities. The focus in

Bismarckian Germany was on *Realpolitik* – allegedly non-ideological power politics (though in fact the concept was itself ideological).[73] This continued in Wilhelmine Germany, with its ambitions on the world stage. Discussions on international relations became driven not by civilizational ideas but by economic deliberations, as in the *Weltreichslehre* around the turn of the century,[74] or alternatively by pan-ethnic notions of a battle between Germanic, Romanic and Slavic 'races'.[75] Liberal thinkers, who, from the 1820s through to the 1850s had espoused the concept of the West, now invested their hopes in the nation state, which they saw as the true progressive force. Progress would be rooted in the strength of the nation, and needed measuring according to national parameters. The Hegelian idea that progress in history would advance from east to west lost credence.

Elsewhere, of course, civilizational ideas were common currency. Established imperial powers such as Britain had long been advancing the moral necessity of civilizing missions.[76] What was more, a specifically 'Western civilization' became a powerful concept in Britain and the United States around the turn of the century.[77] While the racialization of political thought undermined conceptions of the West in Germany, the language of 'Western civilization' was reconcilable with racist and social Darwinist assumptions in the established colonial empires. Not least because the language of 'Western civilization' now provided Germany's main colonialist competitors with their major rhetorical device, the concept of the West lost its appeal in the Wilhelmine era: Germans who were eager to find their own, particular role in the world political game could not simply copy their competitors' ideological underpinning of colonialism. This remained a problem throughout the period of German colonialism, as embarking on a 'German cultural mission' did not have a power of persuasion comparable to the concept of spreading 'Western civilization'.[78] As far as it is possible to judge on the basis of current research, even in the colonies 'German culture' does not appear to have been commonly used as a means to distinguish the German civilizing mission from those of colonial competitors.[79] Indeed, the binary opposition of 'culture' and 'civilization', associated respectively with 'Germanness' and 'the West' and coming to great prominence during the First World War, was only rudimentarily developed from the turn of the century onwards.[80]

To sum up: from the 1860s the concept of the West was marginalized in the political language of Germans. It had largely lost its future-oriented meanings and barely provided an effective rhetorical tool for framing ideological views and advancing political agendas. Its sweeping rise in 1914 was not to be expected.

Germany against 'the West': The First World War and the Intellectual Roots of a War of Words

During the First World War, 'the West' reappeared as a powerful concept in German political discourse. It became a weapon deployed to mobilize people, a rallying cry that wielded affective power and was used to forge a united body politic. While it had been endowed with a relatively wide range of meanings in the nineteenth century, between 1914 and 1918 its frame of reference was narrowed down and its content largely stripped of ambiguities. The enemy Allies, Britain, France and the U.S., were 'the West' and it was around them that the geographical and power-political contours of the concept were redefined. Values such as individual freedom, constitutional government and the rule of law formed the ideological core of this 'West' and were typically subsumed as 'the ideas of 1789'.[81] Most prominently, Thomas Mann propagated the 'ideas of 1914' in his *Reflections of a Nonpolitical Man* (*Betrachtungen eines Unpolitischen*), written between 1915 and 1918 and particularly directed against France. While the *Reflections* were primarily concerned with aesthetic traditions and conceptions, they were also a devastating denunciation of democracy, which was presented as an eminently 'Western' and thus 'un-German' institution.[82] Characteristically, Mann merged the civilization-versus-culture antithesis with his semantics of 'the West': 'civilization' was all 'West', 'culture' all German and there was no reconciliation possible, for the antithesis was exclusive. This binary logic was easily transferable to a concept like 'the West', which – a relational concept from its inception – had been shaped more by its antonyms than by anything else. While previously the most prominent antonym of 'the West' had been the Russian 'East', 'Germany' now became an equally prominent antonym, as most Germans seemed determined to resist any 'Westernization' (*Verwestlichung*). The concept of the West was repoliticized and retemporalized only to create a distance from the horizons of expectation inscribed in it and to throw German visions of the future into sharp relief.

The amalgamation of the semantics of 'civilization versus culture' with those of 'the West' was decisive in the formation of conflicting political conceptions that satisfied Germans' need for clarity, coherence and an unambiguous ideological edge in the war of words waged from 1914. Following the breakdown of Russian tsardom and the U.S. entry into the war, these political conceptions were made more specific through another semantic amalgamation, that of 'democracy' and 'the West'. As Marcus Llanque explains, 'Western democracy' became both the Allied shibboleth and, for Germans, the 'un-German Other'. This polarization was furthered, moreover, by the restriction of public debate in wartime.[83]

On an unprecedented scale, the concept of the West was deployed to homogenize space, to reduce complexity and to polemicize in political battle.

Despite the absence of a pronounced concept of the West in political discourse at the turn of the century, Germany's new self-image as 'the West's' counterpart was fuelled by various intellectual sources: perception of Russia as conveyed through the writings of Dostoevskiĭ; the reception of Nietzsche; geopolitical thought situating Germany in the centre of Europe; imperial politics; and civilizational ideas about 'cultural areas' (*Kulturkreise*). Together these paved the way for the notion of a Germany opposed to 'the West'.

Most important in the formation of this stance were German-Russian entanglements in the discursive construction of national identities. Thomas Mann's *Reflections* drew strongly on Dostoevskiĭ's anti-Western writings, which provided rich insights into the conceptual cosmos of pan-Slavism.[84] It was, above all, Arthur Moeller van den Bruck who had introduced Dostoevskiĭ's works to Germans from 1906 onward, in the wake of the Russo-Japanese War and the 1905 Revolution.[85] Conservative intellectuals, sceptical about liberalism and the values of the Enlightenment, believed they could find mysticism, spirituality and authenticity in Russia. To Moeller van den Bruck, who in 1916 demanded the 'abandonment of the West', Dostoevskiĭ was the transmitter of new values radicalizing his critique of modernity.[86] The positive reception of Dostoevskiĭ's works in Germany furthered a certain recoding of German notions of the East, which became more multifaceted after the turn of the century.[87] It is true that German soldiers of the First World War envisioned 'the East' as an 'apocalyptic space' – a 'godforsaken slime-desert', as a German lieutenant put it.[88] But it was not solely the appreciation of Russian culture that rendered German concepts of the East more complex than before. Equally relevant were visions of a 'holy German East' and Germany's actual territorial conquests in the East, as confirmed by the treaty of Brest-Litovsk.[89] That 'the West' rather than 'the East' was to become Germany's 'Other' in the First World War also reflected the growing complexity of attitudes towards 'the East'.

A second source impelling Germans to form a distinct concept of the West had particular importance for Thomas Mann and the intellectual Right as well. This was the writings of Friedrich Nietzsche.[90] Nietzsche was one of the very few commentators in late nineteenth-century Germany who had actualized the conceptual tradition of an ideological East–West antithesis. In his 1889 book *Twilight of the Idols or How to Philosophize with a Hammer* (*Götzen-Dämmerung oder Wie man mit dem Hammer philosophirt*) he framed his anti-liberal critique of 'modernity' in terms of a critique of 'the West': 'The whole of the West has lost those instincts, from which institutions grow, from which future grows'. It was not 'the West' but the Russian 'East' that would provide the intellectual sources for the future.[91]

Thirdly, notions of German exceptionalism flourished during the First World War. The geopolitical situation of the *Kaiserreich* lent credence to the idea of a Germany situated between 'East' and 'West' – both in European terms and, with the U.S. entry into the war, in global terms as well. The semantics of international relations that had been established by the mid nineteenth century and had reached their climax in the Crimean War suddenly seemed to make sense again. The revival of this sense of geopolitical position was a vital intellectual source for the perception of Germany as a counter-model to 'the West' that developed during the First World War. The connection between geographical position and political stance was no more obvious than in the *Mitteleuropa* conceptions that stretched back to the mid nineteenth century and had then been invested with 'East–West' terminology.[92]

Fourthly, the new antagonistic language of 'Germany versus the West', encapsulated in the 'ideas of 1914', provided Germany with an effective rhetorical tool to legitimize its imperial politics. German nationalists could now promote the idea of a German cultural mission that was fundamentally different from the 'civilizational' model of the established imperial powers.[93] As Mark Hewitson demonstrates in this volume, these claims of a virtuous German resistance to 'the West' were also fuelled by notions of 'American civilization', whose materialism and consumerism were supposedly threatening German 'culture' and indeed the 'culture' of Europe as a whole.

Fifth and lastly, belief in a 'German-Western antagonism' received support from new theories of *Kulturkreise*. Around the turn of the century, the rising disciplines of ethnography and geography advanced the idea of transnational spaces of coexisting civilizations. Scholars identified cultural patterns of simultaneity rather than of temporality, and this ran counter to the belief in one universal civilization attainable (in principle) in every part of the world. Theories of *Kulturkreise*, which were compatible with ethnic, biological and racial thought, provided a means of bringing spatial and cultural categories together, and made reasoning about different kinds of culture or civilization appear sensible. This could be applied both to 'the East' and to 'the West'. Establishing difference between large-scale spaces in a globalizing world, theories of 'cultural areas' contributed to what Jürgen Osterhammel has called a 'coarsening of global perceptions' (*Vergröberung der Weltwahrnehmung*).[94]

These five intellectual sources and discursive spaces together gave defining outlines to the idea of the West for the German public during the

First World War. That 'the West' rose to such prominence, however, did not mean that neighbouring concepts such as the 'Occident' (*Abendland / Okzident*) became irrelevant. One of the most prominent examples of the latter concept's continuing use is to be found in Max Weber's theory of Occidental rationalization, advanced in his book *The Protestant Ethic and the Spirit of Capitalism*. Contrary to the impression one gains from Talcott Parsons' English translation of 1930, Weber's central concept was the 'Occident' (*Okzident*), not 'the West'.[95] As a frame of reference, 'the West' had become too narrowly focused on political values to be of any use for Weber's wide-ranging examination of Occidental phenomena such as religion, science, law, accounting, capitalism, bureaucracy and so on. More importantly still, the term 'the Occident' allowed Weber to include in his investigation countries that had styled themselves as 'anti-Western' powers. Towards the end of the war, moreover, Weber was one of the very few commentators to repudiate the notion of a German-'Western' antagonism as the key to making sense of the First World War. Instead, he conceived of the war as a conflict of modern societies: he did not see it as a clash of 'culture' and 'civilization'.[96]

Conceptual Reconfigurations: 'The West' in Interwar Germany and among German Émigrés

After the lost war and the Treaty of Versailles the antagonistic meanings of the concept 'the West' continued to reverberate in the German public sphere. Given the intense debates on democracy in Germany's new-founded republic, it is no wonder that the constitutional dimensions of the concept were the dominant ones. 'The West' was discussed with respect to types of government and forms of popular representation. The fact that parliamentary democracy continued to be associated with the Allied forces of the West worked against attempts to spread pluralist conceptions of democracy and to stabilize the Weimar Republic. It was easy to denounce Weimar democracy as 'Western democracy' – the democracy of the victors of the First World War. Many Germans were driven by the search for a distinctly German type of government, and exceptionalist notions beyond 'Eastern' and 'Western' models continued to flourish.[97] Often, these notions were part of grander designs. Ideas of *Abendland*, *Mitteleuropa* or *Reich* each entailed different visions of a German (and European) identity, but were all endowed with a polemical thrust against 'the West'.[98]

A decidedly anti-'Western' stance was particularly pronounced in the New Right circles of Weimar's so-called 'young conservatives', amongst whom 'thinking in terms of compass points' (*Denken in Himmelsrichtungen*) was a common feature.[99] Anti-Westernism, however, was not as widespread among the Weimar Right as one might think. Though usually a prominent reference point in scholarly discussion of German ideas of the West, Oswald Spengler, for instance, preferred spatially contained concepts such as 'Occident' and 'Western Europe' over the more open concept 'the West'. This differentiation is lost in the English translation of his two-volume work *Der Untergang des Abendlandes* (1918/22), which, first published in 1926/28, employs the expression 'the West' for the German term *Abendland*. 'The West', however, did not appeal to Spengler as an overarching concept, because it had come to carry universal meanings and visions of 'modernity'.[100] The marginalization of 'the West' among sections of the Weimar Right becomes equally obvious when one considers the National Socialist use of the concept, as Philipp Gassert does in this volume. From the mid 1920s the National Socialists abandoned the idea of an 'anti-Western' mission for Germany. Their worldview was primarily social Darwinist and racist; and notions of a homogenous 'West' were barely compatible with this.[101]

For liberals of the Weimar Republic 'the West' proved as difficult and ambivalent a concept as it had been for their predecessors in the nineteenth century. As Austin Harrington shows, these liberals embraced 'the West' insofar as it expressed a commitment to republicanism and the Enlightenment, but were opposed to the Western political hegemony of France, Britain and the U.S. with their demands on Germany: instead of the Wilsonian project, they favoured a 'European' solution. The complexity of the liberal appropriations of 'the West', in a situation somewhat reminiscent of their nineteenth-century predicament, throws into sharp relief how exceptional a time the years of the First World War were – politically as well as semantically. While the frame of reference of 'the West' had been narrowed down in wartime Germany, the conceptual horizon widened again soon afterwards.

To social democrats, however, 'the West' was a category of only marginal relevance. Stefan Berger argues that 'the West' remained largely absent from their political language from the nineteenth century until the end of the Second World War. Following Marx, the social democrats were bound to believe that the most progressive societies were situated in the West, and they closely observed political developments in America, France and, especially, Britain. But their ideological preconceptions – with the possible exception of the 'Young Right'[102] – were generally guided by non-spatial, or spatially open, concepts such as 'class struggle', 'bourgeois democracy', 'proletarian revolution' and the like. Their socio-political language was the universal language of internationalism.

Only gradually, as the need to distance themselves from Bolshevik dictatorship and 'Asiatic despotism' became more pressing, did they begin to take a positive stance towards a 'West' deemed capable of social reform and progressive change. Often, as Stefan Berger and Anselm Doering-Manteuffel both highlight in their respective chapters, it was exile in Britain and the U.S. that provided the decisive experiences paving the way to a new German view of 'the West'. Socialist rémigrés like Fritz Heine, Erich Ollenhauer and Richard Löwenthal came sooner or later to the conclusion that Germany's future was inside 'the West'. Their notions of the West, however, were anything but static – the term was a cipher for various horizons of expectation. The post-war project of 'Westernization' was thus guided by a constructed template that was the product of multi-layered transfers and processes of adaptation.[103]

Going 'West': Divided Germany and Cold War Languages

Before 'arriving' in 'the West', however, many left-wing intellectuals, including Löwenthal, advanced projects of a socialist Europe acting as a 'third force' between American capitalism and Soviet communism. The writers and intellectuals who gathered around the journals *Der Ruf*, *Frankfurter Hefte* and *Ost und West* are good examples of these proponents of a European 'third way'. As Dominik Geppert shows in this volume, they also assigned Germany a special place as mediator between 'East' and 'West'.[104] When the binary logic of the Cold War crystallized, however, and found embodiment in the separation of Germany into a communist East and a liberal West, the emerging rhetorical register of the Cold War began to take root in German political culture. Contemporaries were aware of the need for a new political language after the semantic 'pollution' through National Socialism.[105] Concomitantly, they soon began investigating the historical roots of the climaxing East–West antagonism. Classic studies by Heinz Gollwitzer and Dieter Groh provide the most prominent examples of this trend, which prevailed through the 1950s and early 1960s.[106] Often, these studies could be read as a 'due reminder' that Germany's place had originally been inside 'the West', before the 'seminal catastrophe' of the First World War triggered a transformation.

The concept of the West was critical to the discursive negotiation of the FRG's self-understanding. From early on, *Westbindung*, integration with 'the West', constituted its core political rationale. The U.S., in particular, became West Germany's lodestar – a process decisively fostered by the Western superpower itself.[107] Yet, despite the clear alignment of Adenauer's foreign policy with the U.S. as beacon of 'the West', West

German society's intellectual appropriation of 'Western democracy' was a protracted process. Conservatives, who had hitherto kept themselves at a critical distance from liberal democracy, or had categorically rejected it, appropriated the concept of the West via their reception of Alexis de Tocqueville's works on American democracy in the 1830s. Searching for a contemporary 'West', they entered into dialogue with this nineteenth-century advocate of an older 'West'. This discourse, which Martina Steber introduces, extended from the 1950s to the 1970s and shows the multifaceted new engagement of conservative politicians and intellectuals with democracy. They took a convoluted path from mere acceptance to a confident defence of democratic institutions. In conservative discourse in the late 1940s and the 1950s, the concept of the West had been shaped not only by opposition to 'the East' (still laden with hostile stereotypes) but also in distinction to the more popular notion of a Romano-Germanic Christian *Abendland*.[108] When this *Abendland* image lost its power of persuasion at the end of the 1950s, the concept of the West took its place, and an essentially liberal understanding of democracy became entrenched in West German conservatism. From then on, the great majority of the West German public regarded itself unequivocally as part of 'the West'.

One of the most influential liberal thinkers helping anchor West German political culture in a community of Western values was the academic rémigré and former socialist Ernst Fraenkel. Riccardo Bavaj argues that Fraenkel used the concept of 'Western democracy' as a rhetorical tool of persuasion to counter anti-Westernism and to spread his theory of neo-pluralism. Like Ernst Troeltsch in the early Weimar period, he tried to convince the German public of the historical fallacy of contrasting the 'German state' with 'Western democracy'. Without a doubt, the 'Westernization' of the FRG was a complex process. Conceived as a liberalization of politics and society oriented towards 'Western models',[109] it was characterized both by the appropriation of American, British and French ideas and by a resort to German traditions of political thought and practice. The concept of the West, by nature a transnational category, opened up manifold opportunities of combining political conceptions drawn from a variety of sources. The space within which 'the West' could be interpreted, however, was confined by the conceptual framework of the Cold War and by the reverberations of discursive patterns that had been formed through German history. 'Democracy', which had been a particularly contested concept in the interwar period,[110] was increasingly envisioned in terms of 'Western democracy' as the intellectual Cold War narrowed down significant discursive spaces. Both terms, 'democracy' and 'the West', were deprived of some of the layers of meaning that had previously been part of their frames of reference.¹¹¹ At the same time, German concepts of the West remained steeped in the semantic history from the post-Napoleonic era – still shaped by distinctly liberal ideas, still characterized by notions of 'modernity' and still endowed with horizons of expectation that were markedly progressive. Yet there was enough room to allow for the conceptual negotiations over the 'correct' meaning of 'the West' that were part and parcel of the liberalization of the FRG.

The complexity of this process of liberalization also becomes evident when looking at the student movement of the late 1960s, which challenged the socio-political order of the FRG and took a critical stance towards 'the West'. While appropriating new techniques of protest from their fellow activists in the U.S., radical students in West Germany attacked core tenets of 'consensus liberalism', the fundamental 'ideology of the West' from the late 1940s.¹¹² Parliamentary government, liberal pluralism, opposition to totalitarianism, anti-Marxism, private property and the market economy, to name only the most important components of 'consensus liberalism', all came under attack in 1968. As many commentators fell back on the *Sonderweg* interpretation that had gained currency in the previous decade, they perceived as a peculiarly German deviation *from* the West what outside Germany was typically viewed as a crisis *of* the West.¹¹³ For those who had become avowed advocates of 'Western values', nothing less than the success of their cherished political project appeared to be at stake: their hope of situating the FRG firmly in the realm of 'Western democracies'. Eventually, however, while the upheaval of 1968 did prompt a significant recoding of West Germany's political culture, left-wing critics like Jürgen Habermas bought into the language of 'Westernization' as well. In the context of the *Historikerstreit* of 1986, Habermas praised the 'unreserved opening up [*vorbehaltlose Öffnung*] of the FRG to the political culture of the West', calling it the 'great intellectual achievement of our post-war period, of which my generation, in particular, could be proud'.¹¹⁴

Access to the 'Western haven' was still closed to Germans east of the border, however. Officially, of course, access to the Western 'class enemy' was nothing a declared socialist would aspire to. The German Democratic Republic's (GDR) raison d'être was to prove 'the West' wrong. Building a socialist country so close to the West meant fighting Western capitalism, liberalism and imperialism on a daily basis. However, as Katherine Pence shows, East Germany's actual relationship to 'the West' was more complex, and even paradoxical. The GDR's conflicted relationship to 'the West' undermined and 'sabotaged' its socialist experiment, 'creating fissures in socialist society right up to its collapse in 1989'.

Seemingly the end of the Cold War brought victory to 'the West', but it did much to destabilize and undermine it semantically.[115] The West was experiencing increasing uncertainty about its political contours, cultural identity and epistemological status when all Germans – purportedly – became part of it. That German politicians such as Lothar de Maizière and Volker Rühe argued, in 1990, that their country and political party, respectively, would now become 'more Eastern' and 'more Protestant', did not do much to alleviate this uncertainty – nor did the subsequent developments of EU and NATO *Osterweiterung* (enlargement to the East).[116] It does indeed seem that Germany 'arrived in the West' just when the concept was starting to lose its power of persuasion. Historians' current wish to historicize 'the West', and Germany's relationship to it, can certainly be attributed to transformations within the academic field such as the 'cultural turn' and a revival of intellectual and conceptual history, but it is also prompted by the weakening and waning appeal of formerly unquestioned assumptions about what 'the West' stands for. Both developments are, of course, related to each other: academic historicization of 'the West' is both a product and an accelerator of its being called into question. To be sure, 'the West' is still a central leitmotif in German public discourse. Its enduring relevance testifies to the perseverance of a new vocabulary formed in the *Sattelzeit* and the prominence to which the resulting concept rose at crucial junctures of German history.

That 'the West' still has vocal advocates today has already been illustrated. Even more important for its lasting significance are its entanglements with the so-called non-Western world. After all, 'the West' is a particularly prominent point of reference among non-Westerners – both those 'hating the West' and those appreciating 'Western values' against the background of regimes that disregard civil rights and the rule of law. Whether Westerners themselves (Germans included) will 'reboot' the programme of Western civilization remains to be seen. But conceptual history teaches that 'the West' has often been 'in crisis' and 'in decline', and that horizons of expectation attached to it have often faded only to reappear soon after. It may be safe to assume that its last chapter is yet to be written.

Notes

1. The authors would like to thank Günther Kronenbitter, Paul Nolte and the anonymous referees for their valuable comments on earlier drafts of this introduction.
2. Heinrich August Winkler, *Geschichte des Westens*, 3 vols, Munich, 2009–2014.

3. Heinrich August Winkler, *Der lange Weg nach Westen*, 2 vols, Munich, 2000 (quotation from vol. 2, 648). The title of the English translation is: *Germany. The Long Road West*, 2 vols, Oxford, 2006–2007. For an apt comment on Winkler's much-debated work see Anselm Doering-Manteuffel, 'Eine politische Nationalgeschichte für die Berliner Republik. Überlegungen zu Heinrich August Winklers "Der lange Weg nach Westen"', *Geschichte und Gesellschaft* 27 (2001), 446–62. See also Stefan Berger, 'Rising Like a Phoenix… The Renaissance of National History Writing in Germany and Britain since the 1980s', in Stefan Berger and Chris Lorenz (eds), *Nationalizing the Past. Historians as Nation Builders in Modern Europe*, Basingstoke, 2010, 426–51, here 432.
4. See, for instance, Karl Dietrich Bracher, 'Staatsbegriff und Demokratie in Deutschland' (1967/68), in Karl Dietrich Bracher, *Das deutsche Dilemma. Leidenswege der politischen Emanzipation*, Munich, 1971, 11–40; Alexander Schwan, 'Deutschland und der Westen. Eine wieder aktuelle Diskussion', in Klaus W. Hempfer and Alexander Schwan (eds), *Grundlagen der politischen Kultur des Westens. Ringvorlesung an der Freien Universität Berlin*, Berlin and New York, 1987, 3–26; or Kurt Sontheimer, 'Deutschland und der Westen', in Kurt Sontheimer, *Von Deutschlands Republik*, Stuttgart, 1991, 64–81.
5. See Ralf Dahrendorf, 'Demokratie und Sozialstruktur in Deutschland' (1959), in Ralf Dahrendorf, *Gesellschaft und Freiheit. Zur soziologischen Analyse der Gegenwart*, Munich, 1961, 260–99; Ernst Fraenkel, *Deutschland und die westlichen Demokratien*, Stuttgart, 1964; and Richard Löwenthal, *Gesellschaftswandel und Kulturkrise. Zukunftsprobleme der westlichen Demokratien*, Frankfurt/Main, 1979.
6. See Udo Di Fabio, *Die Kultur der Freiheit*, Munich, 2005; and Udo Di Fabio, 'Last der Freiheit', *Frankfurter Allgemeine Zeitung*, 16 September 2013, 7.
7. See especially James C. Bennett, 'America and the West. The Emerging Anglosphere', *Orbis*, Winter 2002, 111–26; James C. Bennett, *The Anglosphere Challenge. Why the English-Speaking Nations Will Lead the Way in the Twenty-First Century*, Lanham, 2004; Robert Kagan, 'Power and Weakness', *Policy Review*, June & July 2002, 3–28; and Robert Kagan, *Paradise and Power. America and Europe in the New World Order*, revised edn, London, 2004 (first published 2003). See also Jeffrey Anderson, G. John Ikenberry and Thomas Risse (eds), *The End of the West? Crisis and Change in the Atlantic Order*, Ithaca and London, 2008; and Christopher S. Browning and Ben Tonra, 'Beyond the West and towards the Anglosphere?', in Christopher S. Browning and Marko Lehti (eds), *The Struggle for the West. A Divided and Contested Legacy*, London and New York, 2010, 161–81.
8. See, for example, Axel Schildt, *Ankunft im Westen. Ein Essay zur Erfolgsgeschichte der Bundesrepublik*, Frankfurt/Main, 1999; or Axel Schildt, 'Westlich, demokratisch. Deutschland und die westlichen Demokratien im 20. Jahrhundert', in Anselm Doering-Manteuffel (ed.), *Strukturmerkmale der deutschen Geschichte des 20. Jahrhunderts*, Munich, 2006, 225–39. See also the critical comments on the West as Germany's new 'national myth' by Philipp Gassert, 'Ex Occidente Lux? Der Westen als nationaler Mythos der Berliner Republik', *Vorgänge* 40/2 (2001), 15–22. For an extended version of this essay see Philipp Gassert, 'Die Bundesrepublik, Europa und der Westen', in Jörg Baberowski, Eckart Conze, Philipp Gassert and Martin Sabrow, *Geschichte ist immer Gegenwart. Vier Thesen zur Zeitgeschichte*, Stuttgart and Munich, 2001, 67–89. A certain unease about the inflationary reference to 'the West' and its one-dimensional and present-minded deployments can be gleaned from Klaus Hildebrand, 'Der Westen. Betrachtungen über einen uneindeutigen Begriff', in Dieter Hein, Klaus Hildebrand and Andreas Schulz (eds), *Historie und Leben. Der Historiker*

als Wissenschaftler und Zeitgenosse, Munich, 2006, 595–603; and Michael Hochgeschwender, 'Was ist der Westen? Zur Ideengeschichte eines politischen Konstrukts', *Historisch-Politische Mitteilungen* 11 (2004), 1–30.
9. Christopher Coker, *Twilight of the West*, Boulder, 1998.
10. Kagan, *Paradise and Power*, 3.
11. Niall Ferguson, *Civilization. The Six Killer Apps of Western Power*, London, 2012 (first published in 2011 with the subtitle *The West and the Rest*), 325; Niall Ferguson, 'How American Civilization Can Avoid Collapse', *Newsweek*, 30 October 2011; and see also Niall Ferguson, *The Great Degeneration. How Institutions Decay and Economies Die*, London, 2012.
12. Arnold J. Toynbee, 'The Unit of Historical Study' (1934), in Arnold J. Toynbee, *The Study of History. Abridgement of Volumes I–VI* by D.C. Somervell, Oxford, 1946, 1–11. For a good example of this literature see, most recently, Ricardo Duchesne, *The Uniqueness of Western Civilization*, Leiden, 2011; Ricardo Duchesne, 'Defending the Rise of Western Culture against its Multicultural Critics', *The European Legacy* 10 (2005), 455–84; and Ricardo Duchesne's review article on Ian Morris, *Why the West Rules – for Now*, London, 2010, in *Reviews in History*, 31 May 2011, No. 1091. See also Christopher Coker, *Rebooting the West. The US, Europe and the Future of the Western Alliance*, Abingdon, 2009; Lazaros Miliopoulos, *Atlantische Zivilisation und transatlantisches Verhältnis. Politische Idee und Wirklichkeit*, Wiesbaden, 2007; and David Gress, *From Plato to NATO. The Idea of the West and its Opponents*, New York, 1998, which is less deconstructive than the ironic title may suggest.
13. See Gilbert Allardyce, 'The Rise and Fall of the Western Civilization Course', *American Historical Review* 87 (1982), 695–725; Peter Novick, *That Noble Dream. The 'Objectivity Question' and the American Historical Profession*, Cambridge, 1998, 311–14; and Daniel A. Segal, '"Western Civ" and the Staging of History in American Higher Education', *American Historical Review* 105 (2000), 770–805.
14. See, for instance, Johann Baptist Müller, *Deutschland und der Westen*, Berlin, 1989, which offers a brief overview of twentieth-century commentaries on Germany and the West from the perspective of a traditional history of ideas, and the same author's collection of primary sources: Johann Baptist Müller (ed.), *Deutschland. Eine westliche Nation. Konzeptionen und Kontroversen*, Goldbach, 1993. See also two volumes dealing with the history of international relations: Jürgen Elvert and Michael Salewski (eds), *Deutschland und der Westen im 19. und 20. Jahrhundert*, part 1, Stuttgart, 1993; and Klaus Schwabe and Francesca Schinzinger (eds), *Deutschland und der Westen im 19. und 20. Jahrhundert*, part 2, Stuttgart, 1994.
15. See, however, the instructive essays by Egbert Klautke, 'Auf den Spuren des Sonderwegs. Zur Westorientierung der deutschen Geschichtswissenschaft in der Bundesrepublik', in Manfred Berg and Philipp Gassert (eds), *Deutschland und die USA in der Internationalen Geschichte des 20. Jahrhunderts. Festschrift für Detlef Junker*, Stuttgart, 2004, 98–112; and Thomas Welskopp, 'Identität ex negativo. Der "deutsche Sonderweg" als Metaerzählung in der bundesdeutschen Geschichtswissenschaft der siebziger und achtziger Jahre', in Konrad H. Jarausch and Martin Sabrow (eds), *Die historische Meistererzählung. Deutungslinien der deutschen Nationalgeschichte nach 1945*, Göttingen, 2002, 109–39.
16. See Otto Brunner, Werner Conze and Reinhart Koselleck (eds), *Geschichtliche Grundbegriffe. Historisches Lexikon zur politisch-sozialen Sprache in Deutschland*, 8 vols, Stuttgart, 1972–2004. For possible reasons behind this omission see Bernhard Struck's chapter in this volume.

17. Heinz Gollwitzer, *Europabild und Europagedanke. Beiträge zur deutschen Geistesgeschichte des 18. und 19. Jahrhunderts*, Munich, 1964 (first published 1951); Heinz Gollwitzer, *Geschichte des weltpolitischen Denkens*, 2 vols, Göttingen, 1972/82; Dieter Groh, *Russland und das Selbstverständnis Europas. Ein Beitrag zur europäischen Geistesgeschichte*, Neuwied, 1961 (republished as *Russland im Blick Europas. 300 Jahre historische Perspektiven*, Frankfurt/Main, 1988).
18. See especially Steffen Bruendel, *Volksgemeinschaft oder Volksstaat. Die 'Ideen von 1914' und die Neuordnung Deutschlands im Ersten Weltkrieg*, Berlin, 2003; Peter Hoeres, *Krieg der Philosophen. Die deutsche und die britische Philosophie im Ersten Weltkrieg*, Paderborn, 2004; Marcus Llanque, *Demokratisches Denken im Krieg. Die deutsche Debatte im Ersten Weltkrieg*, Berlin, 2000; Thomas Rohkrämer, *Eine andere Moderne? Zivilisationskritik, Natur und Technik in Deutschland 1880–1933*, Paderborn, 1999; Jeffrey Verhey, *The Spirit of 1914. Militarism, Myth and Mobilization in Germany*, Cambridge, 2000; and also Barbara Beßlich, *Wege in den 'Kulturkrieg'. Zivilisationskritik in Deutschland 1890–1914*, Darmstadt, 2000.
19. See Vanessa Conze, *Das Europa der Deutschen. Ideen von Europa in Deutschland zwischen Reichstradition und Westorientierung (1920–1970)*, Munich, 2005; Dagmar Pöpping, *Abendland. Christliche Akademiker und die Utopie der Antimoderne 1900–1945*, Berlin, 2002; Axel Schildt, *Zwischen Abendland und Amerika. Studien zur westdeutschen Ideenlandschaft der 50er Jahre*, Munich, 1999; Axel Schildt, 'Zur Hochkonjunktur des "christlichen Abendlandes" in der westdeutschen Geschichtsschreibung', in Ulrich Pfeil (ed.), *Die Rückkehr der deutschen Geschichtswissenschaft in die 'Ökumene der Historiker'. Ein wissenschaftsgeschichtlicher Ansatz*, Munich, 2008, 49–70; Barbara Baerns, *Ost und West – Eine Zeitschrift zwischen den Fronten. Zur politischen Funktion einer literarischen Zeitschrift in der Besatzungszeit (1945–1949)*, Münster, 1968; and Christian Bailey, 'The Continuities of West German History. Conceptions of Europe, Democracy and the West in Interwar and Postwar Germany', *Geschichte und Gesellschaft* 36 (2010), 567–96.
20. Patrick Thaddeus Jackson, *Civilizing the Enemy. German Reconstruction and the Invention of the West*, Ann Arbor, 2006. See also Wilfried Mausbach, 'Erdachte Welten. Deutschland und der Westen in den 1950er Jahren', in Berg and Gassert (eds), *Deutschland und die USA*, 423–48.
21. See, especially, Julia Angster, *Konsenskapitalismus und Sozialdemokratie. Die Westernisierung von SPD und DGB*, Munich, 2003; Anselm Doering-Manteuffel, *Wie westlich sind die Deutschen? Amerikanisierung und Westernisierung im 20. Jahrhundert*, Göttingen, 1999; Anselm Doering-Manteuffel, 'Amerikanisierung und Westernisierung', *Docupedia-Zeitgeschichte* (2011), online: http://docupedia.de/zg/Amerikanisierung_und_Westernisierung; Michael Hochgeschwender, *Freiheit in der Offensive? Der Kongress für kulturelle Freiheit und die Deutschen*, Munich, 1998; and Hochgeschwender, 'Was ist der Westen?'. See also the helpful comments by Holger Nehring, '"Westernization". A New Paradigm for Interpreting West European History in a Cold War Context', *Cold War History* 4/2 (2004), 175–91. For a variant of Doering-Manteuffel's Westernization approach, see Konrad Jarausch, *Die Umkehr. Deutsche Wandlungen 1945–1995*, Munich, 2004, especially 137–70 ('Hinwendung zum Westen'). The English version of Jarausch's book is: *After Hitler. Recivilizing Germans, 1945–1995*, Oxford and New York, 2006.
22. The literature on this subject is vast. For an overview, see Riccardo Bavaj, '"The West". A Conceptual Exploration', *Europäische Geschichte Online* (2011), online: http://www.ieg-ego.eu/bavajr-2011-en. See also Vera Tolz, *Russia's Own Orient. The*

Politics of Identity and Oriental Studies in the Late Imperial and Early Soviet Periods, Oxford and New York, 2011, especially 47–68; and Vera Tolz, 'The West', in William J. Leatherbarrow and Derek Offord (eds), *A History of Russian Thought*, Cambridge, 2010, 197–216.
23. See Ezequiel Adamovsky, 'Euro-Orientalism and the Making of the Concept of Eastern Europe in France, 1810–1880', *Journal of Modern History* 77 (2005), 591–628; and Ezequiel Adamovsky, *Euro-Orientalism. Liberal Ideology and the Image of Russia in France (c. 1740–1880)*, Oxford, 2006. See also John H. Gleason, *The Genesis of Russophobia in Great Britain. A Study of the Interaction of Policy and Opinion*, Cambridge Mass, 1950.
24. Michael David-Fox, 'Transnational History and the East-West Divide', in György Péteri (ed.), *Imagining the West in Eastern Europe and the Soviet Union*, Pittsburgh, 2010, 258–68, here 261–62. See especially Péteri (ed.), *Imagining the West in Eastern Europe* (the volume contains two chapters on the GDR as well); and Andrew Kier Wise, 'Russia as Poland's Civilizational "Other"', in Alexander Maxwell (ed.), *The East–West Discourse. Symbolic Geography and its Consequences*, Oxford et al., 2011, 73–92. See also Robert D. English, *Russia and the Idea of the West. Gorbachev, Intellectuals, and the End of the Cold War*, New York, 2000. An overview of the relationship between Russian/Soviet and European identity formation over the past two centuries is offered in Iver B. Neumann, *Russia and the Idea of Europe. A Study in Identity and International Relations*, London and New York, 1996; and Iver B. Neumann, *Uses of the Other. 'The East' in European Identity Formation*, Minneapolis, 1999.
25. See, above all, Valérie Aubourg, Gérard Bossuat and Giles Scott-Smith (eds), *European Community, Atlantic Community?*, Paris, 2008; Marco Mariano (ed.), *Defining the Atlantic Community. Culture, Intellectuals, and Policies in the Mid-Twentieth Century*, London and New York, 2010; and Marco Mariano, 'The U.S. Discovers Europe. *Life Magazine* and the Invention of the "Atlantic Community" in the 1940s', in Maurizio Vaudagna (ed.), *The Place of Europe in American History. Twentieth-Century Perspectives*, Turin, 2007, 161–85. See also Volker R. Berghahn, *America and the Intellectual Cold Wars in Europe*, Princeton and Oxford, 2001; Frank Costigliola, 'Culture, Emotion, and the Creation of the Atlantic Identity, 1948–1952', in Geir Lundestad (ed.), *No End to Alliance. The United States and Western Europe*, New York, 1998, 21–36; Dianne Kirby, 'Divinely Sanctioned. The Anglo-American Cold War Alliance and the Defence of Western Civilization and Christianity, 1945–48', *Journal of Contemporary History* 35 (2000), 385–412; and Giles Scott-Smith, *Western Anti-Communism and the Interdoc Network. Cold War Internationale*, Basingstoke and New York, 2012.
26. See Christopher GoGwilt, *The Invention of the West. Joseph Conrad and the Double-Mapping of Europe and Empire*, Stanford, 1995.
27. See Alastair Bonnett, *The Idea of the West. Culture, Politics and History*, Basingstoke and New York, 2004, 14–39.
28. For an alternative meaning within the field of postcolonial studies, see Fernando Coronil, 'Beyond Occidentalism. Toward Nonimperial Geohistorical Categories', *Cultural Anthropology* 11 (1996), 51–87; and Gabriele Dietze, Edith Wenzel and Claudia Brunner (eds), *Kritik des Okzidentalismus. Transdisziplinäre Beiträge zu (Neo-)Orientalismus und Geschlecht*, Bielefeld, 2009.
29. See especially Bonnett, *The Idea of the West*, 63–122; James G. Carrier (ed.), *Occidentalism. Images of the West*, Oxford, 1995; James G. Carrier, 'Occidentalism. The World Turned Upside-Down', *American Ethnologist* 19/2 (1992), 195–212; Xiaomei Chen, *Occidentalism. A Theory of Counter-Discourse in Post-Mao China*, New York

et al., 1995; Carter Vaughn Findley, 'An Ottoman Occidentalist in Europe. Ahmed Midhat Meets Madame Gülnar, 1889', *American Historical Review* 103 (1998), 15–49; and Harald Fischer-Tiné, '"Deep Occidentalism"? Europa und "der Westen" in der Wahrnehmung hinduistischer Intellektueller und Reformer ca. 1890–1930', *Journal of Modern European History* 4/2 (2006), 171–203. See also some early examples of this field that do not deploy the terminology of Occidentalism: Carmen Blacker, *The Japanese Enlightenment. A Study of the Writings of Fukuzawa Yukichi*, Cambridge, 1969; Stephen N. Hay, *Asian Ideas of East and West. Tagore and his Critics in Japan, China, and India*, Cambridge, Mass, 1970; and Tapan Raychaudhuri, *Europe Reconsidered. Perceptions of the West in Nineteenth-Century Bengal*, 2nd edn, Oxford, 2002 (first published 1988). Much quoted but less typical of the field is the polemical essay by Ian Buruma and Avishai Margalit, *Occidentalism. A Short History of Anti-Westernism*, London, 2005.

30. This is the title of the oft-quoted but analytically flawed book by Theodore H. von Laue, *The World Revolution of Westernization. The Twentieth Century in Global Perspective*, New York, 1989.
31. See, for instance, Iwo Amelung, Matthias Koch, Joachim Kurtz, Eun-Jeung Lee and Sven Saaler (eds), *Selbstbehauptungsdiskurse in Asien. China – Japan – Korea*, Munich, 2003.
32. Jürgen Osterhammel, 'Fremdbeschreibungen. Spuren von "Okzidentalismus" vor 1930', in Lutz Raphael (ed.), *Theorien und Experimente der Moderne. Europas Gesellschaften im 20. Jahrhundert*, Cologne, 2012, 287–311, here 297. For a good example of the process of non-Western 'Othering' see Cemil Aydin, *The Politics of Anti-Westernism in Asia. Visions of World Order in Pan-Islamic and Pan-Asian Thought*, New York, 2007; and Cemil Aydin, 'Beyond Civilization. Pan-Islamism, Pan-Asianism and the Revolt against the West', *Journal of Modern European History* 4/2 (2006), 204–22. See also Andreas Eckert, 'Anti-Western Doctrines of Nationalism', in John Breuilly (ed.), *The Oxford Handbook of the History of Nationalism*, Oxford, 2013, 56–74.
33. For the context see the stimulating volume by Sebastian Conrad and Dominic Sachsenmaier (eds), *Competing Visions of World Order. Global Moments and Movements, 1880s–1930s*, Basingstoke, 2007.
34. A starting point for a discussion of German mediators can be found in the studies by Suzanne L. Marchand, *German Orientalism in the Age of Empire. Religion, Race, and Scholarship*, Cambridge, 2009, and Douglas T. McGetchin, *Indology, Indomania, Orientalism. Ancient India's Rebirth in Modern Germany*, Madison, 2009. See also Suzanne L. Marchand, 'German Orientalism and the Decline of the West', *Proceedings of the American Philosophical Society* 145 (2001), 465–73.
35. See Martin W. Lewis and Kären E. Wigen, *The Myth of Continents. A Critique of Metageography*, Berkeley, 1997, especially 47–103 (on the 'spatial' and 'cultural constructs of Orient and Occident, East and West'); and Frithjof Benjamin Schenk, 'Mental Maps. Die Konstruktion von geographischen Räumen in Europa seit der Aufklärung', *Geschichte und Gesellschaft* 28 (2002), 493–514. The literature on the 'spatial turn' is vast. For recent overviews see Jörg Döring and Tristan Thielmann (eds), *Spatial Turn. Das Raumparadigma in den Kultur- und Sozialwissenschaften*, Bielefeld, 2008; and Stephan Günzel (ed.), *Raum. Ein interdisziplinäres Handbuch*, Stuttgart, 2010.
36. See Reinhart Koselleck, *Vergangene Zukunft. Zur Semantik geschichtlicher Zeiten*, Frankfurt/Main, 1979; Reinhart Koselleck, *Begriffsgeschichten. Studien zur Semantik und Pragmatik der politischen und sozialen Sprache*, Frankfurt/Main, 2006; Jörn

Leonhard, *Liberalismus. Zur historischen Semantik eines europäischen Deutungsmusters*, Munich, 2001; Willibald Steinmetz, 'Neue Wege einer historischen Semantik des Politischen', in Willibald Steinmetz (ed.), '*Politik*'. *Situationen eines Wortgebrauchs im Europa der Neuzeit*, Frankfurt/Main and New York, 2007, 9–40; and Willibald Steinmetz, '40 Jahre Begriffsgeschichte. The State of the Art', in Heidrun Kämper and Ludwig M. Eichinger (eds), *Sprache – Kognition – Kultur*, Berlin, 2008, 174–97. See also Iain Hampsher-Monk et al. (eds), *History of Concepts. Comparative Perspectives*, Amsterdam, 1998; Niklas Olsen, *History in the Plural. An Introduction to the Work of Reinhart Koselleck*, New York and Oxford, 2012; and Melvin Richter, *The History of Political and Social Concepts. A Critical Introduction*, New York and Oxford, 1995.

37. It goes without saying that this transformation did not eliminate the directional sense of the term.
38. Jon May and Nigel Thrift (eds), *TimeSpace. Geographies of Temporality*, London and New York, 2001.
39. See Reinhart Koselleck, 'Zur historisch-politischen Semantik asymmetrischer Gegenbegriffe', in Reinhart Koselleck, *Vergangene Zukunft*, 211–59. See also Helmut Hühn, 'Die Entgegensetzung von "Osten" und "Westen", "Orient" und "Okzident" als begriffsgeschichtliche Herausforderung', in Ernst Müller (ed.), *Begriffsgeschichte im Umbruch? (Archiv für Begriffsgeschichte, Sonderheft 4)*, Hamburg, 2005, 59–67.
40. See Jürgen Osterhammel, *Die Verwandlung der Welt. Eine Geschichte des 19. Jahrhunderts*, Munich, 2009; and Iris Schröder, *Das Wissen von der ganzen Welt. Globale Geographien und räumliche Ordnungen Afrikas und Europas, 1790–1870*, Paderborn et al., 2011.
41. See, for example, Dominique George Frédérique de Pradt, *L'Europe et L'Amérique en 1821*, vol. 1, Paris, [1822], 116; and, with a critical stance towards the 'Western powers', Karl Eduard Goldmann, *Die europäische Pentarchie*, Leipzig, 1839, 111–12.
42. Major encyclopaedias of the eighteenth and early nineteenth centuries define 'the west', if at all, in a purely directional sense. See, for example, Johann Hübner, *Reales Staats-Zeitungs- und Conversations-Lexicon …*, Leipzig, 1711, col. 1676; Heinrich Adam Meissner, *Philosophisches Lexicon …*, Bayreuth et al., 1737, 721; *Grosses vollständiges Universal-Lexicon aller Wissenschaften und Künste …*, vol. 25, ed. Johann Heinrich Zedler, Halle and Leipzig, 1740, col. 840; Johann Samuel Ersch, Johann Gottfried Gruber and Moritz Hermann Eduard Meier, *Allgemeine Enzyklopädie der Wissenschaften und Künste in alphabetischer Folge*, vol. 2/8, Leipzig, 1831, 230–33. Neither the *Walch* (1775) nor the *Brockhaus* (1796) encyclopaedia includes an entry for 'the west'.
43. Großherzoglich Hessischer Rat [Ludwig] von Meseritz, 'Rußland und die vereinigten Staaten von Amerika. Eine Parallele', *Jahrbücher der Geschichte und Staatskunst* 9/2 (1836), 314–42, here 315: 'östliches Kaiserreich' – 'westlicher Freistaat'.
44. See Ernst Benz, 'Ost und West in der christlichen Geschichtsanschauung' (1933), in Ernst Benz, *Endzeiterwartung zwischen Ost und West. Studien zur christlichen Eschatologie*, Freiburg, 1973, 90–117.
45. See Helmut Hühn, 'Westen; Okzident, I', in *Historisches Wörterbuch der Philosophie*, vol. 12, Darmstadt, 2004, col. 661–68.
46. Georg Wilhelm Friedrich Hegel, *Lectures on the Philosophy of World History. Introduction: Reason in History*, trans. H.B. Nisbet, Cambridge et al., 1975, 197.
47. See Claude D. Conter, *Jenseits der Nation – Das vergessene Europa des 19. Jahrhunderts. Die Geschichte der Inszenierung und Visionen Europas in Literatur, Geschichte und Politik*, Bielefeld, 2004, 248–49. See also Ernst Schulin, *Die weltgeschichtliche Erfassung des Orients bei Hegel und Ranke*, Göttingen, 1958, 138–40.

48. See Jürgen Osterhammel, 'Transkulturell vergleichende Geschichtswissenschaft', in Jürgen Osterhammel (ed.), *Geschichtswissenschaft jenseits des Nationalstaats. Studien zu Beziehungsgeschichte und Zivilisationsvergleich*, Göttingen, 2001, 11–45, here 19. See also Lawrence Krader, *The Asiatic Mode of Production. Sources, Development and Critique in the Writings of Karl Marx*, Assen, 1974; and Marian Sawer, *Marxism and the Question of the Asiatic Mode of Production*, The Hague, 1977.
49. See Conter, *Jenseits der Nation*, 253–57, 312–18.
50. See ibid., 140.
51. See Hans-Günther Schwarz, *Der Orient und die Ästhetik der Moderne*, Munich, 2003; Andrea Polaschegg, *Der andere Orientalismus. Regeln deutsch-morgenländischer Imagination im 19. Jahrhundert*, Berlin and New York, 2005; and for German Orientalism, Marchand, *German Orientalism in the Age of Empire*.
52. See Hans Lemberg, 'Zur Entstehung des Osteuropabegriffs im 19. Jahrhundert. Vom "Norden" zum "Osten" Europas', *Jahrbücher für Geschichte Osteuropas* 33/1 (1985), 48–91. Lemberg's analysis is more convincing than Larry Wolff's thesis, which situates the geographical shift as early as in the second half of the eighteenth century: *Inventing Eastern Europe. The Map of Civilization on the Mind of the Enlightenment*, Stanford, 1994. For the idea of a German 'drive to the East' (*Drang nach Osten*), which also originated in the first half of the nineteenth century, see Wolfgang Wippermann, *Der 'deutsche Drang nach Osten'. Ideologie und Wirklichkeit eines politischen Schlagwortes*, Darmstadt, 1981.
53. See Bavaj, 'The West'; Peggy Heller, 'The Russian Dawn. How Russia Contributed to the Emergence of "the West" as a Concept', in Browning and Lehti (eds), *The Struggle for the West*, 33–52; and Martin Schulze Wessel, 'Westen; Okzident, II: Russland', in *Historisches Wörterbuch der Philosophie* 12, col. 668–72.
54. For a broad overview see Lothar Gall, 'Liberalismus und auswärtige Politik', in Klaus Hildebrand and Reiner Pommerin (eds), *Deutsche Frage und europäisches Gleichgewicht. Festschrift für Andreas Hillgruber zum 60. Geburtstag*, Cologne and Vienna, 1985, 31–46.
55. See Groh, *Russland und das Selbstverständnis Europas*, 198.
56. See ibid., 249–50; Stephan Walter, *Demokratisches Denken zwischen Marx und Hegel. Die politische Philosophie Arnold Ruges. Eine Geschichte der Demokratie in Deutschland*, Düsseldorf, 1995, esp. 307–81.
57. See Groh, *Russland und das Selbstverständnis Europas*, 198–222. See also Florian Gassner, *Germany versus Russia. A Social History of the Divide between East and West*, Ph.D. thesis, Vancouver, 2012; and Florian Gassner, 'Becoming a Western Nation. German National Identity and the Image of Russia', in Maxwell (ed.), *The East–West Discourse*, 51–71. For Prussia see Hans-Christof Kraus, 'Wahrnehmung und Deutung des Krimkrieges in Preußen. Zur innenpolitischen Rückwirkung eines internationalen Großkonflikts', in Georg Maag, Wolfram Pyta and Martin Windisch (eds), *Der Krimkrieg als erster europäischer Medienkrieg*, Berlin, 2010, 235–56.
58. Gustav Diezel, *Deutschland und die abendländische Civilisation. Zur Läuterung unserer politischen und socialen Begriffe*, Stuttgart, 1852, 392. See also Harald Biermann, *Ideologie statt Realpolitik. Kleindeutsche Liberale und auswärtige Politik vor der Reichsgründung*, Düsseldorf, 2006, 57.
59. Diezel, quoted in Biermann, *Ideologie statt Realpolitik*, 70. See especially Gustav Diezel, *Russland, Deutschland und die östliche Frage*, Stuttgart, 1853.
60. See, for instance, Jakob P. Fallmerayer, 'Deutschland und die orientalische Frage' (1855), in *Gesammelte Werke von Jakob Philipp Fallmerayer, vol 2: Politische und*

culturhistorische Aufsätze, ed. Georg Martin Thomas, Leipzig, 1861, 110–54. See also Gassner, *Germany versus Russia*, 188–89.

61. See Biermann, *Ideologie statt Realpolitik*; Christian Jansen, 'Das Bild der Französischen Revolution im deutschen Liberalismus der 1850er und 1860er Jahre', in Gudrun Gersmann and Hubertus Kohle (eds), *Frankreich 1848–1870. Die Französische Revolution in der Erinnerungskultur des Zweiten Kaiserreiches*, Stuttgart, 1998, 175–87; Ulrike von Hirschhausen, *Liberalismus und Nation. Die Deutsche Zeitung 1847–1850*, Düsseldorf, 1998, 251–52; and Oscar J. Hammen, 'Free Europe versus Russia, 1830–1854', *American Slavic and East European Review* 11/1 (1952), 27–41, here 38.
62. Friedrich Schlegel, 'Die Signatur des Zeitalters', in Friedrich Schlegel, *Studien zur Geschichte und Politik* (*Kritische Friedrich-Schlegel-Ausgabe*, vol 7, part 1), introd. and ed. Ernst Behler, Munich et al., 1966, 483–596, here 500–507. See Conter, *Jenseits der Nation*, 244–48; and Gollwitzer, *Europabild und Europagedanke*, 204–206.
63. A. Widmann, *Frankreich, Russland und die Vereinigte deutsche Großmacht*, 2nd edn, Jena, 1854, 3.
64. See J.E. Jörg, 'Die kaiserliche Restauration in Frankreich und die fremden Mächte', G. *Philips' und G. Görres' historisch-politische Blätter für das katholische Deutschland* 31 (1853), 1–12; J.E. Jörg, 'Unsere Lage. Zum neuen Jahre', G. *Philips' und G. Görres' historisch-politische Blätter für das katholische Deutschland* 32 (1854), 1–23; and J.E. Jörg, 'Motivirte Gedanken über osteuropäische Thesen', G. *Philips' und G. Görres' historisch-politische Blätter für das katholische Deutschland* 33 (1854), 509–30, 607–44, 681–724, 760–820.
65. Jörg, 'Motivirte Gedanken über osteuropäische Thesen', 722, 802. For an extensive analysis, see Gollwitzer, *Europabild und Europagedanke*, 291–95; and Groh, *Russland und das Selbstverständnis Europas*, 283–93. For conservative notions of the West in Prussia at the time of the Crimean War see, moreover, Barbara Vogel, '"Option gegen den Westen". Anfänge eines politischen Schlüsselworts zwischen Revolution und "Neuer Ära" in Preußen', in Dagmar Bussiek and Simona Göbel (eds), *Kultur, Politik und Öffentlichkeit. Festschrift für Jens Flemming*, Kassel, 2009, 134–55.
66. See Jürgen John, '"Deutsche Mitte" – "Europas Mitte". Zur Verschränkung der "Mitteldeutschland"- und "Mitteleuropa"-Diskurse', in Detlef Altenburg, Lothar Ehrlich and Jürgen John (eds), *Im Herzen Europas. Nationale Identitäten und Erinnerungskulturen*, Cologne et al., 2008, 11–80, here especially 27–36, 62–70.
67. See also Troy R.E. Paddock, *Creating the Russian Peril. Education, the Public Sphere, and National Identity in Imperial Germany, 1890–1914*, Rochester, NY, 2010; and Maria Lammich, *Das deutsche Osteuropabild in der Zeit der Reichsgründung*, Boppard/Rhein, 1978.
68. See also the relevant chapters in Dagmar Lorenz and Ingrid Spörk (eds), *Konzept Osteuropa. Der 'Osten' als Konstrukt der Fremd- und Eigenbestimmung in deutschsprachigen Texten des 19. und 20. Jahrhunderts*, Würzburg, 2011.
69. See Gollwitzer, *Geschichte des weltpolitischen Denkens* 2, 63–70.
70. See Paddock, *Creating the Russian Peril*; Troy R.E. Paddock, 'Creating an Oriental Feindbild', *Central European History* 39 (2006), 214–43; and Troy R.E. Paddock, 'Still Stuck at Sevastopol. The Depiction of Russia during the Russo-Japanese War and the Beginning of the First World War in the German Press', *German History* 16 (1998), 358–76.
71. See, for example, Hugo Ganz, *Vor der Katastrophe. Ein Blick ins Zarenreich. Skizzen und Interviews aus den russischen Hauptstädten*, Frankfurt/Main, 1904. See also Denis Sdvižkov's chapter in this volume.

72. See Anselm Doering-Manteuffel, 'Internationale Geschichte als Systemgeschichte. Strukturen und Handlungsmuster im europäischen Staatensystem des 19. und 20. Jahrhunderts', in Wilfried Loth and Jürgen Osterhammel (eds), *Internationale Geschichte. Themen – Ergebnisse – Aussichten*, Munich, 2000, 93–115.
73. See Gollwitzer, *Geschichte des weltpolitischen Denkens* 2, 218. See also Biermann, *Ideologie statt Realpolitik*; and Karl-Georg Faber, 'Realpolitik als Ideologie. Die Bedeutung des Jahres 1866 für das politische Denken in Deutschland', *Historische Zeitschrift* 203 (1966), 1–45.
74. See Sönke Neitzel, *Weltmacht oder Untergang. Die Weltreichslehre im Zeitalter des Imperialismus*, Paderborn et al., 2000; and Sönke Neitzel, 'Außenpolitische Zukunftsvorstellungen in Deutschland um 1900', in Sönke Neitzel (ed.), *1900. Zukunftsvisionen der Großmächte*, Paderborn et al., 2002, 55–79.
75. Gollwitzer, *Geschichte des weltpolitischen Denkens* 2, 223–24.
76. See Boris Barth and Jürgen Osterhammel (eds), *Zivilisierungsmissionen. Imperiale Weltverbesserung seit dem 18. Jahrhundert*, Konstanz, 2005.
77. See, especially, Brooks Adams, *The Law of Civilization and Decay. An Essay of History*, London and New York, 1895; W. Cunningham, *An Essay on Western Civilization in its Economic Aspects*, 2 vols, Cambridge, 1898–1900; Benjamin Kidd, *Social Evolution*, London and New York, 1894; Benjamin Kidd, *Principles of Western Civilisation*, London and New York, 1902; James Stanley Little, *Doom of Western Civilization*, London, 1907; and Ramsay McDonald, 'The Propaganda of Civilization', *International Journal of Ethics* 11 (1901), 455–68.
78. See Gollwitzer, *Geschichte des weltpolitischen Denkens* 2, 229–30.
79. Research offers conflicting interpretations on this point. Jörg Fisch rejects the view that an antithesis between 'German culture' and 'Western civilization' was constructed in the context of imperial politics, whereas Birthe Kundrus finds proof for the relevance of the notion of 'German culture' for the self-understanding of German colonizers. See Jörg Fisch, 'Zivilisation, Kultur', in Brunner, Conze and Koselleck (eds), *Geschichtliche Grundbegriffe* 7, 679–774, here 749–52; and Birthe Kundrus, *Moderne Imperialisten. Das Kaiserreich im Spiegel seiner Kolonien*, Cologne et al., 2003. See also Beßlich, *Wege in den 'Kulturkrieg'*, esp. 25–27.
80. See Fisch, 'Zivilisation, Kultur'; and *Europäische Schlüsselwörter. Wortvergleichende und wortgeschichtliche Studien*, vol. 3: *Kultur und Zivilisation*, ed. Sprachwissenschaftliches Colloquium (Bonn), Munich, 1967.
81. See Hermann Lübbe, 'Die philosophischen Ideen von 1914', in Hermann Lübbe, *Politische Philosophie in Deutschland. Studien zu ihrer Geschichte*, Basel and Stuttgart, 1963, 173–238. See also Bruendel, *Volksgemeinschaft oder Volksstaat*; and Hoeres, *Krieg der Philosophen*.
82. Thomas Mann, *Betrachtungen eines Unpolitischen*, 2 vols, ed. and annotated by Hermann Kurzke, Frankfurt/Main, 2009 (first published 1918).
83. See Marcus Llanque's chapter in this volume and Llanque, *Demokratisches Denken im Krieg*.
84. See, for example, Harald Bluhm, 'Dostojewski und Tolstoi-Rezeption auf dem "semantischen Sonderweg"', *Politische Vierteljahresschrift* 40/2 (1999), 305–27, here 314–16.
85. See Christoph Garstka, *Arthur Moeller van den Bruck und die erste deutsche Gesamtausgabe der Werke Dostojewskijs im Piper-Verlag 1906–1919*, Frankfurt/Main et al., 1998; see also Bluhm, 'Dostojewski und Tolstoi-Rezeption auf dem "semantischen Sonderweg"'; Theoderich Kampmann, *Dostojewski in Deutschland*, Münster, 1931; Volker Weiß, 'Dostojewskijs Dämonen. Thomas Mann, Dmitri Mereschkowski und

Arthur Moeller van den Bruck im Kampf gegen "den Westen"', in Heiko Kauffmann, Helmut Kellershohn and Jobst Paul (eds), *Völkische Bande. Dekadenz und Wiedergeburt – Analysen rechter Ideologie*, Münster, 2005, 90–122; and Volker Weiß, *Moderne Antimoderne. Arthur Moeller van den Bruck und der Wandel des Konservatismus*, Paderborn et al., 2012, 163–73, 181–86. From a Marxist perspective, see Leo Löwenthal, 'Die Auffassung Dostojewskis im Vorkriegsdeutschland', *Zeitschrift für Sozialforschung* 3/3 (1934), 343–82. For the Russian context see Effi Böhlke, 'Endzeit. Zukunftsvorstellungen im russischen politisch-philosophischen Denken um 1900', in Neitzel (ed.), *1900*, 31–54.

86. Arthur Moeller van den Bruck, 'Abkehr vom Westen', *Der Tag*, 16 October 1916. See Bluhm, 'Dostojewski und Tolstoi-Rezeption auf dem "semantischen Sonderweg"', 314; and André Schlüter, *Moeller van den Bruck. Leben und Werk*, Cologne et al., 2010, esp. 267–72.
87. See Gerd Koenen, *Der Russland-Komplex. Die Deutschen und der Osten, 1900–1945*, Munich, 2005; and Gregor Thum (ed.), *Traumland Osten. Deutsche Bilder vom östlichen Europa im 20. Jahrhundert*, Göttingen, 2006.
88. Bernhard von der Marwitz, quoted in Vejas Gabriel Liulevicius, *The German Myth of the East. 1800 to the Present*, Oxford, 2009, 137. See also Vejas Gabriel Liulevicius, 'Der Osten als apokalyptischer Raum. Deutsche Frontwahrnehmungen im und nach dem Ersten Weltkrieg', in Thum (ed.), *Traumland Osten*, 47–65; and Vejas Gabriel Liulevicius, *War Land on the Eastern Front. Culture, National Identity and German Occupation in World War I*, Cambridge and New York, 2000.
89. Liulevicius, *German Myth of the East*, 130–54, here 134.
90. See Christoph Schmidt, *'Ehrfurcht und Erbarmen'. Thomas Manns Nietzsche-Rezeption 1914 bis 1947*, Trier, 1997.
91. Friedrich Nietzsche, 'Götzen-Dämmerung oder Wie man mit dem Hammer philosophirt' (1889), in *Nietzsches Werke*, vol. 8, Leipzig, 1899, 59–182, here 151. See also Friedrich Nietzsche, *Menschliches Allzumenschliches*, vol. 1 (*Nietzsches Werke*, 1. Abtl., Bd. II/1), Leipzig, 1917, 262.
92. See, especially, Friedrich Naumann, *Mitteleuropa*, Berlin, 1915.
93. See Gollwitzer, *Geschichte des weltpolitischen Denkens 2*, 82, 230.
94. Osterhammel, *Die Verwandlung der Welt*, 143. See also Sebastian Conrad, *Globalisierung und Nation im Deutschen Kaiserreich*, Munich, 2006, 64. The discovery of an alleged 'yellow peril' at the turn of the century was also part of this wider redesign of global perceptions. See Heinz Gollwitzer, *Die gelbe Gefahr. Geschichte eines Schlagworts. Studien zum imperialistischen Denken*, Göttingen, 1962.
95. Compare Max Weber, *Gesammelte Aufsätze zur Religionssoziologie*, vol. 1, 9th edn, Tübingen, 1988 (first published 1920), 1–16, with Max Weber, *The Protestant Ethic and the Spirit of Capitalism*, trans. Talcott Parsons, with a foreword by R.H. Tawney, 3rd edn, New York and London, 1950 (first published 1930), 13–31.
96. See Marcus Llanque's chapter in this volume.
97. See, especially, Bernd Faulenbach, *Ideologie des deutschen Weges. Die deutsche Geschichte in der Historiographie zwischen Kaiserreich und Nationalsozialismus*, Munich, 1980.
98. See Conze, *Das Europa der Deutschen*; Pöpping, *Abendland*.
99. Armin Mohler, *Die Konservative Revolution in Deutschland 1918–1932. Ein Handbuch*, 3rd revised edn, Darmstadt, 1989 (first published 1950), 64. See especially the works by Moeller van den Bruck, but also Friedrich Hielscher, *Das Reich*, Berlin, 1931; Edgar Julius Jung, *Die Herrschaft der Minderwertigen. Ihr Zerfall und ihre*

Ablösung, Berlin, 1927; Ernst Niekisch, *Entscheidung*, Berlin, 1930; and Giselher Wirsing, *Zwischeneuropa und die deutsche Zukunft*, Jena, 1932.
100. See Oswald Spengler, *Der Untergang des Abendlandes. Umrisse einer Morphologie der Weltgeschichte*, 2 vols, Munich, 1918/22; and Oswald Spengler, *The Decline of the West*, trans. Charles Francis Atkinson, New York, 1926/28. For a summary of Spengler's argument, see Jacinta O'Hagan, *Conceptualizing the West in International Relations. From Spengler to Said*, Basingstoke and New York, 2002.
101. See, for example, Alfred Rosenberg, *Der Zukunftsweg einer deutschen Außenpolitik*, Munich, 1927; and Alfred Rosenberg, *Der Mythus des 20. Jahrhunderts. Eine Wertung der seelisch-geistigen Gestaltenkämpfe unserer Zeit*, Munich, 1930.
102. See Stefan Vogt, *Nationaler Sozialismus und Soziale Demokratie. Die sozialdemokratische Junge Rechte 1918–1945*, Bonn, 2006.
103. See Anselm Doering-Manteuffel's chapter in this volume and Doering-Manteuffel, *Wie westlich sind die Deutschen?* See also Angster, *Konsenskapitalismus und Sozialdemokratie*.
104. For concepts of a European 'third way' see also Christian Bailey, *Between Yesterday and Tomorrow. German Visions of Europe, 1926–1950*, New York and Oxford, 2013; Christian Bailey, 'The Continuities of West German History'; Friedrich Kießling, *Die undeutschen Deutschen. Eine ideengeschichtliche Archäologie der alten Bundesrepublik, 1945–1972*, Paderborn et al., 2012, 212–17, 359–75; and Wilfried Loth, *Der Weg nach Europa. Geschichte der europäischen Integration 1939–1957*, Göttingen, 1990, 28–34. For neutralist conceptions see Alexander Gallus, *Die Neutralisten. Verfechter eines vereinten Deutschland zwischen Ost und West, 1945–1990*, Düsseldorf, 2001.
105. See A. Dirk Moses, *German Intellectuals and the Nazi Past*, Cambridge et al., 2007; and Tillmann Bendikowski and Lucian Hölscher (eds), *Political Correctness. Der sprachpolitische Streit um die nationalsozialistischen Verbrechen*, Göttingen, 2008.
106. See Gollwitzer, *Europabild und Europagedanke*; and Groh, *Russland und das Selbstverständnis Europas*. See also Bernhard Fabian, *Alexis de Tocquevilles Amerikabild. Genetische Untersuchungen über Zusammenhänge mit der zeitgenössischen, insbesondere der englischen Amerika-Interpretation*, Heidelberg, 1957; and with a critical intent: Kurt Goldammer, *Der Mythus von Ost und West. Eine kultur- und religionsgeschichtliche Betrachtung*, Munich and Basel, 1962.
107. See now Reinhild Kreis, *Orte für Amerika. Deutsch-Amerikanische Institute und Amerikahäuser in der Bundesrepublik seit den 1960er Jahren*, Stuttgart, 2012.
108. See Conze, *Das Europa der Deutschland*; Schildt, *Abendland*; and Stephen Brockmann, 'Germany as Occident at the Zero Hour', *German Studies Review* 25/3 (2002), 477–96.
109. See Ulrich Herbert, 'Liberalisierung als Lernprozess. Die Bundesrepublik in der deutschen Geschichte', in Ulrich Herbert (ed.), *Wandlungsprozesse in Westdeutschland. Belastung, Integration, Liberalisierung, 1945–1980*, Göttingen, 2002, 7–49.
110. See Jan-Werner Müller, *Contesting Democracy. Political Ideas in Twentieth-Century Europe*, New Haven, 2011.
111. Michael Hochgeschwender makes this point with respect to 'the West' in his article 'Was ist der Westen?'.
112. Ibid., 27.
113. Richard Löwenthal, however, was able to combine both explanatory models. See Riccardo Bavaj, '"Western Civilization" and the Acceleration of Time. Richard Löwenthal's Reflections on a Crisis of "the West" in the Aftermath of the Student

Revolt of "1968"', *Themenportal Europäische Geschichte* (2010), online: http://www.europa.clio-online.de/2010/Article=434.
114. Jürgen Habermas, 'Eine Art Schadensabwicklung. Die apologetischen Tendenzen in der deutschen Zeitgeschichtsschreibung', *Die Zeit*, 11 July 1986, reprinted in '*Historikerstreit*'. *Die Dokumentation der Kontroverse um die Einzigartigkeit der nationalsozialistischen Judenvernichtung*, Munich and Zurich, 1987, 62–76, here 75.
115. See most recently Paul Nolte, 'Jenseits des Westens? Überlegungen zu einer Zeitgeschichte der Demokratie', *Vierteljahrshefte für Zeitgeschichte* 61 (2013), 275–302, here 280–82. See also David Marquand, *The End of the West. The Once and Future Europe*, Princeton and Oxford, 2011, esp. 1–23, 100, 176–77.
116. See Doering-Manteuffel, *Wie westlich sind die Deutschen?*, 5–6.

Part 1

Rises and Silences of 'the West'

Chapter 1

IN SEARCH OF 'THE WEST'
The Language of Political, Social and Cultural Spaces in the *Sattelzeit*, from about 1770 to the 1830s

Bernhard Struck

In 1835 Richard Otto Spazier published a travel account entitled *East and West. Travels in Poland and France*.[1] The journalist and author, born in Leipzig in 1803, grew up in Dresden and, by the early 1830s, had became an ardent supporter of Polish national independence. Following the violent suppression of the November Insurrection by Russian troops in Poland in 1830, Spazier decided to travel through the Prussian parts of the former *Rzeczpospolita*, the Polish-Lithuanian noble republic, mainly through the Grand Duchy of Posen. Thus in 1833 he travelled for several weeks from Leipzig via Landsberg (Gorzów Wielkopolski), Gnesen (Gniezno) to Posen (Poznań) and back via Glogau (Głogów) in Silesia and Dresden. Deeply frustrated with the politically stagnant situation in the German lands during the *Vormärz* and saddened that the war for Polish independence that he was hoping for had not materialized, Spazier eventually decided to leave his home country. As with many of his generation and with figures in the *Junges Deutschland* like Heinrich Heine, Karl Gutzkow and Ludwig Börne, his chosen destination was Paris. It was only in 1854, shortly before his death, that he returned from France.

Today there is nothing surprising in the linkage of Spazier's travel and exile destinations, Poland and France, and the geographical categories East and West, which he chose to describe these two neighbouring countries from a German perspective. A traveller in the late twentieth century, say on a train from Berlin to Warsaw, would easily subscribe to Spazier's geographical categories and think of travelling 'eastwards'. Around 1830, however, this was a novelty.

From a German perspective Richard Spazier was one of the first travellers to refer to Poland and France as belonging to the East and to the West: previous travellers had located these countries along a North–South axis. Why did Spazier do this? What led him to choose spatial categories encompassing macro-regions with specific normative connotations that are familiar to the modern reader but which had not been applied previously? Did travellers like Spazier have an image of the West that was shared by others? Basing its insights mainly, though not exclusively, on travelogues, this chapter aims at reconstructing the use of spatial categories by German authors during the *Sattelzeit* ('saddle period') – to use the term coined by Reinhart Koselleck. Since spatial categories most often coexist in binary oppositions such as 'Orient' and 'Occident', 'East' and 'West', this is done from a perspective that takes into account journeys into areas that today are recognized as parts of Western and Eastern or East Central Europe.

Travelogues feature prominently in this contribution for a number of reasons. First, during the decades corresponding with the *Sattelzeit* – roughly from 1770 to 1830 – travel and travel writing flourished. The decades around 1800 were the heyday of the *bürgerliche Bildungsreise*, the bourgeois practice of gaining an education through travel. Following the Enlightenment ideal of personal self-improvement, extended travels that enabled Europeans to learn from the world were seen as an integral part of rounding off their education and experience as well as enriching their personal culture.[2]

As part of the travel culture of the time, it was an imperative to write about the travel experience in order to pass the acquired knowledge on to a wider public. Thus the genre of the travelogue was not just widely read; from the late eighteenth century onward it was a genre that only the novel could match in popularity.[3]

Due to the wide circulation of travel writing – about a quarter of all books in lending libraries were works on geography, most of which were travelogues – the genre is indicative of how space was perceived and described.[4] Prior to the specialization of the sciences and the emergence of geography as a discipline in its own right from the 1830s onwards, travelogues covered information on political, geographical, cultural and statistical issues.[5] Geographers of the late eighteenth century, such as August Ludwig Schlözer and Anton Friedrich Büsching, compiled their geographical and statistical works primarily from travelogues.[6]

This chapter is divided into two main sections. The first will go into further detail on the concepts of the *Begriffsgeschichte* and *Sattelzeit* as well as look at spatial concepts people held during that period. The latter will be examined with reference to the work of Larry Wolff and his thesis regarding the invention of Eastern Europe during the late eighteenth century. The second part will then seek to reconstruct spatial concepts from a German perspective. In contrast to Larry Wolff's interpretation it will be argued that, from a German perspective, an inner-European East–West divide did not emerge during the late eighteenth century but towards the end of the *Sattelzeit*. It was only after 1815 that authors started referring more frequently to an inner-European East–West divide and thus, perhaps, contributed to the emerging idea of the West.

The Challenge of *Begriffsgeschichte*: Geography and Spatial Concepts during the *Sattelzeit*

The year Spazier published his travel account, 1835, roughly corresponds with the end of what Reinhart Koselleck has famously named the *Sattelzeit* – the period between about the 1770s and the 1830s, during which modern socio-political language was shaped.[7] Browsing through the alphabetically arranged volumes of the *Geschichtliche Grundbegriffe* (*Basic Concepts in History*), the monumental core of *Begriffsgeschichte*, we find that the entries primarily engage with concepts related to social, legal and constitutional history. What are absent are entries related to space or to geographical categories. This void could be seen as surprising, since modern political language and discourse operates with geographical concepts such as 'the West', 'the East', 'Orient' or 'Occident'. On a functional level, such geographical concepts serve as a *Kollektivsingular* (collective singular), first, in order to demarcate a specific spatial entity based on political and cultural patterns. Second, and perhaps more important, they carry normative implications by creating binary oppositions and dichotomies between alleged levels of modernity, between 'progress' and 'backwardness', between 'civilization' and 'barbarism'. From a twentieth- or twenty-first-century perspective it is difficult to imagine political discourses without these powerful and suggestive spatial concepts – powerful, since all of these *Kollektivsingulare* have the ability to evoke images, identifications and emotions.[8]

The reasons for not including, implicitly or explicitly, any spatial concepts are arguably speculative. Three reasons, however, seem plausible, two of them derived from the theoretical and methodological concept of *Begriffsgeschichte*, a third stemming from the intellectual and political context from which the history of concepts evolved. The first reason could be the simple one that none of the spatial concepts 'East', 'West', 'Orient', 'Occident' belongs to the core of socio-political and legal language. The close interrelation between social history and *Begriffsgeschichte*, as explicated by Koselleck, is certainly one reason for their absence.[9]

A second reason derives from the explicit methodological choice of a *longue durée* perspective and the idea of diachronic comparisons of the shifting semantics of words and concepts.[10] With their semantic variations, of course, concepts such as 'nation' or 'democracy' have distant etymological origins. Even though forms of alterity constructions are at least as old as human intercultural interaction, including travel or commerce, as well as forms of scripture – one could think of Herodotus's *Histories* – spatial collective singulars such as 'the West' did not exist before the *Sattelzeit*, hence their absence from the *Geschichtliche Grundbegriffe*.[11]

A third reason that might explain the absence of any spatial concepts could be the wider political and intellectual context from which the history of concepts emerged. *Begriffsgeschichte*, conceived as an extension as well as an integral part of *Sozialgeschichte*, has its roots in the 1960s and when the volumes of the *Geschichtliche Grundbegriffe* were published, between 1972 and 1992. During these decades, politically dominated by the Cold War and its static geopolitical East–West dichotomy, spatial history and its concepts were simply not on the agenda. It is not by accident that an interest in space only reemerged after 1989/91 and the fall of communism.[12] This 'spatial turn' became manifest in a number of publications on borders and their fluidity as well as publications on spatial issues, their etymological origins and the shifting semantic content of concepts such as 'Eastern Europe'.[13]

One of the most influential and inspiring books here is Larry Wolff's *Inventing Eastern Europe*. The book was published only a few years after the fall of the Berlin Wall and Wolff's starting point is the Cold War and Churchill's famous speech in 1946 that evoked the existence of an 'iron curtain' dividing Europe into an 'East' and a 'West'. What Wolff is interested in is the genealogical origin of the concept of 'Eastern Europe'.[14] He analyses an array of primary sources, mainly of British and French origin from the eighteenth century – including maps, memoirs and philosophical works as well as travel writing. His main thesis is that it was the Enlightenment that invented 'Eastern Europe' as a geographical concept, with its normative, mainly negative, connotations. As Wolff argues, this process was shaped by real encounters, such as travel, as well as through the imagination, though there is certainly not a clear line between the two.[15] Since it was the Enlightenment that invented 'civilization' as a measurable scale of human development, philosophers, travellers and geographers of the late eighteenth century, according to Wolff, saw Eastern Europe as the inner-European 'other', the negative normative counterpart of the allegedly civilized parts of Western Europe, mainly France and England.[16] Loosely following Edward Said's concept of 'Orientalism', Wolff states that Western philosophers and travellers 'orientalized' the eastern parts of Europe, including Poland, Russia, Bohemia and the Baltic provinces, depicting them as backward, barbaric or (semi-)oriental. The traditional North–South dichotomy that had split Europe into a civilized South and a barbaric North since Tacitus had thus shifted to an East–West divide.[17]

Wolff gives some compelling evidence for the poor conditions of roads, inns and infrastructure, and for the destitution of the rural and urban populations in what is today known as East Central or Eastern Europe between Riga, Warsaw, Moscow and Budapest.[18] The question remains, however, to what extent this was specific to an allegedly backward and barbaric Eastern Europe in contrast to the self-identification of the travellers and philosophers with an allegedly modern and progressive Western counterpart.[19] Despite this evidence from the primary sources, among which travelogues feature prominently, there is a key problem in Wolff's argument which harks back to the theoretical background of *Begriffsgeschichte*. There is little evidence from the sources themselves that travellers, cartographers or philosophers actually used terms such as 'East' or 'Eastern Europe' around 1800 in order to circumscribe an inner-European other or 'orient'. Terms like 'Eastern Europe' or 'Oriental Europe' are rare in sources of the time before 1800. If found at all, they derive from French terms translated into English, such as *'Prusse orientale'* or *'l'orient de l'Europe'*.[20] Linked with descriptions of rural conditions, which were indeed poor, and with accounts of the neediness of the peasants and the condition of serfdom, these terms are interpreted as part of the invention of Eastern Europe and of an increasing awareness of a growing inner-European East–West divide, a divide between backwardness and civilization.

The absence of the actual spatial concepts is, however, problematic. Without the terms 'Eastern Europe' and 'Western Europe' or 'West' actually being used by contemporaries around 1800, Wolff seems to be projecting the post-1945 Cold War division of Europe back into the eighteenth century.[21]

With very few exceptions Wolff's analysis is based on English and French authors. Thus the question emerges to what extent German travellers shared this image of an 'Eastern' and a 'Western' Europe. How did travellers from the German lands describe areas, which – to the modern mind – belong to Western Europe, the West or, following the logic of Reinhart Koselleck's *'asymmetrische Gegenbegriffe'*, Eastern Europe respectively?[22]

Shifting Language of Space:
From North to East, from South to West

Travel writing is a key source for the reconstruction of the perception of space as well as for the change of spatial concepts. Accounts in this genre are not, however, the only source available to historians. Encyclopaedias from the later eighteenth century might as well serve as a starting point. There are a number of entries hinting at geographical directions such as 'westlich' (western), 'Norden' (north), 'östlich' (eastern) and 'Süd' (south) to be found in both Johann Heinrich Zedler's *Universal-Lexicon* and Johann Christian Adelung's *Grammatisch-kritisches Wörterbuch*.[23] None of these terms, however, shares the modern semantic connotation of a spatial concept such as 'the East' or 'the West'. What the terms in both encyclopaedias indicate is a relation between geography, on the one hand, and culture and climate on the other. Typical of eighteenth-century climate theory is the way in which the rather brief encyclopaedia entries refer to a North–South rather than an East–West dichotomy. According to proponents of climate theory, such as Montesquieu and Jean-Baptiste Dubos, Europe was divided into 'southern and northern nations', long influenced by different climates that shaped culture and people as well as forms of government and institutions.[24] None of the terms given in Zedler's or Adelung's encyclopaedias, however, indicate the idea of a macro-region that encompasses several countries; nor, semantically, do these terms share the characteristics of a *Kollektivsingular* such as 'the West', with its modern normative implications.

Aside from the encyclopaedias, the corpus of travel writings is arguably one, and perhaps the most relevant, source for reconstructing spatial categories in the *Sattelzeit*.[25] In the late eighteenth century, a typical *bürgerliche Bildungsreise* would have gone through France and Italy, often with at least a brief stop in the Netherlands. Throughout the second half of the eighteenth century, England and Switzerland became increasingly popular travel destinations as well.[26] Certainly less high in numbers but not uncommon were tours through Poland, through the Baltic provinces, and into tsarist Russia, at times touching Bohemia and other parts of the Habsburg monarchy. Though, of course, financial and temporal resources varied from traveller to traveller, a typical journey would usually last between a few weeks (as a minimum) to several months – the more usual length. In these times prior to railway travel, the tourists covered vast distances in stagecoaches, usually travelling along the network of the postal system. Longer spells during such a journey were most commonly spent in cities such as Paris, London, Rome, Warsaw or Saint Petersburg. But the time spent in the coach and in smaller towns, inns and villages gave ample opportunities for observation of the spaces in-between, enabling individuals to make comparisons between different regions.[27]

The search for geographical terms and spatial concepts in travelogues around 1800 highlights that the authors generally referred to three different spatial levels: the subnational or regional; the national; and a macro-regional level that transcended state boundaries. The use – or rather the hierarchy – of these different scales changed during the *Sattelzeit*. Before Richard Spazier, who in 1835 explicitly entitled his travelogue *East and West*, thus referring to Poland and France as parts of larger East–West macro-regional entities, it was usual for the title of a travel journal to list the different countries visited rather than subsume them under larger macro-spatial units. A typical example from the late eighteenth century is that of the physician Johann Friedrich Carl Grimm, who published an account of his journeys under the title *Remarks of a Traveller through Germany, France, England and Holland in Letters to his Friends*.[28] As in numerous other accounts of this time, the national level featured prominently in the title. Prior to the 1830s, individual national destinations were hardly ever subsumed under a larger macro-region such as the West or the South and, in this respect, Spazier's *East and West* was indeed a novelty for its time.

The spatial level referred to most frequently in accounts before the early nineteenth century was the regional or local one. Once a traveller had crossed a state border, for instance from the Holy Roman Empire into France, the precise description of individual regions within that country, such as Alsace, Provence or Lorraine, dominated the spatial perception.[29] The same was true for travels into other European regions. In Poland, for instance, travellers would distinguish between Little Poland, Great Poland and Podolia as subnational historical regions with distinctive characteristics.[30] In this proto-ethnographic discourse, travellers spent considerable time and numerous pages on detailed descriptions of the economy and agriculture, social relations, architecture, costumes, culture and language, all at a subnational local and regional level.[31]

Relatively small-scale observations and descriptions at local and regional level were the dominant spatial frame through which travellers observed the other until at least 1800. There are reasons for this. First, these small-scale descriptions need to be seen within the nature and function of travel at that time. Due to the vastness of the territory covered during weeks and weeks in a stagecoach, spatial awareness was predominantly regional or local prior to the 1840s. Only with the rapid expansion of railways from the mid nineteenth century onward did travellers start to perceive space in a panoramic manner.[32] Second, within the logic and rules of the genre of the period, it was imperative to make use of the time (and money) spent travelling by passing on precise knowledge to a wider readership. This is reflected in the detailed, often multivolume travelogues: the travellers' focus was largely on aspects like social conditions, culture or the state of agriculture and how to improve it. Third, despite the application of conjectural histories in the works of Rousseau, Diderot, Condorcet and Kant during the Enlightenment and despite an emerging historical awareness (especially during the 1790s),[33] travelogues did not take a grand overview of developments. The genre crossed disciplines, including history, geography, description of the state, ethnography and statistics, but it did not (yet) hint at the kind of historical awareness that would, for instance, subsume the French and American Revolutions under one unifying spatial concept such as 'the West'. Hence none of the travelogues published in the German lands about France during the 1790s made explicit references to American independence and the events of the 1760s and 1770s in the North American colonies within a spatial concept that bracketed France with the new transatlantic republic. Influential commentators such as Georg Forster, Gerhard Anton von Halem and Johann Wilhelm von Archenholz, to name but a few, described the unfolding of the French Revolution in detail, often with fascination, but saw it as a historical event in its own right.[34] While there are occasional reflections on either the French Revolution or American independence and their respective wider repercussions on Europe, no relation to a spatial concept such as 'the West' is to be found.[35]

Compared to frequent references to the nation (most importantly in the titles of travelogues) and the detailed proto-ethnographic descriptions of landscape, agriculture, architecture and culture on a regional and local level, references to larger macro-regions were rare until the early nineteenth century. If they made such references at all, German travellers would allude to the long-standing North–South divide within Europe that dated back to Tacitus and that saw a revival during the Renaissance and the Reformation with a Europe divided into Protestant and Catholic blocs.

Carl Feyerabend, a historian and author of travelogues from Danzig, for instance, referred to Poland and Russia as the 'northern states' within a context of physiocratic discourse in the late 1790s. Even a city such as Lemberg (Lviv in today's Ukraine) could be referred to as being part of 'the North', as it was by Joseph Rohrer.[36] In a similar vein, one of the most widely read travel accounts of the early-nineteenth century, Johann Gottfried Seume's *Mein Sommer 1805*, subsumed a journey from Dresden via Warsaw and Saint Petersburg and through Scandinavia under a concept of being in 'the North'.[37] References to the North, however, were not exclusive to German travellers. As a spatial framework the North was widely referred to by other European authors until the early nineteenth century.³⁸

If there was a North, it followed that there was a South. This was the geographical notion German travellers regularly applied to France. With extended travel routes through France, Italy and often Switzerland – less so Spain – destinations were subsumed under the macro-regional concept of the South. With continuous references to eighteenth-century climate theory, travellers and geographers referred to a spatial unit that was unified by climate, which in turn had an impact on the state, customs, architecture and history in general. Thus, both North and South were largely referred to as historical and cultural regions beyond the national or state level.

With regard to the North, many travellers referred to historical periods and events such as the Deluge, the Polish-Swedish wars of the 1650s and 1660s, and the 'northern wars' of the early-eighteenth century, which left a visible impact on the region, especially parts of Poland-Lithuania, lasting until around 1800.³⁹ On the other hand frequent references to antiquity and the classics invoked the South as a broader concept. The focus here was mainly on Italy and southern France with their Roman heritage. The North–South divide, still visible in most travel accounts up to the 1830s and 1840s, was not a clear-cut one, however. Destinations like northern France were seen as border regions within this inner-European divide. Johann Daniel Mutzenbecher, a merchant from Hamburg, still referred to an inner-European North–South cleavage and stressed the many similarities between northern Germany and the northern parts of France with respect to architecture, customs and urbanization around 1820.⁴⁰ Reference to 'the West' as a spatial reference point remained largely absent for another ten years or so until Spazier published his *East and West* in 1835.

As early as 1830, however, Karl Gustav Helbig, a theologian and philologist from Saxony, travelled through parts of Russian Poland and – as one of the first travellers and political commentators of the time to do so – referred to an inner-European 'West' that contained France and England.⁴¹ It was during the two decades following the Congress of Vienna that authors started referring, slowly but certainly more frequently and explicitly, to an inner-European East–West dichotomy rather than to the traditional North–South divide. Following the classics and the legacy of Tacitus, the older North–South concept was primarily a climatic, historical and cultural-religious spatial division of Europe. By contrast, the newly emerging East–West opposition was primarily determined by political criteria. Many people, and especially the so-called *Junges Deutschland* generation, were becoming increasingly disappointed, if not frustrated, with the stagnant political situation in Prussia and Austria after 1815. Most importantly, the political alliance of the two largest German states with tsarist Russia during the Metternich era was seen as a betrayal of a generation that had hoped for more liberal political developments after the Napoleonic Wars.

One of the first travelogues to hint at the shift of geographical concepts after 1815 was written by Heinrich Heine. In 1822, Heine, who was only a few years older than Spazier, travelled through parts of Prussian and Russian Poland. To the young law student, Poland was a country 'in-between', influenced by 'barbarism from the East' (which was how Heine thought of tsarist Russia) and 'high culture [*Überkultur*] from the West'.[42] The West, to Heine, meant France, the country that would become his long-term home in exile, as it was for so many of his generation. In contrast to earlier authors, the generation of Heine and Spazier saw Europe after 1815 divided by a political rift. They associated the West with positive political values, most importantly the reign of law and constitutionalism. They saw the East, on the other hand – especially tsarist Russia – as the opposition, a region of illiberal, autocratic regimes. The latter corresponded to the *Ancien Régime* that had successfully survived the 1790s and 1800s, a political system that stood for the past and, according to Heine, fostered backwardness if not outright 'barbarism'.

The 1820s, however, seem to have been a period of transition. Despite Heine's quite clear-cut East–West dichotomy, there were other voices. In his *Lectures on the Philosophy of History*, Hegel suggested a tripartite division of Europe. According to his vision of history, there was first a 'southern Europe' around the Mediterranean. The 'heart of Europe' next consisted mainly of France, England and Germany. Last, according to Hegel, there were the 'north-eastern states of Europe', primarily Poland, Russia and the 'Slavic Empires'. His idea of a distinct 'north-eastern' part of Europe indicates a period of transition since Poland and Russia were located in the North prior to 1815.[43] It seems that in a period roughly from 1820 to 1835 – between Heine and Hegel and the later Spazier – the idea of an inner-European 'East' emerged first. The image of the East was based on the perception of its political and cultural backwardness. Another aspect of the idea of this newly emerging East was its Slavic character as opposed to the Germanic and Romanic linguistic regions. The idea of 'Slavic Empires', to which Hegel and others referred, was new in the early nineteenth century. Following the linguistic research of Johann Gottfried Herder and Wilhelm von Humboldt, Slavic-speaking areas drifted away from the traditional and geographically broader concept of the North, which had previously encompassed the Scandinavian countries as well as Poland, the Baltic provinces and Russia.[44]

If the *Sattelzeit* shaped modern socio-political language, the shift towards an idea of East and West as oppositional *Kollektivsingulare*, and thus towards a new spatial concept of Europe, was part of this process. The idea of an inner-European West, not a transatlantic one, only prevailed once 'the East' had started to take shape towards the end of this period of transition.

Notes

1. Richard Otto Spazier, *Ost und West. Reisen in Polen und Frankreich*, Stuttgart, 1835.
2. Thomas Grosser, 'Reisen und soziale Eliten. Kavalierstour – Patrizierreise – bürgerliche Bildungsreise', in Michael Maurer (ed.), *Neue Impulse der Reiseforschung*, Berlin, 1999, 135–76; James Buzard, *The Beaten Track. European Tourism, Literature, and the Ways to Culture, 1800–1918*, Oxford, 1993.
3. Peter J. Brenner (ed.), *Der Reisebericht. Die Entwicklung einer Gattung in der deutschen Literatur*, Frankfurt/Main, 1989; Uwe Hentschel, *Studien zur Reiseliteratur am Ausgang des 18. Jahrhunderts. Autoren – Formen – Ziele*, Frankfurt/Main et al., 1999; Bernhard Struck, *Nicht West – nicht Ost. Frankreich und Polen in der Wahrnehmung deutscher Reisender zwischen 1750 und 1850*, Göttingen, 2006, 79–93.
4. Marlies Stützel-Prüsener, 'Die deutschen Lesegesellschaften im Zeitalter der Aufklärung', *Nation und Nationalismus in Deutschland 1770–1990*, ed. Otto Dann, 3rd edn, Munich, 1996, 71–86.
5. Justin Stagl, *Geschichte der Neugier. Die Kunst des Reisens*, Vienna, 1995, 71–122.
6. Rainer Baasner, '"Unser Staatsgeographus ist beständig auf Reisen". Zur Ausdifferenzierung von Reiseliteratur und Geographie 1750–1800', in Maurer (ed.), *Neue Impulse der Reiseforschung*, 249–65; David N. Livingstone and Charles W. Withers (eds), *Geography and Enlightenment*, Chicago and London, 1999.
7. See Reinhart Koselleck, 'Einleitung', in Otto Brunner, Werner Conze and Reinhart Koselleck (eds), *Geschichtliche Grundbegriffe. Historisches Lexikon zur politisch-sozialen Sprache in Deutschland*, 8 vols, Stuttgart, 1972–2004, vol 1, 13–28, here 18–20.
8. See Reinhart Koselleck, *Vergangene Zukunft. Zur Semantik geschichtlicher Zeiten*, 3rd edn, Frankfurt/Main, 1995, 38–66, here 50–53.
9. Ibid., 107–29; Reinhart Koselleck, *Begriffsgeschichten. Studien zur Semantik und Pragmatik der politischen und sozialen Sprache*, Frankfurt/Main, 2006, 9–31, here 13.
10. Ibid., 22.
11. See for instance François Hartog, *Le miroir d'Hérodote. Essai sur la représentation de l'autre*, Paris, 2001; Gabriele Scheidegger, *Perverses Abendland – barbarisches Russland. Begegnungen des 16. und 17. Jahrhunderts im Schatten kultureller Missverständnisse*, Zurich, 1993; or Michael Harbsmeier, *Wilde Völkerkunde. Andere Welten in deutschen Reiseberichten der Frühen Neuzeit*, Frankfurt/Main, New York, 1994.
12. Doris Bachmann-Medick, *Cultural Turns. Neuorientierungen in den Kulturwissenschaften*, Reinbeck, 2006, 284–328, here 286–87; Jürgen Osterhammel, 'Die Wiederkehr des Raumes: Geopolitik, Geohistoire und historische Geographie', *Neue Politische Literatur* 43 (1998), 374–97; Frithjof Benjamin Schenk, 'Mental Maps. Die Konstruktion von geographischen Räumen in Europa seit der Aufklärung', *Geschichte und Gesellschaft* 28 (2002), 493–514; Jörg Döring and Tristan Thielmann, 'Einleitung: Was lesen wir im Raume? Der *Spatial Turn* und das geheime Wissen der Geographen',

in Jörg Döring and Tristan Thielmann (eds), *Spatial Turn. Das Raumparadigma in den Kultur- und Sozialwissenschaften*, Bielefeld, 2008, 7–45, here 7–8.

13. Maria Todorova, *Imagining the Balkans*, New York, 1997; Gerard Delanty, *Inventing Europe. Ideal, Identity, Reality*, Basingstoke, 1995; Martyn P. Thompson, 'Ideas of Europe during the French Revolution and Napoleonic Wars', *Journal of the History of Ideas* 55/1 (1994), 37–58.
14. Larry Wolff, *Inventing Eastern Europe. The Map of Civilization on the Mind of the Enlightenment*, Stanford, 1994, 1–4.
15. See also Struck, *Nicht West – nicht Ost*, 95–112.
16. Wolff, *Inventing Eastern Europe*, 8, 12–13. On the idea of 'culture' as a 'new category of inquiry to the comparative study of human history' see Michael C. Carhart, *The Science of Culture in Enlightenment Germany*, Cambridge (Mass.) and London, 2007, 3; Sankar Muthu, *Enlightenment against Empire*, Princeton, 2003; and Larry Wolff and Marco Cipollini (eds), *The Anthropology of the Enlightenment*, Stanford, 2007. See also Johannes Fabian, *Time and the Other. How Anthropology Makes its Object*, New York, 1983.
17. Wolff, *Inventing Eastern Europe*, 4–5.
18. Ibid., 27, 28, 32.
19. Critically from a comparative perspective, see Bernhard Struck, 'Historical Regions between Construction and Perception. Viewing France and Poland in Late-18th and Early-19th Century', *East Central Europe/L'Europe du Centre Est* 32/1–2 (2005), 79–97.
20. Wolff, *Inventing Eastern Europe*, 6, 17–25, 141, 287.
21. For a critique of Wolff see Guido Franzinetti, 'The Idea and the Reality of Eastern Europe in the Eighteenth Century', *History of European Ideas* 34/4 (2008), 361–68; Michael Confino, 'Re-inventing the Enlightenment. Western Images of Eastern Realities in the Eighteenth Century', *Canadian Slavonic Papers/Revue canadienne des slavistes*, 36/3–4 (1994), 505–22.
22. Koselleck, *Vergangene Zukunft*, 211–59, here 217.
23. Johann Heinrich Zedler (ed.), *Großes vollständiges Universal-Lexicon aller Wissenschaften und Künste …*, 64 vols, Leipzig and Halle, 1732–1750 (reprint Graz, 1961–1964); Johann Christian Adelung, *Grammatisch-kritisches Wörterbuch der hochdeutschen Mundart. Mit beständiger Vergleichung der übrigen Mundarten, besonders aber der Oberdeutschen*, 4 vols, Vienna, 1808, 1510; Johann Christian Adelung, *Versuch eines vollständigen grammatisch-kritischen Wörterbuches der hochdeutschen Mundart*, 4 vols, Leipzig, 1780, vol. 3, 520–21, 624 and vol. 4, 190.
24. Roberto M. Dainotto, *Europe (in Theory)*, Durham and London, 2007, 51, 206–207; Regina Hartmann, *Deutsche Reisende in der Spätaufklärung unterwegs in Skandinavien. Die Verständigung über den 'Norden' im Konstruktionsprozeß ihrer Berichte*, Frankfurt/Main et al., 2000, 41–42.
25. Struck, *Nicht West – nicht Ost*, 113–21.
26. Michael Maurer (ed.), *O Britannien, von deiner Freiheit einen Hut voll*, Munich, 1992; Thomas Grosser, *Reiseziel Frankreich. Deutsche Reiseliteratur vom Barock bis zur Französischen Revolution*, Opladen, 1989.
27. Struck, *Nicht West – nicht Ost*, 230–69.
28. Johann Friedrich Carl Grimm (anonymous), *Bemerkungen eines Reisenden durch Deutschland, Frankreich, England und Holland in Briefen an seine Freunde*, 3 vols, Altenburg, 1775.
29. See for instance Heinrich Sander, *Beschreibung seiner Reisen durch Frankreich, die Niederlande, Holland, Deutschland und Italien, in Beziehung auf Menschenkenntnis,*

Industrie, Litteratur und Naturkunde insonderheit, 2 vols, Leipzig, 1783/84; or Marie Sophie von La Roche (anonymous), *Journal einer Reise durch Frankreich, von der Verfasserin von Rosaliens Briefen*, Altenburg, 1787.
30. See for instance Johann Joseph Kausch, *Nachrichten über Polen*, 2 vols, Salzburg, 1793, vol. 2, 103; Johann Bernoulli, *Reisen durch Brandenburg, Pommern, Preußen, Curland, Russland und Pohlen, in den Jahren 1777 und 1778*, 6 vols, Leipzig, 1779/80, vol. 1, 136–39, vol. 6, 294–96; or Johann Rhode, *Reisen durch einen Theil Rußlands und Deutschlands in den Jahren 1797 und 1798 vom Mahler Anton*, 2 vols, Altona, 1798, vol. 1, 58–59.
31. Struck, *Nicht West – nicht Ost*, 39; Peter Bugge, '"Something in the View that Makes You Linger": Bohemia and Bohemians in British Travel Writing, 1836–1857', *Central Europe* 1/7 (2009), 3–29, here 5–6.
32. Wolfgang Schivelbusch, *Geschichte der Eisenbahnreise. Zur Industrialisierung von Raum und Zeit im 19. Jahrhundert*, 3rd edn, Munich and Vienna, 2000, 51–66.
33. Ernst W. Becker, *Zeit der Revolution! – Revolution der Zeit? Zeiterfahrungen in Deutschland in der Ära der Revolutionen 1789–1848/49*, Göttingen, 1999.
34. At least seventy-seven travel accounts were published in the German lands during the 1790s. See Struck, *Nicht West – nicht Ost*, 85; and Thomas Grosser, 'Der lange Abschied von der Revolution. Wahrnehmungen und mentalitätsgeschichtliche Verarbeitung der (post)revolutionären Entwicklung in den Reiseberichten deutscher Frankreich-Besucher', in Gudrun Gersmann and Hubertus Kohle (eds), *Frankreich 1800. Gesellschaft, Kultur, Mentalität*, Stuttgart, 1991, 163–91.
35. See for instance Karl Friedrich Häberlin, 'Ueber den Einfluß der Unabhändigkeit der vereinigten Staaten von Nord-America, auf den politischen Zustand Europens', *Göttingesches Magazin der Wissenschaften und Literatur* 3/5 (1783), 685–734. The same is true for journals at the time: see Werner Greiling and Matthias Middell, 'Frankreich-Berichterstattung in deutschen Zeitungen. Kursachsen und Thüringen zur Zeit der Französischen Revolution', in Hans-Jürgen Lüsebrink and Rolf Reichardt (eds), *Kulturtransfer im Epochenumbruch. Frankreich–Deutschland 1770 bis 1815*, vol. 1, Leipzig, 1997, 197–237.
36. See Carl B. Feyerabend, *Kosmopolitische Wanderungen durch Preußen, Liefland, Kurland, Litthauen, Vollhynine, Podolien, Gallizien und Schlesien, in den Jahren 1795 bis 1797*, 4 vols, Germany, 1798–1803, vol. 2, 367; Joseph Rohrer, *Bemerkungen auf einer Reise von der türkischen Gränze über die Bukowina durch Ost- und Westgalizien, Schlesien, Mähren nach Wien*, Vienna, 1804, 157.
37. Johann Gottfried Seume, *Mein Sommer 1805*, 2nd edn, Leipzig, 1815, 3.
38. John A. Carr, *A Northern Summer; or, Travels round the Baltic through Denmark, Sweden, Russia, Prussia, and Part of Germany in the Year 1804*, London, 1805. See also Hendriette Kliemann, *Koordinaten des Nordens. Wissenschaftliche Konstruktionen einer europäischen Region 1770–1850*, Berlin, 2005; Hartmann, *Deutsche Reisende in der Spätaufklärung unterwegs in Skandinavien*.
39. Johann Philipp von Carosi, *Reisen durch verschiedene polnische Provinzen, mineralogischen und andern Inhalts*, 2 vols, Leipzig, 1781/84; Feyerabend, *Kosmopolitische Wanderungen*, vol. 2, 460.
40. Johann Daniel Mutzenbecher, *Bemerkungen auf einer Reise aus Norddeutschland über Frankfurt nach dem südlichen Frankreich im Jahr 1819*, Leipzig, 1822, 139. See also Karl Friedrich von Jariges, *Bruchstücke einer Reise durch das südliche Frankreich, Spanien und Portugal im Jahr 1802*, Leipzig, 1810, 10–14; and Benjamin Schenk and Martina Winkler (eds), *Der Süden. Neue Perspektiven auf eine europäische Geschichtsregion*, Frankfurt/Main, 2007.

41. Karl Gustav Helbig (Pseud. K.G. Freimund), *Bemerkungen über den Zustand Polens unter russischer Herrschaft im Jahr 1830. Nach dem im Lande selbst gemachten Beobachtungen zusammengestellt*, Leipzig, 1831.
42. Heinrich Heine, 'Über Polen' (1823), in *Reisebriefe und Reisebilder*, Berlin, 1981, 83–117, here 93.
43. Georg Friedrich Wilhelm Hegel, *Vorlesungen zur Philosophie der Geschichte*, Frankfurt/Main, 1999, 132–33. Very similar is August von Behr, *Meine Reise durch Schlesien, Galicien, Podolien nach Odessa, der Krimm, Konstantinopel und zurück über Moskau, Petersburg durch Finnland und die Insel Rügen im Sommer 1832*, Leipzig, 1834, 172–73, which located Russia in the 'North' while attributing France to the 'West'.
44. Hans Lemberg, 'Zur Entstehung des Osteuropabegriffs im 19. Jahrhundert. Vom "Norden" zum "Osten" Europas', *Jahrbücher für Geschichte Osteuropas* 33 (1985), 48–91, here 61–72.

Chapter 2

THE KAISERREICH AND THE KULTURLÄNDER
Conceptions of the West in Wilhelmine Germany, 1890–1914

Mark Hewitson

Historians disagree about the role of 'the West' as an idea, affiliation or aspiration. The concept often seemed peripheral, they hold, because of the demise of the Concert of Europe in the late nineteenth century and the subsequent instability of diplomatic relations before 1914, upset by the rise of powerful new nation states – especially Germany – and the slow disintegration of the Ottoman and Austro-Hungarian Empires.[1] The various concepts of 'Europe', '*das Abendland*', '*der Westen*' and '*der Okzident*', although often used interchangeably, remained potentially distinct and contradictory.[2] The movement away from Europe altogether towards an imagined global system of 'world empires' appeared to cause further uncertainty. While Germany's 'European' or 'Central European' position might have been emphasized in such a process, its ties to 'the West' seem to have been attenuated by its rivalry with Western world powers such as the British Empire and the United States.[3] How important and enduring the shift from Europe towards *Weltpolitik* actually was, and for which parties and journalists – not to mention voters and readers – it mattered, is still disputed.[4] What is beyond dispute is the fact that the Great Powers, within and beyond Europe, were changing places as a consequence of industrialization and two arms races involving the navies of Germany and Britain, and the armies of France, Russia and the *Kaiserreich*.[5] The newfound military power of states such as Germany and Russia, together with corresponding fears about the future, exacerbated other processes of nationalization, pushing Berlin, St Petersburg, Rome, Paris, London and Vienna to cast around for further colonies and spheres of influence.[6] The resulting conflicts of allegedly rising and falling nation states and empires seemed to preclude the formation of regional blocs. The most significant regional axis, the Dual Alliance between France and Russia, notoriously appeared to unite 'East' and 'West' for the overriding purpose of opposing Germany. 'Globalization', accompanied by changing means of communication, transport, patterns of trade and migration, purportedly redirected the gaze of contemporaries beyond national borders and the paradigm of the nation state, but its impact – even in the opinion of historians who pay most attention to transnationalism – was variable, serving amongst other things to underline the importance of passport controls, citizenship laws and myths of racial descent and ethnic belonging.[7] In Wilhelmine Germany the conceptualization of 'the West' was subject to these transformations. Its content, development and contestation give an indication of how important such processes were in the creation and destruction of the transitory imagined landscapes in which contemporaries lived and acted.

Nation States and 'Western' States

The actuality and necessity of national unification and the primacy of the nation state worked against a straightforward alignment of 'Western' powers or cultures, of which Germany was a part or from which it was excluded. Thus, when political geographers or Pan-Germans spoke of a 'western territory' (*Westland*) or 'western space' (*Westraum*) during the Wilhelmine era, they were referring to the borderlands to the west of the unquestioned 'core' of the German nation state, and, modifying the notion of a fixed, unchanging boundary, were regarding these as territory into which Germany might expand.[8] The main repository of power remained the state, which had not only come to monopolize the means of violence, as Max Weber – among many contemporaries – had pointed out, but which had also, in its most successful form, converged with national cultures. 'In fact, today, "nation-state" has become conceptually identical … with "state"', wrote Weber on the eve of the First World War.[9] The territories of states, whether monarchies, empires or republics, had been consolidated during the nineteenth century itself, furnishing – in Charles Maier's opinion – 'the properties, including power, provided by the control of bordered space' and creating 'the spatially anchored structures for politics and economics that were taken for granted from about

1860 to about 1970 or 1980 but that have since begun to decompose'.[10] The concentration of territories, which in Germany had been (in the words of the economist Adolph Wagner in 1900) 'almost independent and half-sovereign' under the Holy Roman Empire and the Confederation, had been combined with the demarcation, mapping and defence of national borders. Along with this came the enumeration and classification of populations, with censuses beginning in the early nineteenth century, and greater demands made by the state on national populations through conscription and higher taxation. People had greater contact with government, as literacy increased and elementary education became the rule. Political parties emerged between the 1840s and early 1870s, and press circulation grew.[11] These processes, encompassing what Wagner termed 'the nation's more general political and economic tasks', often antedated the main phases of industrialization and the rapid expansion of trade – processes accompanied by large-scale migration, improvements in transport (rail from the 1840s onwards, ocean-going steamships from the 1830s, automobiles from the 1900s) and new forms of communication, with the first commercial telegraph patented in 1837 and the first telephone in 1876. Such developments have all been associated with 'globalization'.[12] 'Scholars of globalization, such as Sebastian Conrad, who have been most anxious to 'rescue' 'history from the nation', concede that '*die Nation* served around 1900 as the hegemonic paradigm of social and historical imagination'.[13]

Most Wilhelmine commentators were convinced that a German identity, described as a national 'character' or set of 'values', existed in contradistinction to other national identities. 'Without overrating itself, a people does not arrive at knowledge of itself at all', Heinrich von Treitschke argued in his lectures on politics, published posthumously in 1898.[14] Of course, the Berlin historian's obsession with the German cause derived in part from his sense of its precariousness. He accused 'the Germans' of being always 'in danger of losing their nationality', yet also betrayed a certainty that nation states had become the norm in nineteenth-century Europe and elsewhere, as sources of unprecedented power and as guarantors of culture.[15] Race, culture, politics and history were usually combined in such accounts of national unity, in different fashions and with different degrees of intensity, but they generally drew on an enduring framework of images and ideas. Sometimes national imagery and affiliations were merely implied; at other times they were stated explicitly and violently, as in the pronouncements of the Pan-German League, whose newspaper, the *Alldeutsche Blätter*, claimed to have detected 'a broadly based conspiracy ... with the aim of harming Germandom'.[16] In most cases, national identity was assumed to entail what Treitschke called 'a different picture and a different conception of the divinity' that marked out each culture and made it incommensurable with others.[17] This national paradigm, combined with continuing Eurocentrism, undermined the idea that Germany, as a long-established, unique national culture and a new *Nationalstaat*, could belong to a 'Western' bloc.

Kultur and Zivilisation

The relationship between Germany and 'the West' was understood in terms of culture, science, technology and power. Like Spengler, who began his sprawling, classically inspired thesis on the 'decline of the Occident' before the First World War, the majority of Wilhelmine onlookers believed that they belonged to a shared 'European' culture. This extended to the British dominions and the United States and was based, in different combinations, on the traditions of Greek philosophy, Roman law and conceptions of property, Christianity, the Enlightenment, capitalism, industrialization and imperialism. By the early twentieth century, Germany was believed to be in competition with France, Britain and the United States for the intellectual and political leadership of the modern, 'European' world of 'cultured lands' (*Kulturländer*). Although the rivals of the Reich were treated as separate national entities, with their own geography and traditions, they were seen to share certain values, which could be contrasted – especially by those on the Right – with German values. Germany, it was implied, offered the sole modern alternative system of thought and institutions to the dominant, overlapping systems of the 'Western' states.[18] During the eighteenth and nineteenth centuries, German culture had been defined primarily through a reaction against French administration, etiquette, learning and art, manifested in the occupied territories of the Napoleonic wars, in the princely courts of the German states and in the monarchical, Bonapartist and republican regimes of the 'hereditary enemy' (*Erbfeind*) of the Confederation and the Reich.[19] From the mid nineteenth century onwards, Britain, which had earlier been depicted as a 'Germanic' self-governing society, and the United States, which had been portrayed as a romantic, wild and free-spirited antithesis to Europe, were both gradually transformed – if German accounts were to be believed – into calculating, capitalist, industrial powers and oppressive, Puritan, empirical and materialist cultures, that more closely resembled the strict social form, rational science and commercialism of France.[20] There were still thought to be marked differences between 'Romanism' and 'Germanism', of course, and between the 'Old World' and the 'New World', as Karl Lamprecht spelled out in his popular diary,

Americana, in 1906: 'If the present American civilization disappeared: what would remain for posterity? Practically nothing … . It has to be expressed in no uncertain terms: vis-à-vis the old culture of the European population, both the Germanic and the Romance, the Americans are still behind.'[21] Yet, with the democratization of British politics, the growth of French financial capitalism and the emergence of French, British and American positivism, few Germans questioned the political and cultural propinquity of France, the United Kingdom and the United States, for it seemed that the populations of all three countries were preoccupied with external form, observation, numbers, utility and, increasingly, equality. Many Wilhelmine commentators assumed that Germany was different.[22]

The critical question for such commentators seemed to concern *Zivilisation*, or the adaptation and harnessing of technology, and *Kultur*, or the profound, historical, organic and mysterious sources of creativity and identity. The United States, as the world's largest industrial economy, became the focus of many Wilhelmine critiques. In 1900, the country already accounted for 23.6 per cent of global industrial production, compared to 18.5 per cent for the United Kingdom and 13.2 per cent for the Reich. By 1913, the share of the United States had risen to 32 per cent. The pre-war debate about the U.S.A. centred on materialism, economic growth and efficient management. The most salient watchword was 'Taylorism', a system of 'scientific management', in the words of Frederick W. Taylor's most famous work, based on time-and-motion studies and a strict separation of the different elements of the production process.[23] For Georg Schlesinger, the first chair of *Betriebswissenschaft* in Germany at the Technische Hochschule of Berlin-Charlottenburg, Taylorism in the United States had increased productivity at the same time as improving conditions for workers by giving them better machines. Schlesinger was opposed by union leaders and Social Democrats, with Kurt Eisner – in the *Neue Rundschau* (1913) – seeing in 'the person of Taylor the soul of the sensible and rule-bound engineer and the cold passion of a prophet of capitalism'.[24] It was also opposed by technical experts such as the economist Emil Lederer and the banker Wilhelm Kochmann, who concluded in an assessment of Taylorism in the *Archiv für Sozialwissenschaft und Sozialpolitik* (1914) that 'the principle of systematic rationalization' had ensured that machines had become 'overpowerful', determining the rhythm of human labour.[25] For the engineer and author Franz Erich Junge, there was a real danger of an imposition 'of the routine of material quantities on the ethical and state principles of the old *Kulturvölker*, of the marginalization of the national and moral ideas of the latter by the uncontrolled individualism, opportunism and commercialism of the former, of the overshadowing of European culture by American civilization'.[26] Such criticism frequently involved a broad denunciation of 'materialism' in the U.S.A., spilling over into descriptions of a corrupt political system, which had 'become a business' in the opinion of the publicist Paul Dehn and which could 'eventually degenerate into a plutocracy' in the view of Wilhelm von Polenz.[27] Most importantly, materialism in its American manifestation appeared to endanger culture itself. Unsurprisingly, this fear was articulated by Pan-Germans like Dehn, who welcomed 'the modernization of methods in industry, trade and agriculture' but deplored 'Americanization' in a 'wider social and political sense', and it was also voiced by cultural critics like Stefan George:

> About Prussianness and Anglo-Americanism: earlier, in the papers, there was only Prussianness, the *Reichsdeutsche*, the lieutenant, the corps student, the enemy of anything cultural. Since about 1900, the other [Anglo-Americanism] has been recognized as a worse enemy, which destroys life itself: the advocacy of this American way of thinking, which always sees only antitheses, and always makes transpositions; that is, draws correct conclusions from fundamentally wrong premises. The advocatory is a reversal of the human.[28]

For the novelist and playwright Polenz, 'the new world still has much to learn from us', with 'their civilization' set to benefit from the 'penetration of a Teutonic spirit'; yet it also threatened to push European culture back 'from a higher level of culture to a lower one'.[29] To the historian Karl Lamprecht, American high culture was like American cuisine: 'the choice is great, there is no lack of invention and openness, and one sees future trends more or less in advance, but everything remains according to the programme; it is badly presented and dyspepsia lurks in the background'.[30] Americans tended to see things in terms of 'quantitative methods' and had a 'proclivity towards statistics', hindering them from the 'building up of their own culture, which can only be constructed on qualitative judgements and values'.[31] Amongst academics, Werner Sombart went furthest, trying to prove that Jews had been largely responsible for the establishment of modern capitalism and of a modern United States, which was 'in all its parts' a 'Jew-land'.[32] 'What we call Americanism', he continued, was 'to a great extent nothing other than a Jewish spirit'.[33] Few commentators or mainstream politicians followed Sombart's lead, leaving anti-Semitism and anti-Americanism as substantially separate sets of ideas until after 1914. Many more, though, equated capitalism, the United States and other 'Western' states such as Britain and France with 'civilization'. That such a constellation of ideas was associated with specifically 'Western' opponents in and after the First World War was neither inevitable nor surprising.³⁴

The Menace of 'the East'

Germany was widely assumed to be in the West – though with '*Kulturländer*' and 'Europe' referred to more frequently than 'the Occident' or, indeed, 'the West'. This was because the nation did not belong to the 'East' – a label commonly used in the Wilhelmine era – but rather defended Europe against the 'Slavs'. It is true that there was still a surprisingly high incidence of intermarriage, social interaction, bilingualism and cultural exchange between Poles and Germans in Prussia's eastern provinces, yet government policy aimed, with increasing rigour, to 'Germanize' the region (as the popular term dating from the 1850s put it).³⁵ Such policies included deportations of Poles and Jews, as non-citizens, from Prussia between 1883 and 1887, with thirty-two thousand removed in 1883 alone. With this came the establishment of the Royal Prussian Settlement Commission in 1886, set up to buy land for the settlement of 130,000 Germans in 'Polish' areas during the pre-war period; it had a reserve of 500 million marks by 1913. Polish was replaced by German in schools, causing sixty thousand schoolchildren in Posen – encouraged by their parents – to go on 'strike' in 1906; and a Prussian Expropriation Act was passed in 1908, which enabled the confiscation of Polish estates for redistribution to Germans. The measures were at once aggressive and defensive, as were popular attitudes to Poles and other 'Slavs'. Their effect was to underline differences between the 'East' and 'Europe' or, though more rarely invoked, 'the West'.

The most feared source of a flood of 'Slavs' was Russia, whose population had increased from 74 million inhabitants in 1861 to 150 million in 1905 and which, as an unpredictable Great Power, was the primary sponsor of pan-Slavism. At times, Russians – like other 'Slavs' – were portrayed as racial inferiors. *Simplicissimus*, for example, showed them variously as primitive and subhuman: as lice and rats.³⁶ On the whole, however, Russians provided a cultural rather than a racial foil for German identity, partly because 'Slavs' were sometimes included – for example, in Houston Stewart Chamberlain's *Foundations of the Nineteenth Century* (1899) – in the family of Aryan or Indo-European peoples.³⁷ Russian culture, in particular, which had already been described as barbaric in the eighteenth century, came to represent 'Asia', menacing the borders of Germany and Europe.³⁸ To the German Left, such representations dated back to the Karlsbad Decrees in 1819 and the revolutions of 1848 and

1849, when Russian armies had helped to enforce the reactionary policies of the Habsburg monarchy. By the mid nineteenth century, it was common, as Friedrich Engels demonstrated, to move from criticism of a despotic, centralized Russian state to the denigration of Slavic cultures in their entirety: 'Peoples which have never had a history, which, from the very moment when they reached the first, rawest levels of civilization, fell under foreign domination or which were first forced up to the first stage of civilization, have no capacity for life, will never be able to attain any degree of independence.'[39] Such hierarchies of culture persisted in socialist circles until the Russian Revolution in 1917. Thus references by Engels and Bebel to the barbarity of 'the East' were reiterated in 1914 by an unofficial SPD (Sozialdemokratische Partei Deutschlands) statement to the press justifying the party's decision to go to war:

> Defeat would be something unthinkable, something frightful. If war is the most horrible of all horrors, the frightfulness of this war will be intensified by the fact that it will not only be waged by civilized nations. We are sure that our comrades in uniform of all sorts and conditions will abstain from all unnecessary cruelty, but we cannot have this trust in the motley hordes of the tsar, and we will not have our women and children sacrificed to the bestiality of Cossacks.[40]

On the German Right, the picture had traditionally been more complicated, with reactionaries such as August von Haxthausen, who was one of the best-known mid-nineteenth century foreign observers of Russian culture, interpreting the peasant commune or *mir* as a pre-revolutionary, pre-industrial barrier against European decadence.[41] Most conservative commentators, however, saw Russia as a culture that had been little influenced by Greek thought, Western Christianity, Roman law or the Enlightenment. By the 1900s, Russia's defeat in the Crimean and Russo-Japanese Wars (1856 and 1905), Russo-German hostility following St Petersburg's Dual Alliance with France in 1894, and the collapse and partial restoration of tsarism in the 1905 Revolution all damaged Russia's reputation; and émigré Baltic Germans like Friedrich von Bernhardi and Theodor Schiemann, who dominated the academic study and newspaper reportage of Russian affairs, wrote articles discrediting both state and society there as the products of a backward and violent '*Unkultur*'.[42] This remained the dominant image of Russia until the outbreak of the First World War, increasingly interlaced – as one correspondent of the *Alldeutscher Verband* made plain in a reference to the struggle of 'blonds' against 'Slavs' – with racial stereotypes, despite the endeavours of the historian Otto Hoetzsch and other reform-minded conservatives to portray the Russian regime as an imitation of the German Empire in the years before 1914. Most commentators, by contrasting themselves with their 'Asiatic' Russian or Slav neighbours, placed the Reich at the centre of 'Europe'.[43]

'Asia', the 'East' and the 'Orient' stretched, apparently without end, beyond Russia and the lands of the 'Slavs', to the Ottoman Empire, China and Japan. In terms of faith, the different territories seemed to be connected by the absence of Western Christianity, which contrasted with the exotic rituals and beliefs of Russian Orthodoxy, Islam and various types of eastern 'mysticism'. Politically they all seemed to languish under Oriental 'despotism', from the arbitrary but declining powers of the Ottomans prior to the uprising of 1908 to the partly new, partly archaic prerogatives of the emperors of Japan. These stereotypes, in turn, were frequently intertwined with anti-Semitism, as more than two million Jews fled pogroms in the Russian Empire between 1870 and 1914, with most passing through Austria-Hungary and Germany. Such 'Eastern Jews', often speaking Yiddish and wearing long caftans and black hats, were subjected to quarantine, blamed for the outbreak of a cholera epidemic in Hamburg in 1892 and labelled 'half-Asian', even by Jewish writers like Karl Emil Franzos.[44] They were joined, as nebulous symbols of 'the East', by other migrants, most notably from China. Unlike 'Eastern Jews', Chinese workers, who came to be associated with recurrent alarms of a 'yellow peril' (*gelbe Gefahr*) and a 'coolie trade' (*Kulihandel*), rarely travelled to or settled in Germany, despite mass migrations to South East Asia and the Pacific (19 million between 1840 and 1940), Manchuria and Siberia (30 million) and South Africa, Australia and both North and South America (2.5 million). Hamburg, originally with perhaps the largest community, counted only 207 Chinese inhabitants by 1910.[45] Xenophobic panics – usually triggered by rumours of landowners or manufacturers applying to recruit 'coolies' – seem to have rested on cross-party concerns about foreign competition in the labour market and, more importantly, on deep-seated anxiety about the arrival of supposed racial and cultural aliens from the East. 'The three great colonial states which have come into contact with the Chinese – North America, Australia and South Africa – have had terrible experiences with them and now defend themselves passionately against the yellow plague', wrote the *Deutsche Volkszeitung* in 1906.[46] As part of the European force, under General Alfred von Waldersee, that put down the 'Boxer' Rebellion in 1900 and effectively consolidated the seizure of Kiaochow in 1897, Germany had become increasingly entangled in the Far East at the same time as extending its activities in the Middle and Near East – helping, for instance, to train the Turkish army and build the Berlin–Baghdad railway. Such interventions appear to have made the 'Orient' or 'Asia' more newsworthy without rendering it more familiar. In contrast to 'the West', 'the East' was a relatively stable, commonplace term, representing, in the opinion of many Wilhelmine commentators, Germany's most consistent and constitutive 'other'.

Conclusion

Nation states were too powerful and their conflicts of interest too pressing to permit a straightforward identification with any cultural, territorial or diplomatic 'Western' bloc. The international system appeared to contemporary onlookers such as Hintze to be slowly detaching itself from 'the normal nation-state-type form' dominated by the traditional European Great Powers; yet the new order of 'world powers' was still 'emerging' and remained unpredictable.[47] During a succession of international crises from the turn of the century onwards – Fashoda (1898), the Boer War (1899–1902), the Moroccan crises (1905–1906 and 1911–1912), the annexation of Bosnia-Herzegovina (1908) and the Balkan Wars (1912–1913) – it was difficult to avoid the impression that the most important enmities threatening to provoke a conflagration were intra-European, with flashpoints overseas or on the periphery of the continent, but with the most likely theatre of war on the European mainland and along its Atlantic seaboard. Any conception of the West in these circumstances appeared to contradict the vital interests of the *Kaiserreich* as a newly established nation state in a 'question', as a contemporary phrase put it, 'of its own existence' (*eine Existenzfrage*). At times, even Social Democrats seemed sympathetic to the argument that the 'youthful' Reich was being thwarted by a conservative French and British-dominated balance of power and that it had a right, as Bernhard von Bülow had proposed in his first, oft-repeated speech to the Reichstag on 6 December 1897 – to its 'place in the sun'.[48] Conservatives, National Liberals, Catholics and Left liberals, although differing in their attitudes to war and their views of other Great Powers, all appeared unwilling to sacrifice Germany's perceived national interests for the sake of vague cultural and ideological affinities and oppositions. Shifting European points of conflict and alliances, with hopes of a rapprochement entertained by many observers throughout the period before 1914, undermined a sense on the part of contemporaries of a shared or opposing set of 'Western' values, traditions or interests. The movement towards *Weltpolitik* and 'globalization' was too contradictory and inchoate to overcome such intra-European rivalries. While that movement tended to point Germans away from 'Europe', the concept of a 'European' culture and continent continued to be a relevant point of reference. Indeed, alongside other concepts such as 'nation' and *Kulturländer*, 'Europe' signified a more prominent socio-spatial entity than the newly emerging concept of 'the West', with which it partly overlapped. Germany's position on the continent remained an object of dispute, and the relationship between Germany, 'Europe' and 'the West' remained a confused one.

Diplomatic relations, national antipathies and competition were not all-important, however. Many Wilhelmine commentators seem to have had in mind constellations of ideas which, although varied, facilitated a loose grouping of 'Western' cultures or states. In particular, virtually all contemporaries agreed that the *Kaiserreich* was not part of the 'East' – even conservatives who emphasized Germany's 'bridging' role and Baltic German and other experts such as Theodor Schiemann, Friedrich von Bernhardi, Otto Hoetzsch and Friedrich Meinecke. Such commentators either reiterated their belief in Russia's weakness after the Russo-Japanese War in 1904–1905 and the 1905 Revolution – rendering Moscow unable 'to wage war with a European Great Power of the first rank', in Paul Rohrbach's estimation – or distanced themselves from exaggerated representations of Russian and 'Slav' 'backwardness' and 'barbarity'.[49] Furthermore, many people, well beyond the circles of cultural critics on the Right, appear to have sympathized with a distinction between deep-rooted national 'cultures' and artificial, mechanized, exclusively rational 'civilizations', of which the main exemplar was usually held to be the United States. They seem, too, to have felt threatened, as well as excited, by an irresistible and uncertain movement away from Europe altogether. In many accounts, such anxieties – frequently coexisting with more realistic assessments of the *Kaiserreich*'s position within a continental balance of power – gave credence to the notion that Germany lay at the centre of a 'European' or 'Central European' bloc. The borders of this bloc were undefined – variously including or excluding France, Britain, the Low Countries, Scandinavia, Bohemia, Moravia, the Baltic provinces and different areas of the Adriatic and Balkans – and its relationship to conceptions of the West was double-edged. The *Okzident*, here, could be seen, in Max Weber's sense, to have produced many problems – capitalism, industrialization, bureaucratization, an obsession with efficiency and an overreliance on rationality and instrumental action at the expense of meaningful values, political debate, individual freedom and creativity.[50] These now appeared to menace Germany on its western flank through the policies and proclivities of the United States, the United Kingdom and, even, France. Germany, in other words, was both in 'the West' and threatened by it – a paradox resulting from the 'internal' and 'external' natures of 'Western' achievements and challenges, and also a corollary of Europe's very expansion and success. This paradox remained relevant during the

1920s, as criticism of the 'Western' Allies, *Zivilisation* and 'the ideas of 1789' came to rest uneasily alongside premonitions of the decline of a 'West' which had Germany at its core.

Notes

1. The classic account of the end of the Concert of Europe remains Francis H. Hinsley, *Power and the Pursuit of Peace*, Cambridge, 1963; see also Klaus Hildebrand, *Das vergangene Reich. Deutsche Außenpolitik von Bismarck bis Hitler 1871–1945*, Stuttgart, 1995. On the persistence and successes of the system see Jost Dülffer et al. (eds), *Vermiedene Kriege. Deeskalation von Konflikten der Grossmächte zwischen Krimkrieg und Erstem Weltkrieg 1856–1914*, Munich, 1997.
2. The term '*der Westen*' sometimes connoted 'the Wild West' but was also pitted against '*der Osten*'. '*Das Abendland*' often had religious connotations, yet was also distinguished, for example by Spengler, from cultures or empires in the Near and Far East (China, India, Persia), where the sun rose. '*Der Okzident*' was closely tied to the French term '*l'occident*' and was likewise contrasted with the cultures of 'the Orient', as can be seen in the religious sociology of Max Weber. On 'Europe' see Heinz Gollwitzer, *Europabild und Europagedanke. Beiträge zur deutschen Geistesgeschichte des 18. und 19. Jahrhunderts*, Munich, 1964, 328–35, and Paul Michael Lützeler, *Die Schriftsteller und Europa*, Munich, 1992, 190–224.
3. See especially Sönke Neitzel, *Weltmacht oder Untergang. Die Weltreichslehre im Zeitalter des Imperialismus*, Paderborn et al., 2000; and Heinz Gollwitzer, *Geschichte des Weltpolitischen Denkens*, 2 vols, Göttingen, 1972/82.
4. For more on this see Mark Hewitson, *Germany and the Causes of the First World War*, Oxford, 2004, 145–94.
5. David G. Herrmann, *The Arming of Europe and the Making of the First World War*, Princeton, 1996; David Stevenson, *Armaments and the Coming of War. Europe, 1904–1914*, Oxford, 1996.
6. Much of the work of the 'Hamburg' and 'Bielefeld' schools was predicated on a controversial interpretation of the nefarious effects of late and incomplete national unification. For a later statement of this point of view, see Harold James, *A German Identity, 1770–1990*, Oxford, 1989. A good study of national antagonism, its causes and effects, remains Paul M. Kennedy, *The Rise of the Anglo-German Antagonism, 1860–1914*, London, 1980.
7. Sebastian Conrad, *Globalisierung und Nation im Deutschen Kaiserreich*, Munich, 2006; Sebastian Conrad and Jürgen Osterhammel (eds), *Das Kaiserreich transnational*, Göttingen, 2004; Jürgen Osterhammel, 'Transnationale Gesellschaftsgeschichte. Erweiterung oder Alternative?', *Geschichte und Gesellschaft* 27 (2001), 367–93; Kiran Klaus Patel, *Nach der Nationalfixiertheit. Perspektiven einer transnationalen Geschichte*, Berlin, 2004.
8. See Thomas Müller, *Imaginierter Westen. Das Konzept des 'deutschen Westraums' im völkischen Diskurs zwischen Politischer Romantik und Nationalsozialismus*, Bielefeld, 2009.
9. Max Weber, *Wirtschaft und Gesellschaft*, 5th edn, Tübingen, 1972, 242.
10. Charles S. Maier, 'Consigning the Twentieth Century to History. Alternative Narratives for the Modern Era', *American Historical Review* 105 (2000), 808.

11. Adolph Wagner, *Vom Territorialstaat zur Weltmacht*, Berlin, 1900, 6.
12. Ibid., 8.
13. Conrad, *Globalisierung und Nation im Deutschen Kaiserreich*, 334.
14. Heinrich von Treitschke, *Selections from Treitschke's Lectures on Politics*, London, 1914, 10.
15. Ibid.
16. *Alldeutsche Blätter* in 1908, quoted in Roger Chickering, *We Men Who Feel Most German. A Cultural Study of the Pan-German League, 1886–1914*, London, 1984, 123.
17. Treitschke, *Selections from Treitschke's Lectures on Politics*, 10.
18. See Mark Hewitson, 'The *Kaiserreich* in Question', *Journal of Modern History* 73 (2001), 738–80.
19. Friedrich Naumann in *Die Hilfe*, 1900, no. 28; Oscar A.H. Schmitz, *Das Land der Wirklichkeit*, Munich, 1914, 22–23, 38, 56–57, 61, 67–68, 73, 111, 114–15, 142, 146; Karl Hillebrand, *Frankreich und die Franzosen*, 4th edn, Strasbourg, 1898, 9.
20. See Mark Hewitson, 'The Wilhelmine Regime and the Problem of Reform', in Geoff Eley and James Retallack (eds), *Wilhelminism and its Legacies*, New York, 2003, 76–86.
21. Karl Lamprecht, cited in Frank Trommler, 'Inventing the Enemy. German-American Cultural Relations, 1900–1917', in Hans-Jürgen Schröder (ed.), *Confrontation and Cooperation. Germany and the United States in the Era of World War I*, Oxford, 1993, 113; David E. Barclay and Elisabeth Glaser-Schmidt (eds), *Transatlantic Images and Perceptions. Germany and America since 1776*, Cambridge, 1997, 65–86, 109–30; Dan Diner, *America in the Eyes of the Germans*, Princeton, 1996, 3–51; Charles E. McClelland, *The German Historians and England*, Cambridge, 1971; Kennedy, *The Rise of the Anglo-German Antagonism*, 59–145, 306–437.
22. In keeping with the preeminence of national discourses, most contemporaries did not, however, use the term 'the West' to express this difference.
23. Frederick Winslow Taylor, *The Principles of Scientific Management*, New York, 1911.
24. Kurt Eisner, 'Taylorismus', *Neue Rundschau*, 24 (1913), 1448.
25. Wilhelm Kochmann, 'Das Taylorssystem und seine volkswirtschaftliche Bedeutung' and Emil Lederer, 'Die ökonomische und sozialpolitische Bedeutung des Taylorsystems', *Archiv für Sozialwissenschaft und Sozialpolitik* 38 (1914), 391–424, 769–84.
26. Franz Erich Junge, *Amerikanische Wirtschaftspolitik*, Berlin, 1910, 286.
27. Paul Dehn, *Weltwirtschaftliche Neubildungen*, Berlin, 1904, 191; Wilhelm von Polenz, *Das Land der Zukunft oder was können Deutschland und Amerika voneinander lernen?* 5th edn, Berlin, 1904, 121.
28. Stefan George, cited in Egbert Klautke, *Unbegrenzte Möglichkeiten. 'Amerikanisierung' in Deutschland und Frankreich (1900–1933)*, Stuttgart, 2003, 105, 103.
29. Polenz, *Das Land der Zukunft*, 402, 405.
30. Karl Lamprecht, *Americana*, Freiburg, 1906, 9.
31. Ibid., 67–71.
32. Werner Sombart, *Die Juden und das Wirtschaftsleben* (1911), cited in Klautke, *Unbegrenzte Möglichkeiten*, 104.
33. Ibid.
34. This was usually expressed as 'Americanism' – and opposition to Americanism – and it was not related consistently or specifically to 'the West'. See Dieter Heimböckel, 'Zivilisation auf dem Treibriemen. Die USA im Urteil der deutschen Literatur um und nach 1900', in Frank Becker and Elke Reinhardt-Becker (eds), *Mythos USA. 'Amerikanisierung' in Deutschland seit 1900*, Frankfurt/Main, 2006, 49–69.
35. See Mark Tilse, 'Synthesis between Nationalisms'. *Identity, Culture and Politics in the German-Polish Provinces of the Prussian East, 1871–1914*, Ph.D. thesis, London, 2008.

36. See Mark Hewitson, 'Nation and Nationalismus: Representation and National Identity in Imperial Germany', in Mary Fulbrook and Martin Swales (eds), *Representing the German Nation*, Manchester, 2000, 19–62.
37. Houston Stewart Chamberlain, *Die Grundlagen des neunzehnten Jahrhunderts*, Munich, 1899.
38. See, for instance, Dieter Groh, *Russland im Blick Europas. 300 Jahre historische Perspektiven*, 2nd edn, Frankfurt/Main, 1988.
39. Friedrich Engels, cited in Lew Kopelew, 'Zunächst war Waffenbrüderschaft', in Mechthild Keller (ed.), Russen und Russland aus deutscher Sicht. 19. Jahrhundert: Von der Jahrhundertwende bis zur Reichsgründung (1800–1871) (*West-östliche Spiegelungen*, series A, vol. 3), Munich, 1992, 11–81, here 51.
40. August Bebel, cited in Nicholas Stargardt, *The German Idea of Militarism*, Cambridge, 1994, 59; Friedrich Stampfer, cited in Philipp Scheidemann, *Memoirs of a Social Democrat*, vol. 1, London, 1929, 189.
41. Christoph Schmidt, 'Ein deutscher Slawophile? August von Haxthausen und die Wiederentdeckung der russischen Bauerngemeinde 1843/44', in Keller (ed.), *Russen und Russland aus deutscher Sicht 3*, 196–216; Gerd Voigt, *Rußland in der deutschen Geschichtsschreibung 1843–1945*, Berlin, 1994, 66–114. .
42. Troy R.E. Paddock, 'Still Stuck at Sevastopol: The Depiction of Russia during the Russo-Japanese War and the Beginning of the First World War in the German Press', *German History* 16 (1998), 358–76.
43. Holger H. Herwig, *Hammer or Anvil? Modern Germany, 1648–Present*, Lexington, 1994, 180.
44. Vejas Gabriel Liulevicius, *The German Myth of the East. 1800 to the Present*, Oxford, 2009, 115.
45. See Conrad, *Globalisierung und Nation im Deutschen Kaiserreich*, 206 and Heinz Gollwitzer, *Die gelbe Gefahr. Geschichte eines Schlagworts*, Göttingen, 1962.
46. Conrad, *Globalisierung und Nation im Deutschen Kaiserreich*, 198.
47. Otto Hintze, 'Die Hohenzollern und ihr Werk' (1915), cited in Michael Fröhlich, *Imperialismus. Deutsche Kolonial- und Weltpolitik 1880–1914*, Munich, 1994, 76.
48. Cited in ibid., 75.
49. See Troy R.E. Paddock, 'Historiker als Politiker', in Mechthild Keller (ed.), *Russen und Russland aus deutscher Sicht. 19./20. Jahrhundert: Von der Bismarckzeit bis zum Ersten Weltkrieg* (*West-östliche Spiegelungen*, series A, vol. 4), Munich, 2000, 307–25; and Troy R.E. Paddock, *Creating the Russian Peril. Education, the Public Sphere, and National Identity in Imperial Germany, 1890–1914*, Rochester, NY, 2010. See also Friedrich von Bernhardi, *Deutschland und der nächste Krieg*, Stuttgart, 1912, 97–98.
50. See Max Weber, *Gesammelte Aufsätze zur Religionssoziologie*, vol. 1, 9th edn, Tübingen, 1988 (first published 1920).

Chapter 3

THE FIRST WORLD WAR AND THE INVENTION OF 'WESTERN DEMOCRACY'

Marcus Llanque

At the time of the First World War, the term 'West' was not at first used to mark a central ideological difference between the enemy countries. During the fighting, the term was mainly used to describe the Western Front as distinct from the other theatres of war, namely the Eastern Front and the front in the Alps. In the collective memory of the warring nations, the Western Front came to stand as a symbol of the cruelty and senselessness of the war as a whole. At the same time, however, an ideological debate took place which gave 'the West' a political meaning over and above its geographical one. This manifested itself in the concept of 'Western democracy'. With this development, 'the West' came to describe one side of a line of demarcation that ran not only between the enemy countries but also between 'civilizations' and their respective political cultures. A clashing juxtaposition was created between 'Western democracy' and the 'German idea of freedom'.

This was the main ideological feature of the discursive constellation during the Great War. The military dispute between the European powers over political supremacy was turned by intellectuals and scientists into an ideological argument over whose political system should be regarded as the best, the most modern and the one that would prevail in the future.[1] The debate took up a large part of the German discourse and was amplified by the nation's defeat. Its long-term effect was to foster the belief that Germany did not belong to 'the West' but should seek its own path of political development.

The Discursive Constellation of the First World War: A War of Words

The Great War was a struggle not only of military weapons but also of words; it was a war of propaganda, a war of political thrusts and counter-thrusts.[2] In the last days of 1914, some British historians and politicians issued a book claiming that the war was essentially a testing time for democracy, that Britain and the Dominions stood in the tradition of democracy and that they were opposing a brand of militarism that, tyrant-like, was prepared to dishonour obligations of international law for mere purposes of might. In the introduction to the book, the authors stated that by democracy they did not mean so much a form of government as 'a spirit and an atmosphere'[3] and that the bond between government and the governed was one built on trust. What seemed at first to be an apology for the British government's policies turned out to be a programmatic statement of what the war stood for and what the task in the near future should be in domestic politics. 'Full democracy', the authors wrote, was not to be achieved through 'changes in the machinery of democratic control' of government but through a proper education of the people.[4] They found it necessary to draw a distinction between an elected government and its reform by changing the ballot (on the one side) and the idea of a democratic government as one thriving on exchanges of opinion and an informed public (on the other) because Germany had already introduced universal male suffrage, while Britain had not. This needed some explaining. So the authors claimed that, without parliamentary control and the 'habit of free discussion and practical criticism of public affairs', which the German people so lacked in stark contrast to the British, there was insufficient democracy and any institutional reform was meaningless. Upon this argument they based their opinion that British democracy did not 'depend upon our popular franchise or on any legal rights and enactments. It depends upon the free spirit and self-respect of the British people'.[5] It took the Representation of the People Act of 1918 to grant universal male suffrage in Britain, and this was mainly to pay respect to the returning soldiers for their sacrifices at the front. Having given so much, they deserved to be treated as equal citizens at home.[6]

Patriotism dictated the polemics on both sides and caused oversimplifications instead of clear-cut analysis. The most intriguing oversimplification in this war of words was the claim that there was a complete ideological abyss between the Entente allies and Germany. The Germans condensed the differing guiding principles of the two political cultures into the terms 'ideas of 1789' (for the French and British) and 'ideas of 1914' (for Germany), while the Allies spoke of an opposition between democracy and autocracy. Such arguments had a very doubtful basis in the actual history of political ideas, but they served the polemical atmosphere of the day. Britain and France based their criticisms on Germany's resort to war and conduct in it, and they claimed to be defending European humanism and civilization against Teutonic militarism. This same 'militarism', however, was interpreted by German authors as the epitome of modern collectivism and statehood. This clash of 'the ideas of 1914' with 'the ideas of 1789' epitomized the divided interpretations being made of the current state of civilization(s) and included projections of what future developments should be.

On the surface, the political debate during the First World War was dominated by questions of territory and security. Were the combatants seeking to secure a peace with or without annexations? Did they want to restore the status quo ante or establish a new order? Discussions of war aims tend to focus on matters of foreign policy; but there was a subtle connection between foreign and domestic policy.[7] Who was in charge of the German political leadership, for instance: the government, the emperor or the military high command? In France and the U.K, the governments feared that another war would come if the current political system in Germany remained intact. Prime Minister Lloyd George expressed his concerns in many speeches and even in a meeting of the Imperial War Cabinet in March 1917: 'If Germany had had a democracy, like France, like ourselves, or like Italy, we should not have had this trouble.'[8]

The propaganda that surrounded the war and the gravity of the enduring military conflict amplified and extended the causes for which war was being waged. What, on the British side, began as a conflict caused by the breach of Belgian neutrality intensified into a confrontation of political systems, culminating in a Manichaean opposition between the Entente allies, who claimed they were defending freedom, and the Central Powers who, it was said, were ruled by a military caste.[9] Many of the British publications that hymned democracy were addressed to the American public, and sought to give the impression that the Entente allies and the United States held the same democratic values (though they did not clarify what the concept of democracy actually meant).[10] The Americans joined the debate soon after the United States had declared war against Germany in 1917[11] and the war hysteria that was common to all countries involved in the conflict erupted there as well.[12]

German intellectuals were deeply impressed by the experience of the first war months. During those months of sudden solidarity, it seemed that all party conflict had diminished and that the gaps between social milieux, religious communities and economic interests were reduced: it was as though an entirely new German people had emerged. The appeal of the 'ideas of 1914' was largely due to the political unity demonstrated in these first months of the war. The 'ideas of 1914' connected the war with domestic politics, too, and it became accepted that a certain kind of Prussian militarism belonged to the very heart of German political culture. The 'ideas of 1914' also included a model of popular government, though it may seem a crude model by today's standards: German supporters were keen to demonstrate that their nation could serve modern democratic aspirations in a way that did not follow the path of individualism but took a path of collectivism. Accordingly, the German debate was full of talk about 'socialism'. This meant not only 'war socialism' – as a means of gaining total control of the economy and society in order to improve the war effort – but also socialism as a peacetime German tradition, in which a broad front could be formed, including Marxist socialism as well as Prussian statehood. So they could understand the 'ideas of 1914' better, people discussed authors like Heinrich von Treitschke more intensely than they had before the war. In these ideas, 'freedom' for individuals meant voluntarily accepting their dependency on the 'welfare state' the German *Kaiserreich* was already in the process of becoming. In a later decade, Leonard Krieger, referring to Treitschke's article on *Freiheit*, summed this up as 'the German idea of freedom'.[13] The 'ideas of 1914' were not part of the Romantic legacy; rather, they exemplified a way of thinking that was deeply concerned to have a sound grasp of contemporary social, technical and cultural developments. Such convictions did not end with the termination of the war but had a long afterlife in the Weimar Republic.

It fairly soon became obvious that German intellectuals and scientists were arguing without any political experience of their own. Day-to-day politics were unfamiliar to them; they had no understanding of procedure. Power politics, strategic thinking and planning, parliamentary tactics, the necessity to communicate in public and to negotiate in private – all these features of politics common to so many countries were considered to belong to 'non-German' political culture. The political principles thought to differentiate the political culture of the 'Western' Powers from that of the Central Powers were listed as follows: in the West there was a professional power broker representing group interests, whereas in Germany there was a bipartisan government of experts in administration; on the 'Western' side there were 'politicians' and on the German side, 'statesmen'.[14]

There were moderate authors, too. Hans Delbrück, for instance, a famous conservative historian of warfare at Berlin University, had, prior to the war, presented a realistic analysis of the advantages and disadvantages of popular government in 'the West',[15] and during the war he expressed his belief in the common heritage of European cultures. He stressed the common features of countries of Germanic origin, among which he counted Britain as well as Germany, and he maintained that cultural exchange between Romanic and Germanic countries was mutually stimulating.[16] The publicist and essayist Otto Flake warned against the tendency to create an 'artificial China' in which all European nations tried to insulate themselves from the influence of other cultures and aspired to live in splendid cultural isolation. He presented a model of European nations as cultural systems communicating with each other, using the analogy of communicating pipes permanently exchanging their contents and balancing themselves.[17] But those moderates did not have a wide audience. It was zealous partisanship that dictated the hour – all the more so since an intense debate on the ambiguity of the 'Western' interpretation of democracy was raging.

Democratic Critiques of Western Democracies

Before the war, French, British and American intellectuals and scientists did not gather round the banner of democracy as the foundation of their political ideology, nor did they rally to an idea of the West. Albert Vernon Dicey, a distinguished scholar in English public law, spoke of the United States as the 'Western' democratic power ('the vast republic of the West'), together with the republic of France. These two leading democratic states were both seen as different from Britain. What all three states had in common was the idea of popular government. However, that did not mean they were democratic in the strict sense, but simply that their governments had to take public opinion into account.[18] To Dicey the debate on democracy in Europe centred round the question of whether, in the first years of the twentieth century, socialism was to be the primary political aim and whether democracy could be considered a gateway to that.[19]

In general, English and American authors spoke more readily of 'popular government' than of 'democracy', tending to consider that democracy was just one way of carrying out the people's will, parliamentarianism being another. Many of these authors, like Sidney Low and Abbot Lawrence Lowell, were concerned that improvements in democracy might endanger the effectiveness of parliamentarian rule,[20] but their criticisms stopped short of rejecting democracy as such.

Even in the U.S. the idea of democracy was losing supporters. This was out of disillusionment. Observation of democratic practices in the U.S. had raised doubts about whether democracy was a proper model for modern political government of a mass society. In a critique that drew on experiences with Tammany Hall in the local government of New York City, Edwin Lawrence Godkin, founder of the journal *The Nation* and later editor of the *New York Evening Post*, coined the phrase: 'unforeseen tendencies of democracy'.[21] Godkin's critique could be applied to all political systems with universal (male) suffrage, huge numbers of voters and vast powers for self-government institutions. Godkin underlined what James Bryce, the British historian and probably the leading analyst of the United States' political system, also maintained: that there were tendencies towards demagogy in the United States.[22] Bryce did not, however, make a case for dismissing democracy as such; he stressed the advantages of democracy in terms of people's control of government and the influence of public opinion on it. The feature that made it possible to criticize aspects of democratic government and at the same time favour democracy as a political system was the distinction between democracy as a concept of government and democracy as a social condition – a distinction originally made by Alexis de Tocqueville and discussed extensively, by Dicey among others.[23] Critics could therefore find fault with aspects of democracy as a concept of government but stay loyal to the democratic social condition.

Some recognized experts on democratic political systems in Germany, like Wilhelm Hasbach, reflected on the distinction between 'political' and 'social' democracy[24] but were, on the whole, unsympathetic to the democratic idea and distinguished it from liberalism. Shortly after the outbreak of the war, Hasbach repeated his critique of democracy and supported his objections against the system by citing English and French authors (such as James Bryce, Brougham Villiers and Walter E. Weyl) who, in his view, also distanced themselves from any naive advocacy of democratization.[25] But Hasbach missed the difference between criticizing democracy from within and doing so from outside the fold of believers.

The Germans were especially confused by the fact that the idea of democracy had been criticized from within before the war but was now used as the focal concept in the 'Western' Allies' political ideology. Many aspects of the pre-war democrats' self-criticisms were taken up in the German debate on democracy during the First World War. Scientists from neutral countries like the Netherlands and Sweden were highly esteemed sources of independent evaluation and were quoted extensively by German authors, who believed they could take their assessments as objective analysis. Among these authors were the Dutchman J.H. Valckenier Kips[26] and the Swedes Rudolf Kjéllen[27] and Gustav Steffen.[28] Additionally, the German debate relied on a huge amount of literature written before the war which condemned both the features and the effects of democratic political regimes. Given the pre-war criticism of democracy that had formerly come from the 'West', German authors concluded that the Allies' use of legitimacy claims founded on the idea of democracy was to be considered a mere propaganda technique.

A strategy to support democratic political reform without being vulnerable to accusations of defeatism was to avoid the semantics of 'Western' democracy altogether. Hugo Preuß was among the first authors to support the democratization of Germany's political regime. In *Das deutsche Volk und die Politik*, published as early as 1915, he refrained from using the term 'democracy'. Instead he talked of *Volksstaat* in opposition to *Obrigkeitsstaat* to characterize current trends in the German Empire.[29]

1917: The Turning Point of the Debate

At the beginning of 1917, against the advice of Chancellor Bethmann Hollweg, the German Military High Command succeeded in getting unrestricted submarine warfare approved as the keystone of the German war strategy. It was clear that a direct reaction to such a move would be the entry of the United States into the war, but the Americans' military capacity to change the course of the fighting was underestimated. The United States declared war in April 1917. No Allied government was more vehement in its demands for political reform towards democratization in Germany than was Woodrow Wilson.[30] In his address to Congress on 2 April 1917, he proclaimed the war to be a fight to make the world safe for democracy.[31] Wilson's address was a crucial turning point in the debate over democracy in the First World War. It was with the American public in mind that English intellectuals and scientists had stressed the idea of democracy before 1917. The need for democracy now became the central focus of the Allies' war propaganda both at home and abroad.

Before the *Lusitania* affair and the declaration of unrestricted submarine warfare, the American public had been undecided, and Wilson had won the 1916 election through his official attitude of keeping the U.S.A. out of the remote European war. Intellectuals with strong ties to German culture had challenged British accusations of German militarism. For instance, in 1915 John Burgess had published a book in which he praised the achievements of the German Empire – achievements beginning with universal male suffrage and ending with compulsory military service (which he saw as an advantage).[32] Against this trend, we find philosophers like John Dewey making an issue out of the differences between German and 'Western' philosophy and historical thinking[33] and elaborating on the American way of educating people into the practice of democracy.[34]

But there were sceptical voices, too. Liberals of the Left, like John Atkinson Hobson, argued against the impression that the West had already achieved democracy and that it was only the enemy states that lacked appropriate political and social systems. Hobson feared that the impact of the war on Britain would lead to the decoupling of the political executive – sponsored and supported by industrial as well as imperial interests – from social reform. Hence, he included in his notion of democracy all progressive forces that were opposed to reactionaries and militarists of every kind.[35] He also reminded the public that in Germany there had been strong intellectual currents of cosmopolitanism, as in the works of Goethe and Kant, who clearly belonged to the 'Western' liberal tradition.[36] It is true that these appeals for more democracy provoked some conservative reactions favouring 'imperial democracy', for example (meaning a government centred round the king and independent from parliament),[37] while others rejected the idea of democracy by identifying it with a 'pure' form based on a plebiscite and the politics of the street.[38] But the declaration of war on Germany had largely changed the discourse. Now many intellectuals and historians published books on the democratic cause for the war.[39] Collections of war poems and speeches were common;[40] and Wilson's idea of a League of (democratic) Nations was found especially inspiring amongst concerned people in the United States.[41]

As long as tsarist Russia was part of the alliance against the empires of Germany and Austria, the Allies' claim that they were fighting for the rule of popular government was relatively easy for the Germans to reject as mere propaganda. With the downfall of Russian tsarism in the east and the entry of the United States into the war in 1917, the constellation changed dramatically. From August 1917, reactionary groups in Germany started to form a pressure group, the *Vaterlandspartei*, aimed at turning public opinion against any aspirations towards democratization, and flooding the public with pamphlets and articles that condemned any democratic reforms as 'un-German'. This pressure group became huge. Against it, those who favoured political reform, as well as supporters for a peace of reconciliation, formed their own pressure group, the *Volksbund für Freiheit und Vaterland* (The Peoples' League for Freedom and Country).

Coming to Terms with the 'Attack of Western Democracy'

The discourse on political reform came to a peak in Germany during the summer and autumn of 1917. In his widely discussed book on Bismarck's legacy in the constitution of the Reich, *Bismarcks Erbe in der Reichsverfassung*, Erich Kaufmann could already speak of the war as a conflict not merely of military and economic supremacy but also of contrasting constitutions and ideologies. Kaufmann's aim was to demonstrate that the German political system did not fall short in development apt for modern times by playing down the parliamentary system; rather that the constitution of the German Empire had its own worth and tradition. To Kaufmann it was evident that the Allies' claim that they were defending the 'democratic cause' was a sophisticated propaganda technique, emanating from imperial powers that aimed at world domination. He therefore warned against their 'sermon' of democracy and their 'gospel' of alleged political freedom.[42]

Among the first public responses to the entry of the United States into the war was a series of lectures given at the House of Representatives of Prussia in Berlin in May 1917. The speakers were Adolf von Harnack, Ernst Troeltsch, Otto Hintze, Max Sering and Friedrich Meinecke, five distinguished scholars, and their lectures were printed in a published collection. Troeltsch, the famous Protestant theologian, historian and sociologist of religion, tried to draw a fair picture of the conflict. His contribution was entitled *Der Ansturm der westlichen Demokratie* ('The Attack of Western Democracy'). At the start of it, it seems as if he was singing the same old tune, confirming antagonistic worldviews; but in fact, Troeltsch tried to analyse the real differences between Germany and the 'Western' powers that had been concealed by polemical talk. His résumé ended with the observation that the heated debate had arisen from competition for the same collective good: liberty and the appropriate interpretation of its idea.[43] Liberty had to be considered the point of departure for any European nation, whereas its implementation followed different paths due to the differing circumstances of its practice. Every path of development from that original point of departure had its own advantages and disadvantages. Liberty in the Anglo-Saxon world was primarily a principle of individual self-realization: its advantage happened to be a much higher awareness in political matters. It was true, Troeltsch continued, that German political culture tended to shift political responsibilities to the state: this was mainly caused by an understanding of individual liberty strongly influenced by an attitude prizing intellectual inwardness rather than social involvement. But there was another side to the coin: Anglo-Saxon liberty tended to feed egoism and pursuit of profit at the expense of the common good; while, contrastingly, Germany had developed a welfare state whose principles were derived from the concept of collectivism. Troeltsch regarded this as the specific 'non-Western' contribution Germany had made to the broad idea of liberty and he believed it was important enough to compensate for the nation's less developed political participation. To Troeltsch, however, it seemed imprudent to support a development towards socialism without guaranteeing individual rights and political control by the people, and that meant nothing less than moving in pursuit of greater democracy.[44] Troeltsch emphasized the advantages of the 'ideas of 1789' while simultaneously stressing the future, which would owe its basic character to the 'ideas of 1914'. He believed in individualism as well as collectivism, in human rights as well as voluntary acceptance of the importance of the state. He rejected the idea that it was possible to develop in just one direction without having accepted the necessity of establishing balancing features from the other. He expressed the hope that, in the future, it would be possible for all cultures to learn from one another. But, for the present, he claimed the right of self-determination for the German people: they must choose their own path of liberty. He denied all the Allies' accusations that it was an autocracy and a military caste that ruled German politics without any approval from the people.

Rather than mediate between the claims the West made to be democratic and the counterclaims of German intellectuals, who wanted to follow their own path to democracy, Max Weber, the towering figure in German sociology, refused to contemplate ideological juxtapositions at all. When Weber spoke of *Westmächte* he was referring to the Allies of the Western Front, with no allusion at all to any differences in ideology.[45] Weber tried to analyse the war as a rational conflict of interests: his aim was to discuss ways and means of ending the war by a settlement of interests that would be acceptable to both sides. For Weber, democracy was the political result of modernization, and modernization was a social development that all countries were bound to experience sooner or later.

In the first years of the war, Weber could not resist joining in with the common cry of patriotism. However, in light of the crisis in domestic politics of July 1917, when Bethmann Hollweg was removed from office and the dictatorship of the Army High Command began, Weber changed his public standpoint and pleaded for democratization. The alternative to 'Western' democracy was not, he argued, a 'German' way of democracy: the question turned on whether democratization would be with or without political responsibility. Weber revealed his fury at the demagoguery that had caused recent events, which he found more despicable than any of the demagoguery of which the 'Western' democracies were regularly accused. Right from the beginning, Weber charged, those in favour of uncontrolled government by bureaucratic administrators had tried to exploit the war in order to secure an *ancien régime* preserving the interests of industry and the east Prussian landed estates. It was mostly a band of naive *littérateurs* who had invented the contrast between an allegedly 'German' way of democracy – with strong bureaucracy but without parliamentarian control – and a supposed conspiracy of 'Western European democracies'.[46] Though in earlier days Weber had tended to reiterate the wartime polemic discourse, he realized that this discourse led to irrational thinking and was contributing to Germany's defeat. To his mind now, the war was not about a clash of cultures but about modern societies' ability to accept unavoidable developments and to master the challenges they represented. But Weber was the exception to the rule.

Notes

1. Marcus Llanque, *Demokratisches Denken im Krieg. Die deutsche Debatte im Ersten Weltkrieg*, Berlin, 2000.
2. Bernadotte E. Schmitter and Harold C. Vedeler, *The World in the Crucible, 1914–1919*, New York, 1984, 306–16; Roger Chickering and Stig Förster (eds), *Great War, Total War. Combat and Moblization on the Western Front, 1914–1918*, Cambridge, 2000.
3. R.W. Seton-Watson, J. Dover Wilson, Alfred E. Zimmern and Arthur Greenwood (eds), *The War and Democracy*, London, 1914, 1.
4. Ibid., 4.
5. Alfred E. Zimmern, 'Germany', in ibid., 75–120, here 93.
6. Ian Machin, *The Rise of Democracy in Britain, 1830–1918*, Houndmills, 2001, 139–49; David Marquand, *Britain since 1918. The Strange Career of British Democracy*, London, 2008, 9–75.
7. David Blackbourn, *History of Germany, 1780–1918. The Long 19th Century*, 2nd edn, Malden, 2003, 360–68.
8. Cited in Lloyd C. Gardner, *Safe for Democracy. The Anglo-American Response to Revolution, 1913–1923*, New York, 1984, 118.
9. Ibid., 97; Stuart Wallace, *War and the Image of Germany*, Edinburgh, 1988.
10. James Bryce (ed.), *The War of Democracy. The Allies' Statement*, New York, 1917, reproducing an interview of Lord Haldane with the *Chicago Daily News*.
11. David M. Esposito, *The Legacy of Woodrow Wilson. American War Aims in World War I*, Westport, 1996, 137.
12. Jörg Nagler, 'Pandora's Box. Propaganda and War Hysteria in the United States during World War I', in Chickering and Förster (eds), *Great War, Total War*, 485–500.
13. Leonard Krieger, *The German Idea of Freedom. History of a Political Tradition*, Boston, 1957, 367–68.
14. Ferdinand Tönnies, *Der englische und der deutsche Staat*, Berlin, 1917; Erich Kaufmann, *Bismarcks Erbe in der Reichsverfassung*, Berlin, 1917, 78–82.
15. Hans Delbrück, *Regierung und Volkswille*, Berlin, 1914.
16. Hans Delbrück, *Krieg und Politik*, Berlin, 1918, 156.
17. Otto Flake, 'Demos', in *Frankfurter Zeitung*, 4 December 1917, first morning edition, 1–2.
18. Albert Vernon Dicey, *Lectures on the Relation between Law and Public Opinion in England during the 19th Century*, London, 1914, 440.
19. Ibid., lxxi–lxxxii.
20. Sidney Low, *The Governance of England*, New York and London, 1904; Abbot Lawrence Lowell, *The Government of England*, New York, 1909.

21. Edwin Lawrence Godkin, *Unforeseen Tendencies of Modern Democracy*, Westminster, 1898.
22. James Bryce, *The American Commonwealth*, vol. 2, completely revised with additional chapters, Norwood/Mass., 3rd ed., 1907, 563–80.
23. Dicey, *Lectures on the Relation between Law and Public Opinion*, 50.
24. Wilhelm Hasbach, *Die moderne Demokratie. Eine politische Betrachtung*, Jena, 1921 (first published 1912), 290–357.
25. Wilhelm Hasbach, 'Neuere Literatur über die moderne Demokratie', *Zeitschrift für Politik* 7 (1914), 471–76, here 476.
26. J.H. Valckenier Kips, *Der deutsche Staatsgedanke*, Leipzig, 1916.
27. Rudolf Kjéllen, *Die Ideen von 1914. Eine weltgeschichtliche Perspektive*, Leipzig, 1915.
28. Gustav Steffen, *Demokratie und Weltkrieg*, Jena, 1916; Gustav Steffen, *Das Problem der Demokratie*, Jena, 1917.
29. Hugo Preuß, *Das deutsche Volk und die Politik*, Jena, 1915.
30. David Stevenson, *The First World War and International Politics*, Oxford, 1988, 77–83. For a recent reassessment of Wilson see John Milton Cooper (ed.), *Reconsidering Woodrow Wilson. Progressivism, Internationalism, War and Peace*, Baltimore, 2008.
31. *Papers Relating to the Foreign Relations of the United States 1917, Supplement 1: The World War*, Washington, 1931, 195–201.
32. John William Burgess, *The European War of 1914. Its Causes, Purposes and Probable Results*, Chicago, 1915.
33. John Dewey, *German Philosophy and Politics*, New York, 1915.
34. John Dewey, *Democracy and Education. An Introduction to the Philosophy of Education*, New York, 1916.
35. John Atkinson Hobson, *Democracy after the War*, London, 1917, 7.
36. Ibid., 115 and 134.
37. James B. Halcrow, *Imperial Democracy and United Empire. An After-the-War Programme*, Tracts for the Times, London, 1917, 6.
38. William H. Mallock, *The Limits of Pure Democracy*, 2nd edn, London, 1918.
39. Christian Frederick Gauss, *Democracy Today. An American Interpretation*, Chicago and New York, 1917; Hartley Burr Alexander, *Liberty and Democracy*, Boston, 1918; John Firman Coar, *Democracy and the War*, New York and London, 1918.
40. Lyman W. Powell and Gertrude B. Powell (eds), *The Spirit of Democracy*, Patriotism by Literature series, Chicago and New York, 1918.
41. Norman Angell, *The Political Conditions of Allied Success. A Plea for the Protective Union of Democracies*, New York, 1918.
42. Kaufmann, *Bismarcks Erbe in der Reichsverfassung*, 3–4, 148–49.
43. Ernst Troeltsch, 'Der Ansturm der westlichen Demokratie', in *Die deutsche Freiheit. Fünf Reden von Adolf von Harnack u.a.*, Gotha, 1917, 79–113.
44. Ernst Troeltsch, 'Plenges Ideen von 1914', *Annalen für soziale Politik und Gesetzgebung* 5 (1917), 309–43, here 321.
45. Max Weber, 'Deutschland unter den europäischen Weltmächten', in Max Weber, *Zur Politik im Weltkrieg. Schriften und Reden 1914–1918*, edited by Wolfgang J. Mommsen and Gangolf Hübinger (Max Weber Gesamtausgabe I/15), Tübingen, 1984, 161–95, here 172.
46. Max Weber, 'Die Lehren der deutschen Kanzlerkrise', in Max Weber, *Gesammelte Politische Schriften*, Munich, 1921, 262; Max Weber, *Suffrage and Democracy in Germany*, in Max Weber, *Political Writings*, ed. Peter Lassman, trans. Ronald Speirs, Cambridge, 1994.

Chapter 4

PERCEPTIONS OF THE WEST IN TWENTIETH-CENTURY GERMANY

Anselm Doering-Manteuffel

This chapter argues that during the period of the two world wars, from 1914 to 1945, the opposition between 'Germany' and 'the West' was more important for the coherence of the European-American West than the West's opposition to the Stalinist Soviet Union. After 1945 the antagonism between 'Germany' and 'the West' gradually dissolved – if by 'Germany' one means the Federal Republic.

The chapter is divided into three parts. The first part examines the First World War and the Treaty of Versailles, and the following 'crisis of liberalism' in the modern industrialized world between 1918 and 1939. The impact of this last was greater in Central Europe than in France, Britain or the U.S. During the 'crisis of liberalism', the contrast between 'Germany' and 'the West' hardened into a hostile political-ideological opposition.

The second part investigates the period of fascism and National Socialism from a specific point of view, namely the connection between emigration and remigration. From 1933 onwards, many intellectuals and artists emigrated from Central Europe. In Washington and London, a number of them participated in planning occupation policy for the time after the demise of the Third Reich. They influenced re-education policy, the reorganization of the social sciences at German universities and the restructuring of the media; and they were among the most important protagonists of the 'Westernization' of German political and intellectual culture.

The third part analyses the measures, forms of action, goals and impact of 'Westernization' in the Federal Republic during the 1950s and early 1960s. In the course of that process, German, Western European and American intellectuals sought to overcome the political-ideological hostility that had come about in the wake of the First World War.

The Rise of 'the West' out of First World War Propaganda

Before 1914, the German Reich was usually regarded as part of a group of nations characterized by a shared European and North American intellectual and cultural heritage. From this perspective 'the West' had emerged from the tradition of the Enlightenment in the second half of the eighteenth century. The Enlightenment, concerned with the individual's rights to economic, political and cultural freedom, had been shaped by French, British and German influences. In Britain, John Locke's theory about the freedom of the market was influential, with his defence of life, liberty and property. In France, Montesquieu's theory presented freedom as human equality: *liberté* and *égalité*. In Germany it was Immanuel Kant who wanted freedom to be seen primarily as rational self-determination. In the United States, the influence of the European Enlightenment was visible in the Declaration of Independence and the Constitution. Lockeanism and the French Enlightenment came together here: freedom of property and the market on the basis of equality, understood as the legal order of the white Anglo-Saxon Protestant population.[1]

Indeed, the European-Atlantic traditions of the Enlightenment provided reference points for the identity-building of European and North American nations in the nineteenth century.[2] After 1815, in continental Europe, Britain and the U.S., liberalism developed out of these traditions and became the political philosophy of 'progress'. 'Progress' and 'liberty' formed the core concepts of social thinking in Europe from about 1830. Political emancipation, the revolutions of 1848, technological modernization with scientific development and, finally, industrialization were all processes largely driven by the liberal paradigms of 'progress' and 'liberty'.[3]

At the end of the nineteenth century, from about 1880, technological progress and industrialization had reached such a pace in Central Europe that contemporaries felt increasingly uneasy in the face of constant change. *Nervosität* (anxiety or nervousness) was the first slogan to express unease at the impact of progress, from 1890. Added to this was criticism of the lifestyles of the middle classes from 1900 onwards, whether in Wilhelmine Germany or Edwardian Britain. Before the First World

War, liberal thinking on progress, the bourgeoisie as its agents, and the constantly accelerating pace of everyday life as a result of industrialization and urbanization had become the focus of increasing criticism.[4]

In 1889 Friedrich Nietzsche gave voice to a 'critique of modernity' in his book *Twilight of the Idols or How to Philosophize with a Hammer* (*Götzen-Dämmerung oder Wie man mit dem Hammer philosophirt*).[5] Nietzsche, who was a sharp observer of the currents of the time, understood 'modernity' as encompassing the following phenomena: accelerated change, democracy and freedom. Nietzsche's critique lists the manifestations of 'modernity' under the heading 'the West': democracy, liberalism, accelerated change, *Nervosität*, haste. The opposite of 'the West', in Nietzsche's eyes, was a condition of tradition and permanence, guaranteed by institutions such as the monarchy, the church and the (nation) state. Modernity and progress destroyed a historical awareness that linked the past with the future. For Nietzsche, 'the West' was a cipher for modernity and progress; and Germany, alas, was part of it.[6]

In 1914 the First World War began. Only a few weeks after the first military battles, the propaganda war between the enemy camps broke out between France and Britain as Entente powers on the one side, and Germany on the other. The German Reich had violated international law on the first day of the war by allowing German armies to march through Belgium in order to reach a better position from which to start hostilities against the French forces. In Belgium, the German troops displayed unbelievable aggression, even against the civilian population. They murdered women and children. After a few weeks, the German artillery bombed the library of the University of Leuven (Louvain), which contained innumerable manuscript sources on the medieval history of Western Europe. Most of the documents were destroyed. Soon afterwards the German artillery in eastern France damaged the cathedral of Reims.[7]

This was the background against which the *Krieg der Geister* (the 'war of the intellectuals') self-mobilized in support of the policies of their respective governments. It began in October 1914. Propaganda in the French press soon described the Germans as 'barbarians', while in Britain the Germans were called 'Huns'. Yet in the years before the First World War the German Reich had achieved an extremely high cultural level. At that time, the majority of Nobel Prizes went to Germans, in the natural sciences as well as in the arts and literature. And now the propaganda from France and Britain was calling them barbarians and Huns! In October 1914 the *Aufruf an die Kulturwelt* or 'Manifesto of the Intellectuals of Germany' was published with the signatures of ninety-three academics and artists. Many of them were supporters of a bourgeois intellectual liberalism. In this manifesto they expressed their support for the policies of the German imperial government and for the way in which the German Imperial Army Supreme Command was conducting the war. In the nationalist enthusiasm of the first weeks of the war they denied the contrast, clearly developed in the German Reich, between the liberalism in scholarship and the arts on the one hand, and the monarchical semi-absolutism of the government – known as Kaiser Wilhelm II's 'personal rule' – on the other. Before 1914, most liberal academics had distanced themselves from the *Kaiserreich*'s political system. Now, in October 1914, they joined the nationalist intellectuals in the right-wing political camp and unreservedly endorsed the German Reich's military policies. The most important sentence in the Manifesto read: 'The German army and the German people are one, and today this awareness makes brothers of 70 million Germans without distinction of education, rank and position, or political party'.[8]

This legitimization of Wilhelmine Germany's political system and the cultural arrogance towards all other nations expressed in the Manifesto did a great deal of damage to Germany in the First World War. In France, Britain and the U.S. arguments were developed elaborating on the contrast between these 'Western countries' on the one side, and Germany on the other.

Britain, France and the U.S. began to think about a tradition of intellectual values and philosophical and academic orientations. A tradition of this sort did not really exist, because (as already explained) the British, French and American varieties of Enlightenment philosophy and liberalism were quite different from one another. Yet, for the first time, the Western Entente powers now constructed a common tradition – and very effectively. Its main feature was that it differed fundamentally from the intellectual fabric of German-speaking Central Europe. 'The West' was moulded into a coherent value system; and Germany was not part of it. Instead, German scholars and writers formulated the 'ideas of 1914', which provided the philosophical basis for a dissociation from 'the West'.[9]

The construction of 'the West' included the notion of an established connection between the political and economic order, social culture, science and technology. It was tied to the assumption that only this comprehensive structural pattern could guarantee constant progress for the benefit of mankind. Progress along these lines meant 'civilization', and 'civilization' was identical with 'Western civilization' – the most highly developed social order. It was not limited to one country or a single nation. Its geographical range was potentially worldwide. 'Civilization' was a universal project based on a liberal worldview. The components of this worldview were Lockeanism ('life, liberty and property') and the understanding that every individual had the right to feel 'free' in the context of the legal order and within the framework of the free market. During the First World War, this theory of progress and modernity was elaborated as the essence of 'Western civilization'.

In 1915, American social scientists, interested in society's capacity for progress, investigated cultural developments following the Industrial Revolution in the English-speaking countries, on the one hand, and German-speaking Central Europe on the other. Germany, with its modern industry and efficient economy, appeared to have a backward social and political order. The political order, it seemed, was shaped by the rule of a constitutionally limited absolutism, while the social order was characterized by an unquestioning acceptance of dynastic authoritarianism. In contrast, Britain seemed to provide the yardstick for a coherent cluster of political-social and economic-industrial progress, the epitome of 'Western civilization'. The most important authors to develop this argument were the sociologist Thorstein Veblen and the philosopher John Dewey. Their writings laid the foundation for the theory of the German *Sonderweg* (special path). In the course of West Germany's 'Westernization', this theory was later to be appropriated, along with modernization theory, by German scholars from the early 1960s onward. In other words, the *Sonderweg* thesis was the product of the division between 'Germany' and 'the West' during the First World War. 'Western values' were pitted against 'German ideas' – and vice versa.[10]

U.S. President Woodrow Wilson's Fourteen Points of January 1918 were a manifesto of the liberal thought of the U.S.A.'s Progressive Era. They called for free trade and freedom of the seas, transparent political negotiations between states eschewing secret diplomacy, and democracy and self-determination. The peoples of Europe who had been liberated from the spell of monarchies (the Habsburg monarchy, the Ottoman Empire, the Russian Empire and the German *Kaiserreich*) were to receive the right to found their own nation states and to establish the political order of freedom: parliamentary democracy. Wilson's plan turned out to be unrealizable.[11]

The demand for 'self-determination' presupposed that this right would be granted to all peoples of Europe. But this would have meant that after the end of the Hohenzollern monarchy in Germany and the disintegration of the multinational state of Austria-Hungary, Germans and Austrians would receive the right to create a state in line with their notions of self-determination. The desire of the German-speaking population of Austria for a union with the German Reich would have made defeated Germany the biggest state in Europe after the end of the First World War in territory, population and economic strength. Germany's European wartime adversaries, France and Britain, could not accept this, and the German people were not granted the right of national self-determination.

For this reason alone, Western liberalism on the Wilson model was discredited in Germany after 1919. The hostility towards 'the West' which had been stirred up by wartime propaganda since 1914 was now intensified by the impact of the peace treaty. Ideology and power politics worked hand in hand. What is more, liberalism was increasingly considered an obsolete worldview whose only purpose was to secure the interests of the middle classes against those of the workers' movement.[12]

The First World War, moreover, had confirmed that industrial progress was not an unmixed blessing. Rather, industrialized warfare had demonstrated that modernity and progress, in the first instance, led to death and destruction. After the war, any talk of 'progress' no longer held out the promise of a good, better future. Eric Hobsbawm refers to the period from 1918 to 1945 as 'the fall of liberalism'. This phenomenon, to be sure, can be observed in many countries at the time. The crisis of liberalism in the interwar period was a cultural problem of pan-European proportions.[13]

In Germany, however, an additional aspect came into play. As a result of the Versailles Treaty, the liberal ideas of progress, self-determination and liberty were politically discredited as well. The peace treaty was imposed on Germany, not negotiated. Therefore the value system of the Western powers, especially of the United States, was perceived as something foreign and antagonistic. It could not serve as a model for Germany's new democratic order following the end of the monarchy. Nor did the influences of American modernity, felt in the 1920s in both industry and everyday culture, change anything in respect of Germany's ideological distance from 'the West'. 'Americanism' was, to be sure, received with a certain amount of enthusiasm by some Germans, and adherents of National Socialism, in particular, regarded the United States' technological modernity as a model and a challenge. But this did not change Germany's hostility to the West, which it associated with the social and political order of the Anglo-American victors.[14]

National Socialism's Enemy Images and German Émigrés in the West

The Nazis swiftly appropriated the widespread protest against the Versailles Treaty in Germany. From the early 1920s on, they combined it with a vehement anti-Bolshevism. In the years following the First World War, the most popular enemy images were of the victorious Western powers and the revolutionary Soviet Union. The Nazis used the resentment against 'the West' in German society that had manifested itself in the 'ideas of 1914' in order to attack parliamentary democracy and the republican constitution of the Weimar state. Their smear campaigns were directed against the political culture and social order of Western-style democracies, as well as against the socialist and communist powers. Anti-Semitism transcended and linked both enemy images. The Nazis spoke simultaneously of the 'Jewish Republic' and of 'Jewish Bolshevism'. After their seizure of power in 1933, anti-Semitism, anti-communism and hostility to democracy merged together into a comprehensively destructive policy. In the so-called Nazi revolution, communists, Jews and democrats – Social Democrats and left-wing liberals – were all equal targets of persecution. During the Second World War, the Third Reich cultivated a comprehensive enemy image constructed on a global scale. Its hatred was directed at the 'Jewish-Bolshevik world conspiracy', which was allegedly related to American 'plutocrats', as well as at 'Americanism', which the SS in 1944 described as a 'world danger'. Nazism aimed to destroy all these 'enemies'.[15]

It is not surprising that responses to Germany after the Second World War were different from those after the First World War. This time, it was not a matter of rivalry between different ideas of a socio-cultural and political order but, vice versa, of vanquishing National Socialism in Germany and sweeping away the ideological understanding of '*Deutschtum*' ('Germanness') that had been disseminated from 1914, and most strongly from 1933 on. The political values of 'the West' were to be applied to Germany, and anti-Western notions had to be overcome. In other words, Anglo-American ideas about political order in a modern society were to be brought to bear against Germany's anti-Western ideas.

After 1945, this transformation of political and social thought was substantially influenced by intellectuals who had fled Germany from the Nazis in 1933. Many had been persecuted for political reasons; many also because they were Jewish. The crucial factor was that, before 1933, most of them had belonged either to socialist groups or to a small minority of Left-liberal intellectuals. They were opponents of the anti-Western 'ideas of 1914', but most countries of the West were unknown to them, because few had ever travelled abroad. They often emigrated first to Britain or Scandinavia, sometimes to France, but in most cases, their paths ultimately led to the United States.

In the U.S. they came face to face with a different political culture. They became familiar with the interplay between market economy and liberal democracy, and could observe how divergent social interests were reconciled in the era of the New Deal. The free market, individualism, democracy and social consensus in a pluralistic society taken together made up a free, progressive order, which many emigrants came to regard as an ideal. During the years of emigration, they revised the political convictions they had brought from Germany and combined them with elements of American political culture. In the U.S., socialist opponents of capitalism were transformed into cautious supporters of a market economy. Others recognized that parliamentary democracy and a pluralist society presupposed each other.

In other words, many emigrants who influenced the political reorganization of Germany after 1945 had experienced an amalgamation of contrasting worldviews. To be sure, from the First World War onwards they had all been opponents of the narrow-minded German nationalism that related to the 'ideas of 1914'. They had all been opponents of *völkisch* ideology. But they had regarded antagonism between the social classes, between the bourgeoisie and the working class, as a fact of social life. The socialists among them, moreover, had gone to the U.S. as committed opponents of capitalism and the market economy. In the American New Deal they could observe how capitalism, democracy and social consensus worked together.[16]

In 1943–1944, a group of German professionals, mostly trained as lawyers or historians, worked at the Office for Strategic Services (OSS) in Washington. They wrote experts' reports about Germany that provided the foundation for the policy of reorientation after the war.[17] In their reports they analysed Germany's political culture since the establishment of the German Reich in 1871, judging it in more or less the same terms as Thorstein Veblen had done in his book of 1915, *Imperial Germany and the Industrial Revolution*. In addition, they focused on the anti-individualistic and non-pluralistic orientation of the bourgeois reform movements before 1914 that nowadays are usually recognized as aspects of anti-liberal modernity and, in the decade following the First World War, as precursors of fascist modernism.[18]

After 1945, German emigrants cooperated with Americans and Britons working in the occupation policy areas of de-Nazification and re-education. The aim of this policy was to combat Nazi ideology in the German population, to introduce the rules of parliamentary democracy and to bring leading Nazis to justice, removing them from public life. In parallel with occupation policy, a transformation of political worldviews and notions of social order began from 1947, producing far-reaching results ten to fifteen years later. This process of ideologically orienting West German society towards 'the West', however, was not set in motion by occupation policy. Rather, American and German institutions and individuals worked together in order to influence perceptions of the West, so that in the end, Germans would naturally see themselves as 'Western'.

The occupation policy pursued by the victorious Western powers – the U.S., Britain, and France – was undoubtedly crucial in persuading the people of the Western zones to favour parliamentary democracy, the market economy and the lifestyles of a consumer society. The turn towards 'the West' was to be carried out as a material and moral turning away from dictatorship – as a rejection of the brown dictatorship and a clear separation from the red variety. The intellectual protagonists of Westernization worked in parallel with the occupying authorities, but mostly independently of them, for they had a different goal. While occupation policy pursued the short- and middle-term goals of 'reorientation' and de-Nazification, the supporters of Westernization had the middle- and long-term goals in view. They wanted to displace the older traditions of German idealism, which, since 1914, had turned into anti-liberalism and become the force driving ideological anti-Westernism. Their aim was to change the cultural value-orientation of the German elites, and to commit them to 'Western' standards.

Transatlantic Cultural Transfer, Westernization and the Ideological Transformation of West Germany's Intellectual Elites

Between 1948 and 1950, West Berlin and West Germany witnessed the foundation of a number of institutions that presented themselves as agents of Westernization and were, on the whole, highly successful. They included universities, the media, congresses and public campaigns, and a close cooperation with representatives of the Social Democratic Party and the trade unions. Three examples follow.

The Free University Berlin was founded in 1948 and, from the start, was the most important centre of political and social science oriented towards the U.S. in Germany. Its lecturers and professors were not Americans or Britons, but Germans who had remigrated back from Britain and the U.S. In Berlin they created the foundations of political science as a discipline for the analysis and promotion of parliamentary democracy and pluralism. They turned the Free University into Germany's earliest centre of political science as the 'science of democracy'. In addition, they supported the university constitution which, from the start, provided for parity between lecturers and students, between research and teaching. Liberal also in many other respects, the constitution prohibited any institutions which, like student corporations, were regarded as forging the cadres of *völkisch* and anti-Western ideology.[19]

From 1950 onwards the journal *Der Monat* became the most important publishing outlet of critical German intellectuals receptive to 'the West'. *Der Monat* was financed by the Congress for Cultural Freedom (CCF) and published pieces by Western European, American and German intellectuals who pursued two goals in particular. The first was to combat the tradition of ideological *'Deutschtum'* dating from 1870/1890 and to spread the values of the 'liberal consensus' from the U.S.'s New Deal era. This particular current of liberalism, tried and tested through the Great Depression and the war, was supposed to replace the tradition of German anti-liberalism. The second goal was to convince the German (and West European) Left that social democracy could only be successful if it underwent a consensual union with capitalism. The influence of the New Deal could also be felt here, because 'consensus liberalism' was now supplemented by 'consensus capitalism'. The purpose of these efforts was obvious. During the Cold War, the United States sought to inoculate European social democratic parties and trade unions against the influence of communist countries and the Communist parties in Western Europe. For this reason, the CCF was also committed to working in France, Italy and the U.K. The respective media outlets of the CCF were called *Preuves*, *Tempo Presente* and *Encounter*. In Germany, success came at the end of the 1950s. In 1959 the German Social Democratic Party (SPD) made a commitment to the market economy in its Godesberg programme; in 1962 the German trade union organization followed suit.[20]

The editors of *Der Monat* were in close contact with German broadcasters, book and newspaper publishers and numerous writers. A dense network of intellectual propagators was built up, whose aim was to bring the principles of consensus liberalism to bear in the Federal Republic. This involved overcoming the view, both in society and in the self-understanding of political parties, that a modern industrial society was necessarily class-based. In a liberal consensus, notions of a socialist political order were to be combined with those of a market economy in a consensual way. Only then would it be possible, during the East–West confrontation of the Cold War, to inoculate West European and German Social Democratic parties against the influence of thinking in terms of class conflict that emanated from the communist camp.

From about 1965, consensus capitalism and consensus liberalism became the norm in West Germany. It is crucial to note that it was by no means only Western Anglo-American influences that were brought to bear here. Rather, the Federal Republic's 'social-liberal consensus' contained numerous elements of German tradition as well, for instance in the way relations between entrepreneurs and workers and between unions and the government were treated. This is why the model of consensus capitalism, which, after all, derived from the New Deal, was to some extent Germanized as it was implanted into Germany. Today this model is usually referred to as 'Rhenish capitalism'.[21]

The more significant consensus liberalism became in West Germany, the more alien certain strands of recent German history appeared. It seemed as though the political system of the *Kaiserreich* – a semi-absolutist monarchy and a parliament with little control over government – had been responsible for provoking the First World War in 1914. It is no coincidence that Fritz Fischer's pioneering book *Der Griff nach der Weltmacht* (in English, *Germany's Aims in the First World War*) was published in 1961. In its wake, the anti-Western and anti-liberal traditions within the history of the German nation state came under harsh scrutiny. From the Fischer debate on, Germans could acknowledge these anti-Western traditions as part of their history while, at the same time, distancing themselves from them. These anti-Western traditions, dating from around 1900, were increasingly overcome in a political culture more in tune with 'Western values'. A later challenge presented itself in 1990 with the integration of the East Germans and the fight against a dual anti-Westernism – for in the German Democratic Republic (GDR), anti-liberalism dating from the interwar period continued while, in addition, 'the West' had always been considered the archenemy of communism.[22]

Looking back at Germany in the twentieth century, three phases in the struggle for a particular model of order can be discerned. From the time of the First World War, this struggle was dominated by the influential presence of Britain and the U.S., initially with France too. At that time an awareness of the West developed that was determined by both ideology and power politics. This 'West' represented the liberal model of order consisting of parliamentarianism and the market economy after the British and U.S. pattern. France's significance in this configuration of power was marginal from as early as 1923/25, which explains why 'the West', with its claim to hegemony, has since been understood as an exclusively Anglo-American model. Its main rivals in Europe during the twentieth century were: first, the semi-autocratic and corporatist model of order represented by the German *Kaiserreich*; following that, the National Socialist model of a racially defined empire with a corporative structure; and finally, the Soviet empire with a communist dictatorship and an economic system under state control that dominated the GDR. Germany's struggle against 'the West' was decided in 1945, but the country was divided and the GDR, thrust into the 'Eastern' orbit, continued to display an ideological enmity to 'the West' until 1989/90.

Notes

1. See Jörn Leonhard, 'From European Liberalism to the Languages of Liberalisms. The Semantics of "Liberalism" in European Comparison', *Redescriptions. Yearbook of Political Thought and Conceptual History* 8 (2004), 17–51; and Jörn Leonhard, 'Progressive Politics and the Dilemma of Reform. German and American Liberalism in Comparison, 1880–1920', in Maurizio Vaudagna (ed.), *The Place of Europe in American History. Twentieth-Century Perspectives*, Turin, 2007, 115–32. This article was translated by Angela Davies, London.
2. See Michael Hochgeschwender, 'Was ist der Westen? Zur Ideengeschichte eines politischen Konstrukts', *Historisch-Politische Mitteilungen* 11 (2004), 1–30.
3. See Jörn Leonhard, *Liberalismus. Zur historischen Semantik eines europäischen Deutungsmusters*, Munich, 2001, 96–126.
4. See Stephen Kern, *The Culture of Time and Space, 1880–1918*, Cambridge Mass. and London, 2003; Philipp Blom, *The Vertigo Years. Change and Culture in the West 1900–1914*, London, 2008; and Joachim Radkau, *Das Zeitalter der Nervosität. Deutschland zwischen Bismarck und Hitler*, Munich, 2000.
5. Friedrich Nietzsche, *Twilight of the Idols, or, How to Philosophize with a Hammer. Translated with an Introduction and Notes by Duncan Large*, Oxford and New York, 1998 (German original 1889).
6. 'Europe's ... nervousness ... has reached a critical condition with the founding of the German Reich ... . The whole of the West [der ganze Westen] has lost those instincts from which institutions grow, from which future grows: nothing perhaps goes against the grain of its "modern spirit" so much. People live for today, they live very quickly – they live irresponsibly: and this is precisely what is called "freedom".' Ibid., 66.
7. See Hew Strachan, *The First World War, Vol. 1: To Arms*, Oxford, 2001, 163–280.
8. See Jürgen von Ungern-Sternberg and Wolfgang von Ungern-Sternberg, *Der Aufruf 'An die Kulturwelt!' Das Manifest der 93 und die Anfänge der Kriegspropaganda im Ersten Weltkrieg*, Stuttgart, 1996.
9. See Martha Hanna, *The Mobilization of Intellect. French Scholars and Writers during the Great War*, Cambridge Mass. and London, 1996; Peter Hoeres, *Krieg der Philosophen. Die deutsche und die britische Philosophie im Ersten Weltkrieg*, Paderborn, 2004; and Steffen Bruendel, *Volksgemeinschaft oder Volksstaat. Die 'Ideen von 1914' und die Neuordnung Deutschlands im Ersten Weltkrieg*, Berlin, 2003.
10. Thorstein Veblen, *Imperial Germany and the Industrial Revolution* (1915), New Brunswick, 1990; John Dewey, *German Philosophy and Politics*, New York, 1915; George Santayana, 'Egotism in German Philosophy', in *The Works of George Santayana*. Triton edition, vol. 6, New York, 1936, 143–250. See Anselm Doering-Manteuffel, *Wie westlich sind die Deutschen? Amerikanisierung und Westernisierung im 20. Jahrhundert*, Göttingen, 1999; and Anselm Doering-Manteuffel, 'Westernisierung. Politisch-ideeller und gesellschaftlicher Wandel in der Bundesrepublik der 60er Jahre', in Axel Schildt, Detlef Siegfried and Karl-Christian Lammers (eds), *Dynamische Zeiten. Die 60er Jahre in den beiden deutschen Gesellschaften*, Hamburg, 2000, 311–41.
11. See Thomas J. Knock, *To End All Wars. Woodrow Wilson and the Quest for a New World Order*, Princeton, 1992.
12. See Rudolf von Thadden (ed.), *Die Krise des Liberalismus zwischen den Weltkriegen*, Göttingen, 1978.
13. See Eric Hobsbawm, *Age of Extremes. The Short Twentieth Century, 1914–1991*, London, 1994; Anselm Doering-Manteuffel, 'Mensch, Maschine, Zeit.

Fortschrittsbewusstsein und Kulturkritik im ersten Drittel des 20. Jahrhunderts', in *Jahrbuch des Historischen Kollegs 2003*, Munich, 2004, 91–119.

14. See Frank Costigliola, *Awkward Dominion. American Political, Economic, and Cultural Relations with Europe, 1919–1933*, Ithaca and London, 1984; Philipp Gassert, *Amerika im Dritten Reich. Ideologie, Propaganda und Volksmeinung 1933–1945*, Stuttgart, 1997.
15. See Richard J. Evans, *The Coming of the Third Reich*, London, 2003, 77–153; see also Reichsführer SS and SS Hauptamt (eds), *Amerikanismus – eine Weltgefahr*, Berlin, 1944.
16. See Donald Fleming and Bernard Bailyn (eds), *The Intellectual Migration. Europe and America, 1930–1960*, Cambridge Mass., 1969; Claus-Dieter Krohn, *Wissenschaft im Exil. Deutsche Sozial- und Wirtschaftswissenschaftler in den USA und die New School for Social Research*, Frankfurt/Main and New York, 1987; and Mitchell G. Ash and Alfons Söllner (eds), *Forced Migration and Scientific Change. Emigré German-Speaking Scientists and Scholars after 1933*, Washington, D.C. and Cambridge, 1996.
17. The most prominent example is the book by Franz Neumann, *Behemoth. The Structure and Practice of National Socialism*, Toronto and Oxford, 1942, 1944. See Alfons Söllner, 'Franz L. Neumann – Skizze zu einer intellektuellen und politischen Biographie', in Franz L. Neumann, *Wirtschaft, Staat, Demokratie. Aufsätze 1930–1954*, Frankfurt/Main, 1978, 7–56.
18. See Alfons Söllner (ed.), *Zur Archäologie der Demokratie in Deutschland*, 2 vols, Frankfurt/Main, 1986; Petra Marquardt-Bigman, *Amerikanische Geheimdienstanalysen über Deutschland 1942–1949*, Munich, 1995; and Tim B. Müller, *Krieger und Gelehrte. Herbert Marcuse und die Denksysteme im Kalten Krieg*, Hamburg, 2010.
19. See James F. Tent, *The Free University of Berlin. A Political History*, Bloomington, 1988; and James F. Tent, 'The Free University and its Americans. Shifting Perceptions among U.S. Officials and Visiting Scholars', in Uta Gerhardt (ed.), *Zeitperspektiven. Studien zu Kultur und Gesellschaft*, Stuttgart, 2003, 143–70.
20. See Peter Coleman, *The Liberal Conspiracy. The Congress for Cultural Freedom and the Struggle for the Mind of Postwar Europe*, London, 1989; and Michael Hochgeschwender, *Freiheit in der Offensive? Der Kongress für kulturelle Freiheit und die Deutschen*, Munich, 1998. See also Charlotte A. Lerg and Maren M. Roth (eds), *Cold War Politics. Melvin J. Lasky: New York – Berlin – London*, Munich, 2010.
21. See Julia Angster, *Konsenskapitalismus und Sozialdemokratie. Die Westernisierung von SPD und DGB*, Munich, 2003; The term 'Rhenish capitalism' was coined by Michel Albert in *Kapitalismus contra Kapitalismus*, Frankfurt/Main, 1992. See also Werner Abelshauser, 'Der Rheinische Kapitalismus im Kampf der Wirtschaftskulturen', in Volker R. Berghahn and Sigurt Vitols (eds), *Gibt es einen deutschen Kapitalismus? Tradition und globale Perspektiven der Sozialen Marktwirtschaft*, Frankfurt/Main and New York, 2000, 186–99.
22. See Doering-Manteuffel, 'Westernisierung', 333–39.

Part 2

East–West Entanglements

Chapter 5

RUSSIAN AND GERMAN IDEAS OF THE WEST IN THE LONG NINETEENTH CENTURY
Entanglements of Spatial Identities

Denis Sdvižkov

This chapter explores the Russian discourse on 'the West' during the long nineteenth century[1] and its entanglement with discussions that were taking place in the German lands. The chapter discusses where Germany was seen to belong on Russian mental maps of the time and investigates parallels and intersections between the ways Russians and Germans defined themselves in relation to 'the West'.

The discourse was shaped by some basic developments in the Russian concepts of space. From the time of Peter the Great up until the early nineteenth century, Russia largely regarded itself as belonging to 'the North'. Aside from its straightforward meaning describing geographical direction, the concept of the West had mainly temporal connotations. This changed in the first half of the nineteenth century. Under the direct influence of German Romanticism, 'the West' developed a spatial dimension, which was culturally and politically loaded. Then, in the second half of the nineteenth century, the borders of 'the West' became more precisely defined and divisions more differentiated. This development happened, above all, in an interplay with recognition of an emerging 'Eastern Europe'. In addition, the increasingly 'European' nature of Russia after the Great Reforms of the 1860s together with the changed geopolitical situation in Europe after the founding of the German Empire gave new impetus to a mutual exchange of ideas between Germany and Russia.

This period of exchange ended with the radicalization of spatial categories before and during the First World War.

From 'the North' to 'the East'

During the eighteenth and early nineteenth centuries, 'the west' in Russian discourse was primarily understood in a temporal sense: it referred to the last stage of a human being's life – 'the west of my days' (*zapad dneĭ moikh*), or life 'inclined towards the west' (*klonilas' k zapadu*).[2] Concomitantly, 'the west' was associated with the Last Judgement, depictions of which appeared, in the Orthodox tradition, on the western walls of churches. Geographically, a distinction between 'eastern' and 'western' – the terms 'east' and 'west' were not used – tended to refer to the schism between religious traditions and dogmas that developed after the separation of the Eastern and Western Churches in 1054.[3]

On the secular mental maps people held from the Renaissance till the beginning of the nineteenth century, Russia was widely perceived as a 'Northern' country, putting it in a different camp from the civilized 'South'.[4] For some, however, this identification included the promise that, coming 'from the South', the sun of the Enlightenment would eventually reach 'the North'. At the same time, the old idea of a barbaric 'North' was increasingly undermined by the shift in values that came with Romanticism. Both in Germany and Russia, for instance, the works of the Scottish poet James Macpherson received much attention. The author of *Ossian* was elevated to the status of the 'Homer of the North' (in Madame de Stael's phrase).[5]

Not only Russia but also parts of Germany were widely perceived as 'Northern' – Prussia especially. These territories were all on the same side of an inner-European 'North–South' divide that was further influenced by the Napoleonic Wars. The common stand of Prussia and Russia against France brought about a 'Nordic solidarity' that climaxed in 1813–1815.[6] The 'North–South' discourse surrounding the Napoleonic Wars was largely dominated by belief in an opposition between civilization and barbarism. Russian writers often inverted the dichotomy, which was routinely upheld by thinkers of the French Enlightenment. 'Having become a national affair,' the Russian scholar Aleksandr Turgenev wrote in 1812, 'the war has now taken a direction in which the north has to triumph and brilliantly avenge the senseless evils and crimes of the southern barbarians'.[7] This inversion of the cultural meaning of spatial categories could also be found in German debates. In both cases, alternative mental maps emerged in the course of the nineteenth century, and these claimed a central role for the German lands and Russia based on their alleged superiority in terms, respectively, of 'culture' (*Kultur*) and 'spirituality' (*dukhovnost'*).[8]

Between the late eighteenth century and the mid nineteenth century the geographical 'South–North' axis was largely displaced on European mental maps by one with a 'West–East' alignment.[9] The optimistic paradigm of the Enlightenment was challenged by nineteenth-century historism (*Historismus*); and spatial categories developed by German philosophers, above all Hegel, became widespread in Russia. There, the emerging social group of the intelligentsia, searching for key concepts with which to create a new social consciousness and a new national identity, was particularly sensitive to these spatial categories. German idealism became influential – from the 1820s in particular – feeding into the mental geography of the Western 'Promised Land' which educated Russians liked to imagine.[10] While the prominent poet Ivan Dmitriev exclaimed, 'I am in Paris! I have begun to live, not just breathe!',[11] this type of Gallocentric exclamation was supplemented, if not increasingly replaced, in the new Romantic generation by the expression of sentiments more like the following one from an exchange of letters in 1836: 'You are in Berlin! You have reached the end of your journey! I imagine how your heart leapt when you saw this German city upon which each of us laid his hope!'[12]

In 1858, the poet Mikhail Dmitriev held the Russian Hegelians responsible for the politicization of traditional spatial categories: 'Hegel here and Hegel there! – That's all you hear! – The East and the Slavs! The West and the Germans! One could think the West was battling with the East! But the sun continues to travel from the east to the west as it always has!'[13] Under the influence of Hegel, the traditional concept of a balance of power was gradually superseded by the notion of a dialectic tension between 'West' and 'East'. As the historian Nikolaĭ Polevoĭ stated in 1846, 'Asia and Europe, East and West, are two opposites, two halves of the world; their struggle is supposed to constitute the life of humanity, for life is nothing more than the struggle of two fundamental principles'.[14] The 'Westernizer' and critic Vissarion Belinskiĭ, however, warned his contemporaries not to forget that concepts like 'the West! The East! The Teutonic tribe! The Slavic tribe!' eventually all meant the same: 'humanity'. To claim that 'the happiness of one brother comes at the expense of the other's death', he wrote in 1844, was 'an un-philosophical, uncivilized, and un-Christian thought'.[15]

Yet Russian Slavophiles had no time for mediating positions such as Belinsky's. They emphasized the struggle between what they perceived as fundamentally different civilizations. They imagined Russia as a truly Christian – that is, European – civilization, which differed fundamentally from both the Asiatic 'East' and the modern 'West'. With respect to the latter, they pitted Russian religious spirituality against Western secularity, the principle of evolution against the urge for revolution and conquest; and, most importantly, they stressed the Orthodox idea of a harmonious spiritual community (*sobornost'*) versus a 'Western' way of life caught up in individualism and divisiveness. Russia was destined to form a synthesis incomparably superior to anything achieved by either side of the Hegelian dualism of 'East' and 'West'. For Slavophiles, Berlin was no longer the blessed end of a long journey but the 'capital of complacent discord'. Against the background of the Revolution of 1848, the poet Aleksei Khomiakov wrote to the Anglican clergyman William Palmer, who had close relations with the Russian Orthodox Church: 'I am writing to you from the capital of complacent discord, from Berlin, and I am starting with the word "unity". Nowhere else have I felt the need ... for this divine principle so intensely ... . An almost limitless development of individualism is the most prominent characteristic of Germany, especially of Prussia'.[16]

Russia's growing international isolation after 1848, which went hand in hand with an emerging 'fortress mentality', ensured that Hegel's philosophical model acquired polarizing political meanings. Fëdor Tiutchev, a long-time diplomat in the German lands and a prominent writer, wrote to his German-born wife in the midst of the Crimean War: 'This horrible clash has to happen. It is caused not only by England's stingy egoism or France's base foulness ... and not even by the Germans. There is something greater and more fateful at work here. That is the eternal antagonism between what, for lack of better terms, we have to call: the West and the East.'[17] The Crimean War established a situation similar to that of 1812, when Russia found itself opposed to the whole of Europe. Now this confrontation was no longer thought of in terms of 'South' versus 'North' but in terms of 'West' versus 'East'. Watching the smoke from the Anglo-French ships from the quayside at Kronstadt, Tiutchev found his views confirmed: 'The entire West has arrived to demonstrate its negation of Russia and to bar her way to the future.'[18]

The Emergence of 'Eastern Europe'

The dualism between 'West' and 'East' (in the sense of an 'Asiatic East') was further shaped by the emergence of the concept of 'Eastern Europe' (*Vostochnaia Evropa*). This concept allowed Slavophiles in particular to claim their 'Europeanness' without losing their non-Western identity. In general during the 1830s and 1840s, Russians began to conceive of themselves as belonging to 'Eastern Europe'. In this trend, the entanglement between Russian and German discourses was of particular note. The same Tiutchev, who was well acquainted with German literature and strongly influenced by Schelling, used the concept of 'Eastern Europe' as a means of Russian self-assertion. Interestingly, he referred to the Orientalist Jakob Philipp Fallmerayer's Russophobic diary from 1843, which articulated the 'idea of a great independent Eastern Europe in contrast to a Western one'.[19] What Fallmerayer perceived as a threat, Tiutchev saw as a desirable development for 'another Europe'.

In contrast to their old identification with 'the North', the Russians' self-conception of belonging to 'the East' was not unambiguous. As there is no separate word for 'the Orient' in the Russian language, 'the East' and 'the Orient' were semantically identical. Hence, the concept of 'the East' was usually qualified by an adjective so as to avoid any confusion between 'Eastern Europe' and Russia's own 'East'/'Orient'[20] which was located in Asia. Two sets of terms were in common use. First, there was the 'Christian' or 'Orthodox East' – the realm of the former Byzantine Commonwealth[21] including the European 'Orient'. Use of this term played down the mental borders between Europe and Asia. Second, there was 'Eastern Europe', regarded as a supranational and regional entity. The 'Eastern Question' was often interpreted as an issue concerning both the 'Christian East' and 'Eastern Europe'. For the prominent pan-Slavist writer (and general) Rostislav Fadeev, and for the famous philosopher Vladimir Solov'ev, Russia's mission was to 'resurrect the East of Christ' by separating it from the despotic 'Asiatic East' (the region Solov'ev referred to as 'the East of Xerxes').[22]

In the wake of the Crimean War, established notions of *Staatsräson* were eclipsed by nationalist ideas, which came to dominate Russian mental maps. 'Russia' and 'Eastern Europe' were no longer considered to be territorially encircled political entities but were perceived as the expansive space of the Slavic race, which transcended the boundaries of Imperial Russia. Nikolaiĭ Danilevskiĭ's pan-Slavist tract *Russia and Europe* (1869) became a milestone in this context. Influenced as it was by the works of the historian and Germanist Heinrich Rückert from Breslau, Danilevsky's book also became known in Germany.[23] It was based on the notion that 'Europe' was identical with its 'Western' territories and that 'Russia' was identical with the 'Eastern' (Slavic) areas, and that these two broad areas represented two distinct civilizations. As Danilevskiĭ wrote, 'the only way for Russia to play an historic role worthy of itself and of Slavdom is to become the head of a separate, independent political system of states that, with its community of interests and unity, will act as a counterweight to Europe ... [A] pan-Slavic union is the only firm foundation from which a self-sufficient Slavic culture can grow'.[24]

Against this background of a shifting geopolitical fabric following the Crimean War, Germanophobic overtones became ever more vigorous in the discourse on 'Eastern Europe'. In his influential *History of Russia from the Earliest Times* (1851–1880), for instance, the eminent historian Sergeï Solov'ev attributed the peripheral status of 'Eastern Europe' to the fact that 'before the eighteenth century, the Slavs constantly retreated before the onslaught of the German tribe, which pushed them further and further east'.[25] Subsequent post-Petrine history thus consisted of a *reconquista* of German-occupied lands. On the eve of German unification, Fadeev claimed that 'our historical movement from the Dnieper to the Vistula was a declaration of war on Europe, which had invaded a part of the continent that did not belong to it'. The final goal was 'an emancipated East of Europe'.[26]

Hence 'Eastern Europe' was primarily pitted against 'Germandom' and only secondarily against 'the West': 'Our main enemy is not at all Western Europe but the German tribe with its excessive territorial claims'.[27] So, in the struggle for 'Eastern Europe', Germany became Russia's main opponent. A key role in consolidating feelings of enmity was played by the slogan *'Drang nach Osten'*, referring to Germany's 'thrust to the East'. This initially emerged in Polish discourse towards the end of the 1840s and entered Czech and Russian discourses during the 1860s and 1870s.[28] In the Russian context, it was another example of a rhetorical inversion, which this time inverted the widespread Western notion of an expansionist Russia making raids on the West (*'Raubzug nach dem Westen'*)[29] and a belief that Russian ambitions comprised the greatest threat to the *Abendland*.[30]

German-Russian Entanglements, 1870–1918

From the late 1860s and 1870s onwards the concept of the West acquired fresh interpretative nuances. This was due to the fundamental changes in Russia in the wake of the so-called Great Reforms and also to the geopolitical shifts in Europe after the founding of the German Empire. Characteristic of this phase was a progressive differentiation of the concept of the West according to political camps, which also created a new basis for mutual conceptual transfers. A discourse had started in Germany on how a new, united German nation could form a 'middle' between 'East' and 'West', and this debate was followed in Russia with great interest and attention. The eventual founding of a 'European Empire of the Middle' in 1871 was perceived as the collapse of 'the West' into two worlds: the Roman (Celtic-Latin) and the Germanic.[31] The Russian mental map now distinguished between three different confessional and geographic spheres: a Roman world, a German one and a Slavic one.

Initially, there was some sympathy for the new Germany in the Russian conservative camp, grounded in resentments against the old Anglo-French 'West' and fed on hopes of a new strategic balance of power. Fëdor Dostoevskiĭ saw the year 1871 as the harbinger of an 'amicable' partition of Europe into a Russian 'East' on the one hand and a German 'West' on the other, which would differ significantly from the 'old West' that had gone before:

> What is Germany to do with us? Her goal is the entire Western humanity. She has set her sights on Europe's western world and is intending to inject into it her principles instead of Roman and Romance [*rimskich i romanskich*] principles, and to become its leader, leaving the East to Russia. Two great peoples are therefore destined to change the face of this world.[32]

However, the Congress of Berlin, which followed the end of the Russo-Turkish War of 1877–1878 and – in Russia's eyes – did not take due account of Russian military achievements, demonstrated that Dostoevskiĭ's visions of the future were baseless. Russian conservatives returned to Slavophile perceptions of a 'German tribe' (in Germany and Austria) as an imminent threat to the Slavic Eastern Europe and an enemy much worse than the 'old West' had been. This phobia of the Germans served as one of the few political themes that conservative nationalists and liberal democrats could share.

For Russia's liberal-democratic camp the concept of the West was defined in terms of 'revolution', 'constitution' and 'progress'. The deeply rooted Gallocentric traditions of the liberal intelligentsia were reinforced through the establishment of the Third Republic in France and the reorientation of Russian foreign politics. As *Vestnik Evropy*, one of Russia's most influential reviews (or 'thick journals'[33]) stated before the end of the century: 'The French republic … symbolizes the extreme realization of political ideals that are considered Western European in our country. The French are undoubtedly the most Western people in the specific [liberal-democratic] sense that our political literature imparts to the word "West"'.[34] For liberal democrats, the unified German Empire became not only the antithesis of the democratic 'West' but a projection of the Romanov Empire's militarized bureaucracy into Western Europe.[35]

In the German discourse, the conceptual mapping of 'Russia' and the 'West' also varied between different political camps. Around the turn of the century, Hugo Ganz, a journalist on the liberal *Frankfurter Zeitung*, stressed the dichotomy between Russia and 'the West'. In his widely read book *Before the Catastrophe* (*Vor der Katastrophe*), written in Saint Petersburg during the first months of the Russo-Japanese War of 1904–1905, he spoke of 'the civilized peoples of the West' and 'us in the West', in contradistinction to Russia and its people.[36] Spokesmen for those political forces closely aligned with the newly founded German Reich, however – ranging from national-liberals to the far Right – talked rather in terms of 'Germany' and its dominance in the 'East', and they focused strongly on the influence of German 'culture' (*Kultur*) in 'Central Europe'.[37] In this camp, the Russian pan-Slavists were cited abundantly and with obvious delight, as an eminent proof of an inevitable 'struggle between the Germanic and Slav worlds' (*Kampf zwischen Germanentum und Slawentum*) that was to come.[38]

Russia's demonizing of the German Reich was countered in Germany through the practice of distinguishing between a Russian 'East' and a German 'East' – the latter being a field of a German *mission civilisatrice*. The Russian 'East' was supposed to belong not to the east of Europe but to Asia, where Russia's expansionist aims were deemed legitimate. One of the Baltic German 'Kremlinologists' of the late nineteenth century, Ernst von der Brüggen, wrote about the Germanophobic rantings of General Mikhail Skobelev, the conqueror of Central Asia: 'We Germans can find it surprising that we are accused of a peaceful push towards the East by a man who ... has just returned home from the battlefields of Asia as a representative of the old Russian push towards the East'.[39]

At the same time, there were groups in Germany that looked on Russia more favourably. First, there was a Russophile tradition which harked back to the 'Nordic solidarity' that had been propagated in German conservative periodicals during the early nineteenth century.[40] In the second part of his autobiography, published in 1898, the German novelist Theodor Fontane recalled a veritable passion for Russia (*Russlandschwärmerei*) that had been shared by the whole of 'official Prussia' (*das ganze offizielle Preußen*) and was particularly strong among the inhabitants of the 'old' Prussian provinces in the East.[41] Second, the seeds of German Romanticism that had been sown in Russia half a century earlier had grown and were beginning to burgeon, so that there were shared cultural values. With the emergence of a Europeanized intelligentsia, Russian 'cultural conquests in the West'[42] – above all the success of Russian literature in Germany[43] – went hand in hand with 'Western cultural conquests in Russia'. August Scholz, a Polish-born critic of Jewish origin and one of the most popular translators of Russian literature at the time, saw a considerable degree of 'Westernization' permeating Russia's cultural sphere. In 1886, he wrote in *Westermanns illustrierte deutsche Monatshefte*: 'In Russia we are gradually encountering the same phenomena that we are used to seeing in the civilized West, and we are not disinclined to recognize that country as "belonging to us", as a new area conquered for European culture, even if not entirely so'.⁴⁴

So, German observers acknowledged that Russians were moving closer to the 'West'. In particular, developments in Russia affected the attitudes of German Social Democrats. The 'awakening of the ahistorical peoples of Russia'⁴⁵ aroused the interest of Friedrich Engels and Karl Kautsky, for instance. In 1902, Kautsky wrote in his article 'The Slavs and the Revolution', which also appeared in Russian translation in Vladimir Lenin's newspaper *Iskra*: 'The revolutionary centre [has] shifted from West to East … . Russia, which has received so many revolutionary impetuses from the West, is now perhaps giving revolutionary impetuses of its own'.⁴⁶

At the same time, there were German cultural critics around the turn of the century who responded sympathetically to Russian anti-Westernism. Fëdor Dostoevskiĭ played a particularly striking role in this respect. Representatives of the German 'Conservative Revolution' invoked Dostoevskiĭ as an ally against the 'civilization' of Western Europe which they deemed soulless and mechanistic.⁴⁷ During the First World War, when the concepts 'West' and 'East' began to refer to Germany's battle fronts, Russian anti-Westernism was harnessed to 'substantiate' Germany's 'ideas of 1914'. While German military propaganda on the Eastern front placed 'Russian culture' in quotation marks,⁴⁸ proponents of the 'Conservative Revolution' mentioned it liberally in rants against 'the West'. Thomas Mann's *Reflections of a Nonpolitical Man* (1918) provides a particularly salient example of the reception of Russian anti-Westernism in Germany. Mann praised Dostoevskiĭ for articulating, well before the turn of the century, what he believed was a fundamental opposition between the soulless materialism of Western Europe and the 'humanity' of Russia and Germany. 'The history of the emergence of German and Russian humanity', Mann wrote, was the same *Leidensgeschichte*: 'What similarity there is in the relationship of the two national souls with "Europe", the "West", "civilization", politics, democracy! Don't we, too, have our Slavophiles and Zapadniki (Westerners)?'⁴⁹ Moreover, Arthur Moeller van den Bruck, who was to author the book *The Third Reich* (*Das dritte Reich*) in 1923, was instrumental in getting Dostoevskiĭ's complete works published in German (1906–1919).⁵⁰ In his foreword to the completed edition he stated:

> What we need in Germany is Russia's unconditional spirituality [*Geistigkeit*]. We need it as a counter-balance to the Westernness [*Westlertum*] to whose influences we too were exposed, just as Russia has been exposed to them. … After looking over to the West for so long that we became dependent on it, we are now looking over to the East – and are searching

for independence ... . The questions of the East ... are at the same time a question of spiritual [*geistig*] sovereignty. Having lost it to the West in the nineteenth century, we want to get it back for Germany in the twentieth century.[51]

Conclusion

The Russian concept of the West had mainly temporal connotations initially, but, from the first half of the nineteenth century on, it came increasingly to refer to the geographical space of western Europe. The concept became politicized at a relatively early stage. Along with events such as the Napoleonic Wars and the confrontation between the Russian Empire and 'the West' on the eve of the Crimean War, the reception of German Romanticism played an important role in this politicization. In Russia particular attention was paid to Germany's peripheral position vis-à-vis the Anglo-French 'Roman West' and observers there noted how Germany identified itself at different times as 'Northern', 'Western' and 'Central European'. From watching this soul-searching they derived the idea of a multiplicity of European identities, instead of equating 'Europe' with 'the West'. In Russia this idea became the main source of a notion of 'Eastern Europe' as 'the other Europe'. However, Russian and German mental maps collided when it came to their respective 'thrusts towards the East'. This led to Germany becoming more and more peripheral on Russian mental maps until the new nation was eventually completely excluded from what they saw as 'the West'.

Germany, for its part, recognized the changing face of Russia after the Great Reforms of the 1860s and acknowledged Russia's new status in Europe's cultural balance of power. Germans assessed this development in two ways: on the one hand as proof of the unstoppable 'Westernization' of Russia; on the other, as evidence supporting the idea of a plurality of European identities. This last idea culminated in the anti-Western 'ideas of 1914' and in the tenets of the 'Conservative Revolution'.

Notes

1. See Vera Tolz, 'The West', in William J. Leatherbarrow and Derek Offord (eds), *A History of Russian Thought*, Cambridge, 2010, 197–216; Riccardo Bavaj, '"The West". A Conceptual Exploration', *Europäische Geschichte Online* (2011), online: http://www.ieg-ego.eu/bavajr-2011-en (accessed 10 December 2011). I am grateful to Anton Fedyashin for translating the text from Russian to English, as well as to Ingrid Schierle (GHI Moscow) and the editors of the present volume for their careful reading of this chapter and their helpful suggestions.

2. See Nikolaĭ Karamzin, *Stikhotvoreniia [Poems]*, Leningrad, 1966, 139.
3. 'Zapad' / 'zapadnyi', in [Ivan Geĭm], *Novyi rossiisko-frantsuzsko-nemetskii slovar'. Nouveau dictionnaire russe-français & allemand / composé d'après le Dictionnaire de l'Académie Russe par Jean Heym*, vol. 1 (A–K), Moscow, 1799, 404.
4. See Natalia Kazakova, *Zapadnaia Evropa v russkoi pismennosti XV–XVI vekov. Iz istorii mezhdunarodnykh kul'turnykh sviazei Rossii [Western Europe in Russian Writing of the 15th and 16th Centuries. On the History of Russia's International Cultural Relations]*, Leningrad, 1980, 109–10, 115. Several volumes in the series *Imaginatio Borealis. Bilder des Nordens* have examined 'Northern' spatial categories. Russia is dealt with by, amongst others, Dennis Hormuth and Maike Schmidt (eds), *Norden und Nördlichkeit. Darstellungen vom Eigenen und Fremden*, Frankfurt, 2010.
5. See Wolf Gerhard Schmidt, *'Homer des Nordens' und 'Mutter der Romantik'. James Macphersons Ossian und seine Rezeption in der deutschsprachigen Literatur*, 4 vols, Berlin and New York, 2003–2004; Jury Levin, *Ossian v russkoj literature. Konec XVIII – pervaja tret' XIX veka [Ossian in Russian Literature. From the Late 18th to the Early 19th Century]*, Leningrad, 1980; and Howard Gaskill (ed.), *The Reception of Ossian in Europe*, London, 2004. See also Frithjof Benjamin Schenk, 'Mental Maps. Die Konstruktion von geographischen Räumen in Europa seit der Aufklärung', *Geschichte und Gesellschaft* 28 (2002), 493–514, here 506.
6. On the Napoleonic 'North–South' division see Käthe Panick, *La race latine. Politischer Romanismus im Frankreich des 19. Jahrhunderts*, Bonn, 1978, 70 f. On 'Northern' self-conceptions in the German lands – Prussia and elsewhere – see Hans Lemberg, 'Zur Entstehung des Osteuropabegriffs im 19. Jahrhundert. Vom "Norden" zum "Osten" Europas', *Jahrbücher für Geschichte Osteuropas* 33/1 (1985), 48–91, here 53–55.
7. Aleksandr Turgenev to Pëtr Viazemskiĭ, 27–29 October 1812, SPb, in *Ostafievskii arkhiv kniazei Viazemskikh [The Prince Viazemskiĭ Archive in Ostafievo]*, 5 vols, Saint Petersburg, 1898, vol. 1, 5–8.
8. For the opposition between 'culture' and 'civilization' see Klaus Städtke, 'Kultur und Zivilisation. Zur Geschichte des Kulturbegriffs in Russland', in Christa Ebert (ed.), *Kulturauffassungen in der literarischen Welt Russlands. Kontinuitäten und Wandlungen im 20. Jahrhundert*, Berlin, 1995, 18–46.
9. See Lemberg, 'Zur Entstehung des Osteuropabegriffs'; Larry Wolff, *Inventing Eastern Europe. The Map of Civilization on the Mind of the Enlightenment*, Stanford, 1994.
10. For an introduction see Donald Treadgold, *The West in Russia and China. Religious and Secular Thought in Modern Times*, vol. 1: *Russia, 1472–1917*, Cambridge, Mass, 1973, 152–79; and Nicholas V. Riasanovsky, *Russia and the West in the Teaching of the Slavophiles. A Study of Romantic Ideology*, Gloucester, Mass, 1965.
11. Ivan Dmitriev, 'Puteshestvie N.N. v Parizh i London' [The Journey of N.N. to Paris and London] (1803), in Ivan Dmitriev, *Polnoe sobranie stichotvorenii [Complete Poems]*, Leningrad, 1967, 348.
12. Nikolaĭ Stankevich to Timofeĭ Granovskiĭ, 14 June 1836, Piatigorsk, in Nikolaĭ Stankevich, *Izbrannoe [Selected Poems]*, Moscow, 1982, 139. 'Germany opened the eyes of the people of the Forties [of the nineteenth century]', remembered the literary critic Nikolaĭ Shelgunov. Nikolaĭ Shelgunov, 'Liudi sorokovykh i shestidesiatykh godov' [The People of the Forties and Sixties] (1869), in Nikolaĭ Shelgunov, *Literaturnaia kritika [Literary Reviews]*, Leningrad, 1974, 63.
13. Mikhail Dmitriev, 'Gegelisty' [Hegelists] (1858), in Mikhail Dmitriev, *Moskovskie elegii. Stikhotvoreniia. Melochi iz zapasa moiei pamiati [Moscow Elegies. Poems. Trifles from the Stock of My Memory]*, Moscow, 1985, 69.

14. Nikolaĭ Polevoĭ, *Obozrenie russkoi istorii do edinoderzhaviia Petra Velikogo* [*A Survey of Russian History until the Autarchy of Peter the Great*], Saint Petersburg, 1846, xxi.
15. Vissarion Belinskiĭ, 'Sochineniia kniazia V. F. Odoevskogo' [The Works of Prince V.F. Odoevskiĭ] (1844), in Vissarion Belinskiĭ, *Polnoe sobranie sochinenii* [*Complete Works*], 13 vols, Moscow and Leningrad, 1953, vol. 8, 317.
16. Alekseĭ Khomiakov to William Palmer, 18 September 1847–14 May 1848, Berlin, quoted in Alexej Peskov, 'Der deutsche Komplex der Slavophilen', in Dagmar Herrmann and Alexander Ospovat (eds), *Deutsche und Deutschland aus russischer Sicht. 19. Jahrhundert. Von der Jahrhundertwende bis zu den Reformen Alexanders II* (*West-östliche Spiegelungen*, series B, vol. 3), Munich, 1998, 844–72, here 869.
17. Fëdor Tiutchev to Ernestina Tiutcheva, 24 February and 8 March 1854, Saint Petersburg, in Fëdor I. Tiutchev, *Polnoe sobranie sochinenii i pisem* [*Collected Works and Letters*], 6 vols, Moscow, 2002, vol. 5, 160.
18. Fëdor Tiutchev to Ernestina Tiutcheva, 9 June 1854, Saint Petersburg, in ibid., 175.
19. Quoted from the diary of Jakob Philipp Fallmerayer (1843) in Georg von Rauch, 'J. Ph. Fallmerayer und der russische Reichsgedanke bei F. I. Tjutčev', *Jahrbücher für Geschichte Osteuropas* 1 (1953), 54–96, here 68.
20. See Vera Tolz, '*Russia's Own Orient*'. *The Politics of Identity and Oriental Studies in the Late Imperial and Early Soviet Periods*, Oxford, 2011, discussing among other things the German influence on the Russian-Orient discourse; see also David Schimmelpenninck van der Oye, *Russian Orientalism. Asia in the Russian Mind from Peter the Great to the Emigration*, New Haven, 2010.
21. See Dimitri Obolensky, *The Byzantine Commonwealth. Eastern Europe, 500–1453*, London, 1971.
22. Rostislav Fadeev, *Mnenie o vostochnom voprose. Po povodu poslednikh retsenziĭ na 'Vooruzhennyia sily Rossii'* [*Reflections on the Eastern Question. On the Occasion of the Last Review of the 'Armed Forces of Russia'*], Saint Petersburg, 1870, 87, 98. 'O Rus'!... What kind of East do you want to be: the East of Xerxes or of Christ?' Vladimir Solov'ev, 'Ex Oriente lux' (1890), in Vladimir Solov'ev, *Sobranie sochinenii* [*Collected Works*], Brussels, 12 vols, 1970, vol. 12, 27.
23. See Robert E. MacMaster, 'The Question of Heinrich Rückert's Influence on Danilevskij', *The American Slavic and East European Review* 14 (1955), 59–66; and Max-Rainer Uhrig, 'Im Bann des Russenschrecks. Heinrich Rückerts byzantinisch-asiatische Slawenlegende', in Mechthild Keller (ed.), *Russen und Russland aus deutscher Sicht. 19./20. Jahrhundert. Von der Bismarckzeit bis zum Ersten Weltkrieg* (*West-östliche Spiegelungen*, series A, vol. 4), Munich, 2000, 275–98, here 291–95.
24. Nikolaĭ Danilevskiĭ, *Rossiia i Evropa. Vzgliad na kul'turnye i politicheskie otnosheniia slavianskogo mira k germane-romanskomu* [*Russia and Europe. An Inquiry into the Cultural and Political Relations of the Slavic World to the Romano-Germanic World*], Moscow, 1995, 341 (first published 1869).
25. Sergeĭ Solov'ev, *Istoriia Rossii s drevneishikh vremen* [*The History of Russia from the Earliest Times*], 29 vols, Moscow, 1867, vol. 17: *Istoriia Rossii v epokhu preobrazovaniia* [*The History of Russia in an Age of Transformation*], part 5, 382–83.
26. Fadeev, *Mnenie o vostochnom voprose*, 91, 93.
27. Ibid., 86.
28. See Henry Cord Meyer, *Drang nach Osten. Fortunes of a Slogan-Concept in German-Slavic Relations, 1849–1990*, Bern, 1996; Wolfgang Wippermann, *Der deutsche 'Drang nach Osten'. Ideologie und Wirklichkeit eines politischen Schlagwortes*, Darmstadt, 1981; and Helena Ulbrechtová, 'On the History of the "East–West" Concept and on the Possibilities of Its Further Use in the Slavonic Literary and Cultural Studies', in

Siegfried Ulbrecht and Helena Ulbrechtová (eds), *Die Ost-West-Problematik in den europäischen Kulturen und Literaturen. Ausgewählte Aspekte*, Prague, 2009, 19–52.
29. August Scholz, 'Graf L. N. Tolstoj', *Westermanns illustrierte deutsche Monatshefte* 30/60 (1886), 498–511, here 499. See also Lew Kopelew, 'Am Vorabend des großen Krieges. Rückblick auf ein Jahrhundert', in Keller (ed.), *Russen und Russland aus deutscher Sicht* A 4, 11–107, here 38.
30. See Fritz T. Epstein, 'Der Komplex "Die russische Gefahr" und sein Einfluss auf die deutsch-russischen Beziehungen des 19. Jahrhunderts', in Imanuel Geiss and Bernd Jürgen Wendt (eds), *Deutschland in der Weltpolitik des 19. und 20. Jahrhunderts*, Düsseldorf, 1973, 143–59.
31. See Dagmar Herrmann, 'Die neue europäische Ordnung – eine Vision Fëdor Dostojevskijs', in Dagmar Hermann (ed.), *Deutsche und Deutschland aus russischer Sicht. 19./20. Jahrhundert. Von den Reformen Alexanders II. bis zum Ersten Weltkrieg* (*West-östliche Spiegelungen*, series B, vol. 4), Munich, 2006, 488–549, here 532.
32. Fëdor Dostoevskiĭ, *Dnevnik pisatelia [A Writer's Diary]*, in Fëdor Dostoevskiĭ, *Sobranie sochinenii [Collected Works]*, 15 vols, Saint Petersburg, 1995, vol. 14, 369.
33. The term 'thick journals' (*tolstye zhurnaly*) alludes to the usual 200-plus pages making up each issue.
34. 'Inostrannoe obozrenie' [Foreign Review], *Vestnik Evropy* [*Messenger of Europe*] 8 (1891), 828–29. See also Robert F. Byrnes, 'Russia and the West. The Views of Pobedonostsev', *Journal of Modern History* 40 (1968), 234–56, here 238: 'For the nobility, the West began west of Berlin and Vienna, while for the court and the state officials Berlin and Vienna were the centres of the Western world'.
35. See Aaron J. Cohen, 'Bild und Spiegelbild. Deutschland in der russischen Tageszeitung "Russkoe slovo" (1907–1917)', in Herrmann (ed.), *Deutsche und Deutschland aus russischer Sicht* A 4, 258–79, here 265.
36. Hugo Ganz, *Vor der Katastrophe. Ein Blick ins Zarenreich. Skizzen und Interviews aus den russischen Hauptstädten*, Frankfurt/Main, 1904, 42, 169, 233. The book was also translated into French and English.
37. See for instance the definition of 'Central Europe' as a 'part of the earth that has come to flourish today under the leadership of German culture', as suggested by Josef F.M. Partsch, *Mitteleuropa. Die Länder und Völker von den Westalpen und dem Balkan bis an den Kanal und das Kurische Haff*, Gotha, 1904, vii. This definition is lacking in the preceding English edition: Joseph Partsch, *Central Europe*, New York, 1903.
38. Generalstabschef Helmut von Moltke (1913), quoted in Conrad von Hötzendorf, *Aus meiner Dienstzeit 1906–1918*, 5 vols, Vienna, 1922, vol. 2, 146.
39. [Ernst] von der Brüggen, 'Die Lage in Russland', *Deutsche Rundschau* 31/2 (1882), 134.
40. See Olga Zaichenko, *Nemeckaia publicistika i formirovanie obraza Rossii v obshestvennom mnenii Germanii v pervoi polovine XIX veka* [*German Journalism and the Formation of Russia's Image in German Public Opinion in the First Half of the 19th Century*], Ph.D. thesis, Moscow, 2004, 225–58.
41. Theodor Fontane, *Von Zwanzig bis Dreißig*, Berlin and Weimar, 1982 (*Autobiographische Schriften*, vol. 2), 249–50 (first published in 1898).
42. Kopelew, 'Am Vorabend des großen Krieges', 82.
43. See Siegfried Hoefert (ed.), *Russische Literatur in Deutschland. Texte zur Rezeption von den Achtziger Jahren bis zur Jahrhundertwende*, Tübingen, 1974.
44. Scholz, 'Graf L. N. Tolstoj', 498.
45. 'Das Erwachen der geschichtslosen Völker Russlands', *Die Neue Zeit* 34/1 (1916), 387.

46. Karl Kautsky, 'Die Slaven und die Revolution', in *Märzfeier 1902. Festschrift der Wiener Volksbuchhandlung Ignaz Brand zum Gedenktag der Revolution von 1848*, Vienna, n.d., 3.
47. A view of the following epoch is provided by Leonid Luks, '"Eurasier" und "konservative Revolution". Zur antiwestlichen Versuchung in Russland und in Deutschland', in Gerd Koenen and Lew Kopelew (eds), *Deutschland und die russische Revolution, 1917–1924*, Munich, 1998, 219–39.
48. See http://www.dhm.de/lemo/html/wk1/propaganda/deutsch/objekte.html (accessed 10 December 2011). See also *Das Land Ober Ost. Deutsche Arbeit in den Verwaltungsgebieten Kurland, Litauen und Bialystok-Grodno*, ed. on behalf of the Oberbefehlshaber Ost, Berlin and Stuttgart, 1917, 210: 'But this Russian culture, as transmitted historically so far, and dependent on selfish rulers, was nothing more than the night of apathy and the emptiness of nothingness.'
49. Thomas Mann, *Betrachtungen eines Unpolitischen*, Frankfurt/Main, 1974 (first published in 1918) (*Gesammelte Werke*, vol. 12), 441.
50. Herrmann, 'Neue europäische Ordnung', 547 ff. See Gerd-Klaus Kaltenbrunner, 'Von Dostojewski zum Dritten Reich. Arthur Moeller van den Bruck und die "konservative Revolution"', *Politische Studien* 20/184 (1969), 184–200; and André Schlüter, *Moeller van den Bruck. Leben und Werk*, Cologne et al., 2010, 271 ff.
51. Arthur Moeller van den Bruck, 'Zur Einführung in die Ausgabe', in Fjodor Dostojewski, *Sämtliche Werke*, vol. 1/1: *Rodion Raskolnikoff (Schuld und Sühne)*, ed. Arthur Moeller van den Bruck, Munich, 1922 (first edited 1908), v–vi, here v.

Chapter 6

'ORIENT' AND 'OCCIDENT', 'EAST' AND 'WEST' IN THE DISCOURSE OF GERMAN ORIENTALISTS, 1790–1930

Douglas T. McGetchin

During the period from the end of the eighteenth century to the beginning of the twentieth, German interest in Asia went through remarkable transformations. An initial Romantic fascination with Sanskrit and Indian languages developed into a scientific, philological and Eurocentric examination of Asian texts. Finally, by the end of the era, when German colonialism had become established, some German scholars showed interest in a new, more open approach to Asian topics. How exactly did German orientalists view Asia from the 1790s to the 1920s? They went from initial admiration of Asia as the home of Europeans, to a Eurocentric belittling of its culture through philological analysis, to a new openness in the aftermath of the First World War, when Europeans had self-doubts and hoped that Asia could provide answers to their troubles. So Asia went from up on a pedestal down to the gutter, then back up onto a pedestal. One can trace these shifting fortunes through a detailed look at the varying German orientalist use of the terms 'Orient'/'Occident' ('Orient'/'Occident') and 'East'/'West' ('Osten'/'Westen').

Romantic Attraction to Asia (c. 1790–1820)

A key element at the end of the eighteenth century was acknowledgement that Europe owed its origins culturally and linguistically to Asia. This was based on Sir William Jones's discovery and shocking pronouncement at the Asiatic Society of Bengal in 1786 that Greek and Latin had a long-lost linguistic relation, Sanskrit.[1] Jones translated a classical Sanskrit play, Kalidasa's *Sakuntala*, into English in 1789, and Georg Forster retranslated the work into German the next year. This play had a tremendous impact on the German Romantics, providing not only a non-European classical ancestor, but also one that echoed their own modern interests. Sanskrit became a focus for German orientalists in the early nineteenth century both because Ancient Indian literature held such an interest for the Romantics and because German nationalists found it served their cause by providing a non-Roman/Gallic ancient cultural pedigree. This discovery of Sanskrit in the Romantic era comprised the beginning of what Friedrich Schlegel called an Oriental Renaissance. He thought it would be as profound as the Renaissance of classical learning that had occurred several centuries before in Italy. While the Oriental Renaissance was in fact more limited, it did have an important impact within certain cultural circles in Germany.[2]

If one examines important texts during the early nineteenth century era for the terms 'Orient', 'Occident', 'East' and 'West', one finds frequent use of them in more popular sources, but little or no use among orientalist scholars. The orientalists typically used terms such as 'Europe', 'Asia' or 'India'. For example, Friedrich Schlegel, who inspired the so-called Oriental Renaissance, did not use the terms 'Orient', 'Occident', 'East' or 'West' but 'Asia', 'Indian' and 'Europe' in the introduction to his influential *Ueber die Sprache und Weisheit der Indier* (On the Language and Wisdom of the Indians) of 1808. His usage conformed to the contemporary view that Europe owed its linguistic roots to Asia. He promoted 'Indian studies' as a 'rich treasure'.[3] At the end of his introduction he asserted that 'Indian studies' could rival the Italian Renaissance in their potential to bring a 'reawakened knowledge of antiquity' that would in turn lead to a rebirth of 'European intelligence'.[4] This passage was very significant in helping to inspire the growth of linguistic studies in the German states, especially the study of Sanskrit. But Schlegel's promotion of Ancient Asia had negative consequences as well: he helped condemn China to obscurity in nineteenth-century Germany because, he argued, Chinese lacked any linguistic affinity with Indo-European languages. German orientalist interest in the Far East thus atrophied through the nineteenth century, in stark contrast to the explosive growth of interest in Ancient India.[5]

The Romantics' interest in classic Indian drama also opened the eyes of Germans to the possible relevance of Ancient India for contemporary German nationalist and cultural concerns. The aesthetic representations in *Sakuntala* made it an important play for the Romantics: Goethe copied the format of its prologue while Novalis used the title character as a nickname for his girlfriend.[6] Through these oriental studies and what, they argued, was the linguistic closeness of German to Sanskrit, Germans could use an affiliation with Aryan roots against the Graeco-Roman Francophile culture of what would become 'the West'. German nationalists used India as a cultural touchstone, a source of independence from the Franco-Graeco-Roman heritage. This was particularly true in the early nineteenth century as they fought to overcome the Napoleonic military and cultural invasion. Germans were interested in Sanskrit because they believed there was a deep affinity between modern German and what they thought was its ancient linguistic roots. Thus the study of oriental languages and the Indo-European language tree would help them understand themselves, as well as provide prestige to German linguistic science and its patron, the Prussian state.[7]

In Vienna, the orientalist Joseph von Hammer-Purgstall (1774–1856) founded with Baron Rzewuski the *Fundgruben des Orients* (Treasure Trove of the Orient), which ran through six volumes from 1805 to 1819.[8] Hammer-Purgstall's translations were popular among German poets, including Goethe and the orientalist poet Friedrich Rückert.[9] In the introduction to the first issue, amidst their call for the development of orientalist studies, the authors cited the Qur'an sura that also appeared on their cover page:

> We feel ourselves called to the true path of perfecting oriental [*orientalischen*] studies and with it our undertaking in the sense of our epigraph, 'God is the Orient and God is the Occident. He leads whom he wills to the true path.' Thus everything faced in the Orient about the Occident and in the Occident about the Orient should meet here a helping hand arising out of the buried treasures of insight and knowledge.[10]

Similar Qur'an-inspired expressions and the word 'Orient' appeared frequently in an influential poetic work of Goethe, the *West-östlicher Divan* (1820): 'God is the Orient / God is the Occident / North and south lands / Rest in peace in his hands'.[11] In authoring this collection of poems, Goethe drew upon his reading of the fourteenth-century Persian poet Hafiz, his own attempts to learn Arabic, a life-long study of the Qur'an, and his creative adaptation of stories in the *One Thousand and One Nights*.[12]

Eurocentric Philological-Racial Backlash (c. 1820–1900)

Even if German poets and orientalists were most enthusiastic about Ancient India, the Romantics' Oriental Renaissance nevertheless faced challenges from the traditional forces of theology, classicism and philosophy. Theological problems with Asia among Western scholars emerged in the Creuzer *Streit* and the Higher Criticism. The Creuzer *Streit* emerged after Friedrich Creuzer (1771–1858), a philologist at Heidelberg, published a four-volume work on ancient symbols and myth in 1812.[13] Like the Romantics, Creuzer saw Asia as a source of religion and Ancient Greek culture. His critics included Goethe and Johann Voss, who discredited Creuzer and his regard for Asia as crypto-Catholic and politically suspect.[14] Creuzer's orientalist predecessor, Friedrich Schlegel, had converted to Catholicism after publishing *Ueber die Sprache und Weisheit der Indier*, moving on to medieval studies and turning his back on the orientalist studies he had founded. The impact of the Creuzer *Streit* was profound, and oriental studies were no longer acceptable in the academic mainstream.[15] In the Higher Criticism, David Friedrich Strauss called into question the veracity of Biblical miracles in his 1835 book *Das Leben Jesu* (The Life of Jesus), discounting the historicity of Jesus. This orientalist-inspired approach horrified pious Germans by subjecting Christian texts to the same scrutiny that the rival Jewish, Muslim and Hindu scriptures underwent. For daring to challenge the Protestant power structure, Strauss permanently lost his academic post. Despite Strauss's 'drumming' by the religious authorities, many scholars accepted the scientific validity of his critique, and its cultural influence spread widely.[16]

Classicists favoured Greece and resented the orientalists' attempt to place an older, Ancient Indian 'Aryan' heritage before the distinguished place their own Ancient Greek culture had at the root of European history. For Friedrich Schlegel, India may have been a useful alternative, but Johann Winckelmann's 'Graecophilia' had many adherents.[17] The Graecophiles were powerful, and the Graeco-Roman classical heritage was at the foundation of German education through the emphasis in the *Gymnasia* on preparation for higher learning. Replacing the familiarity of an Ancient Greek past with an Asian one would undo the Battle of Marathon, letting the Asian hordes into the Acropolis.

The modern would-be King Leonidas, heroically holding back the Asian mob at Thermopylae, was the 'world-historical' philosopher Georg Friedrich Wilhelm Hegel. In a defence of European philosophy, Hegel worked to refute the Oriental Renaissance by learning as much as he could about Asia, so as to place it in an 'infantile' position within his triumphalist philosophy of unfolding *Geist* (spirit). Applying what might be called a Whiggish sense of the Prussian state as the endpoint, Hegel dismissed Indian philosophy as mere religion, and the 'Orient'/'East' as simply an early step towards the ultimate realization of the 'Spirit of Freedom' in the monarchical Prussian state, ironically enough. Yet Hegel faced a serious fifth column threat at the heart of the German academic establishment: the founder of the modern German university system, Wilhelm von Humboldt, who learned Sanskrit and was so captivated by the philosophy of the Indian *Bhagavadgita*[18] that he gave lectures on it to the Prussian Academy of Sciences in 1825 and 1826, and wrote a lengthy review dealing with it in 1827. Hegel's refutation of the *Bhagavadgita* seriously engaged von Humboldt, who tried to minimize the damage to his own philo-orientalism.[19]

Hegel's attack on the Orient involved several arguments. First he asserted a strong separation between 'East' and 'West'. He argued that '*Asia is, characteristically, the Orient quarter of the globe – the region of origination. It is indeed a Western world for America; but as Europe presents on the whole, the centre and end of the old world, and is absolutely the West* – so Asia is absolutely the *East*'.[20] To support this clear bifurcation between East and West, Hegel next turned to historical arguments. 'It was Alexander's aim to avenge Greece for all that Asia had inflicted upon it for so many years and to fight out at last the ancient feud and contest between the East and the West.'[21] Hegel acknowledged that Roman rule over the eastern Mediterranean fostered an East–West religious transmission: 'In the Roman World the union of the East and West had taken place in the first instance by means of conquest: it took place now inwardly, psychologically, also; – the Spirit of the East spreading over the West', as Alexandria was 'the centre of communication between the East and the West'.[22] Yet this eastern Levant was also the site of bloody Crusades of the Middle Ages, where, he argued, 'the West bade an eternal farewell to the East at the Holy Sepulchre, and gained a comprehension of its own principle of subjective infinite Freedom'.[23]

Hegel's overall goal was to show the progression of the Spirit across time and space, from ancient to modern, from 'East' to 'West', from infancy to adulthood. He freely acknowledged that: 'In Asia arose the Light of Spirit, and therefore the history of the World'.[24] He chose not to refute four decades of mounting linguistic evidence tracing the 'Eastern' origins of Indo-European languages. Instead, he argued that origins were primitive, less developed and undesirable. In his lectures on the philosophy of history, his chapter on 'The Oriental World' argued for the superiority of 'Western' religion over 'Eastern' religion, which he characterized as Nature worship: 'This forms the point of separation between the East and the West; Spirit descends into the depths of its own being, and recognizes the abstract fundamental principle as the Spiritual. Nature – which in the East is the primary and fundamental existence – is now depressed to the condition of a mere creature; and Spirit now occupies the first place'.[25]

Beyond his lumping of all Asia into one 'oriental world', Hegel grouped Western culture into three additional worlds, the Greek, Roman and German, but without developing his concept of the West much further.[26] What was clear, however, was that in the sun's diurnal trajectory, the 'East' formed an infantile position, while Minerva's owl, symbolizing wisdom, flew at dusk, when the sun was setting in the 'West'.

By the 1820s, once Hegel had helped set German views of Asia on a more Eurocentric path, orientalists followed his lead in their detailed philological research. The Eurocentric uses of 'East' and 'West' can be seen more plainly in the work of the German-born and German-educated Friedrich Max Müller, a pivotal and polemical figure in nineteenth-century German orientalism. A charismatic speaker and voluminous writer, Müller helped to popularize the study of Ancient India through his lectures and publications, starting with those on the Hindu epic *Rig Veda*, which he described as the oldest work of literature known to humanity. Müller is celebrated today in India as a European who spoke out in favour of Indian civilization when few Britons were willing to do so. In his Cambridge University guest lectures published as *India: What Can It Teach Us?* (1883) he argued: 'The Sacred Books of the East are no longer a mere butt for the invectives of missionaries or the sarcasms of philosophers [i.e., Hegel]. They have at last been recognized as historical documents, ay [sic], as the most ancient documents in the history of the human mind'.[27]

A quarter of a century before, however, Müller had developed the term 'Aryan race' and had used it to characterize East–West interaction in a way detrimental to 'Easterners'. Germans were interested in Asia not just for spices and trade, but intellectually for the ancient 'Aryan' roots of European language and racial identity. According to Müller there were two branches of the Aryan race, the peoples linguists today call the proto-Indo-Europeans. From somewhere around the Caucasus Mountains in southern Russia, one group migrated northwest into Europe, and the other southeast into the Indian subcontinent. In what was essentially a narcissistically Eurocentric project, Müller characterized each group, looking approvingly at the western European branch: 'The main stream of the Aryan nations has always flowed towards the northwest ... the prominent actors in the great drama of history ... . They have perfected society and morals, and we learn from their literature and works of art the elements of science, the laws of art, and the principles of philosophy'.[28] The 'glorious path' of these Western 'rulers of history', in Müller's account, contrasted sharply with their poor country cousins from 'the East', who pathetically were 'the last to leave this common home ... [. H]e saw his brothers all depart towards the setting sun, and ... then, turning towards the south and the east he started alone in search of a new world'.[29] Yet even this less dynamic, eastern branch of the Aryan race was more powerful than the indigenous eastern natives, who were easy to conquer. Müller summarized the differentiation between West and East by locating the two branches of his Aryan race in Greece and India, which he saw as 'indeed the two opposite poles in the historical development of the Aryan man. To the Greek, existence is full of life and reality; to the Hindu it is a dream, an illusion'.[30]

Müller was not the first German orientalist to invent these ideas. At Bonn August Wilhelm von Schlegel (brother of Friedrich Schlegel) and his student and successor Christian Lassen both wrote about Aryan migrations in explicitly racist terms, arguing that it was miscegenation with 'savage' black-skinned natives that caused the downfall of 'white' Aryan migrants in India.[31] But Müller was working in England and helped to spread these ideas in the Anglophone world. Ironically, by the 1880s, after racist ethnologists had hijacked Müller's arguments about an Aryan race, Müller tried to limit the damage he had done, by opposing the use of 'Aryan' as an ethnological term, rather than as just a linguistic one. He attempted this in his opposition to the anthropologist Karl Penka.[32]

In 1881, Hermann Oldenberg, Professor of Sanskrit and Comparative Linguistics in Berlin, published a highly successful book on the Buddha that further elaborated on these differences between East and West. A 1914 reviewer said it was one of the 'most widely circulated books in all of orientalist literature'[33] and it is still in print today. While Oldenberg's text did not use the terms 'Orient' or 'Occident' at all, it made twenty-one references to 'the East' and nineteen to 'the West'. Following Max Müller's earlier theory about two branches of the Aryan race originating somewhere between Persia and the Caucasus – one going west into Europe, the other east and south into India – Oldenberg likewise divided the ancient Indian Gangetic plain into a distinctive East and West. These sector labels meant more than just geographical directions: they each bore a cultural significance and a hierarchical value. I would argue that this distinction was a representation of the overall colonial relationship of his own era, projected backwards onto the plains of Ancient India. Basing his arguments on textual evidence and nineteenth-century German orientalist biases, Oldenberg made these arguments before the discovery in 1922 of the Indus Valley Civilization (which nurtured the cities of Harappa and Mohenjo Daro) and without the benefits of archaeological evidence. Archaeological findings have done their part to refute and generally discredit the Aryan-invasion theory of Oldenberg's time,[34] but Oldenberg's arguments remained tremendously persuasive well into the twentieth century.

For Oldenberg and the generations of orientalists who followed him, the Aryans of South Asia arrived from the west and so, in his scheme, racial and intellectual purity flowed from west to east. Oldenberg perpetuated such racial characterizations, despite promoting a view of the East as 'inexhaustibly rich'. He elaborated on his East/West division within northern India by differentiating between the intellectual Western Veda worshippers and the slower-paced people of the East.[35] This division corresponds with the contemporary colonial relationship of the British imparting technology and sophisticated ideas to their 'backward' native neighbours, whom Rudyard Kipling characterized as 'half devil, half child'.[36] Oldenberg's climatic argument harked back to eighteenth-century notions of European superiority arising from the cool, moderate climate of Europe as opposed to the enervating heat of the tropics. 'In the sultry, dreamy stillness of India, thoughts spring and grow, every surmise and every sensation grows, otherwise than in the cool air of the west.'[37]

Oriental Resurgence (c. 1900–1930)

For the bulk of the nineteenth century, most German orientalists confined themselves to examining Ancient Asia, until a connection between modern colonial interests and scholarly enquiry in Germany emerged during the short German colonial era between 1884 and 1918. Suzanne Marchand refers to the *Furor Orientalis* at this time: a generation of 'furious orientalist' scholars, all born after 1860, passionately examined previously taboo subjects of Asian religion, art and philosophy – topics ignored by their positivistic, linguistically minded predecessors.[38] This new generation gained its attitude in part from Germany's entry into the scramble for colonies.[39] There was greater contact with a modern Orient, not just a textual ancient one. These orientalists led scholarly expeditions into Central Asia, including those to Turfan from 1902 to 1914, and excavated tons of material, such as the wall murals from the Bezeklik Thousand Buddha Caves (artefacts which Allied bombs destroyed in Berlin during the Second World War).[40] New interest in modern Asia helped to facilitate connections during the First World War between the German Foreign Office and Indian revolutionaries.[41]

The issue of Asian influence on Europe became important again during this later era, which Marchand calls a Second Oriental Renaissance.[42] One can see this development in a growing interest in Buddhism and Eastern religion. Arthur Schopenhauer had written about certain affinities between Buddhism and his own philosophy half a century earlier, but it was only in the 1880s that Buddhism began to gain a real foothold in Europe.[43] Questions emerged about parallels between the teachings of Buddha and Jesus and the possibility of Jesus having travelled to India.[44] Madame Blavatsky's influential theosophical movement blended religions from Europe and Asia, seeking a transcendent truth drawing on all of them.[45] The theosophists were just one manifestation of an international trend of Western intellectuals who cultivated what Stephen Hay argues was 'Orientophilia', in a reaction to disillusionment with their own European culture.[46]

During the Weimar era a revitalized view of the East came into its own. In *Siddhartha* (1923) Hermann Hesse published a personal journey of introspection using a Buddhist ancient Indian setting. Hesse's later novel *Die Morgenlandfahrt* (Journey to the East) (1932) depicted a quest by a small band of Western religious seekers who failed miserably in their attempt to attain Eastern wisdom. In this work Hesse harked back to the late eighteenth-century orientalists' rhetoric of Asian origins – albeit in spiritual rather than linguistic terms – when he described the 'East' as 'the Home of Light', arguing that 'our goal was not only the East, or rather the East was not only a country and something geographical, but it was the home and youth of the soul, it was everywhere and nowhere, it was the union of all times'.[47] Hesse's invocation of a resurgent Asia was the positive side of the coin whose negative flipside questioned the West.[48]

Oswald Spengler's *Der Untergang des Abendlandes* (The Decline of the Occident) (1918) and the great interest in Rabindranath Tagore's lecture visit to Europe reflected the questioning of Western values as a backlash to the horror of the First World War.[49] The theologian and Indologist Rudolf Otto's student, Gustav Mensching, wrote about Tagore's visits to Europe in the 1920s, comparing them with Gandhi's leadership of resistance in India.[50] Tagore's message criticized the materialism and religious shallowness of the West, contrasting these to a largely Buddhist-oriented personal spirituality found in Asia. This message helped make Tagore a celebrity in Europe, although paradoxically he left some Chinese and Japanese cold.[51] After almost a century of subservience to Greek classicism, oriental themes emerged in an 'Indian summer' of German orientalism.[52] This flowering in the Weimar era was not to last, as Nazism opportunistically co-opted features of the orientalist wave, including the swastika and studies that linked the ancient Aryan invasions to racist arguments, casting Jews as the Oriental other.[53] Yet, like Nietzschean philosophy, orientalist material was not always a comfortable fit for Nazi interests, as the new regime had little use for its non-violence (*Ahimsa*) or for Buddhist compassion.[54]

Conclusion

In this brief analysis of 'Orient'/'Occident' and 'East'/'West' in German orientalism we can see two waves of Oriental Renaissance breaking on the shores of German cultural understanding. There was an oscillation between an initial wave of emotional identification with Asia and a withdrawal, followed by a new wave of enthusiasm cut short. During the Romantics' interest in Asia and India, the terms 'Orient'/'Occident' and 'East'/'West' were notably neglected. What followed in the 1820s was a Eurocentric turn led by Hegel and the professional orientalist philologists, who inaugurated a detached, scientific era of perceived superiority of the 'West' over the 'East'. To help bring about this shift, they made ready use of the terms 'Orient' and 'Occident' and especially 'East' and 'West', so as to erect a firm racial and intellectual barrier between the two geographical areas. Hegel's application of 'East'/'West' geographical terms to philosophical realms in turn helped further to magnify the difference when it appeared in the racial arguments of A. W. von Schlegel, Lassen, Müller and Oldenberg as, using linguistic evidence, they tracked what they believed to be the migration of ancient 'Aryan' peoples across Eurasia. Finally, in the aftermath of German colonial contact and the pan-European disaster of the First World War, there was a new surge of more appreciative interest by Westerners in the East – coupled with disillusion with their own culture – in a Second Oriental Renaissance.

Notes

1. William Jones, 'The Third Anniversary Discourse, Delivered 2 February 1786', in *The Works of Sir William Jones*, ed. Lord Teignmouth, vol. 3, London, 1807, 34.
2. Douglas T. McGetchin, *Indology, Indomania, and Orientalism. Ancient India's Rebirth in Modern Germany*, Madison, 2009, 146–48.
3. Friedrich Schlegel, *Ueber die Sprache und Weisheit der Indier. Ein Beitrag zur Begründung der Alterthumskunde*, Heidelberg, 1808, ix.
4. Schlegel, *Ueber die Sprache und Weisheit der Indier*, x.
5. Suzanne L. Marchand, *German Orientalism in the Age of Empire. Religion, Race, and Scholarship*, New York, 2009, 21–22. McGetchin, *Indology, Indomania, and Orientalism*, 67–68.
6. A. Leslie Willson, *A Mythical Image. The Ideal of India in German Romanticism*, Durham, NC, 1964, 69, fn 12; Walter Leifer, *India and the Germans. 500 Years of Indo-German Contacts*, Bombay, 1971, 83.
7. Nicholas A. Germana, *The Orient of Europe. The Mythical Image of India and Competing Images of German National Identity*, Newcastle, 2009, 203; McGetchin, *Indology, Indomania, and Orientalism*, 18. For the larger context, see Tuska Benes, *In Babel's Shadow. Language, Philology, and the Nation in Nineteenth-Century Germany*, Detroit, 2008.

8. Wacław Rzewuski and Gesellschaft Von Liebhabern, *Fundgruben des Orients*, vol. 1, Vienna, 1805.
9. Nina Berman, *German Literature on the Middle East. Discourses and Practices, 1000–1989*, Ann Arbor, 2011, 161.
10. Rzewuski, *Fundgruben des Orients*, vol. 1, iii.
11. Johann Wolfgang von Goethe, *West-östlicher Divan*, Vienna, 1820, 12.
12. Berman, *German Literature on the Middle East*, 141.
13. Friedrich Creuzer, *Symbolik und Mythologie der alten Völker besonders der Griechen*, 4 vols, 1st ed. 1810–12, 2nd ed., 6 vols, Leipzig, 1819–28.
14. Marchand, *German Orientalism in the Age of Empire*, 70.
15. Marchand, *German Orientalism in the Age of Empire*, 66–71; McGetchin, *Indology, Indomania, and Orientalism*, 96–97. Marchand argues: "the outcome of this [Creuzer] Streit was hugely influential…and strong echoes of it can be heard in the 1890s, in the 1920s, and even in the *Black Athena* debate of recent years." *German Orientalism in the Age of Empire*, 66.
16. Marchand, *German Orientalism in the Age of Empire*, 109–10; Robert D. Richardson, *Emerson. The Mind on Fire*, Berkeley, 1995, 12–13.
17. Suzanne L. Marchand, *Down from Olympus. Archaeology and Philhellenism in Germany, 1750–1970*, Princeton, 1996, 7–10; Marchand, *German Orientalism in the Age of Empire*, 63.
18. The *Bhagavadgita* is a short book within the much longer epic *Mahabharata*, a dialogue between the prince Arjuna and his charioteer Krishna, the divine avatar or incarnation of the Hindu god Vishnu. It contains an elegant and short synopsis of Hindu theology, including the aphorism that particularly appealed to von Humboldt, the idea that one should pursue actions but without lusting after their fruits – in other words, that one should act with an outwardly engaged but inwardly stoic detachment.
19. Saverio Marchignoli, 'Canonizing an Indian Text?', in Douglas McGetchin, Peter K.J. Park and Damodar SarDesai (eds), *Sanskrit and 'Orientalism'. Indology and Comparative Linguistics in Germany, 1750–1958*, New Delhi, 2004, 259–65. Wilhelm Halbfass glosses over Hegel's profound animosity to Humboldt over India, stating that Hegel 'praised and studied' Humboldt's *Bhagavadgita* work: Wilhelm Halbfass, *India and Europe. An Essay in Understanding*, Albany, 1988, 86. On the pivotal importance of Hegel's hostility towards German orientalism see Bradley Herling, *The German Gita. Hermeneutics and Discipline in the German Reception of Indian Thought, 1778–1831*, New York, 2006, 203–53; Robert Cowen, *The Indo-German Identification. Reconciling South Asian Origins and European Destinies, 1765–1885*, Rochester, NY, 2010, 131–40; Halbfass, *India and Europe*, 95–99; and Peter Kwan-Joon Park, *Africa, Asia, and the History of Philosophy: Racism in the Formation of the Philosophical Canon, 1780–1830*, Albany, 2013, 113–31.
20. Georg Wilhelm Friedrich Hegel, *The Philosophy of History*, revised edn, trans. J. Sibree, New York, 1899, 99. Emphasis in original.
21. Hegel, *The Philosophy of History*, 272.
22. Hegel, *The Philosophy of History*, 330.
23. Hegel, *The Philosophy of History*, 393.
24. Hegel, *The Philosophy of History*, 99.
25. Hegel, *The Philosophy of History*, 195.
26. Alastair Bonnett, *The Idea of the West. Culture, Politics and History*, Basingstoke and New York, 2004, 24; Patrick Thaddeus Jackson, *Civilizing the Enemy. German Reconstruction and the Invention of the West*, Ann Arbor, 2006, 88–89.

27. Friedrich Max Müller, *India. What Can it Teach Us?* New York, 1883, 274.
28. Friedrich Max Müller, *A History of Ancient Sanskrit Literature so far as it Illustrates the Primitive Religion of the Brahmins*, London, 1860, 12, 14–15.
29. Müller, *A History of Ancient Sanskrit Literature*, 14–15.
30. Müller, *A History of Ancient Sanskrit Literature*, 18.
31. August Wilhelm von Schlegel, *De l'origine des Hindous*, Transactions of the Royal Asiatic Society of Literature of the United Kingdom, vol. 2, London, 1834, 405–46; Christian Lassen, *Indische Altertumkunde*, vol. 1, Bonn, 1847, 408; McGetchin, *Indology, Indomania, and Orientalism*, 164.
32. Pascale Rabault, 'From Language to Man? German Indology and Ethnology in the Epistemological Battlefield of the Nineteenth Century', in McGetchin et al. (eds), *Sanskrit and 'Orientalism'*, 337–60.
33. Marchand, *German Orientalism in the Age of Empire*, 272.
34. See Thomas R. Trautmann, *The Aryan Debate*, New Delhi, 2007 and Edwin F. Bryant, *The Quest for the Origins of Vedic Culture. The Indo-Aryan Migration Debate*, Oxford, 2001.
35. Hermann Oldenberg, *Buddha: His Life, His Doctrine, His Order*, trans. William Hoey, London, Williams and Norgate, 1882, 63–64.
36. Rudyard Kipling, 'The White Man's Burden', *McClure's Magazine*, February 1899.
37. Oldenberg, *Buddha*, 268.
38. Marchand, *German Orientalism in the Age of Empire*, 216.
39. Marchand, *German Orientalism in the Age of Empire*, 213.
40. Peter Hopkirk, *Foreign Devils on the Silk Road. The Search for the Lost Cities and Treasures of Chinese Central Asia*, Amherst, 1984; Marchand, *German Orientalism in the Age of Empire*, 421, 425; McGetchin, *Indology, Indomania, and Orientalism*, 109. On misperceptions of Buddhism in nineteenth-century Europe, see Roger-Pol Droit, *The Cult of Nothingness. The Philosophers and the Buddha*, trans. David Streight and Pamela Vohnson, Chapel Hill and London, 2003.
41. Nirode K. Barooah, *Chatto. The Life and Times of an Indian Anti-imperialist in Europe*, New Delhi, 2004; Douglas T. McGetchin, 'Indo-German Connections, Critical and Hermeneutical, in the First World War', *The Comparatist* 34 (2010), 95–126.
42. Marchand, *German Orientalism in the Age of Empire*, 232.
43. Droit, *The Cult of Nothingness*, 19–93, 149–50.
44. The Russian journalist Nicholas Notovitch published *Vie inconnue de Jesus-Christ* (*The Unknown Life of Christ*), translated from French by Violet Crispe (London, 1895), based on his visit to the remote Tibetan monastery of Himis where he claimed to have found evidence. Max Müller refuted Notovitch's account and theosophy's claims of 'Esoteric Buddhism' in his *Last Essays*, New York, 1901.
45. Marchand, *German Orientalism in the Age of Empire*, 270–71.
46. Stephen Hay, *Asian Ideas of East and West. Tagore and his Critics in Japan, China, and India*, Cambridge, Mass, 1970, 314.
47. Hermann Hesse, *Journey to the East*, New York, 1972, 11, 19.
48. For this multivalent approach to the West, see Bonnett, *The Idea of the West*, 6.
49. Michael Adas, 'Contested Hegemony. The Great War and the Afro-Asian Assault on the Civilizing Mission Ideology', *Journal of World History* 15/1 (2004), 31–63.
50. Leifer, *India and the Germans*, 253.
51. Bonnett, *The Idea of the West*, 88–89.
52. Marchand, *German Orientalism in the Age of Empire*, 478–85.

53. Fritz Stern, *The Politics of Cultural Despair. A Study in the Rise of the Germanic Ideology*, Berkeley, 1974; Laurel Plapp, *Zionism and Revolution in European-Jewish Literature*, New York, 2008.
54. Steven E. Aschheim, *The Nietzsche Legacy in Germany, 1890–1990*, Berkeley, 1992; Timothy W. Ryback, *Hitler's Private Library. The Books that Shaped his Life*, New York, 2008, 68.

Chapter 7

GERMAN JEWS AND THE WEST
Identification, Dissimilation and Marginalization around the Turn of the Century

Stefan Vogt

In German-Jewish thinking, 'the West' has never been a concept as elaborate as 'the East'.[1] From the last decades of the nineteenth century, debates about the East, its significance for the Jews in general, and for German Jews in particular, filled the pages of German-Jewish journals and occupied the minds of many German-Jewish intellectuals. The 'East' referred to Eastern Europe, where the vast majority of Jews resided, and to the East European Jews who came from there. The 'East' also referred to the Orient, which was both the mythical homeland of the Jews and the object of colonial fantasies amongst Jews and non-Jews alike. The emerging Zionist movement added to the significance of this concept, but it was heavily debated among the non-Zionist majority of German Jewry as well. The impact of the East on German-Jewish consciousness can thus hardly be exaggerated.

A considerable amount of scholarly work has been done on this subject, but it was Steven Aschheim's book *Brothers and Strangers*, published thirty years ago, that broke the ground for this research; and even today this book provides the most thorough and comprehensive analysis available.[2] Aschheim compellingly shows how the East and the East European Jew provided both a negative and a positive image, or mirroring, for German Jews' debates on Jewish and German-Jewish identity. In the late nineteenth century, and right up until the early years of the twentieth, the prevailing image of the *Ostjude* (Eastern Jew) was one of backwardness, religious zealotry and unwillingness to integrate into modern society.[3] In order to become proper Germans, and to be accepted by German society as such, German Jews felt that they had to differentiate themselves from the stereotype of the *Ostjude*. This was certainly true for the liberal majority of German Jewry, but was also so, though to a lesser degree, for the first generation of German Zionists. The situation changed dramatically, however, after the turn of the century. A new generation of Zionist intellectuals redrew the image of the *Ostjude*, so that this figure was now seen as both solidly rooted in Jewish traditions and the source of Jewish spiritual renewal. In this view, which was partly adopted by non-Zionists as well, the *Ostjude* came to represent true Jewishness. German Jews realized that they lacked the *Ostjude*'s authenticity. Impelled by the apparent inability of assimilation and liberalism to overcome anti-Semitism, and also by a more general rejection of liberal ideas, a growing section of German Jewry took this image of the *Ostjude* as their model for redefining Jewish identity.

In both its positive and its negative guise, the East, as it was employed by German-Jewish intellectuals to debate Jewish identity in Germany, was conceived as a counter-image of the West. However, it has rarely been spelled out quite what the 'West' actually stood for, either in the historical sources or in the scholarly literature. The West, it seems, was a self-evident concept for German Jews. Yet the fact that the term itself was only sparsely used does not mean that the idea was of no significance in this discourse. A closer look reveals that the image of the West in German-Jewish consciousness was just as complex and ambivalent as the image of the East. This chapter will discuss the various meanings 'the West' had for German Jews and their significance both for the relationship between Jewish and general German discourses on this topic and for internal Jewish debates about assimilation, secularization and belonging to a nation. It will be argued that German Jews' images of the West demonstrated the deep entrenchment they felt in German culture and it will be shown how, at the same time, the Jews in Germany were forced to remain at the margins of this culture until, in the end, they were brutally removed.[4]

The West as an Ideal

From a German-Jewish perspective, the process of emancipation and acculturation that took place roughly between 1780 and 1871 could be seen as a move towards the West.[5] Intellectually and politically, it owed a lot to developments associated with the democratic revolutions in France and North America. Socially and economically, the process was part of a wider one establishing a bourgeois society and capitalist economy, which took place in Germany in a way generally similar to that in other countries of Western Europe. Social and political modernization in the nineteenth century seemed gradually to be integrating Germany into Western Europe and, to an extent, German Jews were becoming 'West European' Jews as part of the process. To be sure, the emancipation and integration were only partial and this meant that Jews in Germany retained their status as a marginalized minority – at least to some degree. So the self-identification of German Jews as German or Western was never uncontested or unambiguous.[6] However, both emancipation and integration had made considerable headway during the century. German Jews could sincerely hope that the move towards German and German-Jewish Westernization they perceived would lead to their full inclusion in German society.

Yet in the last third of the nineteenth century, Germany was not altogether a West European country. Identification with the West was not necessarily part of the dominant concept of national identity that slowly formed after the establishment of the German nation state in 1871. This was not so much despite the fact that, in many ways, Germany increasingly resembled Western European countries, but rather because of it. Already in the 1860s, industrialization had taken off, and by the 1890s Germany's capitalist economy was among the strongest and most advanced in the world. Though unsuccessful in attempts to confront the authoritarian political system head-on, the German middle class (*Bürgertum*) had managed to establish itself as a major and indispensable pillar of the power structure of the Empire and had created a distinctively bourgeois society. Germany was widely held to be one of the most advanced countries in the fields of science and technology. At the end of the 1880s, Germany had also joined the distinguished club of colonial powers.

While these developments tightened the network of relationships between Germany and Western European countries at both personal and institutional levels, significant parts of the bourgeoisie developed an ambivalent image of, and attitude towards, the West. Among those Germans most clearly identifying with it were the majority of the German Jews. As Aschheim and others have shown, this identification was based on a radical distancing of themselves from Eastern European Jews – a distancing that went as far as outright denigration.[7] According to their outlook, the West was everything the Eastern Jew was not. However, the German-Jewish image of the West in the late nineteenth century was not only a foil to set against the 'backward' East but contained positive characteristics of its own. The image implied an identification with German culture and nationhood, which were considered Western. It also implied adherence to a liberal concept of society. And, finally, it included an affirmation and defence of Jewish emancipation. Both the reactive and positive elements of this image were present, for example, in Franz Oppenheimer's seminal but controversial article *Stammesbewusstsein und Volksbewusstsein*, published in *Die Welt* in 1910.[8]

Oppenheimer begins his article by emphatically declaring himself a '*Westeuropäer*', a West European. He makes it perfectly clear that West European culture is quite distinct from East European culture, which, according to Oppenheimer, hardly exists. In Romania, for example, culture is only 'a thin Western European varnish covering oriental barbarism'. But he also considers Jewish culture in Eastern Europe to be 'infinitely far below modern culture, of which our *Völker* are the bearers'. The *Völker* Oppenheimer claims to belong to are, of course, those of Western Europe, including Germany. As part of the West, he explains, Germany has produced world-class thinkers, researchers, artists and engineers. Germany has also developed a liberal civil society which, although weaker than what might be found in other western countries, is far more advanced than those in the East, especially in regard to the status of Jews. This is why Oppenheimer identifies both with German culture and with the German nation. At the same time, however, Oppenheimer, the Zionist, insists on his identity as a Jew.

For German Jews like Oppenheimer, identification with the West meant holding on to German national and cultural identity without giving up Jewishness. Thus, it was a strategy to ensure and enforce legal emancipation and social integration as Jews. For this purpose, Germany needed to be defined as both culturally and politically Western. The concept of the West therefore served also as a means to emphasize what was considered positive in German culture and politics. Moreover, it helped create a specific image of Germany Jews could find worth identifying with. Oppenheimer realized, however, that Germany lagged behind other Western countries in at least one important respect, namely in its anti-Semitism: the Jews were 'socially boycotted everywhere, and unlawfully discriminated by the authorities'. The persistence of anti-Semitism among the elites and in the administrative structures was also a major concern of the liberal *Centralverein deutscher Staatsbürger jüdischen Glaubens*.[9] Yet, so that the presence of anti-Jewish resentment did not compromise identification with Germany, the differences between the situations there and in the East had to be emphasized even more. The fact that anti-Semitism was much worse in the East, and that in Russia and Romania even legal emancipation was far from being achieved, was therefore a proof of Germany's belonging to the West. In a similar way, the cultural differences between Germany and Eastern Europe had to be emphasized.

When German Jews like Oppenheimer described the cultural level of East European Jews as low and deficient, they assured themselves not only that they belonged to German culture but also that Germany belonged to the cultural realm of the West, which in turn seemed to support their position as Jews within German society.

Often, the identification of German Jews with the West also included a notion of Western cultural mission to the Orient. This was, of course, particularly relevant in Zionist attitudes towards Palestine. Early Zionist documents are replete with the belief that Jewish colonization in Palestine would bring Western culture to this land of the East. Theodor Herzl's utopian novel *Altneuland* is the classic example of this notion, but Otto Warburg too claimed that the Jews in Palestine would 'offer the achievements of the Western nations to the Orient'.[10] The most important of these achievements were education and hygiene, two concepts which were conceived as quintessentially Western. As recent literature has shown, this can be seen as part of the Zionist project to 'Westernize' the Jews in Palestine.[11] In the German context, however, these concepts were more prominently aired in general colonialist discourses, to which Warburg and other Zionists directly contributed.[12] From the early Zionists' point of view, Germany's participation in the European colonial project strengthened its belongingness to the West. Yet this was not a Zionist peculiarity. Many liberal Jews agreed in this assessment and likewise supported German colonial endeavours. In the *Allgemeine Zeitung des Judenthums*, for example, German and European colonialism were explicitly seen as part of the 'struggle between Orient and Occident', which was at the same time the 'struggle of culture and humanity against barbarism and half-barbarism'.[13] In Palestine, the dominantly liberal *Hilfsverein der deutschen Juden* worked for the dissemination of Western culture and values and – conceiving it as almost synonymous – for the strengthening of German influence abroad. The *Hilfsverein*'s declared aim was, among other things, to promote the German language in Palestine in order to 'facilitate the connection with the culture of the civilized world'.[14]

Even though colonialism made Germany look more like its western neighbours, it did not necessarily bring these countries any closer together. Rather, it reinforced economic competition and the German nationalists' urge to confront their Western rivals.[15] Overall, German national identity, to which most German Jews felt committed, was much less inclined towards the ideas and values associated with the West, ideas like liberalism and individualism, than the predominantly liberal Jews wished it to be. As a consequence, the self-identification Jews had formed with the West became more and more problematic.

The West as a Problem

It was the second generation of German Zionists especially who began to question the identification of German Jewry with the West. This questioning developed from the turn of the century. Many of the protagonists came from highly acculturated backgrounds but, in contrast to their parents' generation, they strove for 'dissimilation' from German culture.[16] This process was partly fuelled by disappointment over the failure of the assimilationist strategy to achieve full integration and by the persistence, or even radicalization, of anti-Semitism. Another motivation, however, came from the general intellectual trend in Germany that increasingly questioned and rejected the ideas of liberalism, rationalism and the Enlightenment.[17] The new Zionist discourse on the West, which was adopted by a number of non-Zionist Jews as well, was part of this development.

The most obvious sign of it was an increased interest in the histories, cultures and milieux of East European Jews. In many articles, authors such as Nathan Birnbaum (who is said to have coined the term '*Ostjude*') attempted to introduce a positive image of the East European Jew into German-Jewish discourse.[18] Most important in this respect, however, was Martin Buber. Buber was particularly interested in the Hassidic culture of Eastern Europe. Yet rather than investigate this phenomenon historically, he aimed at popularizing it for his German-Jewish readership and at establishing a Jewish version of neo-mysticism, very much along the lines of German neo-Romantic thinking.[19] Buber exerted enormous influence on the younger generation of German and Central European Zionists – this is evident, for example, in the essay collection *Vom Judentum* which was edited by the Prague Zionist student organization *Bar Kochba*.[20] Buber was also the driving force behind the foundation of the *Jüdische Verlag* in 1902 and was editor of the journal *Der Jude*, founded in 1916. Both were to a large degree devoted to the promotion of Eastern Jewish culture.[21] Other journals, such as Fritz Mordechai Kaufmann's *Die Freistatt*, had similar aims.

The journal most exclusively concerned with disseminating a positive image of the East European Jew was *Ost und West*, founded in 1901 and edited by Leo Winz. *Ost und West* did not confine itself to conveying information, descriptions and images of East European Jews. As David Brenner has shown, the journal also engaged in developing a negative stereotype of 'the Western Jew'.[22] In contrast to the East European Jew, who was considered to be rooted in Jewish traditions and mores, the Western Jew was depicted as a parvenu, a social climber who showed off his wealth in order to be accepted in non-Jewish society. The journal repeatedly published brief satirical sketches about wealthy Jews in the affluent western neighbourhoods of Berlin, who desperately, but ultimately unsuccessfully, strove to gain access to German high society.[23]

While *Ost und West* developed a popular stereotype of the Western Jew, other German-Jewish intellectuals embarked on a more thorough and fundamental redefinition of the West and its meanings for German Jews. Again, Martin Buber was at the forefront of this endeavour. In a lecture of 1912, Buber contrasted the 'Occidental' with the 'Oriental' type and claimed that the senses of the former were 'detached from the grounds of organic life'.[24] The Occidental tended always to approach the 'truth of the world' ('*Wahrheit der Welt*') through abstraction and to split this *Wahrheit* up into analytical concepts ('*Begriffe*'). And, while the Oriental would strive for the realization of ideas through deeds, the Occidental would aim only at intellectual understanding. Buber made it clear that, in his view, the approach of the Occidental type towards the world was deficient and less 'fundamental'. The Occidental type, he maintained, was not able to reach wholeness, because he had no immediate relationship to the world. While, for the Oriental, 'the essence and the meaning' of his life were identical with the essence and the meaning of the world, for the Occidental the two spheres were separated from one another and could only be connected by cognitive means.

Buber's characterization of the Occidental type was clearly moulded in terms of a complete *Lebensphilosophie*, and so was the image of the West throughout the discourse of the second-generation Zionists.[25] Robert Weltsch, who later became editor of the *Jüdische Rundschau*, the official journal of the German Zionist organization, wrote in 1913 that emancipation had dismantled the Jewish community and had made individualism triumphant. Instead of participating in the 'stream of life', Weltsch argued, the Western Jew wanted only to evoke 'the semblance of life. He becomes an actor, a counterfeiter, a liar'.[26] In the same collection, Hans Kohn characterized this version of Zionism as part of a general turn against 'soul-eliminating' rationalism.[27] In a similar vein, Birnbaum described the Western Jew as 'rootless and shady', a person lacking character, 'dull, colourless and boring'.[28] From the early years of the twentieth century, this negative stereotype of the Western Jew and of the West in general became increasingly popular in German Zionist circles.

The main purpose behind establishing such an inverted dichotomy between the Eastern and the Western Jew was to create an essentialist concept of the Jewish *Volk* as a basis for a more radical Jewish nationalism. This concept owed a lot to neo-romantic and *völkisch* discourses in German culture. Martin Buber made this unmistakably clear. In the first of his Prague *Reden über das Judentum*, he claimed that awareness of being part of a nation requires the 'discovery of the blood as the root-like, nourishing force inside of each person, the discovery that the most fundamental elements of our being are determined by the blood, that our thinking and our will is fundamentally influenced by it'.[29] The trend also included a negative image of the West. Initially in most cases this was a critique of the Western Jewish condition. The West in this critique represented the idea of assimilation, which was now rejected much more vigorously than it had been by the first-generation Zionists. The assimilation of Western Jews produced 'civilization without culture', as Birnbaum put it.[30] Yet assimilation was conceived as a Jewish version of a much larger problem. In this respect, the West represented the ideas of the nineteenth century: liberalism, rationalism and materialism. Buber claimed that it was especially 'the Western Jew' who had developed an 'intellectuality that is alienated from life, unbalanced and not organic'.[31]

In their most radical version, the Zionist discourses even contributed to the German nationalists' open confrontation with the West during the First World War. In his pamphlet *Von der weltkulturellen Bedeutung und Aufgabe des Judentums*, published in 1916, Nachum Goldmann argued that Germans and Jews were allies in a historic struggle against the individualist and liberal thinking of the nineteenth century.[32] This was because the spiritual roots of German culture could be traced, via the Reformation, to the ancient Middle East, and especially to Judaism, whereas liberalism was based on Greek antiquity, from which a direct line ran through the Renaissance to the ideas now prevalent in the West. While assimilationist Jewry had ignored this affinity between *Deutschtum* and *Judentum*, the Zionists, according to Goldmann, were well aware of it:

> Assimilationist Judaism, which is inclined to cosmopolitanism and hopes to achieve the dissolution of the Jewish nation through an amalgamation of all nations, has its intellectual roots in the Western philosophy of Enlightenment, in English liberal thought and [the] French Encyclopaedists. In contrast, young, national Judaism, which places the national idea at the centre of its vision of life, is intellectually based on German philosophy: Fichte, Hegel, Lagarde, all the classic authorities of German national thinking are its teachers, too.[33]

Yet for all their participation in general ideological developments taking place in Germany, Zionist and German-Jewish discourses on the West must be seen in a different light. Affirmation of the East was strongly encouraged by the fact that the *Ostjude* became the primary target of German anti-Semitism, especially during the First World War and in its aftermath. In 1923, a wave of anti-Semitic violence swept across

Germany and culminated in a pogrom in the largely Eastern Jewish *Scheunenviertel* quarter in Berlin.[34] Many Jews understood that the attacks were in fact directed against all Jews. So the negative redefinition of the West by German Jews was also an attempt to strengthen a specific Jewish identity in the face of increasing exclusion and growing anti-Semitism. Paradoxically, appropriation of German *völkisch* nationalism thus became a means to counter the anti-Semitism that characterized substantial parts of the very same nationalist ideology.

It should be pointed out that the rejection of the West, even by the young Zionists, was much less complete than in the case of German nationalists. In one way or another, most German Zionists strove to combine *völkisch* concepts of identity with central elements of the Enlightenment, namely legal emancipation and universal humanism. Buber, for example, insisted that the ultimate goal of Jewish nationalism was to redeem humanity.[35] He and his followers developed a critique of aggressive forms of nationalism, both in Germany and within the Zionist movement, based on humanistic and universalistic ideas. The liberal majority amongst German Jews indeed became more interested in Jewish culture and, to an extent, less confident in the ideas of liberalism and rationalism which were thought of as Western,[36] but they generally clung to liberal political convictions. They did so right up until the end of the Weimar Republic and thus retained to that time their positive image of the West. To German Jews, the West had become problematic, but its affirmation had not ceased to be an element in the construction of German-Jewish identity.

Conclusion: The Jews and the Margins of the West

This survey of German-Jewish images of the West from the end of the nineteenth to the early twentieth century has shown how strongly they were influenced by developments in German culture and philosophy during that period. This indebtedness should not only be seen as a response to environmental influences. The development of the images demonstrates that German-Jewish thinking in general was deeply embedded in the German intellectual world. In particular, Jews' idea of the West was an important element in their debates on strategies to achieve emancipation and integration in Germany. Throughout the period under consideration, the dominant strategy was to define Germany as a proper part of the West. On this basis Jews could argue that their quest for emancipation was, at the same time, a quest for identification with German culture. When ideologies within that culture developed features apparently contradicting Germany's adherence to the West (as Jews conceived it), this strategy became problematic, and a more sceptical image of the West evolved in Jewish discourses too. Many German-Jewish intellectuals now emphasized their Jewishness in opposition to both German and Western identities; but in doing so they also participated in a general intellectual trend in Germany. German Jews revolted against the West not only as Jews, but also as Germans. Paradoxically, their turning from an affirmative to a negative image of the West was simultaneously an endorsement of, and a counteraction to, developments in wider German society.

Nevertheless, there were significant differences between the German-Jewish and the German nationalist revolts against 'the West'. Even the Zionists, who advocated a non-Western identity for Jews most radically, were not prepared completely to abandon the liberal values and universalistic ideals of the Enlightenment which they associated with the West. Robert Weltsch, for example, insisted that 'it is a vital question for every nationalism to find its way to the idea of humanity'.[37] The Zionists never stopped demanding full civil equality for German Jews and continued to denounce the incomplete state of emancipation in Germany. The Zionists' rejection of liberalism was, to a large degree, another version of the general cultural criticism of the time. It was also, however, a reaction to the fact that the liberalism of the nineteenth century had failed to provide full acceptance and emancipation for the Jews. 'Liberalism', wrote Weltsch, 'did not emancipate the Jews as Jews, but, under the fiction of unified humanity, compelled them to assimilate to the majority'.[38] The revolt of German Jews against the ideals associated with the West was thus at the same time a critique of the failure of the West to realize these ideals. This, to be sure, was a paradoxical attitude; but it was consistent with the German Jews' ambivalent and precarious position at the margins of society – poised between inclusion and exclusion, between particular and universal identities and, indeed, between the West and the rest.

Notes

1. As in other chapters, the terms 'West' and 'East' in their capitalized version refer to intellectual and cultural concepts rather than to geographical or social entities.
2. Steven A. Aschheim, *Brothers and Strangers. The East European Jew in German and German Jewish Consciousness, 1800–1923*, Madison, 1982. Other important work includes Sander L. Gilman, 'The Rediscovery of Eastern Jews. German Jews in the East, 1890–1918', in David Bronsen (ed.), *Jews and Germans from 1860 to 1933. The Problematic Symbiosis*, Heidelberg, 1979, 338–67; Jack Wertheimer, *Unwelcome Strangers. East European Jews in Imperial Germany*, New York, 1987; Paul Mendes-Flohr, 'Fin-de-Siècle Orientalism, the Ostjuden and the Aesthetics of Jewish

Self-Affirmation', *Studies in Contemporary Jewry* 1 (1984), 96–139; Jehuda Reinharz, 'East European Jews in the Weltanschauung of German Zionists, 1882–1914', *Studies in Contemporary Jewry* 1 (1984), 55–95; David N. Myers, '"Distant Relatives Happening onto the same Inn". The Meeting of East and West as Literary Theme and Cultural Ideal', *Jewish Social Studies* 1 (1995), 75–100; Michael Brenner, *The Renaissance of Jewish Culture in Weimar Germany*, New Haven, 1996; Yfaat Weiss, '"Wir Westjuden haben ein jüdisches Stammesbewußtsein, die Ostjuden ein jüdisches Volksbewußtsein". Der deutsch-jüdische Blick auf das polnische Judentum in den beiden ersten Jahrzehnten des 20. Jahrhunderts', *Archiv für Sozialgeschichte* 37 (1997), 157–78; and David A. Brenner, *Marketing Identities. The Invention of Jewish Ethnicity in Ost und West*, Detroit, 1998.

3. The term 'Ostjude' or 'Eastern Jew' is used in this chapter to designate the image of the Eastern European Jew, not the actual person.
4. Due to limits of space this chapter will focus on the period of the German *Kaiserreich* and Weimar Republic.
5. This was often true even in a quite literal sense. During the nineteenth century, many Jews migrated from the eastern provinces of Prussia, some of which had only recently been acquired from Poland, to Berlin or to other cities further west. See Gotthold Rhode (ed.), *Juden in Ostmitteleuropa. Von der Emanzipation bis zum Ersten Weltkrieg*, Marburg, 1989; Avraham Barkai, 'German-Jewish Migrations in the Nineteenth Century, 1830–1910', *Yearbook of the Leo Baeck Institute* 30 (1985), 301–18; and Jakob Lestschinsky, 'Die Umsiedlung und Umschichtung des jüdischen Volkes im Lauf des letzten Jahrhunderts', *Weltwirtschaftliches Archiv* 30/2 (1929), 123–56, and 32/2 (1930), 563–99.
6. On the ambiguous character of German-Jewish emancipation see especially David Sorkin, *The Transformation of German Jewry, 1780–1840*, New York, 1987. German-Jewish Enlightenment also participated in some of the peculiarities of German ideology in the nineteenth century, especially its inclination to Hegelian philosophy and its concept of *Bildung*.
7. See Aschheim, *Brothers and Strangers*, 3–57, and the other work cited in footnote 2.
8. Franz Oppenheimer, 'Stammesbewusstsein und Volksbewusstsein', *Die Welt*, 18 February 1910, 139–43. The following quotations are from this article. Oppenheimer's position was representative of the majority of liberal German Jewry, as well as of the first generation of German Zionists, to which Oppenheimer himself belonged. All translations are mine.
9. The latest and most comprehensive work on the *Centralverein* (CV) is Avraham Barkai, *'Wehr Dich!' Der Centralverein deutscher Staatsbürger jüdischen Glaubens (C.V.) 1893–1938*, Munich, 2002. More specific work on the CV's fight against anti-Semitism in the *Kaiserreich* includes Sanford Ragins, *Jewish Responses to Anti-Semitism in Germany, 1870–1914. A Study in the History of Ideas*, Cincinnati, 1980; and Ismar Schorsch, *Jewish Reactions to German Anti-Semitism, 1870–1914*, New York, 1972.
10. Theodor Herzl, *Altneuland*, Leipzig, 1902; Otto Warburg, 'Palästina als Kolonisationsgebiet', *Altneuland* 1 (1904), 13. Warburg was one of the leading German Zionists and became the third president of the Zionist Organization in 1911.
11. See, for example, Dafna Hirsch, '"We Are Here to Bring the West, Not Only Ourselves". Zionist Occidentalism and the Discourse of Hygiene in Mandate Palestine', *International Journal of Middle East Studies* 41 (2009), 577–94; Amnon Raz-Krakotzkin, 'The Zionist Return to the West and the Mizrahi Jewish Perspective', in Ivan Davidson Kalmar and Derek J. Penslar (eds), *Orientalism and the Jews*, Lebanon, NH, 2005, 162–81. Hirsch rightly points out that the categories of 'East' and 'West'

were rather fluid in the Palestinian discourse, as the majority of the Jewish population was of Eastern European descent.
12. See Derek J. Penslar, *Zionism and Technocracy. The Engineering of Jewish Settlement in Palestine, 1870–1918*, Bloomington, 1991.
13. 'Einige Betrachtungen über die Weltlage', *Allgemeine Zeitung des Judenthums*, 24 March 1885. This leading article was published anonymously.
14. 'Baronin von Cohn-Oppenheim Stiftung für den Hilfsverein der deutschen Juden', in *Dritter Geschäftsbericht (1904) des Hilfsvereins der deutschen Juden, erstattet der Generalversammlung am 26. Februar 1905*, Berlin, 1905, 131. On the *Hilfsverein* see Zeev W. Sadmon, *Die Gründung des Technions in Haifa im Lichte deutscher Politik, 1907–1920*, Munich, 1994; Isaiah Friedman, 'The Hilfsverein der deutschen Juden, the German Foreign Ministry and the Controversy with the Zionists, 1901–1918', *Leo Baeck Institute Yearbook* 24 (1979), 291–319; and Moshe Rinott, *'Hilfsverein der deutschen Juden' – Creation and Struggle. A Chapter of the History of Hebrew Education in Eretz Israel and of the History of German Jews*, Jerusalem, 1971 (in Hebrew).
15. See Paul Kennedy, *The Rise of the Anglo-German Antagonism 1860–1914*, London, 1980; and Peter Walkenhorst, *Nation-Volk-Rasse. Radikaler Nationalismus im Deutschen Kaiserreich 1890–1914*, Göttingen, 2007.
16. The term has been developed by Shulamit Volkov, 'The Dynamics of Dissimilation. Ostjuden and German Jews', in Jehuda Reinharz and Walter Schatzberg (eds), *The Jewish Response to German Culture. From the Enlightenment to the Second World War*, Hanover, 1985, 195–211.
17. There is a plethora of literature on this intellectual development. The classic study is George L. Mosse, *The Crisis of German Ideology. Intellectual Origins of the Third Reich*, New York, 1964.
18. See, for example, Nathan Birnbaum, 'Etwas über Ost- und Westjuden', in Nathan Birnbaum, *Ausgewählte Schriften zur jüdischen Frage*, vol. 1, Czernowitz, 1910 (first published 1904).
19. His most important works in this field are Martin Buber, *Die Geschichten des Rabbi Nachman*, Frankfurt/Main, 1906, and Martin Buber, *Die Legende des Baal-Schem*, Frankfurt/Main, 1908.
20. Verein jüdischer Hochschüler Bar-Kochba Prag (ed.), *Vom Judentum. Ein Sammelbuch*, Leipzig, 1913. The book was the result of cooperation between *Bar Kochba* and Buber, following his famous 'Three Lectures on Judaism', held in Prague between 1909 and 1910. See Martin Buber, *Drei Reden über das Judentum*, Frankfurt/Main, 1911.
21. On the *Jüdischer Verlag* see Anatol Schenker, *Der Jüdische Verlag 1902–1938. Zwischen Aufbruch, Blüte und Vernichtung*, Tübingen, 2003. On the journal *Der Jude* see Eleonore Lappin, *Der Jude, 1916–1928. Jüdische Moderne zwischen Universalismus und Partikularismus*, Tübingen, 2000.
22. Brenner, *Marketing Identities*, 77–97.
23. See for example Lothar Brieger Wasservogel, 'Das Alte Testament', *Ost und West* 1 (1901), 849–54; Siegbert Salter, 'Szene aus Berlin W.', *Ost und West* 5 (1905), 593–96; or Siegbert Salter, 'Das Glück des Hauses Löbenthal', *Ost und West* 5 (1905), 797–802.
24. Martin Buber, 'Der Geist des Orients und das Judentum', in *Der Geist des Judentums. Reden und Geleitworte*, Leipzig, 1916, 9–48. The following quotations are from this text.
25. On the influence of *Lebensphilosophie* on German-speaking Zionism see Yotam Hotam, *Moderne Gnosis und Zionismus. Kulturkrise, Lebensphilosophie und nationaljüdisches Denken*, Göttingen, 2009, 117–237; Jörg Hackeschmidt, *Von Kurt Blumenfeld*

zu Norbert Elias. *Die Erfindung einer jüdischen Nation*, Hamburg, 1997, 78–89; and George L. Mosse, 'The Influence of the Volkish Idea on German Jewry', in George L. Mosse, *Germans and Jews. The Right, the Left and the Search for a 'Third Force' in Pre-Nazi Germany*, London, 1971, 77–115.

26. Robert Weltsch, 'Theodor Herzl und wir', in *Vom Judentum*, 157–58. On Weltsch see Stefan Vogt, 'Robert Weltsch and the Paradoxes of Anti-Nationalist Nationalism', *Jewish Social Studies* 16 (2010), 85–115.
27. Hans Kohn, 'Geleitwort', in *Vom Judentum*, vi.
28. Birnbaum, 'Etwas über Ost- und Westjuden', 279–80.
29. Martin Buber, 'Das Judentum und die Juden', in Martin Buber, *Der Jude und sein Judentum. Gesammelte Aufsätze und Reden*, Cologne, 1963, 13. On the neo-Romantic and *völkisch* elements in German Zionist thinking see Mosse, 'The Influence of the Volkish Idea on German Jewry'; Avraham Shapira, 'Buber's Attachment to Herder and German Volkism', *Studies in Zionism* 14 (1993), 1–30; and Manuel Duarte de Oliveira, 'Passion for Land and Volk: Martin Buber and Neo-Romanticism', *Leo Baeck Institute Yearbook* 41 (1996), 239–60. A recent Hebrew dissertation looks at these elements in the discourse of Prague Zionism: Zohar Maor, *A New Secret Doctrine. Spirituality, Creativity and Nationalism in the Prague Circle*, Jerusalem, 2010.
30. Birnbaum, 'Etwas über Ost- und Westjuden', 281.
31. Buber, 'Das Judentum und die Juden', 15.
32. Nachum Goldmann, *Von der weltkulturellen Bedeutung und Aufgabe des Judentums*, Munich, 1916, 11–18.
33. Ibid., 50.
34. On the anti-Semitic wave of 1923 see Cornelia Hecht, *Deutsche Juden und Antisemitismus in der Weimarer Republik*, Bonn, 2003, 163–86; and Dirk Walter, *Antisemitische Kriminalität und Gewalt. Judenfeindschaft in der Weimarer Republik*, Bonn, 1999, 111–42. On the *Scheunenviertel* pogrom see Trude Maurer, *Ostjuden in Deutschland, 1918–1933*, Hamburg, 1986, 329–32.
35. See for example Buber, 'Das Judentum und die Menschheit', in: Buber, *Der Jude und sein Judentum*, 21–22. It is another question whether this attempted reconciliation of *völkisch* identity and universal humanism was, theoretically and practically, at all possible.
36. See for example Max Dienemann, 'Über die Bedeutung des Irrationalen für das Liberale Judentum', *Liberales Judentum* 13/4–6 (1921), 27–32; Leo Baeck, 'Geist und Blut', in Leo Baeck, *Wege im Judentum. Aufsätze und Reden*, Berlin, 1933, 72–89.
37. Robert Weltsch, 'In der Zeit der Bedrängnis', *Jüdische Rundschau*, 4 December 1931.
38. Anonymous (Robert Weltsch), 'Zeitschriften-Schau', *Jüdische Rundschau*, 25 November 1932.

Part 3

LIBERAL AMBIGUITIES AND STRATEGIES OF 'WESTERNIZATION'

Chapter 8

BETWEEN EAST AND WEST?
A Liberal Dilemma, 1830–1848/49

Benjamin Schröder

The great political events of 1830 and 1831 seemed neatly to divide the European powers into two opposing camps. In France, the July Revolution brought the 'Citizen King' Louis Philippe to the throne; and Belgium, helped by the constitutional powers France and Britain, became an independent parliamentary monarchy. Yet opposing these progressive forces, there were still reactionary powers to be reckoned with. Crushing the November Uprising in Poland, the tsar made it clear that the conservative monarchies were well able to defend the status quo. This chapter seeks to explore how these shifts influenced conceptions of Europe in the German liberal movement from 1830/31 to the Revolution of 1848/49, focusing primarily on the Rhineland.

In the Prussian Rhine Province, David Hansemann, an Aachen merchant and a leading figure in the liberal movement, saw the different European systems of government as being divided into three groups. In an influential memorandum written in 1830, Hansemann described the first system as resolutely adhering to present conditions and, particularly, to the 'most limitless despotism'. The second system was, on the opposing side, that of the constitutional states – nations such as France, Britain and Belgium. Its main features were freedom of the press and a parliament whose members not only represented the people but had an influence on legislation and the principles of government. So as not to offend his king, and not wanting to appear as a radical, Hansemann introduced a third system – enlightenment, justice, clemency, but without true political freedom – and this allowed him to position Prussia 'in the middle between the other two'. He was convinced, though, that in terms of the political system alone and viewed from an outside perspective, the Prussian monarchy would have to be put into his first category. Reaching similar conclusions, Prince Joseph of Salm-Reifferscheid-Dyck claimed to speak for 'almost nine-tenths' of his fellow deputies in the Rhenish Provincial Diet when he argued that it would not be long before the nations of Europe and the German states would be divided into two blocs according to constitutional principles.[1]

At that time, Rhenish liberals were not yet in close contact with fellow progressives from other regions of the German Confederation – were not, indeed, much organized even amongst themselves. They would start to form a more coordinated movement only from around 1840, when the Prussian regime's grip on the press loosened. That liberals in the south of Germany shared the Rhinelanders' views[2] seems therefore to indicate that these perceptions were ubiquitous in Germany. The pervasiveness of other concepts connected with these views, some of which are discussed below, also points in this direction.

The paradigm of a pan-European ideological confrontation between liberal and conservative powers remained plausible up until the Revolution of 1848/49. As late as 1847, the liberal *Kölnische Zeitung*, which was widely read well beyond the Rhine Province, wrote of two 'parties' facing each other in Europe. One of them, clinging to the 'old forms', subscribed to privileges and tradition; the other believed in progress, the spread of universal ideas beneficial to the public, and eventual political emancipation. The newspaper also associated these parties with geographical categories: 'Whilst in the East bondage [*Unfreiheit*] rules almost without confines, and whilst … it still tries to rise as reaction in the South, the reactionary party is suffering decisive losses in the West every day anew.'[3] The newspaper's editors were not the only ones locating progress in the West and despotism in the East. The debate of the Frankfurt Parliament on principles of German foreign policy held in the Paulskirche in July 1848, for instance, was also structured on the assumption of two ideological blocs. The discussion, as the assembly's president, Heinrich von Gagern, put it, revolved around 'our policies towards the East … and the West'.[4]

As was typical of liberal thinking at the time, the division went beyond signifying a mere difference in systems of government. The idea of liberal emancipation accompanied a conviction that progress was a universal process, and that different nations stood at different stages in this process. In this model, those who spoke a Germanic or Romance language were seen to be more cultured than the Slavs. Even a large encyclopaedia like the *Brockhaus* subscribed to this view, claiming that the difference in degree of civilization among the European peoples neatly coincided with the 'natural' division of the continent into an Eastern and a Western part.[5]

Cognitive Cartographies

Contrary to what was stated in the *Brockhaus*, the geographical categories of 'East' and 'West' were not 'natural', even though – still – they seem to suggest some mathematical objectivity. The representations of spatial and other knowledge in the 'maps' we shape in our minds are far from accurate. The function of these 'mental maps' is mainly to reduce the complexity of the world, enabling us to interact with our environment better. However, this makes them susceptible to influence from subjective assessments and value judgements,[6] as the association of East and West with the attainment of a certain stage in the imagined universal process of progress shows. Moreover, the division of Europe into an Eastern and a Western part was a relatively new concept at the beginning of the nineteenth century. Since the Renaissance, it had been more customary to view the continent as split into a North and a South, a view that went back to the humanists' study of antiquity. It was rendered plausible by the different climate zones and the denominational divide of Catholics in the South and Protestants in the North. Only after the Congress of Vienna had drastically changed the political map did the North–South pattern slowly lose its power of shaping perceptions. In the years leading up to the Crimean War, it was gradually superseded by the division into East and West. Even in the 1840s, many contemporaries still thought of different European regions in terms of North and South.[7]

The political camp of reaction can also be found on this older axis. Warnings of Russia as a 'colossus', a 'power' or a 'barbarian of the North' were ubiquitous in the *Vormärz* period leading up to the March 1848 revolution. However, this seldom implied a constitutional or progressive South. In fact, in the Paulskirche, the Saxon democrat Robert Blum set off 'the tyrant of the North' against 'the free West'.[8] And there was another fundamental difference to the East–West division. In the North–South pattern the reaction could also be located in the South. For instance, a 'despotic South and East of Europe' was constructed as a background against which to point out the good treatment of Jews in France, Holland, Belgium and England.[9] By contrast, the normative connotations of East and West could not be switched so easily. If evoked politically, the West always signified progress and freedom, and no liberal wanted to be in the East.[10]

Still, it is difficult to assess how widespread and pervasive the connection of normative judgements with the geographical categories really was. This is chiefly a methodological problem: by what criteria can something like the spread of an idea be 'measured'? A quantitative approach to this question would be burdened not only by the practical problems of compiling a corpus and establishing comparisons. Its underlying assumption of 'representativeness' seems problematic when allowing for the fragmentary and contingent nature of the source material that has survived. Moreover, how significant would it actually be to know how many times 'the West' and 'the East' appeared across a range of *Vormärz* sources? After all, the persuasive power of an interpretation does not depend solely on its numerical presence in a number of texts. Thus a count in itself will ultimately have little to say about an argument's importance in wider political discussions.

A closer look at how the categories were used and what they entailed, however, offers a greater promise of revealing their importance in contemporary political ideas and discourse. Differing from practice in the second half of the twentieth century, the *Vormärz* thinkers' use of 'the West' focused on Europe exclusively. The term was most often used in reference to France, and it almost never included the U.S.A.[11] Furthermore, East/West terms appeared mostly in constructions such as 'from the', 'in the' or 'towards the' East or West. This usage is very different from how, more than a hundred years later, the opposites became codes for differing ideological systems, the mere words 'East' and 'West' implying attributes such as democratic or liberal as against communist or totalitarian (from a liberal perspective, that is). Hence, it is probably safe to assume that references to the East and the West denoting a confrontation of opposing blocs did not come so naturally in the mid-nineteenth century. However, the connection between certain values and these geographical categories seems to have been strong enough for a journalist to expect his readers to understand when he made a passing allusion to 'the hostile principles of the East and the West'.[12] A correspondent of the *Kölnische Zeitung* must also have assumed that the connotation with despotism was common currency when he reported that someone at a celebration of the Treaty of Verdun in Berlin had 'warned of the East'.[13] Likewise, the newspaper contended that 'the civilized West' had left its mark on the Polish nobility.[14]

It is perhaps no coincidence that the West here appears with the attribute 'civilized', whereas to evoke notions of tyranny and barbarism it seems to have been sufficient to talk of 'the East' with no qualification. The image of despotism had been linked with the East for a long time.

'The East' traditionally denoted the Orient, a foreign region in Asia, well outside Europe. Indeed, even in the nineteenth century encyclopaedias still defined 'East' with reference to the Orient.[15] What was new was that this category could now be applied to Russia, which thereby moved further away on the mental map German liberals held. When Tsar Alexander I abandoned his liberal views from 1818 onwards, Russia came to be viewed as a (half-)Asian power. It began its move from the 'North' to the 'East' of Europe, and its image became associated with the elements of danger, violence, tyranny and unpredictability which had been characteristic of descriptions of the Orient since the days when the Ottoman Empire threatened Europe. In the historical process, the *Kölnische Zeitung*'s liberal editor, Karl Heinrich Brüggemann, wrote that Russia had now taken over the role of 'active resistance' against the 'free spirit of the Occident [*Abendland*]'.[16]

Beside the older label of 'power of the North' (or some similar term) it now became customary to call Russians 'barbarians in the East'.[17] Even encyclopaedias adopted this kind of description. Russians were seen as imitators without any inventiveness of their own; they were described as reluctant, deceitful, greedy and, for good measure, prone to alcoholism.[18] All this implied the exclusion of Russia from a civilized Europe which, at the time, quite naturally included nations like Hungary or Poland. However, the normative category of the 'East' frequently extended to the European continent itself, as some of the quotations above show. Poles and other Slavs on the borderlands of Austria, Prussia and Russia were then also described in terms following the pattern of a colonial discourse. These peoples, the *Kölnische Zeitung* contended, had not achieved any cultural accomplishments in their own right, nor could they be trusted to defend themselves (and Europe) against the barbaric Russians and Turks further to the southeast. It was the Germans who had once made them abandon their nomadic life, and only a strong connection with Germany could protect them from 'the flood from Asia'.[19]

The image of a despotic, backward and barbaric 'East' meant, in turn, a positive self-definition of the West as civilized, progressive and free. This self-definition was often only implied, without any explicit use of the term 'West'. There was, however, even a newspaper that carried the very word in its title. In 1831/32 the liberal journalist Philipp Jakob Siebenpfeiffer, one of the organizers of the Hambach Festival, published the short-lived *Bote aus Westen*, which was renamed *Westbote* in January 1832. Its title was meant to announce a programme. In the first issue the newspaper let its readers know that it could not make Germany its centre of attention because the world was divided into the two main camps – one of movement and one of stagnation; and France was leading in the progressive camp.

Figure 8.1. *Der Bote aus Westen* masthead, 1831. Courtesy of the Siebenpfeiffer-Stiftung Homburg, facsimile: Martin Baus.

Therefore, the 'messenger from the West', as it constantly referred to itself, reported particularly on the 'Western countries' of Europe – France, Spain, Portugal, Britain, Belgium and Italy. It was committed to spreading enlightened ideas and to promoting 'liberty', yet also 'order'.[20]

From July to December 1831 the top of its title page depicted a visualization of this mission (see Figure 8.1). According to an explanation by the editors the picture was meant to outline 'the West and the spirit of the time and this paper'. A rising sun in the background symbolized the light; a 'mighty lime tree' stood for 'constitutional liberty'; a Gallic cock, guarding the French constitution, was a reference to 'the West'; and Clio, the Muse of History watching the scene, was inscribing her impressions into the 'loose leaves' of the *Westbote*.[21]

Whether everyone understood these elaborate symbols is difficult to say. After all, the editors of Siebenpfeiffer's newspaper did feel the need to explain them to their readers. The *Bote* shows, however, that the association of the 'West' with positive values and the 'East' as something negative was also understood at a very simple level. In September 1831 a correspondent reported that the little village of Wolfstein had made a collection of money to support the Polish struggle for independence. Three locals were missing from the list of contributors, though. Among them was the Protestant Pastor Jacob, who had, the correspondent wrote, promised to have a sermon printed instead. Jacob himself was not too pleased when his apparent refusal to donate was thus drawn into the public sphere. 'What I do or do not want to do for the Poles is nobody else's business', he wrote in a letter to the editors. Everyone who knew him was aware of his enthusiasm for the good cause of the Polish people and of his sense of community. Reading the contribution that put him in the spotlight, people would now be disappointed with the newspaper, the pastor claimed: 'What a shame! that the messenger from the West, precisely *this* messenger, sometimes seems to be – a messenger from the far East – what a shame! that *this* fighter for truth, justice, and liberty is sometimes – impolite!'[22]

The *Westbote* also demonstrates that there was a European dimension to the normative connotations of geographical concepts in the early nineteenth century. Like many other German newspapers, it had correspondents not only in Germany but in other European countries too. Furthermore, it included translations or synopses of articles from other periodicals. Speaking of a 'civilized Europe', or mentioning that there was not one among four hundred human beings in Russia whose education had raised them above the animals, it sometimes quoted foreign newspapers, in this case the French *Journal des débats* and the English *Courier*.[23] Obviously, German liberals were not the only ones to hold such views.[24] Unfortunately, it is beyond the scope of this chapter to explore such thinking from a European perspective. Some comments on how German, and particularly Rhenish, liberals were placed and where they saw themselves within the bigger European context can, however, be attempted.

Asserting Their Place

Liberals maintained many connections to those European nations they located in their 'West'. Besides the reception of French or English newspapers, there were also the political exiles, most famously Heinrich Heine, who remained in contact with those back home. Moreover, many Germans travelled to Belgium, France and Britain. This is particularly true of entrepreneurs like the aforementioned David Hansemann, who were the leaders of liberalism in the Prussian Rhine Province.[25] Whilst it could be argued that German liberals thus formed part of a larger network of communication and commerce extending over exactly those regions included in their mental concept of the West, the same cannot be said for a reach into Eastern Europe. At least in the Rhineland, liberals saw little reason to go to Russia or Poland. For the latter, what contact there was with Germany broke off when the social, cultural and political elites left Poland in the 'Great Emigration' after the failed uprising of 1830.[26]

So perhaps it is not surprising that many Germans had few qualms about speaking of their neighbours to the East as underdeveloped barbarians.

Of course, there were also negative stereotypes about other peoples in Western Europe. The French, for instance, were thought to be more superficial (and livelier) than the Germans, who in turn were known for their profundity (paid for with a certain ponderousness).[27] But these stereotypes were a far cry from the contemptuous depictions of Russians or Poles. On the whole, German liberals looked towards the West as an example. Here they saw political freedom and the rule of law realized – ideals for which they still had to fight at home. To the entrepreneurs within the liberal movement, the progressiveness of the Western nations was also evident in their economic development. Germany stood only just at the beginning of the industrialization developing in Belgium and, particularly, in England. Within the paradigm of progress as a universal political and social process, these impressions, taken together, showed German liberals the backwardness of their own nation.

In the Prussian Rhine Province, this was probably more evident than elsewhere. Badenese liberals, for instance, could at least boast of having a constitution of their own. Consequently, they probably felt much closer to the 'West', at least during a short period in the early 1830s when there was hardly any conflict between them and their own seemingly liberal prince and government. At that time, some of them even favoured siding with the French against the other German states in a potential armed struggle for freedom in Europe.[28] The Rhine Province, by contrast, had fallen to Prussia in 1816 and there was no constitution in sight. Among Rhinelanders the Prussian regime was noted for its illiberalism and militarism. Clearly, with 'the exception of Russia and Austria, all the important nations of Europe stand at a higher level of political progress than Prussia', Heinrich von Sybel (the historian's father) told fellow deputies at the Eighth Rhenish Provincial Diet in 1845.[29]

At the same time, the Rhinelanders themselves felt very much advanced on the road of progress. They still had the modern judicial system of the Napoleonic period and they fought vigorously against attempts by the Prussian authorities to abolish it in favour of new laws based on the *Allgemeines Landrecht*. As a more urban, trade-oriented society, the Rhine Province was also economically far ahead of the Prussian heartlands, and also of most other German regions, which were still largely rural. Aachen and the Wupper valley were two important centres of early German industrialization, and a city like Cologne, with its rich urban tradition, was seen to be culturally at eye level with the big European metropolises. These views were strong enough to feed a certain sense of mission. David Hansemann, for instance, wrote in his 1830 memorandum that the

Rhineland had come to Prussia to demonstrate what the 'new state of civilization' would eventually look like in the Eastern provinces.[30] It is also indicative that, on some occasions, the Prussian heartland moved further away on Rhenish mental maps. Thus the Hohenzollern crown prince could appear as 'a foreign curiosity from the steppes of Asia' to Gustav Mevissen when he came to Düsseldorf in 1836;[31] and Karl Stedmann, a deputy in the provincial diet and in the Paulskirche, located Berlin 'there in the East', where the monarch, pretending to be a 'personified God-given universal law', still thought he could ignore public opinion and rule with 'bayonets, speeches, much palaver, and uniforms'.[32]

Consequently, liberals, and particularly those in the Rhine Province, found themselves caught in the middle, just as Hansemann suggested in his 1830 memorandum. This could be linked to geographical discourse, which since the seventeenth century had tended to situate Germany in the very centre of Europe.[33] In a publication on the constitutional question, the Bonn lawyer Hugo Hälschner put it in the following way. At the moment Prussia's policies were contradictory and there were two different paths she could choose. If the king summoned a state-wide assembly, this would entail Prussia 'decidedly' joining 'Western Europe' and identifying with Germany outwardly. In order to continue to 'belong to the East', however, it would not be enough to deny the people a representative assembly. Every bit of progress attained so far – Hälschner cited provincial diets, the community constitution, the present condition of the press – would have to be 'retroactively destroyed and nullified'.[34]

Yet the attraction of the West for liberals who saw themselves in the middle was not always so obvious. In fact, there was a certain ambiguity in the liberal rhetoric. This was nowhere more obvious than during the debates in the Paulskirche.

Conclusion

As Manfred Meyer pointed out, in the Frankfurt parliament liberals were far more hesitant in wanting to belong to the West than were the radical democrats on the Left.[35] The Finance Minister of the revolutionary executive in Frankfurt, Hermann von Beckerath, for instance, argued that Germany should 'lean neither to the West nor to the East', instead 'using its own force of gravity, on itself'.[36] Such remarks need to be seen in context, though. In the debate, Beckerath and other liberals were arguing against a motion by the radical Left proposing a closer alliance with France. Liberals, whilst expressing solidarity with their Western neighbour, favoured a more independent German nation state. Their aim was sovereignty as much as liberty. In this sense, positioning Germany in the centre of Europe helped to set it off against the other European nation states. In contrast to radical tactics, putting Germany at the centre was also useful for encouraging a separate, more cautious way of achieving the goal of a united and free nation. This corresponded to the liberals' own fear of revolution and social disorder; it was of tactical use in the fight for political emancipation through agreements with the German princes; and in some way it made a virtue out of necessity. Was there not at least one advantage in lagging behind the progressive powers in the West? By looking at them and following their example, negative aspects of the new developments – such as the poverty associated with industrialization – could be avoided, if progress was adapted to the peculiarities of the German situation. The middle position seemed more attractive if it meant favouring a policy of stepping forward cautiously instead of rushing into a more radical new form of government.

Finally, liberal arguments in the Paulskirche were far from unequivocal. In the same speech in which he saw Germany's future as being in the centre of Europe, Hermann von Beckerath also clearly positioned it in the civilized West, setting it off against a barbaric East. In a climate nervous of a possible armed conflict – characteristic of the Paulskirche debate, and indeed of much of *Vormärz* liberal discourse[37] – Beckerath tried to reassure the parliamentarians that Russia would be wise enough not to start a war. Facing the 'movement of the European West', he argued, it was in the same situation as the European powers had been vis-à-vis the French Revolution (and everyone still knew how that war had ended).[38]

Perhaps this ambiguity goes some way towards answering the question of why German liberals all of a sudden started painting Russia as an underdeveloped tyranny in the early nineteenth century. The image of a despot in the East helped them deal with the cognitive dissonance of feeling progressive themselves whilst at the same time being conscious of their own nation's backwardness compared with France, England and even the small monarchy of Belgium. It was reassuring that, despite everything that was amiss in Germany, at least when they looked at the barbarians in the East, liberals clearly knew where their place was: it was among the civilized peoples of Europe.

Notes

1. Both memoranda are in Joseph Hansen (ed.), *Rheinische Briefe und Akten zur Geschichte der politischen Bewegung 1830–1850*, 2 vols, Essen & Bonn, 1919–1942, vol. 1 (1830–1848), 11–87, here 15–17, 20, 75, 86.

2. See (including a more detailed survey of the political events) Manfred Meyer, *Freiheit und Macht. Studien zum Nationalismus süddeutscher, insbesondere badischer Liberaler 1830–1848*, Frankfurt/Main et al., 1994, 88–95. Meyer did not explicitly analyse *Vormärz* concepts of the 'West', but his own terminology seems to confirm my findings.
3. 'Das Ausland im Januar 1847', *Kölnische Zeitung*, 4 February 1847.
4. *Reden für die deutsche Nation. Stenographischer Bericht über die Verhandlungen der deutschen constituirenden Nationalversammlung zu Frankfurt am Main*, ed. Franz Wigard, Frankfurt/Main, 1848/49, reprint Munich 1979/80, vol. 2, 1098–116, here 1098.
5. 'Europa', *Allgemeine deutsche Real-Encyklopädie für die gebildeten Stände (Conversations-Lexikon)*, 8th edn, 12 vols, Leipzig, 1833–37, vol. 3 (1833), 731–36. The same article can be found from the fifth edition onwards (1819/20). In the fourth edition Europe was also divided into the German-Roman people in the West and the Slavs in the East, but the latter were not mentioned in such a negative light (1817–19: the relevant volume is dated 1817).
6. Frithjof Benjamin Schenk, 'Mental Maps. Die Konstruktion von geographischen Räumen in Europa seit der Aufklärung', *Geschichte und Gesellschaft* 28/3 (2002), 493–514.
7. Hans Lemberg, 'Zur Entstehung des Osteuropabegriffs im 19. Jahrhundert. Vom "Norden" zum "Osten" Europas', *Jahrbücher für Geschichte Osteuropas* 33/1 (1985), 48–91; Bernhard Struck, *Nicht West – nicht Ost. Frankreich und Polen in der Wahrnehmung deutscher Reisender zwischen 1750 und 1850*, Göttingen, 2006, 171–92. For the Rhineland see, as an example, 'Ein Blick auf den Süden Frankreichs', *Rheinische Zeitung*, 12/15 January 1843 (supplements); or Karl Heinrich Brüggemann, 'Rückblick. II. Die kirchliche Bewegung', *Kölnische Zeitung*, 27 January 1846.
8. *Stenographischer Bericht*, vol. 2, 1109. See also 'Rheinbayern. Polen.', *Der Bote aus Westen*, 19 August 1831; Meyer, *Freiheit und Macht*, 99; 'Berlin, 12. August', *Aachener Zeitung*, 16 August 1846; and 'Die Russen im Kaukasus', *Kölnische Zeitung*, 27 July 1847.
9. 'Juden', *Neues Rheinisches Conversations-Lexicon oder encyclopädisches Handwörterbuch für gebildete Stände*, 3rd edn, 12 vols, Cologne, 1833–1837, vol. 7 (1834), 246.
10. I know of one exception: Friedrich List dreamt of 'founding a mighty Eastern German-Magyar Empire' (1842) – cited in Klaus Thörner, *'Der ganze Südosten ist unser Hinterland'. Deutsche Südosteuropapläne von 1840 bis 1945*, Freiburg, 2008, 28 f. It is hard to believe that Carl Vogt should actually have warned of 'a river of barbarism' from 'the West'; see *Stenographischer Bericht*, vol. 2, 1106. The context of his speech suggests he actually meant to say 'the East'. Perhaps it is a typo?
11. Again, I know of one exception: in his *Allgemeine Geschichte* Karl von Rotteck referred to 'reason and the rule of natural law' building an 'exquisite empire in the West, in the young new world' of the U.S.A. (1826). Quoted in Meyer, *Freiheit und Macht*, 93.
12. 'Rheinbayern. Die nächste Aussicht. Zweiter Artikel', *Der Bote aus Westen*, 10 October 1831.
13. 'Berlin, 7. Aug.', *Kölnische Zeitung*, 12 August 1843. See also 'Berlin, 26. Juli', *Rheinische Zeitung*, 30 July 1842.
14. 'Preußen und sein Antheil von Polen', *Kölnische Zeitung*, 31 March 1846.
15. 'Ost, Osten' and 'Orient', *Allgemeine deutsche Real-Encyklopädie*, 8th edn, vol. 8 (1835), 160, 113 and 9th edn, vol. 10 (1846), 560, 508.
16. 'Rückblick', *Kölnische Zeitung*, 11 January 1846 and 8 February 1846. Cf. 'Die politische Lage', *Kölnische Zeitung*, 17 January 1847, where the terms 'East' and

'West' are used in this context. See Lemberg, 'Zur Entstehung des Osteuropabegriffs im 19. Jahrhundert', 67 f., 74 f.; also Stefan Wolle, '"Das Reich der Sklaverey und die teutsche Libertät…" Die Ursprünge der Rußlandfeindschaft des deutschen Liberalismus', and Mechthild Keller, 'Es teilen sich die Geister. Pressestimmen von den Karlsbader Beschlüssen bis zur Reichsgründung', both in Mechthild Keller (ed.), *Russen und Rußland aus deutscher Sicht. 19. Jahrhundert. Von der Jahrhundertwende bis zur Reichsgründung (1800–1871)*, Munich, 1992, 417–34, 739–65.

17. E.g., in 'Österreich, 26. Januar', *Aachener Zeitung*, 4 February 1845.
18. 'Rußland, geographisch-statistisch', *Neues Rheinisches Conversations-Lexikon*, 3rd edn, vol. 10 (1835), 260–87, here 263 f., 274 f.
19. 'Unsere Gränznachbarn. Die Ostseite. II.', *Kölnische Zeitung*, 19 September 1845. See also Struck, *Nicht West – nicht Ost*, 422–27; Thörner, *'Der ganze Südosten ist unser Hinterland'*, 19–67; and Christian Pletzing, *Vom Völkerfrühling zum nationalen Konflikt. Deutscher und polnischer Nationalismus in Ost- und Westpreußen 1830–1871*, Wiesbaden, 2003, 99–117.
20. *Der Bote aus Westen*, 12 March 1831; 'Erklärung der Redaction', *Der Bote aus Westen*, 13 June 1831 (supplement).
21. 'Hony soit qui mal y pense', *Der Bote aus Westen*, 5 July 1831.
22. 'Rheinbayern', *Der Bote aus Westen*, 16 September 1831; 'An die Redaktion des Boten aus Westen', *Der Bote aus Westen*, 27 September 1831.
23. 'Polen', *Der Bote aus Westen*, 20 June 1831; 'Frankreich und England in Bezug auf Belgien', *Der Bote aus Westen*, 25 June 1831.
24. See Larry Wolff, *Inventing Eastern Europe. The Map of Civilization on the Mind of the Enlightenment*, Stanford, 1994; Ezequiel Adamovsky, *Euro-Orientalism. Liberal Ideology and the Image of Russia in France (ca. 1740–1800)*, Oxford, 2006.
25. Joseph Hansen, *Gustav von Mevissen. Ein rheinisches Lebensbild 1815–1899*, vol. 1, Berlin, 1906, 164 f., 230; Martin Schumacher, *Auslandsreisen deutscher Unternehmer 1750–1851 unter besonderer Berücksichtigung von Rheinland und Westfalen*, Cologne, 1968, esp. 123–64.
26. Struck, *Nicht West – nicht Ost*, 319–21, 422–27, 431 f., 452 f.
27. This conviction was not exclusive to Germans. See, for example, an article apparently adapted from a French periodical: 'Der französische und deutsche Charakter', *Rheinische Zeitung*, 28 May 1842.
28. Meyer, *Freiheit und Macht*, 92–99.
29. Hansen, *Rheinische Briefe und Akten*, vol. 1, 817; see also 517, 885.
30. Hansen, *Rheinische Briefe und Akten*, vol. 1, 76; see, for example, James M. Brophy, *Popular Culture and the Public Sphere in the Rhineland, 1800–1850*, Cambridge, 2007, 210 f., 216–52, 308–10; Gerhard Brunn, 'Zentrale und Provinz in der preußischen Geschichte vom Wiener Kongreß bis zur Revolution von 1848', in Dieter Kastner and Georg Mölich (eds), *Die Rheinlande und Preußen. Parlamentarismus, Parteien und Wirtschaft*, Cologne, 1990, 27–39.
31. Hansen, *Gustav von Mevissen*, vol. 1, 189 f.
32. Barbara Schubert, *Karl Stedmann (1804–1878). Kindheit, Jugend und die Zeit seines politischen Wirkens*, Munich, 1985, 43 f.
33. Hans-Dietrich Schultz, 'Fantasies of *Mitte*, *Mittellage* and *Mitteleuropa* in German Geographical Discussions of the 19th and 20th Century', *Political Geography Quarterly* 8/4 (1989), 315–39, here 317.
34. Hugo Hälschner, *Die preußische Verfassungsfrage und die Politik der rheinischen ritterbürtigen Autonomen*, Bonn, 1846, 34 f.

35. Manfred Meyer, 'Das konstitutionelle Deutschland und der Westen. Tradition und Wandel nationaler Konzepte in Südwestdeutschland 1830–1848', in Helmut Reinalter (ed.), *Die Anfänge des Liberalismus und der Demokratie in Deutschland und Österreich 1830–1848/49*, Frankfurt/Main et al., 2002, 191–212.
36. *Stenographischer Bericht*, vol. 2, 1112–14.
37. Alexa Geisthövel, *Restauration und Vormärz 1815–1847*, Paderborn et al., 2008, 46.
38. *Stenographischer Bericht*, vol. 2, 1112–14.

Chapter 9

BEFORE 'THE WEST'
Rudolf von Gneist's English Utopia

Frank Lorenz Müller

The death of Rudolf von Gneist (1816–1895), the London *Times* explained in its obituary, deprived Germany of 'one of her greatest and most renowned jurists and politicians'.[1] This tribute summed up the double role he had played. Throughout most of his adult life, this erudite, prolific and immensely influential legal scholar had also pursued a clear political purpose: to reform and improve the constitutional, legal, administrative and political structures of the Prusso-German body politic. His many years of public duty saw him join the Berlin City Council, the Prussian Landtag and the German Reichstag. He served as a judge, a university professor, Dean of the Berlin Law Faculty and Rector of the University. Gneist tutored the German Crown Prince Wilhelm and was appointed to the Prussian Council of State (*Staatsrat*). A chairman of the *Centralverein für das Wohl der arbeitenden Klassen* and later the founding president of the *Verein für Socialpolitik*, he showed a real and lasting commitment to issues of social policy and he also took a determined public stance against the anti-Semitism of the late Bismarck era.

Looking to England: Gneist and a 'Liberal Tradition'

Notwithstanding the enormous range and variety of Gneist's activities, the intellectual narrative he chose to offer his compatriots remained doggedly focused on a single dominant topic – a single image he spent decades exploring, analysing, describing and presenting to his German audiences. It was in the constitutional history and workings of the English state that Gneist believed he could find the lodestar that would guide Prussians and Germans towards a solution to their current political problems. For 'as Roman law had become an example for the private law of the continent in the late middle ages', Gneist observed in his contribution to a prominent political encyclopaedia in 1859, 'Great Britain has, since the late eighteenth century, become the examplar of public law and, in a manner of speaking, the yardstick against which the nations of the continent have become accustomed to measure their notions of a free constitution'. Since the French Revolution of 1789 the world had been confronted with frightening clashes of opposing interests, he argued a few years later, but this only underlined the 'enormous importance of the English body politic [Staatswesen] for the continent' since it offered 'proof that these clashes were capable of resolution'; proof that 'liberty of the nations has been gained and can be gained'.[2]

It is interesting to note, however, that for all Gneist's concentration on the political example provided by Britain – a polity located in Western Europe – the wider political notion of the West is entirely absent from his analytical horizon and his political lexicon. In the few instances where the word is used at all, it serves a purely geographical function and is never employed to suggest a transnational 'Western' model in a modern sense. By charting the salient contours of Gneist's image of a specifically British form of politics against the background of his own biography and his political preferences and aversions, this chapter seeks to throw light on the political outlook of an important strand of nineteenth-century German liberalism, and illuminate especially its attitude to 'Western' paradigms. Ever since Sherlock Holmes it has been clear that the absence of something that should have happened – the dog that did not bark in the night – can constitute a most remarkable event. Gneist's stubborn refusal to conceptualize or employ the notion of the West thus provides an instructive insight into the political imagery of Germany's liberalism in the nineteenth century. It suggests which vistas were obscured by deeply entrenched attitudes to revolution, democracy and monarchism and lays bare how much men like Gneist said about the West by refusing to speak its name.

By looking to Britain in his search for political solutions, Gneist conformed to a well established pattern amongst post-Enlightenment liberals. Ever since Montesquieu, admiration for what was deemed to be the British order of things had been common across the whole of continental Europe – even amongst conservatives. But there were some particularly outspoken Anglophiles amongst the liberals of the German *Vormärz*. An awe-struck Friedrich Christoph Dahlmann contrasted Britain's status as a 'watchtower of freedom' with the 'nothingness' of the Germans, while Carl Welcker deplored the 'childishness' of German politics which could bear no comparison with the 'totality of English conditions' that together gave that country honour, freedom, power and progress. 'Liberalism has for years pointed to England as the country from which we can learn an endless amount in political terms', the liberal lawyer Hugo Preuß concluded in 1886, welcoming the fact that Britain now had generally replaced France as a guiding example for Germany's development. To prove that the foundations for this development had been laid by the profound insights of German *Staatswissenschaft* – the academic study of the state – Preuß continued, one only had to mention the name Gneist.[3]

Notwithstanding Gneist's prominent role within this liberal discourse and his steady focus on the establishment and protection of political freedom as the hallmark of the 'paragon of a parliamentary state' (*parlamentarischer Musterstaat*)[4] exemplified in Britain, Gneist's record has been criticized on this very count. In his exploration of the 'German Idea of Freedom' Leonard Krieger took Gneist to task for propagating a concept of a legally ordered state (*Rechtsstaat*) from which all 'oppositional elements had been removed'. Instead of granting a guaranteed sphere of individual rights, the state now merely needed to conform to general rules and allow its measures to be open to judicial review. Otto Pflanze similarly chided the group of mid nineteenth-century German liberals for the 'limitations of their understanding of the constitutional systems of Western Europe and America which they thought to emulate'. Erich Angermann's verdict on Gneist, that he combined 'Anglomania' and liberal ideas with 'old Prussian-conservative, sometimes even reactionary thoughts' and 'professorial dogmatism', was also less than complimentary.[5]

Moreover, critics of the great jurist did not only query his liberal credentials and his alleged failure to endorse the Western paradigm of constitutional government. They also questioned the correctness of his interpretation of the English constitution. The liberal jurist Julius Hatschek (1872–1926) pointed out that Gneist's work was not free of a mistake only too common amongst students of British politics: ascribing to British law the very features they considered necessary for their own domestic politics. Legal scholars such as Conrad Bornhak (1861–1944) and Emil Seckel (1864–1924) raised similar concerns.[6] Striking a noticeably harsher tone, the Austrian Josef Redlich (1869–1936) found Gneist's work 'not only obsolete' but wrong: he remarked that 'the general idea of the modern political history of England, as given by Gneist, stood in inexplicable contradiction to the real development and the true nature of the political facts'. More recent appraisals have continued in this critical vein with Hugh Whalen, Reinhard Lamer and Erich Hahn accusing Gneist, respectively, of 'misjudg[ing] the role of the emerging middle classes', of having 'turned the reality of the English constitution onto its head' and of 'glaring and unresolved contradictions'.[7]

Though the thrust of these criticisms is largely justified, Redlich was mistaken in calling the shortcomings and incongruities in Gneist's work 'inexplicable'. On the contrary, the two main accusations against Gneist – the undemocratic, pseudo-parliamentary, non-Western quality of his political endeavour, and the distorted account of British politics given in his work – are certainly capable of a coherent explanation. They are intrinsically linked and help to explain why Britain loomed so large for this eminent German liberal thinker, while the concept of the West did not feature at all. Gneist's commitment to a moderately liberal, anti-democratic monarchical constitutionalism – a political persuasion Angermann has called the 'significantly right-wing liberalism of the notables' – made him seek out a utopian version of eighteenth-century British polity to guide German developments in the nineteenth century. In Gneist's opinion, intellectual examination of the history and system of English self-government would assuredly produce 'principles applicable to our situation'.[8]

The political motives driving this process not only compelled Gneist to offer a reading of Britain's pre-1832 constitution that was, at the very least, selective; they also gave him no option but to regard Britain's development after the Great Reform Act as one of corruption and decline. Moreover, given the strong anti-revolutionary bias characteristic of Prusso-German liberalism in the second half of the nineteenth century and its search for a consensual and elite-driven political transformation within a monarchical framework, Gneist was unlikely to draw inspiration from the French and North American experiences.

'Governmental Through and Through': Gneist's Prussian Career

Rudolf Gneist's professional career and political development fit well into the pattern of moderate national liberalism in nineteenth-century Germany. Born in Berlin in 1816, he belonged, in the words of the American jurist Munroe Smith, 'both on his father's side and on his mother's, to that official class which for more than a century had been the only political class in Prussia'. The son of a low-ranking Prussian judge, he spent much of his youth in the care of his uncle, a Protestant pastor in

Pomerania, before attending the Royal Grammar School in Eisleben and later enrolling at the University of Berlin to study law. This was in 1833. The brilliant student graduated three years later and embarked on a dual career as an official within the Prussian legal service and an academic jurist. Having been appointed a lecturer in 1839, an assistant judge in 1843 and a non-tenured professor in 1845, Gneist was to find that his further advancement would be delayed by the revolutionary events of 1848/9. The young scholar took an active role during those months – pushing for the rights of junior staff within the university, serving as an elected member of the Berlin City Council and arguing forcefully for a constitutional arrangement which respected the rights of both crown and parliament. Though Gneist had never expressed anti-monarchical views, he was out of favour and under police surveillance throughout much of the post-revolutionary period and had to wait until 1858 to secure a full professorship. The 'New Era', which heralded a liberal thaw in Prussian politics, saw Gneist elected to the Prussian Landtag, where he eventually aligned himself with the Left-Centre liberal Bockum-Dolffs caucus. As the 'New Era' gave way to the Constitutional Conflict, the gifted speaker and analytical thinker quickly emerged as a prominent and effective parliamentary opponent of the government. Gneist castigated Bismarck's government for the illegality of its actions in army reform and budgetary control. He even refused to support the 1866 Indemnity Bill by which the government sought retrospective authorization from parliament. Later, however, Gneist did endorse Bismarck's policy of annexations after the Austro-Prussian War.[9]

From then on Gneist, like the bulk of Germany's liberal-national movement, became a wholehearted supporter of the project that Bismarck led, to found and consolidate a German constitutional nation state under the aegis of Prussia. As a Reichstag and Landtag deputy for the National Liberal Party, he played an important part in the reform of Prussia's rural communities (*Kreisordnung*), accepted Bismarck's invitation to join the legal board of the Foreign Office, influenced the reordering of local taxation and took a firmly anti-Catholic line in the *Kulturkampf*. Convinced of the necessity of Bismarck's anti-socialist campaign, and also of its legality, Gneist advocated restricting the activities of the Social Democrats – even after the legislation had lapsed in 1890. Unlike the Left-Liberal wing of the National Liberals, Gneist remained a supporter of the government's policies after 1878/79, so that, by 1888, Bismarck could confidently call him 'loyal and governmental through and through'.[10]

His loyalty, tireless devotion to public service and scholarly productivity earned Gneist a rich harvest of official honours. Among them were: appointment to the Prussian Council of State in 1885; the title *Wirklicher*

Geheimer Oberjustizrat in 1886; ennoblement and decoration with the order *Pour le Mérite* in 1888; and the title 'Excellency' in 1895. Gneist's life was thus a demonstration of the opportunities for public service in the fields that were to play such a central role in the political precepts at the heart of his academic work: law, administration and parliament. His biography shows that one could advance on merit – in his case, from commoner to nobleman, from impecunious student to wealthy professor.

Gneist's England: 'Self-government', Liberty and Power

The second half of Gneist's life, the period of his great successes, was also the time when he engaged with the topic that was to define him as a scholar: Britain's public law and constitution. Gneist travelled to Britain in 1845, 1846, 1848 and 1850, each time staying in London for more than a month and taking a lively interest in legal matters. Beginning with his 1853 treatise *Adel und Ritterschaft in England* (Nobility and Gentry in England) and his *Geschichte und heutige Gestalt der Ämter in England* (History and Present State of Offices in England) of 1857, Gneist embarked on a publishing programme of breathtaking productivity. His 'English Constitutional and Administrative Law' eventually grew to three thousand pages, filling four hefty volumes; and there were numerous further supplementary volumes, monographs and articles. It was clear even to Gneist's contemporaries that the motivation that drove him to visit and revisit this topic in such exhaustive detail (and often with tedious repetition) was not purely scholarly. 'Each of his works on political science had not only a political tendency, but a direct political purpose', Conrad Bornhak wrote in 1896. 'His investigations were not merely to spread information of one of the most important civilized nations of the world … . English law furnished him with the most suitable means from which to deduce general propositions valid for modern Europe, concerning the relation of state and society.' The New York jurist Munroe Smith even detected a 'propagandist character' in Gneist's work that advocated 'the recognition and acceptance of the principles which he found embodied in certain English institutions and the development, in accordance with these principles, of equivalent Prussian and German institutions'.[11]

Gneist was drawn to Britain because it seemed to him to provide a remedy for the political woes of the nineteenth century – the problems for which France was largely responsible, but which it had failed to solve. There was, Gneist argued in 1864, a wonderful contrast between 'the revolutions of the continent, in which enthusiasm for the idea of liberty produce[d] violence and oppression', and eighteenth-century Britain. In the latter he found 'an era of great legislation which established the political freedom of the people'. Stress on the difference between the pernicious revolutionary developments on the European continent and the political idyll in Britain was to become a fundamental theme in Gneist's writing. 'Whereas the course of the French movement appears to result in irreconcilable oppositions, in implacable hostility amongst the social classes, in the impossibility of the ideal of political and individual freedom,' he wrote in 1869, 'the British state [englische Staatsbildung] offers a positive answer to the problems to which the French have so far always offered a negative one'. A few years later, after the events of the Paris Commune, Gneist observed even more starkly that 'the "harmony of interests" which arose as a slogan from the new French society [was] a pious wish after exhausting struggles which end[ed] without reconciliation. The burning of the Louvre and of the Hôtel de Ville in the French capital ha[d] once again thrown light on the social motto égalité, fraternité, liberté'. Germany's failure to keep pace politically in the course of the last generation, Gneist argued disapprovingly in 1872, was connected with the tendency of German society 'almost always to follow French and Belgian examples'.[12]

Gneist identified the magic ingredient that was responsible for Britain's superiority and would also solve Germany's problems in his very first publication on British law. Like the mainstream German liberals of the post-1851 period, he reacted to recent developments in France by abandoning an exclusive belief in the efficacy of parliamentary institutions, and he embraced other perspectives. In *Adel und Ritterschaft in England*, he not only gave a detailed account of the numerous ranks of nobility in Britain but presented a system characterized by dynamism and permeability. He observed that thrift, industry, courage, devotion and ability allowed commoners to join a highly respected and effective elite, making Britain's aristocracy, in Gneist's eyes, not just an aristocracy by birth, but something much more meritocratic: an aristocracy by wealth and achievement. Gneist's praise for this phenomenon was not merely a call for middle-class emancipation – with an unmistakable admixture of autobiographical elements – but also an exhortation to the Prussian nobility of his day.[13]

In Britain it was this social formation, made up 'mainly of the owners of knightly estates, but also of councillors, local lawyers, ecclesiastical and other urban notables' that formed the heart of a system of local 'self-government'. Gneist regarded this as the very root that produced and sustained Britain's superior political structures. As royally appointed justices of the peace and administrators in their localities, these unpaid local notables performed a crucial governmental and educative task. 'Only the daily practice of a communal life exercised with great sobriety can restore the realization that the free state is based on the fulfilment of communal obligation', Gneist declared in 1859. Five years later he added that it was 'the school of communal life in counties, towns and parishes which provides even the most extreme parties ... with an understanding of the state'. He ascribed a 'morally cleansing force to every serious, personal, independent act within the state' (*die sittlich läuternde Kraft jeder ernsten persönlichen Selbstthätigkeit im Staat*).[14]

In 1869 Gneist gave a detailed explanation of how 'self-government', the performance of local administrative and legal roles by the holders of honorific offices, had worked to secure the 'connection between state and society':

> It maintained for centuries the preeminent position of the higher estates [*höhere Stände*] which was lost on the continent; for it linked those elements which had separated on the continent because of a shifting of the burdens of the state: intelligence, efficiency and activity of the professional civil service with the independence and strength of character of property that does not rely on salary and grace.
>
> It maintained the harmony amongst the propertied, middling and working classes by placing upon the higher ones multiple personal duties .... By legalizing and ennobling the unchangeable relationship between property and work through the discharge of official duties [*staatliche Pflichten*] it gains the willing recognition of the other classes. ...
>
> It enables Parliament to control the dispatch of governmental business effectively, for experience teaches us that no one is capable of controlling the kind of business that he does not know how to conduct himself to a certain degree.[15]

For Gneist, the 'prophet of self-government', everything grew out of this fertile local soil. He understood the House of Commons to be a body collectively representing the nation's various localities and a small number of other corporations such as the universities. And as the 'importance and range of self-government' had expanded from century to century, 'so had the power of the lower house, compared to which the upper house, as the representative of the legal status quo, was increasingly receding'. The system of parliamentary government was thus, in Gneist's reading, not the basis of the British constitution, but its final result, and it remained dependent on the functioning of 'self-government'. 'The great characteristic feature of the English state is not the majorities [*Machtverhältnisse*] in the lower house,' he explained, 'but the spirit of patriotism and moderation which has sprung from the essence and custom of communal bodies'. The history of Britain proved to him 'that the habitual exercise of offices of authority [*obrigkeitlichen Amts*] through the propertied classes' produced 'electorally effective [*wahltüchtige*] corporations and a parliament fit to govern'. What was more, the system paid enormous moral and political dividends since the independence fostered by 'self-government' united the 'classes of society in pursuit of a higher common aim, but, above all, endow[ed] the propertied and educated classes with the energy and manly strength that can found a global empire'.[16]

'Self-government', Parliament and Crown: the Tensions within Gneist's Political Idyll

As this success story of the construction of a free, harmonious, well ordered and ultimately powerful body politic hinged on a rising functional elite of aristocrats and notables soberly discharging their honorific local offices, Gneist's account of the British constitution contained an unmistakably Whiggish ingredient. This sat uneasily alongside two further Gneistian tenets British Whigs would have found much less agreeable: his unflattering view of parliament and parliamentary politics and the significant role he accorded to the monarchy.

Gneist's account of the British parliament conveys the image of an unexpectedly weak and susceptible political institution. Basing his views on excessively technical observations, he doubted its possession of full budgetary control. He had no time for internal aspects of party organization and believed that the detoxifying effects of 'self-government' were permanently needed to protect parliament against inherent dangers of selfish party rule. Ultimately, Julius Hatschek concluded, Gneist had 'scant regard for parliamentary government in England'.[17]

This bias is thrown into even sharper relief when Gneist's view of the crown is added to the equation. His strikingly high opinion of Britain's strong local government was mirrored by a belief that the monarch's role was particularly powerful, leaving relatively little room for the parliamentary body sandwiched in between. 'Important as the rights of Parliament are,' Gneist insisted, 'one must not forget that in their origin they were an emanation of royal power' and notwithstanding a steady reduction in the authority of the crown, an important residual role continued to exist for the monarch.[18] After an unhappy decline in the role of the monarchy caused by the deplorable actions of the Stuarts, the kingship again became 'a positive factor in the will of the State, and it exercised great influence' under King George III. Gneist argued that this royal contribution was an essential corrective, since in spite of 'the doctrines of democracy' which held that 'the powers thus taken away [from the crown] were to benefit the national liberties', these powers simply fell to 'the now completely developed aristocracy in Parliament'. The question was thus no longer that of the possible 'misuse of state power against the majority, but simply of its misuses *through* the majority'. This problem was addressed through the revival of the monarch's role under George III, for 'only with the entrance of the kingship into the strife of the parties, does the era of great statesmen begin, respecting whose glory the mind of Europe, in relation to the English constitution, is closely engaged'.[19]

In spite of his clear words about the political paramountcy of parliament, Gneist portrayed an anachronistically powerful British monarch. With a strong emphasis on the importance of the royal prerogative, he gave the impression that there was a constellation allowing the King to act as a mighty umpire above the parties, equipped with the right to veto parliamentary legislation and firmly in control of executive power. Irrespective of the fact that the royal veto had lain dormant since its last application in 1707 – as Gneist well knew – he suggested that the veto still formed part of the monarch's powers. In his 1859 contribution to Bluntschli and Brater's *Staatslexikon*, Gneist simply quoted from Blackstone's *Commentaries on the Laws of England*, which had already described an antiquated state of affairs when published a century earlier: 'royal authority in the exertion whereof lies the executive part of government; this is placed in a single hand for the sake of unanimity, strength and dispatch. The king of England is therefore not only the chief, but properly the sole magistrate of the nation, all others acting by commission from, and in subordination to him'. Gneist, the loyal Prussian liberal, wanted a strong king, and so he found one in the eighteenth-century image he depicted for his nineteenth-century audience.[20]

Reform and Ruin: Gneist and Nineteenth-Century Britain

There were thus considerable tensions between Gneist's concept of a rising 'self-government' elite, his wariness about parliamentary politics and his monarchical proclivities on the one hand, and his accounts of these political forces and a more realistic appraisal of the situation in eighteenth-century Britain on the other. There were even deeper fault lines, however, between Gneist's British utopia – the polity which (chiefly through the blessings of 'self-government') had succeeded in bringing political freedom and harmonious relations between state and society – and the real Britain of Gneist's day. For the parliamentary sceptic and elite-focused monarchist, the changes of 1832 and 1867 marked a sad decline, leaving behind a British constitution which struck him, by the early 1890s, as being 'almost like a ruin'.[21]

Gneist's frustration with Britain's development in the nineteenth century manifested itself in a peculiar disjuncture: he described the unacceptable flaws of the unreformed parliament with great clarity and found warm words of praise for the spirit of those leading the reform process; but he was unrelenting in his damnation of the actual effects of the reform measures. As early as 1859, long before the Second Reform Act, Gneist acidly rejected the 1832 reform: it had 'introduced a new element into the English state which had hitherto not been decisive – practical ignorance of the state. The newly enfranchised classes regarded their easily won right as an automatic share not in duties towards the state, but in political influence on it'. This was a road to perdition, since 'never, in the course of centuries, have mere elections generated the spirit and ability required for public activity'.[22]

Twenty years later, his views had not mellowed at all. The men of 1832 had failed 'to impose upon the new electors the fulfilment of the same personal duties' that, according to Gneist, had to complement the exercise of political rights. This was hardly surprising, since the new urban working classes had previously lived in the countryside, 'as a rule without any personal participation in the self-government of the neighbouring communities', and were thus unfit for political office. The consequences of this ill-advised enfranchisement were far-reaching. 'The Lower House no longer appears as a representation of the various communities, as limbs of the general self-government over the commonwealth, but as a representation of "interests".' With local bonds thus destroyed, 'party government falls into a helpless dependence upon incalculable combinations of social interests, upon the strongest prejudices, upon political agitation and the tactics of party movement, whose equally influential and wavering organ the daily press has now become'. A few generations down the line it would all end in tears: 'in an era of radical action and of violent counter-action on the part of the hitherto ruling classes'.[23]

Britain's fateful mistake had been to become like France. 'The notion, nowadays predominant in England, which regards a representative constitution as a mere representation of "interests" contains the same momentous error as that social direction in France which declares the satisfaction of the drives and proclivities of the individual as the highest aim of the state', Gneist observed in 1859. That an ill-conceived electoral system should produce ministerial despotism, corrupt parties and social conflict was not a development peculiar to France. In this respect, 'the hastily piled-up populations of the urban and industrial districts of England' were just as bad as the French population, which had been kept in an infantile condition by an overbearing bureaucracy. Gneist did not deviate from this interpretation. 'Unconsciously England had entered upon the same path as France', he concluded in the 1880s. 'The manifest result was also in England a progressive extinction of the parochial mind ... a retirement of the best classes from the parochial life, a holding together of this pseudo-government by a more and more extensive system of government commissioners and general rules, which, from the standpoint of the better-ordered German parochial life, is almost unintelligible, and at all events is for any length of time incompatible with the system of changing party governments.'[24]

Modern Britain, having joined France in its political development, was thus no longer a suitable example for Germany. With its enlarged electorate, party politics, degraded local self-government, social strife and public opinion speaking imperiously through the mouth of a daily press, it was heading for a violent crisis. Gneist foresaw a further 'dissolution of the old cohesions', universal suffrage, the 'arithmetical equalization of the constituencies' and a continental-style multi-party system. In spite of all these worrying developments, though, his old belief in the political wisdom of the 'English nation' enabled Gneist to perceive a faint glimmer of political light at the end of the tunnel. It shone with a very characteristic hue: 'And then a time may recur, in which the *King in council* may have to undertake the actual leadership'.[25]

Before 'the West': Locating the British Solution to Prussia's Problems

When illuminated by this light, all the oddities, contradictions and shortcomings in the political image Gneist portrayed fall into place. The key lies in an observation by the great Heidelberg jurist Georg Jellinek (1851–1911). The image of England on the continent, he wrote in his 1908 preface to the German translation of Sidney Low's *The Governance of England*, never depicted 'the political reality of England, but an idealized community, whose features stood out in contrast to certain arrangements on the continent which were to be fought or altered'. The characteristic complexion of Gneist's idealized community arose from the political situation after 1848/49. 'Above all, it was probably the collapse of the constitutional system in France which cast all our postulates into doubt', he wrote to Robert von Mohl in 1860. 'I wanted to try to discover the practical mediation between state and society in England.' Gneist was attracted to Britain by anti-revolutionary conviction and an increasingly strong anti-French bias, but he also rejected the contemporary parliamentary politics of the Victorian age. Instead he sought – and claimed to have found – a politically acceptable example of effective governance in an idealized version of the British post-1688 era. He took it as an example of where Prussia-dominated Germany's future should lie: in a politics sustained by a dutiful, meritocratic elite whose eminence would be gratefully accepted by the wider population; with a parliament that knew its place; and with a monarchical head exercising true leadership on behalf of the whole country. The rewards could be immense: harmony between state and society, the power to found a global empire, and the achievement of the right kind of freedom. The very first line of Gneist's 1859 essay on Britain's representative system – a quotation from the eminent Whig politician Charles James Fox – encapsulates what the author had in mind: 'Freedom is order, freedom is strength'.[26]

Today it is easy to criticize Gneist for his failure to embrace Western values of parliamentary democracy and oppositional pluralism. Accusing him of ignorance, though, would miss the point. The national-liberal jurist was not incapable of understanding the constitutional systems of Western Europe and North America; rather, he rejected them. His *beau idéal* lay elsewhere – in a carefully constructed image of a pre-1789 'old England' that encapsulated the very antithesis of the calamitous political example offered by France. It lay in a land believed to exist before there ever was a West.

Notes

1. *The Times*, 23 July 1895, p. 6.
2. Rudolf Gneist, 'Großbritannien. Verfassung', in Johann Caspar Bluntschli and Karl Brater (eds), *Deutsches Staatswörterbuch*, vol. 4, Stuttgart and Leipzig, 1859, 423–60, here 423; Rudolf Gneist, 'Das Repräsentativ-System in England. Eine historische Skizze', in August Freiherr von Haxthausen (ed.), *Das Constitutionelle Princip*, vol. 2, Leipzig, 1864, 89–180, here 92.
3. Reinhard Lamer, *Der englische Parlamentarismus in der deutschen politischen Theorie im Zeitalter Bismarcks*, Lübeck, 1963, 5–6; Hans-Christof Kraus, 'Die deutsche Rezeption und Darstellung der englischen Verfassung im neunzehnten Jahrhundert', in Rudolf Muhs, Johannes Paulmann and Willibald Steinmetz (eds), *Aneignung und Abwehr. Interkultureller Transfer zwischen Deutschland und Großbritannien im 19. Jahrhundert*, Bodenheim, 1998, 89–126, here 101–109; Charles E. McClelland, *The German Historians and England. A Study in Nineteenth-Century Views*, Cambridge, 1971, 79; Hugo Preuß, 'Finis Britanniae!', in Hugo Preuß, *Gesammelte Schriften*, vol. 1: *Politik und Gesellschaft im Kaiserreich*, ed. Lothar Albertin, Tübingen, 2007, 105–9, here 105–6.
4. Rudolf Gneist, *Der Rechtsstaat*, Berlin, 1872, 19.
5. Leonard Krieger, *The German Idea of Freedom: History of a Political Tradition from the Reformation to 1871*, Chicago, 1957, 460; Otto Pflanze, 'Juridical and Political Responsibility in Nineteenth-Century Germany', in Leonard Krieger and Fritz Stern (eds), *The Responsibility of Power. Historical Essay for Hajo Holborn*, London, 1968, 162–82, here 180. I am indebted to Kenneth F. Ledford, 'Formalizing the Rule of

Law. The Supreme Administrative Law Court, 1876–1914', *Central European History* 37 (2004), 203–24, here 203–204; and Erich Angermann, 'Gneist, Heinrich Rudolf Hermann Friedrich von (preußischer Adel 1888)', in *Neue Deutsche Biographie* 2 (1955), 487–89, online: http://www.deutsche-biographie.de (accessed 18 August 2011).
6. Julius Hatschek, 'Gneist, Heinrich Rudolf', in *Allgemeine Deutsche Biographie*, vol. 49 (1904), 403–13, online: http://www.deutsche-biographie.de (accessed 18 August 2011); Eugen Schiffer, *Rudolf von Gneist*, Berlin, 1929, 26–27; Conrad Bornhak, 'Rudolf von Gneist', *Annals of the American Academy of Political and Social Sciences* 7 (1896), 81–97.
7. Josef Redlich, *Local Government in England*, vol. 1, London, 1903, v; Hugh Whalen, 'Ideology, Democracy and the Foundation of Local Self-Government', *The Canadian Journal of Economics and Political Science* 26, 1960, 377–95, here 379; Lamer, *Der englische Parlamentarismus*, 20; Erich Hahn, 'Rudolf Gneist and the Prussian Rechtsstaat, 1862–78', *The Journal of Modern History* 49, 1977, 1361-81, here 1364. Cf. the more generous account of Gneist's work in Bryan Keith-Lucas, 'In Defence of Gneist', *The Canadian Journal of Economics and Political Science* 27 (1961), 247–51.
8. Angermann, 'Gneist'; McClelland, *The German Historians and England*, 136.
9. Munroe Smith, 'Four German Jurists IV. Bruns, Windscheid, Jhering, Gneist', *Political Science Quarterly* 16 (1901), 641-79, here 642. This biographical sketch is based on Hatschek, 'Gneist', Schiffer, *Rudolf von Gneist* and Erich J. Hahn, *Rudolf von Gneist 1816–1895. Ein politischer Jurist in der Bismarckzeit*, Frankfurt/Main, 1995.
10. Hahn, *Rudolf von Gneist*, 232.
11. Bornhak, 'Rudolf von Gneist', 90, 93; Smith, 'Four German Jurists', 646.
12. Gneist, 'Das Repräsentativ-System in England', 125; Rudolf Gneist, *Verwaltung, Justiz, Rechtsweg. Staatsverwaltung und Selbstverwaltung nach englischen und deutschen Verhältnissen*, Berlin, 1869, 1–2; Gneist, *Der Rechtsstaat*, 9, 19.
13. McClelland, *The German Historians and England*, 135–36; Wolfgang Pöggeler, *Die deutsche Wissenschaft vom englischen Staatsrecht. Ein Beitrag zur Rezeptions- und Wissenschaftsgeschichte 1748–1914*, Berlin, 1995, 80–82.
14. Gneist, 'Großbritannien. Verfassung', 457; Gneist, 'Das Repräsentativ-System in England', 124–25. See also Lamer, *Der englische Parlamentarismus*, 81–82 and Hahn, *Rudolf von Gneist*, 68–73, 145.
15. Gneist, *Verwaltung, Justiz, Rechtsweg*, 38, 43–47, here 45.
16. Pöggeler, *Die deutsche Wissenschaft vom englischen Staatsrecht*, 82, 83–88; Gneist, 'Das Repräsentativ-System in England', 135, 136, 161. See also Gneist, *Verwaltung, Justiz, Rechtsweg*, 43–44.
17. Lamer, *Der englische Parlamentarismus*, 18–20, 27–31, 73; Hahn, *Rudolf von Gneist*, 74–75; Hatschek, 'Gneist'.
18. McClelland, *The German Historians and England*, 139.
19. Rudolf Gneist, *The English Parliament in its Transformations through a Thousand Years*, trans. R. Jennery Shee, London, 1886, 297, 299, 312 (italics in the original).
20. Lamer, *Der englische Parlamentarismus*, 28–31; Gneist, 'Großbritannien. Verfassung', 449; *Blackstone's Commentaries on the Laws of England, Book the First, Chapter the Seventh (1765–1769)*, online: http://avalon.law.yale.edu/subject_menus/blackstone.asp (accessed 27 August 2011).
21. Lamer, *Der englische Parlamentarismus*, 89.
22. Gneist, 'Das Repräsentativ-System in England', 161, 164. See also Lamer, *Der englische Parlamentarismus*, 25, 86, 93.

23. Gneist, *The English Parliament*, 340; Rudolf Gneist, *The History of the English Constitution*, trans. Philip A. Ashworth, vol. 2, London, 1886, 443–45, 448–49, 452.
24. Gneist, 'Das Repräsentativ-System in England', 169, 172; Gneist, *The History of the English Constitution*, 450–52.
25. Ibid., 453 (italics in the original). For Gneist's hope for a monarchical resurgence see also Lamer, *Der englische Parlamentarismus*, 104–105.
26. Jellinek quoted in Pöggeler, *Die deutsche Wissenschaft vom englischen Staatsrecht*, 118; Gneist to Mohl, 20 July 1860, quoted in Hahn, 'Rudolf Gneist and the Prussian Rechtsstaat', 1363; Gneist, 'Das Repräsentativ-System in England', 89.

Chapter 10

WEIMAR AND 'THE WEST'
Liberal Social Thought in Germany, 1914–1933

Austin Harrington

One important part of the story of German relations to 'the West' in the nineteenth and twentieth centuries needs to concern accounts of these relations in the writings of broadly liberal intellectuals active during the years of the Weimar Republic and the last years of the Wilhelmine Empire. The accounts this chapter will consider express discontent and antagonism with Britain, France and the United States in the context of German defeat in the First World War and the emerging terms of the Treaty of Versailles; but they also display a commitment to values of political liberalism and civic enlightenment and argue for a nationally distinctive German form of democratic political modernity, different in content from the cultural traditions of the states of the North Atlantic seaboard but not radically rejecting or deriding these traditions' claim to validity. As this contribution discusses, despite widely felt German national anguish and humiliation over the clause of the Versailles Treaty that ascribed sole guilt to Germany for the waging of the war, significant voices on the German public intellectual scene repudiated dogmas of unbending 'Western' revenge on Germany and still pleaded the case for cooperation and solidarity in European relations over the course of the decade. They offered a kind of view of the West 'from the outside on the inside', different from any simple sentiment of national inwardness and loathing of the foreign.

This chapter briefly reviews three principal aspects of the development of liberal social thought in Germany at the end of the war and the early

Weimar years. A first section considers an emergent theme of integration between German and Western European political ideas and self-understandings in the early Weimar years, notably as articulated by the Protestant theologian and prominent political commentator of the day, Ernst Troeltsch. A second section turns to statements common in broadly liberal (though also in other ways conservative) circles of the period about Europe as a superordinate nexus of diverse national as well as pre-national historical traditions, capable in principle of generating a more 'concrete' framework of international solidarity than the plan for a League of Nations mooted by Woodrow Wilson. A third and final section concludes with a look at an array of commentaries on the question of European relations both to the U.S. as a rising world power and to the indefinite Eurasian boundary, including in the first instance to revolutionary and pre-revolutionary Russia.[1]

'The West' in German Liberal Social Thought after 1918

It is well known that in August 1914 a longstanding German complex of resentment of the Western European powers exploded in a call to arms. In the writings of almost all prominent German intellectuals in 1914, this complex asserted itself in the discourse of a war for the national spirit (*Geist*) and the national culture (*Kultur*), over against something that was denounced as the decadent, individualistic, commercialized civilization (*Zivilisation*) of France, Britain and the United States, or 'the West'.

It needs to be emphasized, however, that not all writers endorsed a wholly militant reading of the motif of German national cultural protest. Among numerous voices that resisted this kind of discourse were men who had been fervent patriots at the war's outbreak but who would go on to publish widely circulated statements against German nationalist belligerence in later stages of the war and during the Weimar years. Max Weber's influential public activities at the end of the war have been very closely documented over the past decades.[2] Yet Weber was by no means the only prominent voice on the progressive left-liberal centre of German professors of social science of the period. The vibrancy of this milieu in Germany would continue to thrive after Weber's death in June 1920, including notably at the University of Heidelberg's Institute for Social and Legal Sciences (*Institut für Sozial- und Staatswissenschaft*), directed by Alfred Weber (younger brother of Max) until 1933, as well as at numerous other metropolitan centres throughout Germany.[3]

Crucially for many broadly left-liberal social science writers of the period, such as the two Weber brothers, as well as Troeltsch, Max Scheler,

Ferdinand Tönnies and others, Germany's need was to trace a path of development toward parliamentary democratization and constitutional reform that respected and learned from Western European political traditions, but not, in so doing, to abandon its sense of national cultural difference from 'the West'. For these authors, in reflectively appropriating 'Western' political ideas into its own national cognitive self-understandings, Germany could find its own culturally and nationally distinct path to universal political modernity. More widely for many of these authors, a consciousness of the crisis of 'Western civilization' could be communicated without reliance on German-centred notions of approaching doom for the North Atlantic world. In their perspective, a sense of the overturning of 'Western hubris' on the stage of world history could be conveyed without any atavistic notion of the decadence and senescence of France and Britain and the menace of 'Americanization'. Comprehension of the European crisis could be gleaned without resort to notions of 'Western decay' and exhaustion in a supposed contrast to 'German youth' and 'vitality' of the spirit.

On one level, not too much should be read into differences between these liberal writers' uses of the terms 'European' and 'Western'/'Occidental' at particular times or in particular textual passages. Often the designations would be used interchangeably, with little explicit thought given to whether North America or other developed former European colonies were appropriately to be included under the scope of the 'European'. But two differentiations can nonetheless be pinpointed in connotations of the term 'Western' in these commentators' statements: one generally positive, the other more negative. 'Western' would be positively connoted for these voices where it signified a heritage of rational, enlightened values of politics and culture nurtured in part by an ancient Latinate, Christian cultural tradition, to which Germany needed to realign itself and thereby overcome its backward and inward-looking love affair with obscurantist and irrationalist nationalist notions. But at the same time, for these liberal writers no less than for more conservative voices, 'Western' would also be deployed in conjunction with references to Britain and France as the two lead nation states of 'Western Europe' that humiliated Germany at Versailles in 1919 and that symbolized a particular tradition of contractarian, individualist politics that Germany did not have to follow, even in its commitment to founding republican principles of liberal democracy. In this negative instance, 'Western' would denote the British, French (and, by extension, North American) hegemony that Germany had a reason to resist in the name of a more continent-centred Europe – a Europe less beholden to the geopolitical interests of the North Atlantic powers and a Europe that in some ways could enlist other sources of cultural and intellectual protest from 'the East', such as from Russia. The challenge in these writers' minds was therefore for Germany to disentangle those aspects of 'the West' in 'Western Europe' it needed to embrace from those aspects it had a right and a vocation to criticize.

This form of spokesmanship began to emerge already in the middle and later phases of the First World War. For Georg Simmel, the insight to be recognized – as he put it in his essay of 1916 *The Dialectic of the German Spirit* (*Die Dialektik des deutschen Geistes*) – was that through negation of itself, German national political and intellectual culture might accede to a deeper realization of its own self-understanding. 'The ideal of the German', as he put it, was 'the complete German – and at the same time his opposite, his other, his supplement'.[4] For Ernst Cassirer, in *Freiheit und Form* of 1916, similarly, the task was one of reunifying a 'German' idea of inner expressive spiritual 'freedom' with a 'Western' Latinate idea of rational 'form'.[5] Max Scheler, in *Der Genius des Krieges und der deutsche Krieg*, published in early 1915, had been a fervent and belligerent patriot in the early phases of the war; but over the course of the war, Scheler's views rapidly changed, moving increasingly toward a more reflective and universalistic ecumenical vision of European normative order more consonant with his own Catholic intellectual and emotional commitments.[6] 'We must not mistake maturity in French civilization for a defect or weakness, as so frequently in Germany', warned Ernst Robert Curtius in November 1918.[7]

Most notably, Ernst Troeltsch, throughout the last five years of his life until his abrupt death on 1 February 1923, would publish a welter of essays and addresses at this time in defence of democratic religious pluralism and constitutional order in Germany, on the menace of German cultural nationalism and on German reconciliation with 'Western Europe'.[8] In the 1920s Troeltsch would be best known for his speech, held on the second anniversary of the foundation of the German College of Politics (*Deutsche Hochschule für Politik*) in October 1922, entitled *Natural Law and Humanity in World Politics*, attended by Friedrich Ebert and other leading members of the Weimar Coalition.[9] The goal, he maintained in this and many other speeches and texts, was not division but rapprochement and critical synthesis between 'Western European' cultural and intellectual tradition and German thought: between naturalism and idealism in the broadest sense. German traditions of thought had genuine contributions to make to the understanding of ideas of individuality, creativity and self-realization, but only alongside 'Western European' ideas of rationality and natural rights and their reflection in politics and literature. 'Western European' traditions of contractarian political thinking needed to be incorporated into distinctive German national-historical understandings of the ethical agency of the state. French and British conceptions of individuals as holders of natural rights, uniting as citizens in a contract of obligation to the sovereign power, Troeltsch insisted, deserved far greater respect than they had received in Germany in recent decades. The teachings and legacies of Locke, Montesquieu and Rousseau, Troeltsch urged, were not to be derided by Germans as mere etiolated doctrines of 'Western individualism'. A recognition of the legitimacy of the state as in some way flowing from an agreement of its citizens as bearers of primordial rights, given by 'natural law', merited equal consideration alongside German ideas of the state as an expressive nexus of belonging that conferred rights on members of the community it instantiated. 'Western European' ideas of liberty of the individual, Troeltsch maintained, belonged together with German ideas of community and ethical life in the state. The task, he wrote, was one of making clear to German audiences how 'a true European ethos', involving recognition of 'rights of man' 'not as the gift of the state, but as ideal postulates of the state, and indeed of society itself', could be 'incorporated into our own ideas'.[10]

A 'Romano-Germanic Nexus'

A common view of many anti-nationalist liberal voices in Germany and elsewhere in Europe in the early 1920s was that some form of continent-centred institution of European supranational political and economic cooperation could have been pursued as an alternative to the Wilsonian project of a League of Nations. Some idea of the priority of 'Europeanism' or *Europäertum* over 'internationalism', it was felt, might have represented a more concrete agency of mediation between national particularities on the one hand and moral-legal universality on the other. Such a conception, it was believed, could have been sufficiently formally universal in normative authority to discourage states against destructive actions towards one another, and nevertheless also sufficiently concretely bounded in regional historical scope to guide and assure its associate members against disorientation in an otherwise highly threatening-seeming arena of global political and economic conflict and competition.[11]

It is true that some elements of this thinking were driven by reactionary and anti-Semitic motives, haunted by a visceral sense of the threat of the U.S. and 'Americanization' on the one hand and the menace of an awakened, darker 'East' mobilized by socialism or 'Bolshevism' on the other. Certainly there was a strand in this thinking that saw a totality of great European states threatened by internal national fragmentation and by external competitor powers on the world stage and remained deeply suspicious of the Wilsonian internationalist agenda emanating from across the Atlantic. Particularly troubling is the revival of ideas of *Mitteleuropa* over the course of the 1920s, based on the doctrine of an Austro-German neo-imperial centre of power at the heart of Europe, as formulated originally by Friedrich Naumann during the First World War. Indeed it is the case that sympathy for a German project of dominance at the heart of Europe increasingly grew in the 1930s in relatively sophisticated intellectual forms among circles that might once have described themselves as broadly 'Europeanist' rather than nationalist in the 1920s.[12]

In this light should be seen the feeding of Europeanist discourse into nascent Eurochauvinist currents of the age that celebrated the oneness of European nations as organic constituents of a superior civilization in world history. Some Catholic visions of a homogeneous European Christian culture belong in this frame, as do Hugo von Hofmannsthal's influential writings on European unity of the period, at first invoking an image of the Austro-Habsburg multinational empire in 1917 as an exemplar of continental 'ecumenical' solidarity, then in 1927 famously propagating the discourse of a 'conservative revolution'.[13] Nor can Richard Nikolaus Graf von Coudenhove-Kalergi's Pan-European League (founded in 1923) be separated from elements of this outlook. The *Europäische Kulturbund* (European Cultural League), a network of German-language literati organized and patronized from 1922 onwards by the Austrian aristocrat Karl Anton Prinz Rohan, who in 1926 openly professed his support for Mussolini, followed a particularly revealing trajectory. In July 1934 the League's journal, the *Europäische Revue*, led with a piece by Goebbels on National Socialism as a harbinger of peace in Europe. The popular literary magazine *Die Tat*, after its abrupt lurch to the right in 1929 under the editorship of Hans Zehrer and Giselher Wirsing – the author of *Zwischeneuropa und die deutsche Zukunft* (1932) – lent an unquestionably insidious slant to Europeanist discourse.[14]

Indeed, it is also true that prophets of the conservative revolution such as Zehrer and Arthur Moeller van den Bruck called for a 'middle way' or a 'third way' and for 'another Europe' in ways that in some respects mirrored liberal Europeanist conceptions of median or mediating politics. Yet a great deal hinges on the essential difference between liberal-centrist conceptions and the overtly social-corporatist notions invoked by conservatives. The left-liberals' middle or third way was not Othmar Spann's 'third way' of an authoritarian *Ständestaat* or Moeller van den Bruck's Third Reich described in his 1923 tract *Das dritte Reich*.[15] It was not something comparable in this sense to any kind of fascist, messianic 'breakthrough' solution that typically juxtaposed a menace of Americanization from the West with Bolshevism from the East. In principle it was not a stubbornly defencist or Eurochauvinist position to hold that, in preference to Wilson's atomizing policy of ethnic national self-determination enshrined at Versailles, some idea of an historically distinctive supranational civilizational constellation of peoples was to be pursued as the proper site of legal and political self-determination in Europe, rather than the ethnic nation in Wilson's sense. It was not intrinsically reactionary to maintain that a more European-centred legal structure could have developed to realize a political community of European peoples, united by more or less shared cultural histories and cognitive traditions.

For several liberal writers, it was important in this spirit to point to various longstanding pre-national constituents of modern European self-understanding – constituents that reached back to the Middle Ages and demonstrated the clustering of European peoples around an awareness of more or less common languages, customs, laws and religious traditions. A number of such writers affirmed in this sense that a particular *Kulturkreis* or 'civilizational circle' of European societies took its point of inception from the legacy of the 're-Romanization' of the continent under the rule of Charlemagne in the eighth and ninth centuries.[16]

For Troeltsch in particular in his major work of 1922, *Der Historismus und seine Probleme*, contemporary 'Western civilization' had to be seen as rooted in a complex history of continuous reciprocal entwinement and interaction between the religious legacy of the Middle Ages and the secular humanist heritage of classical antiquity and its modern transformation after the Renaissance and the Enlightenment.[17] This 'formation of European history' (*Aufbau der europäischen Kulturgeschichte*), Troeltsch argued, expressed a single continuous arc of unfolding, from Mediterranean antiquity and the Middle Ages to the present day. Departing from Ernst Cassirer's and other more classical-humanistic accounts of the unfolding of 'the West', Troeltsch criticized the notion that modern European consciousness crystallized essentially either in the age of the Enlightenment or in the secular humanistic spirit of the Renaissance period. A genealogy of European culture that privileged the age of Enlightenment in this way tended to neglect some of the more religious sources of the formation of modern European norms, ideas and institutions. Enlightenment culture constituted a bridge between religious medievalism and secular modernity, but not any kind of highest point of civilizational consummation – such as in the way it had appeared in Cassirer's book *Freiheit und Form*. In this sense for Troeltsch, the Enlightenment's culture of reason revealed a point of unstable and ambivalent suspension between theology and metaphysics on the one hand and the emergence of modern historism (*Historismus*) and the historical human sciences on the other. As he had emphasized previously in his earlier influential work of 1912, *The Social*

Teachings of the Christian Churches,[18] modern ideas of moral autonomy of the individual in the West needed to be seen as originating from early Judaeo-Christian religious sources of consciousness under the Roman Empire. They were not to be understood as solely products of the secular Enlightenment, the French Revolution or the political and economic transformations of the eighteenth and nineteenth centuries.

In *The Social Teachings of the Christian Churches*, in opposition to German national Protestantism after Ranke, which liked to date the beginning of the modern age to the Protestant Reformation inaugurated by Luther, Troeltsch's narrative of European religious modernity emphasized the retention of medieval elements in Lutheran culture throughout the sixteenth and seventeenth centuries and the markedly long and slow process of their gradual elimination. Troeltsch's synopsis underscored a sense in which the long sequence of events from the Reformation and the confessional wars of the seventeenth century to the gradual return of stability in the eighteenth century needed to be understood in terms of a series of largely unintended adaptations to crises in the structures of inherited religious authority since the Middle Ages. This meant for Troeltsch that the decisive episodes of modernity fell in the watershed of the later seventeenth century and early eighteenth century and the emergence of cultures of religious toleration under the territorial state. The emblematic challenge of modern times in Europe in Troeltsch's reading consisted principally in the late seventeenth- and eighteenth-century experience of demand for agencies of toleration and conciliation capable of mediating across ever more apparently antagonistic standpoints of ultimate valuation of the world. The key drama of European modernity thus lay in the search for responses to the problem of a world broken into radically conflicting social parties, each claiming ultimate, absolute authority for their own actions and assertions. In sum, the great intellectual task of modern times had become one of finding ways of coming to terms with the end of the 'ecclesiastical unified period of European culture' after the dissolution of the 'Christian unity of civilization'.[19]

Europe between 'East' and 'West'

For many of the Weimar liberal sources of social thought considered here, no spatially determinate line marked the moment at which Europe might have been said to shade over into Asia and consequently few definite judgements could be made about bases of inclusion or non-inclusion in Europe's house of civilizational belonging. For self-reflective commentators of the period such as Troeltsch, Scheler, Simmel, Curtius or Cassirer, a recognition existed that particular *Kulturkreise* overlapped and dynamically interacted with one another in various ways over time, that nothing in the predicates 'Romanic' and 'Germanic' implied any statement about definite ethnic bases of membership in Europe, and, most importantly, that all questions of European self-understanding remained in the last instance inseparable from questions of European knowledge and self-knowledge in relation to others. It followed for these writers that any implicit or explicit geographical placement of a region such as the Islamic Middle East or tsarist and post-tsarist Russia beyond the parameters of Europe still did not mean the normative irrelevance of this region to European self-consciousness and self-description. On the contrary, for these authors, any experienced sense of divergence of 'Eastern' cultures and histories from European self-awareness entailed a mentally delimiting horizon that had to be in some way confronted, interpreted, investigated and in this process ultimately to some degree crossed.

For both generally liberal and conservative German audiences at the beginning of the twentieth century, Russian civilizational history in particular in this connection tended to evoke the sense of a competing civilization for European self-understanding, less exhausted by capitalism, individualism and worldly avarice. For many in this vein, Russia connoted what Nikolaiĭ Danilevskiĭ in 1869 had portrayed as Moscow's new 'Third Rome', acquiring the mantle of the new universal centre of Christian civilization, after a perceived spiritual exhaustion of the 'second Rome' of Paris.[20] Familiar to many was the passage in Dostoevskiĭ's *Diary of a Writer* that declared that Russia brought an 'entirely new civilization into the world history of humanity'.[21] The resonance of Dostoevskiĭ's appeal to German spiritual protest at 'the West' in Thomas Mann's *Reflections of a Nonpolitical Man* is only one example of motifs that found broad appeal among a conservative German public increasingly agitated by a sense of dislocation and disarray, by a vaguely sensed threat of modernity emanating abstractly from an ever more relentlessly industrialized world order.[22]

For some more distinctly liberal-cosmopolitan commentators, however, there was equally a concern not to look vaguely to the Russian 'East' in a grand redemptive stand against 'Western' degeneracy, not to neglect Germany's membership of a Europe committed to the affirmation of ideas of enlightenment, progress and reform, and not to capitulate to a view of 'the West' as an entirely spent force of pure secularity, bereft of all powers of spiritual self-direction. These kinds of cross-cutting lines of reflection can, for example, be traced in a representative text of Alfred Weber's from 1924, entitled *Deutschland und die europäische Kulturkrise*. Here the younger Weber brother wrote of Europe as a continent driven by a 'dynamic counterpoint of cultural-political polarities', confronting Germany with a possibility in future of being 'torn into the flood plains of the East' and reborn in a new 'nexus of Europe-Asia'.²³ The question arose, he wrote, as to whether Europe's future 'axial principle' would cease to be a 'Romano-Germanic-Celtic' one and become instead an 'Oriental-Occidental' one; whether the 'Apollonian forming, clearing and ordering principle' of 'the West' stood to be consumed in the renewed orgiastic 'formlessness' of 'the East'.²⁴

Similar in inflection was Max Scheler's thinking about historic Russian Eastern Orthodox challenges to Latin European self-understanding. Even though unmistakably coloured by a virulent Anglophobic animus redolent of the mephitic mood of the early months of the First World War, significant passages in the Catholic philosopher's *Der Genius des Krieges und der deutsche Krieg* of 1915 could convey a nuanced account of Russian civilizational challenges to European preconceptions.²⁵ Europe's need, in Scheler's account, was to comprehend Russian history as composing a distinct civilizational horizon of its own, divergent from 'the West' in its understanding of the place of the individual and its relationship to the moral collective, and nevertheless decisively relevant for 'Western' Latinate self-understanding precisely by virtue of this divergence. A desideratum for Westerners, Scheler urged, was to view Russian historical life as composing neither a nation nor even a composite of nations on a par with Habsburg Imperial Austria but as a civilizational constellation *sui generis* embodying an entirely alternative, normative idea of the fundaments of human sociality. The tsarist ecclesiastical unity of Russian civilization was to be distinguished from pan-Slavic ethno-nationalism, expressing an intrinsically ethico-religious idea of the brotherly equality of the Byzantine multiplicity of its interwoven peoples living together in a loosely inclusive nexus. Western experiences of dogmatic religious splintering since the Reformation period inclined Europeans too often to see only an image of homogeneity in the East compared to a supposed Western heterogeneity and pluralism, overlooking a way in which numerous sectarian heresies could live at odds with the church in Russia yet nevertheless subsist in peace with Christian Orthodoxy under a broadly sheltering umbrella. Though Europeans did not need to surrender their own acquired horizons of ethical and political self-understanding, their challenge, Scheler went on to argue, was potentially to learn from the way in which the social structures of Eastern Christendom expressed ethical feeling and consciousness more in a sense of the solidarity of the congregation in sin and guilt, enjoining affective devotion to God and a collective spirit of sensuous self-immolation, whereas the Western church tended to teach individual ascetic forbearance conducive to an individualistic ethic of self-preservation in contractual relationships of formal law.

In contrast to modern Western post-Reformation experiences of conflicting doctrinal systems, each competing imperiously for command over the faithful, the religious coloration of Eastern Orthodox sociality knew 'no love "for God" or "in God"' that was 'not at the same time essentially a co-loving fellowship of human beings in God's infinite love for man'.[26]

Scheler's and Alfred Weber's preferred term in describing these connections would most often be 'Europe' rather than 'West' but at least part of their motivation in these discussions was to enlist a view of Russia as a symbolic force of solidarity in Germany's own struggle with 'the West' in the sense specifically of the North Atlantic powers of Britain, France and the United States – a 'spiritual' struggle as they saw it; one that affirmed an important sense of cultural difference with francophone and Anglo-Saxon intellectual traditions without necessarily precluding commitments to conciliation and rapprochement on the plane of international politics and diplomacy.

In both Scheler's and Alfred Weber's perceptions, the October Revolution of the Bolsheviks might have swept away the old tsarist autocracy and patriarchal ecclesiastical structure of authority, but it appeared to have retained many aspects of the old structure's attributes of subordination, wherein individuals lived as brotherly members of a collective under the protection of a superior paternal instance, now represented by the Communist Party. For them it seemed ironic that the new socialist empire built at Moscow in the name of workers' soviets around the world had been inspired by the ideas of a thinker from the ancient Roman-German city of Trier in the Rhineland: by Karl Marx, a man steeped in German literary humanism who had lived most of his life in 'the West', in London.

For Scheler and Alfred Weber, the 'Eastern' realization in Russia of Marx's teachings as a political vision of 'Western' provenance posed a challenge to the evolutionistic Eurocentric presuppositions that Hegelian-Marxist and socialist thinking about world history shared in common with the positivistic liberalism of Western European theoretical traditions from Comte and Saint-Simon to John Stuart Mill and Herbert Spencer. It gave the lie to both the Marxist and the liberalist notion of Western European experiences of industrialization and bourgeois political revolutions as a globally generalizable and necessary developmental 'stage' or 'step' on the way to societal conditions of modernity and modernization. For Georg Lukács in *History and Class Consciousness* of 1923, on the other hand, the Eastern fulfilment of Marx's vision in Russia signified precisely an indictment of the hubris and self-contentment of the European liberal humanism of which Lukács had once been a devotee during his time as a member of the Weber circle at Heidelberg before the war. For the recently converted Hungarian theorist, the international proletariat became the new universal class of world history that rose like the sun in the East.[27] Redefining the crisis of 'Western civilization' as a crisis of the bourgeoisie, Georg Simmel's category of 'form' in Lukács's pre-war and pre-Marxist worldview now became a construct of the capitalist 'West', while 'soul' in Simmel's thinking became henceforth for Lukács the promise of revolution in 'the East'.[28] 'Form' and 'soul' – the two dirempted poles of the Romano-Germanic nexus and the two sides of Simmel's liberal-humanistic dialectic – now found synthesis for Lukács only in a new socialist international of workers' struggle, proclaimed from Bolshevik Moscow as the 'Third Rome' of the new century.

A contrasting foil for the pictures of Europe and the West articulated by liberals such a Scheler, Troeltsch and Alfred Weber in the 1920s would be represented by the place of the United States after its entry into the First World War. Here the rising world power of the U.S. signified another kind of challenge to conventional European self-understanding. In many perceptions, the two opposing poles of Soviet Russia and the United States in European relations in the new century raised the question of the future of a distinctively European idea of the individual, which would be seen as differing on the one hand from the situation of revolutionary socialist Russia and from the form taken by individualism in the U.S. on the other. For numerous commentators, radical individualist values in the American West seemed to pose opposite dangers to those spelt by collectivism in the East. In the American West, it was felt, a principle of autonomous individuality seemed to lurch toward a pole of unlimited individual autarchy, with unsettling consequences for general social wellbeing and solidarity.

It deserves underlining at this point, however, that the claim that followed from this among liberal social science circles was not always simply that an 'Anglo-Saxon circle' had no rightful place in Europe's future. The picture was not always equivalent to clichéd images of U.S. Americans as materialistic egoists, superficial optimists and worldly pragmatists. Notably Simmel, for example, intimated in 1918 that a future wellspring of 'culture' far beyond the horizons of old Europe was not to be dismissed. It was, he underlined, questionable whether 'Europe should have a permanent lease on the inheritance of culture'.[29] Rather, it might be 'something great to think and feel beyond the egoism of our own civilization and valuations; for far too long we have assumed the course of world history to unfold on Europe's shores alone, the crest of its waves leaving Asia millennia in the past and now coming to rest for ever in our continent'.[30] Simmel here mused that perhaps there would 'come a time when Europe [would] be to America as Athens to the later Romans: a travel destination for the young in search of culture, a place full of interesting ruins and great memories, a source of supplies for artists, scholars and chattering literati'. Nothing in this prospect, however, he added, contradicted the possibility of a future 'American world culture'. As frightful as this might seem to some Europeans, its inconceivability might be no greater than the imaginability of the modern nation state from the perspective of the ancient Egyptians.[31]

Yet in Simmel's and others' perceptions, a reasonable case nonetheless remained to be made for the conviction that European understandings of the relation of the individual to society and of ethical social solidarity differed from those prevalent in the New World and could be justifiably defended in this difference. European ideas of the ethical social situation of the individual, it was often felt strongly, did not have to be measured against the spirit of a perpetual westward migration of the faithful self across the Atlantic, moving in a continual sea-borne egress, in an energetic 'Pilgrim's Progress', a methodical quest for the New Jerusalem, far from all soiling ambivalence of incorporated social authorities and institutions. European moral life, wrote Troeltsch in 1920, did not have to share Americans' combination of industry with 'a Christian worldview, [with] a spirit of conservative democracy as a legacy of Puritanism'; it was not a cliché to say that German 'mental life stems from Lutheranism and Catholicism, from classicism and romanticism, and has no clear access to the new realist style of life; it dispenses with the synthesis of mind, morality, business and politics possessed by Americans'.[32]

In sum, as many of these German left-liberal social commentators saw matters, the challenge for Europe was to define an intelligent project of modernity beyond both the triumphalist industrial-commercial modernity of the Atlantic West on the one hand and the bureaucratic and paternalist collectivist modernity of the tsarist and post-tsarist Russian East on the other. An array of constellations might have been thinkable for a future Europe, involving different mediating combinations of communalistic and individualist parameters of life. In this sense, 'Eastern' impulses of critique of secular 'Western' materialism and individualism did not need to find expression solely in the Russian Bolshevik Revolution but might also have realized themselves in a variety of regionally distinctive configurations of values of individuality and collectivity, of market and state power, and of material and spiritual orientations of life. Europe in this picture formed a certain kind of 'middle' or mediating element between 'East' and 'West', but not a 'centre' in any overwhelmingly metaphysical, self-congratulatory or unreflexive sense. For these liberal voices at least, even if by no means for all sections of German political commentary of the age, any European 'centre' or 'middle' lay somewhere perplexingly in-between, in a tensile, unresolved location between contradictory poles of orientation, suspended between the familiar and the alien.

Notes

1. These considerations draw on a longer study of mine, *German Cosmopolitan Social Thought and the Idea of the West. Voices from Weimar*, Cambridge, forthcoming. As I consider in that work, new waves of scholarship on early twentieth-century German liberal cosmopolitan social thought over the last twenty or thirty years have increasingly brought to light the relevance of a range of authors in the above connections. Renewed interest in broadly politically liberal or left-liberal as distinct from Marxist thinkers of the age has chimed with a general shift of attention in recent years in the social sciences towards comparative-historical models and global interpretive-civilizational approaches, with an emphasis on civilizational difference and divergence and a move away from postulates of universal structures of class conflict as motors of world history. But while a sizeable amount of biographical and philological scholarship has accumulated on these personalities, less of an attempt has been made so far to put the relevant sources to further theoretical use – to further application and analytical elaboration in contemporary social science practices. A full listing of the new scholarship is impossible here but milestones worth naming at this point are the now complete or near-complete collected critical editions of Georg Simmel (Suhrkamp, 1989–2012), Max Weber (Mohr-Siebeck, 1984–), Ernst Troeltsch (de Gruyter, 1998–), Alfred Weber (Metropolis, 1997–2003) and Helmuth Plessner (Suhrkamp, 1993–2003) and the related extensive scholarship of the lead editors of these volumes.
2. For an overview see Joachim Radkau, *Max Weber. Die Leidenschaft des Denkens*, Munich, 2005.
3. See notably Reinhard Blomert, *Intellektuelle im Aufbruch. Karl Mannheim, Alfred Weber, Norbert Elias und die Heidelberger Sozialwissenschaften der Zwischenkriegszeit*, Munich, 1999; and Dirk Hoeges, *Kontroverse am Abgrund. Ernst Robert Curtius und Karl Mannheim. Intellektuelle und 'freischwebende Intelligenz' in der Weimarer Republik*, Frankfurt/Main, 1994.
4. Georg Simmel, 'Die Dialektik des deutschen Geistes', in Georg Simmel, *Georg-Simmel-Gesamtausgabe* [hereafter GSG], vol. 13, 224.
5. Ernst Cassirer, *Freiheit und Form. Studien zur deutschen Geistesgeschichte*, Berlin, 1916.
6. See Max Scheler, 'Europa und der Krieg' (1915), in Max Scheler, *Gesammelte Werke* [hereafter MSG], vol. 4, 251–66; Max Scheler, 'Von zwei deutschen Krankheiten', in MSG 4, 204–19; and Max Scheler, 'Der Mensch im Zeitalter des Ausgleichs' (1927), in MSG 9, 145–71.
7. Ernst Robert Curtius, *Französischer Geist im zwanzigsten Jahrhundert*, Bern, 1925, 231 (an augmented and retitled edition of *Die literarischen Wegbereiter des neuen Frankreich*, first published in 1919 with a preface dated 22 November 1918).
8. See Ernst Troeltsch, *Schriften zur Politik und Kulturphilosophie (1918–1923)* (*Kritische Gesamtausgabe* [hereafter *ETKG*], vol. 15), ed. Gangolf Hübinger in cooperation with Johannes Mikuteit, Berlin et al., 2002.
9. Ernst Troeltsch, 'Naturrecht und Humanität in der Weltpolitik' (1922/23), in Troeltsch, *Schriften zur Politik und Kulturphilosophie*, 493–512.
10. Ibid., 509.

11. See for example Alfred Weber, 'Die Krise des modernen Staatsgedankens in Europa' (1925), in Alfred Weber, Alfred-Weber-Gesamtausgabe [herafter AWG], vol. 7, 233–346; Scheler, 'Europa und der Krieg'; and Georg Simmel, 'Die Idee Europa' (1917), in GSG 16, 54–58.
12. For a invaluable survey of these and other Europeanist stances in German-language literature and essayism of the period see Paul Michael Lützeler, Die Schriftsteller und Europa. Von der Romantik bis zur Gegenwart, Baden-Baden, 1998 (first published 1992). See also Vanessa Conze, Das Europa der Deutschen. Ideen von Europa in Deutschland zwischen Reichstradition und Westorientierung (1920–1970), Munich, 2005; and Britta Weichers, 'Mitteleuropa oder Paneuropa? Zwei europäische Integrationskonzepte in der Zeit des Ersten Weltkrieges und der Weimarer Republik', in Adolf Schröder (ed.), 'Völker Europas, findet euch selbst!' Beiträge zur Ideengeschichte der Europabewegung in Deutschland, Munich, 2007.
13. Hugo von Hofmannsthal, 'Die Idee Europa. Notizen zu einer Rede' (1917), in Hugo von Hofmannsthal, Reden und Aufsätze, vol. 2, Frankfurt/Main, 1979, 43–54; Hugo von Hofmannsthal, 'Das Schrifttum als geistiger Raum der Nation' (1927), in Hugo von Hofmannsthal, Reden und Aufsätze, vol. 3, Frankfurt/Main, 1980, 24–41. See also Lützeler, Die Schriftsteller und Europa, 253–55.
14. On Coudenhove, Rohan and Wirsing see Lützeler, Die Schriftsteller und Europa, 312–19, 324–31, 340–42. See also Anita Ziegerhofer-Prettenthaler, Botschafter Europas. Richard Nikolaus Coudenhove-Kalergi und die Paneuropa-Bewegung in den zwanziger und dreißiger Jahren, Vienna, 2004.
15. See Arthur Moeller van den Bruck, Das dritte Reich, Berlin, 1923; and Othmar Spann, Der wahre Staat. Vorlesungen über Abbruch und Neubau der Gesellschaft, Leipzig, 1921.
16. The late nineteenth century ethnologist Leo Frobenius is usually seen as the originator of the term Kulturkreis. But Frobenius's use of this term, notable for its rather troubling emphasis on definite ethnicity, was not the only common valence of the word in early twentieth-century German academic writing, as it also need not be today. For a discussion of issues around technical uses of the term 'civilization' and its cognates in the field of comparative historical sociology, see Said A. Arjomand and Edward A. Tiryakian (eds), Rethinking Civilizational Analysis, Thousand Oaks, 2004.
17. Ernst Troeltsch, Der Historismus und seine Probleme (ETKG 16), ed. Friedrich Wilhelm Graf, Berlin et al., 2008 (first published 1922). For an overview of research on this work and of Troeltsch scholarship in general see the introduction by Friedrich Wilhelm Graf as well as Mark D. Chapman, Ernst Troeltsch and Liberal Theology. Religion and Cultural Synthesis in Wilhelmine Germany, Oxford, 2001.
18. Ernst Troeltsch, Die Soziallehre der christlichen Kirchen und Gruppen, 2 vols, Tübingen, 1912.
19. Ibid., vol. 2, 173.
20. Nikolai Danilevsky, Russland und Europa, Stuttgart, 1920 (in Russian 1869).
21. Fyodor Dostoyevsky, Diary of a Writer (1873–81), translated by Boris Brasol, Santa Barbara, 1979, 727 ff., 1003 (May–June 1877).
22. Thomas Mann, Betrachtungen eines Unpolitischen, Frankfurt/Main, 1983 (first published 1918), 66–67.
23. Alfred Weber, 'Deutschland und die europäische Kulturkrise' (1924), in AWG 7, 471.
24. Ibid., 471, 487.
25. In Scheler's Der Genius des Krieges und der deutsche Krieg see for example the sections headed 'Die geistige Einheit Europas und ihre politische Forderung' and 'Der

Weltkrieg und die wissenssoziologische Struktur Europas – Spezifisch europäische Aufgaben', MSG 4, 154–60, 185–90.
26. Ibid., 167, 185.
27. See Georg Lukács, *History and Class Consciousness*, translated by Rodney Livingstone, London, 1967 (in German 1923).
28. See Georg Lukács, *Soul and Form*, translated by Anna Bostock, London, 1974 (in German 1911).
29. Georg Simmel, 'Brief an Hermann Graf von Keyserling' (1918), in Georg Simmel, *Das individuelle Gesetz. Philosophische Exkurse*, ed. and introd. Michael Landmann, Frankfurt/Main, 1968, 245.
30. Georg Simmel, 'Europa und Amerika. Eine weltgeschichtliche Betrachtung' (1915), GSG 13, 142.
31. Simmel, 'Brief an Hermann Graf von Keyserling', 245.
32. Ernst Troeltsch, 'Spektator-Brief' (1920), in Ernst Troeltsch, *Die Fehlgeburt einer Republik. Ein Spektator in Berlin 1918–1922*, ed. Johann Hinrich Claussen, Frankfurt/Main, 1994, 244–45.

Chapter 11

GERMANY AND 'WESTERN DEMOCRACIES'
The Spatialization of Ernst Fraenkel's Political Thought

Riccardo Bavaj

When historians discuss the topic of 'Germany and the West' nowadays, the work of Heinrich August Winkler is typically the key reference point. For many years, however, this topic was primarily associated with one of Winkler's mentors at the Free University Berlin, the rémigré scholar Ernst Fraenkel (1898–1975). During the early decades of Germany's second experiment in liberal democracy, Fraenkel was a major exponent of the newly emerging discipline of political science: strongly committed to both the political education of German citizens and the incorporation of the Federal Republic of Germany (FRG) into a 'Western value community'. This value-based incorporation – which entailed the acceptance of the pluralist make-up of modern society and of the public negotiation of conflicting viewpoints – was to drag German society away from the murky currents of a 'German special consciousness' – namely, authoritarian statism, anti-democratic nationalism and the ideal of an apolitical government representing a homogenous body politic called 'the people'. Fraenkel's widely read collection of essays, *Germany and Western Democracies* (1964),[1] has become a classic in the intellectual history of the FRG and a milestone in the 'Westernization' of its political culture.

As this chapter demonstrates, however, Fraenkel adopted the *language* of 'Western democracy' surprisingly late. A Left-socialist labour law expert in the Weimar Republic, who had fled Nazi persecution in

1938 and had spent most of his exile in the United States, he returned to Germany in 1951 as a missionary of U.S. constitutionalism but only became an avowed 'Westernizer' in the early 1960s. From the perspective of conceptual history, his years in exile brought about an Americanization rather than a 'Westernization' of his political thought. A conceptual Westernization only occurred in the academic environment of the FU, with its direct exposition to the front line of the Cold War. This chapter examines Fraenkel's gradual transformation into a vocal supporter of 'Western democracy' and elucidates the reasons for what amounted to a spatialization of his political thought. It seeks to answer the question as to what Fraenkel was *doing* in using the concept of the West.[2]

While the ways in which he used the term 'Western democracy' have so far not been examined, many facets of his academic output have been extensively analysed.[3] Recently, scholarly engagement with Fraenkel has been given a further boost through the publication of his collected works, comprising more than four thousand pages.[4] In 2009, the first Ernst Fraenkel biography was published, which offers a vivid account of his academic and 'political life' without, however, providing an in-depth analysis of his intellectual development.[5] Most importantly, Fraenkel has been discussed in the context of debates on the 'Westernization' of the FRG. Inspired by the Tübingen-based research cluster on 'Westernization',[6] Alfons Söllner has plausibly argued that Fraenkel engaged in a project of political education geared towards a fundamental transformation of the political culture in West Germany. Söllner refers to this project as 'the normative Westernization of [the FRG's] political culture'.[7] While the intellectual validity of the expression 'normative Westernization' appears questionable – one would be hard pressed to think of any 'non-normative' mode of 'Westernization' – Söllner is certainly correct in pointing out Fraenkel's tendency to idealize U.S. constitutional history.[8] He ends, for instance, his magnum opus on American government, completed in 1959, by claiming that the United States was the 'greatest work of art ever created in the Western hemisphere'.[9] This assertion surely smacks of glorification and must be taken even more seriously in the light of the euphoric statement, to be found in his correspondence, that this book was the 'confession of his life'.[10] Söllner helpfully reminds us of the ironic remark made by the British political scientist Bernard Crick that, so it seems, most German émigrés feel obliged to pay homage to their host country at least once in their lifetimes: 'Every German American', he quipped in a critical review of Hannah Arendt's book *On Revolution*, 'does it once in gratitude'.[11]

America

Fraenkel's experience of the American 'work of art' was manifold. He studied American law at Chicago Law School, from which he graduated, as a 42-year-old, in June 1941.[12] He was then first hired by a law firm in Washington, D.C., before working for the American Federation of Jews in New York – an organization assisting Jewish refugees who had arrived from Central and Eastern Europe. At the end of 1942, he received a grant from the Carnegie Endowment for International Peace to conduct research on the Rhineland occupation in the aftermath of the First World War. He was looking for good or bad examples of managing an occupation regime, as a new occupation was to be expected once Germany was defeated in the world war then raging.

After the war was over, however, Fraenkel declined an offer from the U.S. government to work in the occupied country. He did not say why, but an answer can be gleaned from a letter he wrote to his close friends, Otto and Susanne Suhr, in March 1946. In this letter he highlighted the significance of his émigré years: while his emigration entailed a '*gradual separation [Loslösung]* from Germany' and an increasing 'accommodation [*Hineinwachsen*] to America', the 'decisive turn', as he put it, came in 1943. When he heard for the first time about the gas chambers in Auschwitz, he 'deliberately, and fully realizing what his decision meant, severed the bond between Germany and [himself] and decided never to return'.[13] 'Germany – even if its fate still concerns me – is not my country any more. ... To identify with Germany once again, is out of the question [*geht nicht an*].'[14]

The country he did identify with was now America. In August 1944, Fraenkel was granted U.S. citizenship, and in the spring of 1951, he became a U.S. State Department consultant for education policy with the High Commission for Germany in West Berlin. Hence, as mentioned at the beginning of this chapter, Fraenkel did consent to return to Germany. Actually, however, it was not much of a 'return'. Rather, he came to West Berlin as an intellectual ambassador of the U.S., describing himself as an 'American in Berlin' in an obvious allusion to Gene Kelly's performance in the famous musical *An American in Paris*, which had been released that very year. He appropriated the role of mediator between two political cultures. At the age of fifty-two, Fraenkel reinvented himself, keen to spread the message of the 'true' image of the United States. He soon became Professor of Political Theory and Comparative Government in West Berlin and wanted to build intellectual bridges – bridges, of course, that carried more intellectual goods from the U.S. to West Germany than the other way around.

On numerous occasions, Fraenkel was keen to enlighten his audience to dispel what he considered some of Germany's most deeply entrenched prejudices against America.[15] One of the issues he raised in his endeavour to debunk Germany's anti-American mythology was the commonly held view that Europe was being subjected to an inexorable process of 'Americanization'. This view, he argued, was one-sided at best, as it did not take into account the process he called 'America's re-Europeanization'.[16] What did he mean by that? He claimed that the secular process of bureaucratization, so central to the modern age, reached the United States later than its proliferation in Europe – namely in the first half of the twentieth century. When Fraenkel spoke of 'Europe', he meant 'Continental Europe'. He argued that Britain and the U.S. had skipped having a period of absolutism such as had been experienced in mainland Europe. This omission was beneficial in most respects, but Britain and the U.S. had to catch up with the Continent in one particular area: the introduction of a hierarchically organized bureaucracy, geared towards rational efficiency in the realms of civil and military administration. The seventeenth and eighteenth centuries, he claimed, caused a 'great schism' in the history of the Occident (*'das große Schisma der abendländischen Geschichte des 17. und 18. Jahrhunderts'*). Fraenkel's 'Occidental schism' took Britain and the U.S. on a different path from the Continent (especially Germany and France) – a difference that was intensified by the frequently evoked opposition between 'the common law countries' on the one side and the civil-law-oriented Continent on the other. This critical distinction, which dominated much of Fraenkel's writing in the 1950s, is worth bearing in mind when scrutinizing the deployment of the term 'Western democracy'.[17]

Western Democracy

Fraenkel did not become an outspoken 'Westernizer' until the early 1960s, beginning with a talk on 'Germany and Western Democracies'[18] that he gave on the occasion of the first anniversary of the Otto Suhr Institute in West Berlin (the former German College of Politics [*Deutsche Hochschule für Politik*], now fully incorporated in the Free University). It was only then that he became preoccupied with enlightening his audience and readership alike as to what 'Western' democracy was about, and in what ways the citizens of the FRG could, and indeed should, become one with the 'Western mind'. Before addressing the question as to why Fraenkel embarked on what would become a ceaseless engagement with the contested issue of Germany's place in the realm of 'Western democracies', this section presents a brief summary of his views on that matter and touches upon his earlier usage of the term 'Western democracy'.

The starting point for his reflections on this issue was surprising. In his talk on 'Germany and Western Democracies' given in April 1960 – the only time he examined the term 'Western democracy' itself – Fraenkel claimed that West German political consciousness had changed, and that West Germany was widely considered an integral part of the community of 'Western democracies'. As will be explained later, this should primarily be understood as a prescriptive statement – that West Germany ought to be part of the 'Western value community' – rather than an empirical observation.[19] What was less surprising was his apt reference to Ernst Troeltsch's famous speech of October 1922 on 'Natural Law and Humanity in World Politics'. Fittingly, Troeltsch had given this speech to mark the second anniversary of the German College of Politics. Fraenkel echoed many of Troeltsch's reflections on natural law, his thoughts on Germany's close interconnectedness with 'the West', and his plea for a renewed rapprochement between (as Troeltsch had put it) 'German political-historical-moralist thought' and 'West European-American' thinking.[20] Like Troeltsch, Fraenkel tried to raise people's awareness of the pan-European roots of 'Western democracies'. He included Germany's contribution to the gestation of this particular form of government, notwithstanding some significant peculiarities that had evolved in early nineteenth-century Germany, such as its organic romanticism and a state-centred historism (*Historismus*) prone to glorify the idea of individuality and to relativize universal values.[21] Like Troeltsch, who, in the aftermath of war, had been keen to counter noxious propaganda and to clear things up at home (*'Ordnung und Klarheit im eigenen Hause'*),[22] Fraenkel was adamant in his wish to clean up salient areas of Germany's contaminated political language.[23] Above all, he wanted to reinforce Troeltsch's statement about how untenable it was to maintain the commonly held attitude that pitted the 'German state' against 'Western democracy'.[24]

Indeed, Fraenkel's view of the relationship between Germany and 'Western democracies' was a far cry from the infamous 'ideas of 1914' so well researched by his colleague Hermann Lübbe at the time.[25] First, he argued that Germany had played a vital and enduring part in the development of 'Western democracies' in the late nineteenth and early twentieth centuries. In particular, he referred to the idea of social security (*soziale Geborgenheit*), encompassing job protection, social and health insurance, and pension schemes for civil servants. All this, he argued, had not originated from 'English, French, let alone American soil'.[26] As for the latter, significant socio-economic reforms had not been introduced in the U.S. until the New Deal, which Fraenkel usually referred to as 'the Roosevelt revolution'.[27]

Second, and related to the first point, Fraenkel argued that the expression 'Western democracy' was by no means an immutable concept. Rather, it emerged from a complex symbiosis: mixtures of appeal and rejection, transfer and appropriation, reshaping and reinventing. 'Western democracy' was an amorphous concept that changed over time. Indeed, any narrow geographical definition of the word 'Western' would be misleading. He claimed that it would be wrong to confine the term 'Western' to countries situated to the west of any particular demarcation line such as the Iron Curtain. After all, the lifework of Tomáš Masaryk was as central to the intellectual sphere of 'Western democracies' as was the fight for freedom of the Poles in the nineteenth century or that of the Hungarians in the twentieth. As for divided Germany, the entire nation could in fact belong to the community of 'Western democracies' if only it would explicitly align itself with it. In an effort to make the boundaries of 'the West' more fluid than they appeared to most people at the time, Fraenkel argued that it was up to individual societies to declare whether or not they would like to belong to the sphere of 'Western democracies'. The rationale behind this voluntaristic way of drawing boundaries was to open up the discursive space of 'the West' and to enable the citizens of the FRG fully to participate in it.[28]

Before explaining why Fraenkel found it necessary to resort to the vocabulary of 'Western democracies' in his writings after 1960, I will make another short diversion to shed light on the evolution of his usage of 'the West'. Fraenkel did not use the terms 'the West' and 'Western democracies' in any essays published before the Second World War, nor did he use them in his famous study on the 'dual state' (1941). He first employed these terms in 1943, the very year of his 'decisive turn'. What he meant by 'Western democracies' in 1943, however, was different from the meaning intended when he deployed the term in the 1960s and 1970s – except for the fact that it was always directed against the Soviet Union. In the midst of the Second World War, 'Western democracies' simply meant 'Anglo-Saxon democracies' – in other words the Anglo-American Allies who, he believed, would undoubtedly win the war.[29] This meaning was relatively stable over the next years: in his writings, 'Western democracies' were confronted with 'Eastern dictatorship'.[30] While such a sharply articulated opposition between 'Western democracies' and 'Eastern dictatorship' mirrored the Cold War division, the FRG was still excluded from 'the West'. This was to change over the following years.

However, after a reference to the opposition between 'Western democracies' and 'Eastern dictatorship' in 1951, he did not use the term 'Western democracies' again until 1960. Instead he preferred to speak of the 'free world' and the 'Occident' (*Abendland*) or used the loose geographical term 'Western hemisphere'.[31] Generally, he did not make extensive use of any 'Occidentalist' rhetoric during these years. Even when he discussed the history of human rights in 1953 and when he elaborated on the distinction between pluralism and totalitarianism a year later, he could do without it.[32] To be sure, in a lecture he gave at the *Hessische Hochschulwochen* in October 1957, he referred to the idea of natural law as 'our Western tradition', frequently evoking the notion of a 'Western world' and 'Western humanity' (*Menschheit*) – as defined against the 'Slavic world' and explicitly harking back to the Great Schism of Christendom in 1054. Yet he did not couch his reflections on natural law and democracy in the terminology of 'Western democracies', even though he aimed at elucidating the fundamental opposition between a 'people's democracy' (*'was "die drüben" unter Demokratie verstehen'*) and 'democracy correctly understood', by which he meant an anti-totalitarian, pluralist form of government.[33]

It was only in 1960, when Fraenkel was approaching retirement, that he became obsessed with the term 'Western democracies', used either with or without inverted commas, either in the plural or the singular. From then on, he affirmed a clear-cut opposition between 'Western and Eastern democracies': the one pluralist, the other totalitarian.[34]

Spatializing Pluralist Democracy

This raises the question as to why he started using the rhetorical commonplace of 'Western democracy' so extensively. Did his political thought change in any meaningful way around 1960, or did the subject of his scholarship perhaps change significantly at the time? In fact, neither changed. The basic traits of his theory of neo-pluralism had been developed in all but name by the end of the Weimar Republic. All he did was systematize this earlier conception of pluralist democracies and transform it into an elaborate theory. What did change, therefore, was above all the way he framed his conception of pluralist democracy. Though he started using the term 'pluralism' in the mid 1950s,[35] he only explicitly combined it with 'Western democracy' from 1960. From that time on, it worked as a cipher for pluralist democracies in which Anglo-American and Continental European features were intermingled.

This rhetorical transformation can be attributed to five key factors. First, it can certainly be argued that it was through Fraenkel's experience of U.S. political culture and his engagement with the constitutional history of the U.S. that he discovered 'the West'. What he described as his 'turning point' in 1943 no doubt played a role.[36] Yet as his 'Western' rhetoric only gathered momentum around 1960, other contributing factors must be found.

Second, from the mid and late 1950s, the issue of Germany's historical relationship to 'the West' was increasingly being seized upon by German scholars, including émigrés who had stayed in their countries of exile. The debate not only reflected West Germany's accession to NATO but was also part of wider struggles within the political culture of the FRG. As Sebastian Ullrich has demonstrated, these struggles intensified in the mid and late 1950s.[37] The first significant studies on the Weimar Republic appeared between the mid 1950s and early 1960s and almost all of them, in one way or another, were related to the historical dichotomy between the 'German state' and 'Western democracy'.[38] The names of Karl Dietrich Bracher and Kurt Sontheimer, who had a close working relationship with Fraenkel at the Free University, may come to mind. Given that the issue of Germany's historical relationship to 'the West' featured increasingly prominently on the academic agenda in the mid and late 1950s, it was a natural step for Fraenkel, 'primed' by his Weimar background, to engage with the critical *Sonderweg* discourse on German anti-'Westernism' – as opposed to a more specific focus on German anti-Americanism. Like Bracher, Sontheimer and other liberal colleagues, he was keen to counter the anti-'Westernism' that he believed was still deeply entrenched in German minds. In fact, Fraenkel was convinced that the political culture of the FRG was badly 'polluted', to use A. Dirk Moses' terminology:[39] it was polluted by the persistence of the idea of a 'positive' *Sonderweg* with its supposed roots in the nineteenth century.

As the notion of a fundamental dichotomy between Germany and 'the West' still fuelled the German 'special consciousness', both the term 'Western democracies' and Germany's relationship to that powerful construct needed to be redefined and the imaginary geography of 'Western democracies' needed expanding. In a way, Fraenkel's goal was to decrease the ambiguity reflected in the title of his influential book, *Germany and Western Democracies*. After all, the conjunction ('and') could imply both the separation of two distinct entities as well as their interconnectedness.

Third, Fraenkel needed to close a spatio-political gap identified by his own scholarship. This gap was the assumed hiatus between Anglo-America and the Continent. The rhetorical construct of 'Western democracies' – directed as it was against an 'Eastern Other' and based on the notion of an internal convergence of 'Western countries' – lent itself to a glossing-over of the cracks caused by the 'Occidental schism' mentioned above. Fraenkel, of course, was still well aware of the heterogeneous nature of the 'Western community'. As a specialist in comparative government, he deliberately used the method of comparison not so much to tease out similarities but to identify differences. In a way that recalls the tradition of Rankean historism – ironically enough considering his political agenda – he pointed out that political science 'should be concerned with demonstrating the individual and concrete factors that determine the formation of the political will in different kinds of government'. The political scientist, he maintained, 'does not have the task of making generic and abstract claims about political phenomena'.[40] However, like his liberal colleagues – Bracher, Sontheimer and others – he viewed political science not just as a science *of* democracy but, above all, as a science *for* democracy: for liberal, pluralist, 'Western democracy'. Whether to evoke the existence of a 'Western community' or to emphasize its inner fault lines was also a question of political expediency.

Fourth, Fraenkel's distrust of West Germany's citizens prompted ceaseless efforts to inculcate in their minds what he conceived as the necessary intellectual foundation of the FRG. While he engaged in the political education of Germans right from the start with his arrival in West Berlin in 1951, he was searching for ever more effective strategies of knowledge transfer.[41] This was particularly important, as pluralist democracy entailed a very complicated political system that was 'difficult to understand' and which, as he frequently lamented, was in actuality understood only very poorly.[42] On numerous occasions Fraenkel complained about the lack of any proper political education and the dominance of Schmittian-Rousseauistic political myths that seriously endangered the stability of the FRG.[43] He remained highly sceptical towards what he called the 'political sub-consciousness' of the German population.[44]

Fraenkel, therefore, resorted to the rhetorical construct of 'Western democracy' because he found it a particularly effective way of spreading his message. His frequent use of the term 'Western democracy' was part of his art of persuasion. 'Western democracy' was more powerful and vivid an expression than 'pluralist democracy', let alone 'neo-pluralism'. The conflation of a spatial concept and a key word of political thought allowed him to anchor the FRG's political culture firmly in the realm of pluralist democracies, implicitly making a case for its democratization. By spatializing a political ideology, he constructed a mental map on which West Germany was an integral part of 'the West'. More than once, he used the expression 'Western democracies – including the Federal Republic',[45] and he often talked about 'Western democracies to which the Federal Republic belongs as well'.[46] The recurrence of such phrases in his writings from 1960 onward reveal Fraenkel's assumption that West Germany's embeddedness in the sphere of 'Western democracies' was far from settled. Instead, he was still unsure, indeed worried, about the FRG's moorings in the haven of 'the West'. The phrases implied, in fact, a polemical statement, which was directed against anti-pluralist traditions still haunting West German political culture – one may think, for instance, of the Schmittian legal scholars Ernst Forsthoff and Werner Weber.[47] Fraenkel's spatio-political statements were part of a strategy to place the FRG squarely in an imagined community called 'the West'.

Fifth, and finally, Fraenkel's growing determination to help transform the FRG's political culture manifested itself, around 1960, in a shift in national identity. The self-declared 'American in Berlin', who had sworn never to use the word 'we' again because he could never any more identify himself with 'the Germans',[48] suddenly switched to the 'we' form again, and this was just around the time he started to avail himself of the language of 'Western democracy'. He was, of course, still proud of his U.S. citizenship, which he only gave up, to his great regret, in 1972 for pension-related reasons. Yet from 1960 onward he spoke of 'we – the Germans'.[49] This further transformation of national identity can be explained not only with his increasing commitment to shift West Germany's political culture but also with his growing identification with the Free University Berlin as a place of knowledge transfer. This identification was fostered by an institutional self-conception as a hub of academic reform, political progress and the transnational circulation of ideas. It was also encouraged, though, by the students' appreciation of his teaching and respect for his work – something he found wanting during his research and guest lecturing stints at American universities. He never quite warmed to the more casual codes of conduct in American life, instead sticking to the habitus of a German professor. This attitude was only reinforced by the initial lack of career prospects in American academia and the eventual appointment as a full professor at the Free University.[50]

Fraenkel felt a growing obligation to both the Free University and the city of West Berlin and was acutely aware of their precarious location on the frontline of the Cold War. In times of crisis, he was careful to avoid any move – such as a prolonged research trip to the U.S. – which might have suggested he would abandon the Free University. This was not only because he had become a staunch Cold War liberal engaged in a war of words right on the border between 'East' and 'West'. Being a rémigré, he was also careful to avoid the slightest appearance of cowardice, or worse, treachery. In a nutshell, Fraenkel had become increasingly 'entangled' (*verwachsen*) with the whole 'Berlin problem', as he put it in a letter from January 1959, shortly after the outbreak of the second Berlin crisis.[51] The 'American professor' – as he had been called during his first years of remigration – had metamorphosed into a German 'Westernizer', who was still a loyal U.S. citizen but now also conceived of himself as an integral part of West Berlin and a steadfast defender of 'Western democracy'. It may be argued, therefore, that the full integration of the concept of the West in his rhetorical register allowed Fraenkel to solve, however subconsciously, an identity dilemma: instead of choosing between two national identities (American or German), he transformed into a German-American 'Westerner'.

Farewell to the West?

It was the self-conception as 'Westernizer' and mediator of knowledge that would soon be challenged by student activists in West Berlin and beyond.[52] The disruption of communication that occurred at universities such as the Free University in the late 1960s seriously endangered the fulfilment of what Fraenkel and other liberal academics saw as their central task: the inculcation of West Germany's future elites with the '*right* understanding of democracy',[53] namely a pluralist, parliamentary, 'Western democracy'. While politicized students appeared to be the harbingers of a much-needed democratization at first (in the liberal sense of the word), their teachers gradually realized that the most articulate exponents of student protest envisioned a 'democratized' society that was very different from their own visions of the future. As was the case with so many liberal scholars at the time, Fraenkel's pro-Americanism and pronounced anti-communism came under attack and his commitment to pluralism and parliamentarianism under harsh scrutiny. The progressive 'Westernizer', who had been keen to build bridges to the North American (and also British) worlds of thought, for he was determined to prevent Germany from falling into the abyss once again, was now denounced as a conservative 'reactionary' and apologist of the status quo.

It is no wonder that Fraenkel shared the interpretation advanced by his like-minded colleague Richard Löwenthal, who dismissed the student revolt as a 'romantic relapse': the leftist renaissance of 'anti-liberal', 'anti-Western' traditions of German thought.[54] After all, radical students adopted a critique of liberalism that sounded uncannily familiar to him. Whether this anti-liberal critique stemmed from Herbert Marcuse or Johannes Agnoli, it all reminded him of his intellectual arch-fiend Carl Schmitt. Once again, Germany appeared to deviate from 'the West'. Caught up in the German *Sonderweg* theory, the flip side of the 'Westernization' project, Fraenkel was blind to the transnational dimension of student protest, which, after all, affected universities in many Western countries, not least the U.S. '1968' was a traumatic experience he was unable to come to terms with. That he placed the student revolt in the narrative of German anti-'Westernism' reveals less about the event itself than about the lasting effect of the spatialization of his political thought and the discursive power of a paradigm that revolved around Germany's relationship to 'the West'. Traumatic memories of the 1930s did much to bolster this narrativization: student activism appeared as a left-wing totalitarian reincarnation of Nazism's 'revolt against the West' (Richard Löwenthal).

At a time when the FRG seemed to be on its way to becoming an integral part of 'the West', Fraenkel and other liberal 'Westernizers' feared that, like its Weimar predecessor, the 'second republic' would bid farewell to 'the West', after all. This fear never left Fraenkel, who died in 1975 thinking that his mission had failed. More generally, it would take years, if not decades, for anxieties of German anti-'Westernism' to disappear. They only faded away in post-unification Germany when for some commentators like Heinrich August Winkler the country seemed to have eventually 'arrived in the West', while for others, who questioned the validity of the 'Germany and the West' paradigm, it had never deviated from 'the West' in the first place. It was not merely the 'Weimar syndrome' but the German *Sonderweg* thesis in general (and its close relative modernization theory) that the latter consigned to history.[55] They bid farewell to 'the West' as an analytical construct and paved the way for its historicization.

Notes

1. Ernst Fraenkel, *Deutschland und die westlichen Demokratien*, ed. Alexander von Brünneck, Frankfurt/Main, 1991. Nine editions of *Germany and Western Democracies* were published between 1964 and 2011 – a remarkable success for a work of scholarship.
2. This analytical perspective is indebted to both Reinhart Koselleck and Quentin Skinner.
3. See especially Angelo Bolaffi, 'Dalla "Kollektive Demokratie" al "doppio Stato" nell'analisi di Ernst Fraenkel', *Annali della Fondazione Feltrinelli* 23 (1983/84), 1065–91; Hubertus Buchstein, 'Ernst Fraenkel als Klassiker?', *Leviathan* 26 (1998), 458–81; Hubertus Buchstein, 'Von Max Adler zu Ernst Fraenkel. Demokratie und pluralistische Gesellschaft in der sozialistischen Demokratietheorie der Weimarer Republik', in Christoph Gusy (ed.), *Demokratisches Denken in der Weimarer Republik*, Baden-Baden, 2000, 534–606; Hubertus Buchstein, 'Political Science and Democratic Culture. Ernst Fraenkel's Studies of American Democracy', *German Politics and Society* 21/3 (2003), 48–73; Hubertus Buchstein and Gerhard Göhler (eds), *Vom Sozialismus zum Pluralismus. Beiträge zu Werk und Leben von Ernst Fraenkel*, Baden-Baden, 2000; and Gerhard Göhler, 'Vom Sozialismus zum Pluralismus. Politiktheorie und Emigrationserfahrung bei Ernst Fraenkel', *Politische Vierteljahresschrift* 27 (1986), 6–27. See also Arnd Bauerkämper, 'Demokratie als Verheißung oder Gefahr? Deutsche Politikwissenschaftler und amerikanische Modelle 1945 bis zur Mitte der sechziger Jahre', in Arnd Bauerkämper, Konrad H.

Jarausch and Marcus M. Payk (eds), *Demokratiewunder. Transatlantische Mittler und die kulturelle Öffnung Westdeutschlands 1945–1970*, Göttingen, 2005, 253–72. See most recently Robert C. van Ooyen and Martin H.W. Möllers (eds), *(Doppel-)Staat und Gruppeninteressen. Pluralismus – Parlamentarismus – Schmitt-Kritik bei Ernst Fraenkel*, Baden-Baden, 2009; Reinhard Dorn, *Verfassungssoziologie. Zum Staats- und Verfassungsverständnis von Ernst Fraenkel*, Baden-Baden, 2010; and Michael Wildt, 'Die Angst vor dem Volk. Ernst Fraenkel in der deutschen Nachkriegsgesellschaft', in Monika Boll and Raphael Gross (eds), *'Ich staune, dass Sie in dieser Luft atmen können'. Jüdische Intellektuelle in Deutschland nach 1945*, Frankfurt/Main, 2013, 317–44.
4. Ernst Fraenkel, *Gesammelte Schriften*, 6 vols, ed. Alexander von Brünneck, Baden-Baden, 1999–2011. While the editors have written instructive introductions to each volume, they have used the term 'Western democracies' in an essentialized manner and have simply adopted the way in which Fraenkel used the term from 1960 onward. See, for instance, Gerhard Göhler and Dirk-Rüdiger Schumann, 'Vorwort', in Ernst Fraenkel, *Gesammelte Schriften*, vol 3: *Neuaufbau der Demokratie in Deutschland und Korea*, Baden-Baden, 1999, 30–31.
5. Simone Ladwig-Winters, *Ernst Fraenkel. Ein politisches Leben*, Frankfurt/Main, 2009.
6. See Anselm Doering-Manteuffel, *Wie westlich sind die Deutschen? Amerikanisierung und Westernisierung im 20. Jahrhundert*, Göttingen, 1999.
7. Alfons Söllner, 'Ernst Fraenkel und die Verwestlichung der politischen Kultur in der Bundesrepublik Deutschland' (2002), in Alfons Söllner, *Fluchtpunkte. Studien zur politischen Ideengeschichte des 20. Jahrhunderts*, Baden-Baden, 2006, 201–23, here 221; see also Alfons Söllner, 'Normative Verwestlichung? Die politische Kultur der frühen Bundesrepublik und Arnold Bergsträsser', in Söllner, *Fluchtpunkte*, 181–200.
8. Söllner especially refers to Fraenkel's supposed reluctance to realize what a hiatus there was between the constitutional norm and constitutional practice, and also points out a certain tendency to marginalize issues of racial discrimination in the U.S.
9. Ernst Fraenkel, *Das amerikanische Regierungssystem. Eine politische Analyse*, Cologne, 1960, 347.
10. 'Ernst Fraenkel to Friedrich Middelhauve, 31 Dec. 1959', quoted in Hubertus Buchstein and Rainer Kühn, 'Vorwort', in Ernst Fraenkel, *Gesammelte Schriften*, vol 4: *Amerikastudien*, Baden-Baden, 2000, 23.
11. Bernard Crick, 'Revolution vs. Freedom', *Observer*, 23 February 1964, 26. See also Bernard Crick, *The American Science of Politics. Its Origins and Conditions*, London, 1959.
12. Fraenkel had gained his first law degree in 1921.
13. 'Ernst Fraenkel to Otto and Susanne Suhr, 23 March 1946', in Fraenkel, *Gesammelte Schriften* 3, 389–95, here 389, 391–92 (emphasis added).
14. 'Ernst Fraenkel to Wolfgang Abendroth, 2 Oct. 1949', quoted in Ladwig-Winters, *Ernst Fraenkel*, 234.
15. On anti-Americanism in the early Federal Republic, see Christoph Hendrik Müller, *West Germans against the West. Anti-Americanism in Media and Public Opinion in the Federal Republic of Germany 1949–68*, Basingstoke et al., 2010.
16. Fraenkel, *Das amerikanische Regierungssystem*, 219.
17. Ernst Fraenkel, 'Das Verhältnis zwischen ziviler und militärischer Gewalt in USA' (1958), in Fraenkel, *Gesammelte Schriften* 4, 278–306, here 279–84.
18. Ernst Fraenkel, 'Deutschland und die westlichen Demokratien' (1960), in Fraenkel, *Deutschland und die westlichen Demokratien*, 48–67.

19. See, however, 'Ernst Fraenkel to Paula Sinzheimer, 9 Feb. 1958', in Ladwig-Winters, *Ernst Fraenkel*, 284–85.
20. Ernst Troeltsch, 'Naturrecht und Humanität in der Weltpolitik' (1923), in Ernst Troeltsch, *Schriften zur Politik und Kulturphilosophie (1918–1923)*, ed. Gangolf Hübinger in cooperation with Johannes Mikuteit, Berlin and New York, 2002 (Kritische Gesamtausgabe 15), 493–512, here 494; for Troeltsch, see also Austin Harrington's contribution to this volume.
21. Fraenkel, 'Deutschland und die westlichen Demokratien', 52.
22. Troeltsch, 'Naturrecht und Humanität', 507.
23. 'The cultivation [*Pflege*] of political semantics is one of the most significant political and scholarly tasks of political science.' Ernst Fraenkel, 'Pluralismus als Demokratietheorie des Reformismus' (ca. 1972), in Ernst Fraenkel, *Gesammelte Schriften*, vol 5: *Demokratie und Pluralismus*, Baden-Baden, 2007, 344–53, here 347–48.
24. Fraenkel, 'Deutschland und die westlichen Demokratien', 53.
25. Hermann Lübbe, 'Die philosophischen Ideen von 1914', in Hermann Lübbe, *Politische Philosophie in Deutschland. Studien zu ihrer Geschichte*, Basel, 1963, 171–235.
26. Fraenkel, 'Deutschland und die westlichen Demokratien', 50. For a critical assessment of this view, see Hans-Hermann Hartwich, 'Der soziale Gedanke im deutschen Staatsverständnis. Anmerkungen zu Ernst Fraenkels Aufsatz: Deutschland und die westlichen Demokratien', in Günther Doeker and Winfried Steffani (eds), *Klassenjustiz und Pluralismus. Festschrift für Ernst Fraenkel zum 75. Geburtstag am 26. Dezember 1973*, Hamburg, 1973, 131–47.
27. Roosevelt was Fraenkel's favourite politician, one whom he had greatly admired during the time of his American exile.
28. Fraenkel, 'Deutschland und die westlichen Demokratien', 51.
29. Ernst Fraenkel, 'Aussichten einer deutschen Revolution' (1943), in Fraenkel, *Gesammelte Schriften* 3, 56–57. See also Ernst Fraenkel, '"Rule of Law" in einer sich wandelnden Welt' (1943/44), in Fraenkel, *Gesammelte Schriften* 3, 58–73, here 58–59, where he used the term 'Western democracies' four times.
30. Ernst Fraenkel, 'Korea – ein Wendepunkt im Völkerrecht?' (1951), in Fraenkel, *Gesammelte Schriften* 3, 491–523, here 521.
31. See, for instance, Ernst Fraenkel, 'Diktatur des Parlaments? Parlamentarische Untersuchungsausschüsse, Öffentliche Meinung und Schutz der Freiheitsrechte' (1954), in Fraenkel, *Gesammelte Schriften* 4, 189–224, here 190.
32. Ernst Fraenkel, 'Menschen- und Bürgerrechte' (ca. 1953), in Fraenkel, *Gesammelte Schriften* 5, 370–73.
33. Ernst Fraenkel, 'Staat und Einzelpersönlichkeit' (1958), in Fraenkel, *Gesammelte Schriften* 5, 386–405, here 387, 394–95, 404.
34. Ernst Fraenkel, 'Die Selbstbestimmung in der Demokratie und in der Volksdemokratie' (1960), in Fraenkel, *Gesammelte Schriften* 5, 406–15.
35. See Ernst Fraenkel, 'Selbstentfaltung und Wertverwirklichung in der demokratischen Gesellschaft' (1954), in Fraenkel, *Gesammelte Schriften* 5, 374–82.
36. After all, Fraenkel studied law in Chicago, which was one of the hubs of the 'Western Civilization' course.
37. See Sebastian Ullrich, *Der Weimar-Komplex. Das Scheitern der ersten deutschen Demokratie und die politische Kultur der frühen Bundesrepublik 1945–1959*, Göttingen, 2009.
38. See, especially, Karl Dietrich Bracher, *Die Auflösung der Weimarer Republik. Eine Studie zum Problem des Machtverfalls in der Demokratie*, Stuttgart, 1955; Karl Dietrich Bracher, 'Weimar. Erfahrung und Gefahr', *Die politische Meinung* 2/15 (1957), 35–46; Kurt Sontheimer, 'Antidemokratisches Denken in der Weimarer

Republik', *Vierteljahrshefte für Zeitgeschichte* 5 (1957), 42–62; and Kurt Sontheimer, *Antidemokratisches Denken in der Weimarer Republik. Die politischen Ideen des deutschen Nationalismus zwischen 1918 und 1933*, Munich, 1962. See also Riccardo Bavaj, 'Deutscher Staat und westliche Demokratie. Karl Dietrich Bracher und Erwin K. Scheuch zur Zeit der Studentenrevolte von 1967/68', *Geschichte im Westen* 23 (2008), 149–71; and Riccardo Bavaj, 'Hybris und Gleichgewicht. Weimars "antidemokratisches Denken" und Kurt Sontheimers freiheitlich-demokratische Mission', *Zeithistorische Forschungen/Studies in Contemporary History* 3/2 (2006), 315–21.
39. A. Dirk Moses, *German Intellectuals and the Nazi Past*, Cambridge, 2007.
40. Ernst Fraenkel, 'Eine Selbstanzeige' (1962), in Fraenkel, *Gesammelte Schriften* 4, 857–60, here 860. See also Fraenkel, *Das amerikanische Regierungssystem*, 280.
41. Fraenkel generally considered the 'educational task of free Western democracies' to be the 'central problem of self determination in autonomous democracies based on the rule of law in the age of industrial mass society'. Fraenkel, 'Die Selbstbestimmung in der Demokratie', 413.
42. Ernst Fraenkel, 'Die ordnungspolitische Bedeutung der Verbände im demokratischen Rechtsstaat' (1967/68), in Fraenkel, *Gesammelte Schriften* 5, 311–12.
43. Fraenkel regarded Rousseau's *Contrat Social* as the 'most influential political work in modern times'. Ernst Fraenkel, 'Strukturanalyse der modernen Demokratie' (1969), in Fraenkel, *Gesammelte Schriften* 5, 314–43, here 325; see also Fraenkel, 'Staat und Einzelpersönlichkeit', 400.
44. Fraenkel, 'Die ordnungspolitische Bedeutung der Verbände', 313.
45. 'Western democracies – including the Federal Republic – base their concept of democracy on the anthropology, steeped in Judeo-Christian tradition, that man is ... not able to put the common good fully into practice' (*dass der Mensch zwar in der Lage ist, das Gute zu erkennen, dass es ihm aber verwehrt ist, es jemals voll zu verwirklichen*). Ernst Fraenkel, 'Möglichkeiten und Grenzen politischer Mitarbeit der Bürger in einer modernen parlamentarischen Demokratie' (1966), in Fraenkel, *Gesammelte Schriften* 5, 283–96, here 291.
46. In 'Western democracies, to which the Federal Republic belongs as well, the people's will is constructed autonomously, while in the Eastern states ... it is externally imposed on the people.' Ernst Fraenkel, 'Das Verhältnis von Recht und Politik in Demokratie und Diktatur' (1963/65), in Fraenkel, *Gesammelte Schriften* 5, 517–29, here 521.
47. See Marcus Llanque, 'Ernst Fraenkel und Rätedemokratie', in van Ooyen and Möllers (eds), *(Doppel-)Staat und Gruppeninteressen*, 185–205, here 190–91. For Ernst Forsthoff, see Florian Meinel, *Der Jurist in der industriellen Gesellschaft. Ernst Forsthoff und seine Zeit*, Berlin, 2011.
48. 'What scares me is the necessity of identification, a non-distanced attitude towards Germany. I am not able to bring myself to say the word "we" [*Das Wort "Wir" kommt mir nicht über die Lippen*].' Ernst Fraenkel to Otto Kahn-Freund, 21 Jan. 1959', quoted in Göhler and Schumann, 'Vorwort', 32, fn 91. See also 'Ernst Fraenkel to Otto Kahn-Freund, 9 June 1959', *Bundesarchiv Koblenz, Ernst Fraenkel Papers, NL 1274*, vol. 29.
49. See, for instance, Fraenkel, 'Die Selbstbestimmung in der Demokratie', 414; Fraenkel, 'Verhältnis von Recht und Politik', 529; or Fraenkel, 'Die ordnungspolitische Bedeutung der Verbände', 303. For an earlier exception, see Ernst Fraenkel, 'Startgleichheit und Klassenschichtung' (1956), in Fraenkel, *Gesammelte Schriften* 3, 625–29, here 628.

50. See, for instance, 'Ernst Fraenkel to Otto Kahn-Freund, 9 June 1959', *Bundesarchiv Koblenz, Ernst Fraenkel Papers, NL 1274*, vol. 29; see also Ladwig-Winters, *Ernst Fraenkel*, 271–87.
51. 'Ernst Fraenkel to Rinners, 1 January 1959', quoted in Ladwig-Winters, *Ernst Fraenkel*, 383–84.
52. For the following, see Riccardo Bavaj, 'Turning "Liberal Critics" into "Liberal-Conservatives". Kurt Sontheimer and the Re-coding of the Political Culture in the Wake of the Student Revolt of "1968"', *German Politics & Society* 27 (2009), 39–59; and Riccardo Bavaj, 'Das Trauma von "1968". Liberale Hochschullehrer in Westdeutschland und Frankreich', *Totalitarismus und Demokratie* 6/1 (2009), 101–14.
53. Kurt Sontheimer, *So war Deutschland nie. Anmerkungen zur politischen Kultur der Bundesrepublik*, Munich, 1999, 172 (emphasis added).
54. Löwenthal's interpretation of '1968' was, however, more complex. See Riccardo Bavaj, '"Western Civilization" and the Acceleration of Time. Richard Löwenthal's Reflections on a Crisis of "the West" in the Aftermath of the Student Revolt of "1968"', *Themenportal Europäische Geschichte* (2010), online: http://www.europa.clio-online.de/2010/Article=434; and Riccardo Bavaj, 'Young, Old, and In-between. Liberal Scholars and "Generation Building" at the Time of West Germany's Student Revolt', in Anna von der Goltz (ed.), *'Talkin' 'bout My Generation'. Conflicts of Generation Building and Europe's 1968*, Göttingen, 2011, 177–94.
55. See, especially, Thomas Welskopp, 'Identität *ex negativo*. Der "deutsche Sonderweg" als Metaerzählung in der bundesdeutschen Geschichtswissenschaft der siebziger und achtziger Jahre', in Konrad H. Jarausch and Martin Sabrow (eds), *Die historische Meistererzählung. Deutungslinien der deutschen Nationalgeschichte nach 1945*, Göttingen, 2002, 109–39. See also Christoph Gusy (ed.), *Weimars lange Schatten. 'Weimar' als Argument nach 1945*, Baden-Baden, 2003; A. Dirk Moses, 'The "Weimar Syndrome" in the Federal Republic of Germany. The Carl Schmitt Reception by the Forty-Five Generation of Intellectuals', in Stephan Loos and Holger Zaborowski (eds), *Leben, Tod und Entscheidung. Studien zur Geistesgeschichte der Weimarer Republik*, Berlin, 2003, 187–207; and Ullrich, *Der Weimar-Komplex*.

Part 4

NATIONALIST SELF-CENTREDNESS AND CONSERVATIVE ADAPTATIONS

Chapter 12

'THE WEST' IN GERMAN CULTURAL CRITICISM DURING THE LONG NINETEENTH CENTURY

Thomas Rohkrämer

Images and opinions concerning neighbouring nations in the West played an important role in cultural criticism in Germany throughout the nineteenth century. This chapter will argue, however, that the images of Britain, France and the U.S.A. remained quite distinct in the German imagination until 1914. While some commonalities between these three 'Western' countries were recognized, it took the enmity engendered by the First World War for a polarized dichotomy between Germany and 'the West' to become a significant topos. All through the long nineteenth century, the main focus of German cultural criticism was on the alleged ills of modernization in all advanced nations. With the coming of war, these ills came to be associated chiefly with 'the West', while an idealized 'Germanness' was presented as a potential remedy for the dark side of modernity. Amid continued tensions after 1918, this way of thinking continued throughout the Weimar Republic: it was not only the Versailles Treaty that was blamed for the ills of the times but also the republic, which was frequently seen as an 'un-German' political structure imposed by 'the West'. Thus political supporters of the Weimar Republic also became associated with an allegedly un-German 'Western' orientation, while the conservative forces rallied behind the call for a 'German' reawakening.

Images of France, Britain and the United States in the Nineteenth Century

Defining 'Germanness' against 'the West' played a key role at different times through the whole course of the long nineteenth century – although the naming of France, Britain and the U.S.A. as 'the West' only became common currency with the First World War. It was in opposition to the Napoleonic invasion that a vague belief in national differences turned into the political rallying cry of a nationalist belief: that Germany should demand the ultimate human loyalty.[1] Moreover, for conservatives, France was not just the aggressive neighbour threatening the political order of the German lands and – in particular – Prussia's status as a major power; it was also the nation of the enlightenment questioning the old ways, the nation of radical political thought demanding a political order based on reason, and the nation of revolutionary action for constitutionalism and democratic rights.

Britain, on the other hand, was less criticized for its political system – it was, after all, a more moderate, non-revolutionary constitutional monarchy – than for its economic system. This was a point particularly important for cultural criticism – that is, critical reflection on the process of modernization, which stressed how men and women were increasingly distanced from nature and how traditions, beliefs and natural communities were disintegrating dangerously.[2] From this perspective, Britain was the prime example of an industrialized state with a free market economy that did not integrate its subjects through emotional ties but through the monetary system and self-interest. In an anonymous text of the Romantic period, the author (probably Hegel or Schelling) thus compared the modern state as it emerged in the 'dual revolution' (political in France, industrial in England)[3] with a 'mechanical clockwork',[4] while the early conservative political Romantic Adam Müller declared that the state should not be a machine but an organic unit. Integration solely through material interests was not sufficient, he argued, for a social unit to function properly; a true community also needed a sense of solidarity based on a shared cultural heritage, shared ideals and shared political goals.[5]

The opposition 'organic'/'mechanical' as a basis for criticizing modern society was of Romantic origin, but became a staple argument in the history of cultural criticism. Rejecting the philosophical idea of a social contract, which takes the interest of the individual as its starting point, cultural critics emphasized that humans are, from birth, part of a wider whole: they belong in the family, a particular historical setting and a specific cultural and political unit. It is not the individual that comes first, they argued, but the collective. The rationally constructed state and the freewheeling economic system were criticized as mechanical because they simply served material functions. In contrast to this, cultural critics looked for a communal purpose that would integrate individuals into a wider whole. The nation should not function mechanically, independent of human ideals, but should incorporate and transcend all of its parts. Humans should not be alienated from a purely pragmatic state, but find meaning, fulfilment and self-realization within their community.[6]

Conservatives in particular tried to keep the French and British influence at bay. When they compared the development of Germany with that of France, there was a sense among cultural critics that enlightenment and revolution, liberalism and unrestricted capitalism were essentially alien to Germany. In contrast to the perceived rationalism of its Western neighbours, France and Britain, Germany came to be seen as an 'organic' power building naturally on its past and characterized by an organic political structure and a multilayered hierarchical order. For Schlegel, for example, France was a 'chemical nation', whose dominance would yield place to a future 'organic epoch', in which Germany would set the tone.[7] In contrast to the 'Western' emphasis on the rights of the individual, with all the to-do of parties and interest groups, of political conflict and economic competition, Germany was held to prioritize service to the common good – often believed to be incorporated in the state – and to foster a commitment to the spiritual values of the community. Instead of a reliance on reason, there was a belief in history. It was not acceptance of the nation that determined citizenship, but shared historical roots, a shared language and shared convictions.

While France came to be associated with radical politics and Britain with industry and commerce, Germans liked to see themselves as more cultured. In a rejection of materialism, which also came to be associated with the United States in the second half of the nineteenth century, Germany proudly portrayed itself as the country of poets and thinkers.[8] This permeated into everyday life, at least within the educated middle class. Harry Graf Kessler, for example, who came as a fourteen-year-old from England to stay with the family of a Protestant minister, noted:

> Very strange was the role of 'Bildung' in the ... household. When it was said of somebody that he was uneducated [ungebildet], then this was the same as when it was said in England that somebody was "not a gentleman"; there was nothing more contemptuous. There was something mystical about the cult of Bildung! Also because its actual content was unfathomable. We only knew that the goal of education was to turn us into 'gebildete Menschen', and that we thus had the duty to educate ourselves restlessly day and night.[9]

Perceived and real differences did thus exist, but the question is how important they were for cultural criticism in Germany. While the *Bildung* discussed above was, for example, clearly associated with 'Germanness', the famous distinction between a more spiritual (allegedly German) *Kultur* and a more materialistic (allegedly 'Western') *Zivilisation* was not generally accepted before the First World War. In the nineteenth century, authors such as Langbehn and Chamberlain expressed ideas that can be seen as laying the foundations for the distinction which, as will be shown, became so important later; but the philosopher Leopold Ziegler still concluded in his book of 1903 on the essence of culture 'that civilization and culture are intermingled' and that thus neither a solely civilized nor a solely cultured people could exist.[10] And when engineers vehemently argued in favour of an acceptance of the 'cultural value of technology' towards the end of the nineteenth century, the distinction of a mechanistic and utilitarian civilization in contrast to a spiritual and natural culture was implicitly questioned and undermined.

How important, then, was 'the West' in attempts to define a wholly distinct 'Germanness'? Germany was not like the long-established nations of France and Britain, where a national identity emerged much earlier. Goethe and Schiller could still ask in 1797: 'Germany? But where is it? I don't know how to find such a country.'[11] As nationalism preceded the nation, 'Germanness' had to be defined primarily through an emphasis on a shared history, a shared language and a shared culture. But what could this communal national culture be in a country with two major religious denominations, important regional diversities and a wide variety of political opinions? How could ideas of national identity respond to the failure of unification by revolutionary means and to a later monarchical unification 'from above'? Did cultural critics in the nineteenth century define 'Germanness' in opposition to a contrasting 'other' in 'the West'?

During the Napoleonic wars, 'Germanness' was defined in contrast to what was French – and to some extent also against capitalist Britain; but this polarization became less pronounced among cultural critics in the course of the nineteenth century, and even the Franco-Prussian war did not really change this trend. With the widespread desire in Germany to unite in a nation state, and then with a powerful empire trying to establish itself, the definition of Germans as a *Volk* of 'poets and thinkers', so useful in promoting a culturally based nationalism, came to be rejected as a naïve and dangerous weakness. In Germany's struggle to achieve status as a world power, it had to be put aside in favour of a new, aggressive political assertiveness. Generally, the more radical cultural critics were, the more they rejected portraying Germany as the positive culture in a blunt contrast with a negative 'other'. Those nations later labelled 'the West' frequently appeared as even more 'over-civilized' than Germany and thus served as a negative example of what might occur if the current trends were to continue unchecked; but fundamentally cultural critics diagnosed the same kind of problems in all national variants of modernity. The thinking of the cultural historian and journalist Wilhelm Heinrich Riehl is quite typical of this attitude. He does praise Germany's varied landscapes and its many forests in contrast to France and Britain, but the purpose of his writing is to check what he perceives to be a current trend that will make the German lands indistinguishable from those of its Western neighbours.[12]

A particularly interesting example of a German critic's deeply ambivalent relationship towards other nations in 'the West' is the musician Richard Wagner's attitude to France. Paris was the key place for opera production at this time, and Richard Wagner spent many years there. His attempts to start a career in Paris met with very limited success, and eventually he turned against those who did not recognize his genius. He came to reject the operas of his contemporaries as too 'Romanic'.[13] For him, they were artificial – indeed superficial; there was too much emphasis on musical entertainment rather than on trying to convey any deeper meaning. France, he believed, had dominated the German lands for far too long;[14] what was sorely needed was a truly German art. And he set out to produce exactly this. By using Germanic mythology, he believed he was going to the roots of the German tradition to produce an up-to-date mythology for the whole *Volk*.[15]

Wagner used Germanic mythology with the intention of fostering a national faith. While French art, so Wagner believed, lacked a connection with the common people, his ambition was to produce a new religion for the whole nation. The different understandings of art within the two nations were so fundamental to him that he diagnosed, in 1867, a 'battle between French civilization and German spirit': Germany had a desperate need to find its own voice.[16] Foreign influences could be accepted, but only if German artists had the strength to integrate these into something truly German. While he applauded Germans for being open to foreign influences, the end result had to be a higher, 'authentically German' synthesis.[17] Art thus must have its roots in the context of one ethnic *Volk*, and it should offer a belief system able to unite the whole people. Only in a second step could it then also appeal to, and possibly become a myth for, all humanity.[18]

The Western neighbour thus played an important role in the development of Wagner's work. First, Wagner valued Paris as the place where a musician had to prove himself; then he saw it as standing for something that needed to be negated or superseded. French opera was the standard to compete with, but he also denigrated it as a superficial, purely aesthetically pleasing art, against which he defined his own creations, which aspired to a deep spirituality with the potential of filling the place of religion in the modern age. Two things should be noted: much more important than words about the 'other' over the border was Wagner's attempt to define what it was to be German and how to achieve a single communal faith through art. The perceived need for a communal faith which art was to provide (since traditional religion had lost its force) was central; Wagner's attack on the Western neighbour was at most an attempt to create a space for appreciation of his own work by showing the limits of the then dominant form of opera.[19]

Richard Wagner is only one example of a whole number of cultural critics who were worried about what they saw as a deeply divided and fragmented Germany. With great urgency, they emphasized the need for a 'spiritual unification' of the German people. Their call for change did not claim to be based on universal, enlightened principles, as it was in the American and French revolutions, but on perceived ethnic characteristics. Germans were not to follow the examples of others, but find their own political convictions, political order and communal goals. In this vein, Paul de Lagarde called for a national religion and Julius Langbehn for an authentic German culture, for which Rembrandt served as the prime inspiration. There was a conviction, however, that the highest cultural achievements would emerge only from ethnically specific sources – or even only from those who were truly German. Langbehn thus expected that, once Germany had found its true form, it would gain the same kind of cultural dominance as Greece had had in the classical world.[20] Similarly, Houston Stewart Chamberlain voiced his 'firm conviction' 'that the whole future of Europe – i.e. the civilization of the world – rests in the hands of Germany'.[21]

These were just some of the more prominent voices within a whole chorus that was gaining force towards the end of the nineteenth century. While Wagner and Langbehn had been individual voices, the Bayreuth Circle came to exert a powerful influence during the Wilhelmine period. The publisher Eugen Diederichs offered a forum for such views, and there was a general sense of crisis and expectation, at least within the educated middle class.[22] A sharp critique of current conditions combined with hopes of dramatic change. These tended towards an extreme cultural chauvinism, vaunting the potential of Germany and the Germans; but the critics' view of the actual conditions in Wilhelmine Germany was very negative. And if contemporary Germany was seen as dangerously fragmented and threatened by unchecked modernization, with citizens about to lose every sense of what it meant to be 'German', how could this stark reality be presented as a positive alternative to some generalized 'West'? The cultural critics of the German Empire could not uphold a complete contrast between their country and 'the West'; instead they argued that Germans should be self-critical, realize the serious deficiencies of current conditions and work towards realizing an alternative modernity. This alternative modernity would maintain continuity with the past, unite Germans in a single communal faith and keep them in harmony with nature. The *Lebensreformbewegung* (Life Reform movement) at the turn of the century stressed a general need to respect nature and a natural way of life within modern societies,[23] and the *Heimatschutz* campaign to maintain typically German or regional landscapes and styles of architecture had more to do with valuing historical, often regional, roots than with any general anti-'Western' orientation. In 1887, Ferdinand Tönnies presented an idealized description of communities where personal ties were valued in contrast to anonymous societies, and this subsequently became highly influential; but his main contrast was between the traditional and the modern world.[24] By far the most radical cultural critic of the time was Ludwig Klages, who denounced the modern landscape by comparing it with Chicago; and he dismissed not only democracy and industrialization, but the whole 'Western' tradition of rationality since mythical Greece as a suicidal aberration.[25] He preferred the Germanic or Nordic tradition over the non-Germanic, but his philosophy was directed against a more general '*Geistigkeit des Westens*' ('rationality of the West') in which he included Kant as much as Descartes, and all scientific thinking and modern technology regardless of its national origin.[26] From a very different perspective, Walther Rathenau criticized mechanization as a dangerous force; but he did not close his eyes to the fact that it was a universal trend within the modern world, and no nation or individual could resist it without giving up all aspirations to have some control over their own destinies: individuals would lose a decent standard of living and nations the means to feed a growing population.[27] Even Friedrich Nietzsche, when he criticized English utilitarian philosophy and the restless American 'striving for gold' for destroying opportunities for a '*vita contemplativa*',[28] admitted that 'America's faith will also become Europe's faith'.[29] National characteristics were so flexible in Nietzsche's mind that Germany's international importance after political unification was seen as reason enough for France to emerge as the new nation of poets and thinkers. 'At the very moment when Germany emerges as a great power,' he argues in *Twilight of the Idols*, 'France achieves new importance as a *cultural power*. A lot of new seriousness, a lot of new spiritual *passion* has already emigrated to Paris. ... It's already known everywhere that in what really counts – and what really counts is still culture – the Germans are no longer worth considering.'[30]

Stereotypical images thus existed among cultural critics of their more democratic Western neighbours and the U.S.A. France was associated with cold reason and revolutionary politics; Britain was seen as 'gentlemanly' in outward appearance while ruthlessly pursuing its material interests; and the United States seemed marked by crass, uncultured materialism resulting from a lack of historical tradition. Connections were made between these traits by emphasizing their common root in Enlightenment beliefs of individual rights and self-interest, rather than stemming from historical tradition and a mode of political thought that put priority on the community. The pursuit of individual happiness was not meant to be the ultimate purpose of life; rather it was to be found in community based on a communal faith, and a life of service by its members to the whole. However, throughout the nineteenth century, stress on the roles of France, Britain and the United States as the negative 'other' remained limited among cultural critics, because they identified and attacked very similar dangers within their own country. These foreign nations were often collectively seen as being more extreme in their conditions than Germany; thus they could serve as a warning for what could happen if modernizing developments were to continue unchecked. Mainly, however, the critics pointed out the dangers within Germany itself and emphasized a communal need for self-improvement at home. It is thus not wholly surprising that, among the more extreme cultural critics in the second half of the nineteenth century, it was the 'Jew' who most commonly came to serve as the negative 'other'. As Jews lived in all modern societies, they could be held responsible for perceived ills within Germany and beyond. Richard Wagner, for example, linked the unchecked desire for power and wealth – so uncompromisingly condemned in artistic form in *Der Ring des Nibelungen* – with Jews. 'The Jew', he stated categorically, 'rules and will rule as long as money is the power against which all our activities lose their impact'.[31] For Paul de Lagarde, Jews were the main obstacle preventing the creation of a national religion; and anti-Semitism gained in importance with revised editions of Langbehn's *Rembrandt als Erzieher*. For the *völkisch* movement, race was the very core of their ideology – and the English were always seen as racially more closely related to Germans than any Jew or even the French.[32] For Ludwig Klages, Christianity and its ancestor, Judaism, were core causes for humanity's alienation from nature.[33] And Houston Chamberlain, an Englishman who grew up in France and travelled for years before he became an unsurpassed glorifier of Germany, showed respect for Britain, contempt for France and hatred for the Jews throughout his works.

August 1914: National Stereotypes Amalgamate into One Image of 'the West'

National stereotypes, charged value judgements and ideals of a harmonious community had long been present on German soil, but it took a brutal political conflict for a stark polarization to emerge between Germany and 'the West'. The First World War gave rise to the term 'total war' not only because of its scale and destructiveness but also because it was accompanied by a 'war of words'.[34] While 'the West' claimed it was fighting against a militaristic, authoritarian regime to make the world 'safe for democracy' (in Woodrow Wilson's famous phrase), intellectuals on the other side came to idealize what they believed to be characteristically 'German'. What cultural critics had presented as ideals for which Germans should strive were now taken as a reality to be defended, as shown in the alleged 'August-enthusiasm' at the time of the declaration of war. Cultural critics, who had previously concentrated on lamenting the divisions within Germany, suddenly subscribed to a polarized distinction between an idealized communitarian Germany and a wholly individualistic 'West'. Whereas, before, they had castigated an emphasis on material achievements in Germany as much as elsewhere, they now contrasted an 'intrinsically heroic' Germany with a greedy and materialistic 'West'. Against the claim that German anti-democratic militarism was responsible for a war of aggression and for war crimes, four thousand university professors signed a declaration claiming: 'In the German army no other spirit reigns than in the German people, because both are one, and we are also part of it. ... Our belief is that the whole of European culture is dependent on the victory which German "militarism" will gain, on the free German people's discipline, loyalty and willingness for sacrifice.'[35]

In the thinking of many intellectuals a massive reorientation is evident. Before 1914, Werner Sombart, for example, blamed capitalism for the ills of the modern world: 'Capitalism', he wrote in 1902, 'has brought us mass society, it has robbed us of a life of inner peace, it has alienated us from nature, it has taken from us the faith of our fathers by turning the world into a mathematical exercise and by promoting an overemphasis on worldly things in us, it has brought the mass of the population into a slave-like dependency from a small number of businesses'.[36] In 1915, however, he projected his criticisms onto 'the West', presenting Germany as heroic.[37] Whereas German culture had itself been perceived as under threat from the forces of modernization before 1914, Thomas Mann came to emphasize a polarized distinction between 'Western' civilization and German culture. His understanding of culture was obviously based on the ideals long expressed by cultural critics: 'Culture is a closed order, style, form, attitude, taste, is any specific spiritual organization of one's world', while civilization was seen by Mann to be 'rationality, enlightenment, pacification, moralization, scepticism, decomposition'.[38]

The beginning of war came to be glorified as a great awakening of the nation. Historians have shown the limited nature of the supposed national enthusiasm for war in August 1914, but there can be no doubt that many intellectuals experienced the time as a moment when the ills of the German *Volk* were overcome in an instant. To the historian Friedrich Meinecke it seemed that a fragmented society had suddenly turned into 'a single, powerful, deeply breathing community';[39] and Johann Plenge was highly influential in claiming a stark contrast between the 'Western ideas' of 1789 (those of the French revolution) and the essentially German 'ideas of 1914'.[40] This distinction was the most extreme example of the way in which the 'war between cultures'[41] led to a political mobilization of cultural criticism: the projection of all points of criticism onto 'the West' and of all ideals onto Germany. During the war, 'the West' became one of two opposing 'others'. While military successes and occupation in the Eastern theatre of war increased the sense of superiority in regard to 'the Slavic other',[42] 'the West' became the crucial ideological opponent against which German nationalists defined their own nation. 'The West' was, as Carl Schmitt put it more generally, an enemy that was taken seriously as an equal, but was perceived to have a wholly different ideological orientation. 'It is no good for humans to be without an enemy. The enemy is on a par with me. That's why I have to struggle with him in battle to gain my own measure, my own limitations, my own identity [*Gestalt*].'[43]

The fact that 'the West' – in contrast to 'the East' – was an 'equal other' and that communalities with it were still recognized can also be seen in the retention of a term that included Germany with the 'West': the term 'occident' or *Abendland*. The Catholic movement based around the journal *Neues Abendland* (which aimed for a re-Christianization of Europe) gave this term a particular ideological slant, but the term served more generally as a way of expressing the communalities of a culture emerging from the classical tradition and transcending the new divide between Germany and 'the West'. It was usually used with positive connotations. Oswald Spengler, for example, calls his famous book in German not the 'Decline of the West' (as it was translated into English), but the decline of the '*Abendland*', which literally translates as the 'occident'.[44] Heidegger also uses the term *Abendland* when he discusses the whole culture emerging from the Greek tradition: 'West' is a derogatory term in his work (again a distinction lost in the translation into English, where 'occident' is consistently translated as 'West').[45] What emerged with the First World War was thus a polarization within what was still recognized as one overall culture, an understanding West German conservatives could use again after 1945 when adapting to the nation's integration into the 'Western World'.[46]

The Enmity Continues: Cultural Criticism in the Weimar Republic

The end of the war in 1918 did not bring an end to this polarization. On the contrary: the peace settlement was widely perceived as a continuation of the will to destroy Germany by other means. Cultural criticism was mobilized against the Versailles Treaty. This was partly done within the context of foreign policy when, for example, Arthur Moeller van den Bruck argued for the rights of the allegedly healthy young nations of East and Central Europe against the old and decadent nations of 'the West'.[47] But at least as important was the use of the term 'West' in domestic politics. The legitimacy of the new republic was undermined by derisive accusations that it was a 'Western' import. While the Democrats and those in the Marxist working-class movement were accused of being 'Westerners within', cultural critics such as Oswald Spengler and Arthur Moeller van den Bruck tried to build on the supposed 'Spirit of 1914' by promoting a 'Prussian', 'German' or 'national' socialism.[48] Rejecting all belief in universal principles,[49] they claimed that a political order had to emerge from a nation's individual history. Furthermore, there was an emphasis on community – in contrast to an order build on the 'Western' idea of individuals entering a social contract – and this was seen to be peculiarly 'German'. Germany was the nation portrayed as most suited for realizing a true socialist order. 'Every nation has its own socialism', Moeller van den Bruck claimed, for example, in his book *Das dritte Reich*:[50] he rejected Marxism as an alien 'Jewish' idea and 'the West' as too individualistic. For him, socialism would emerge most naturally from the Prussian-German tradition with its emphasis on the community rather than on the individual.

Cultural criticism in the Weimar Republic was thus marked by strong opposition to 'the West'. The spread of popular culture was seen as a dangerous process of Americanization,[51] parliamentary democracy as a foreign import that only led to further divisions within society[52] and the Versailles Treaty as a straitjacket to keep Germany weak. 'The West' had won the war, but cultural critics did not want to learn from 'the West'. Instead, they called for Germans to find their own direction. Ernst Jünger wrote that accepting 'Western civilization' as the norm was just like losing the world war all over again,[53] and Heidegger emphasized the need to focus on the nation's Greek and German roots, as these were – in his mind

– the only truly philosophical cultures. During the Weimar Republic, he reflected on heritage and historicity and how these gave shape to a collective destiny,[54] and he stressed (in his political phase in 1933) that the fate of the world depended on the German *Volk* finding its collective ethnic identity and will at a time 'when the spiritual strength of the West fails and the West starts to come apart at the seams, when this moribund pseudo-civilization collapses into itself, pulling all forces into confusion and allowing them to suffocate in madness'.[55]

Conclusion

Images of 'the West' became a key theme in cultural criticism in 1914. Different ideas and stereotypes were present before, but they only amalgamated into a powerful unified image with the coming of the First World War. The alleged unity of the nation in facing the enemy in August 1914 seemed to show that the spirit of community, preparedness for service and sacrifice still existed in Germany, and subsequent political conflicts did not destroy the belief that such a sense of community could be achieved again. This had a fundamental effect on cultural criticism. It now tended to project the things it saw as negatives primarily onto 'the West'. In using the term, moreover, cultural critics meant not only the democratic countries – France, Britain and the United States – but also those political forces within Germany they accused of promoting 'Western' ideologies and politics. Above all, they criticized parliamentary democracy and Marxism. A new, truly 'German' order, they believed, would overcome the ills they had, for so long, attacked. This is why ideas of a communal economy (*Gemeinwirtschaft*) or German socialism found so much resonance: all political parties rose to the call to overcome the divisions in society by making – as they believed – a fair community of the people (*Volksgemeinschaft*) reality.[56] In this way, the themes of cultural criticism gained wider currency in the fatal call for a more homogeneous, truly 'German' order.

Notes

1. Thomas Nipperdey captures this by starting his great history of Germany in the nineteenth century with the words: 'In the beginning, there was Napoleon' (*Deutsche Geschichte 1800–1866*, Munich, 1983).
2. Georg Bollenbeck, *Eine Geschichte der Kulturkritik*, Munich, 2007; Thomas Rohkrämer, *Eine andere Moderne? Zivilisationskritik, Natur und Technik in Deutschland 1880–1933*, Paderborn, 1999.

3. Eric Hobsbawm, *The Age of Revolution*, London, 2007.
4. Manfred Frank and Gerhard Kurz (eds), *Materialien zu Schellings philosophischen Anfängen*, Frankfurt/Main, 1975, 110.
5. Adam Müller, *Die Elemente der Staatskunst* (1809), with an introduction by Jakob Baxa, Jena, 1922.
6. Manfred Frank, *Vorlesungen über die neue Mythologie*, vol. 1. Frankfurt/Main, 1982, 161 ff.
7. Friedrich Schlegel, 'Athenäums-Fragment 216: Charakteristiken und Kritiken I' (1796–1801), in Kritische Friedrich-Schlegel-Ausgabe, ed. Ernst Behler, Paderborn, 1979 ff., 1: 248.
8. Georg Bollenbeck, *Bildung und Kultur: Glanz und Elend eines deutschen Deutungsmusters*, Frankfurt/Main, 1996; Wolf Lepenies, *The Seduction of Culture in German History*, Princeton, 2006.
9. Quoted in Bollenbeck, *Bildung und Kultur*, 160.
10. Quoted in Bollenbeck, *Bildung und Kultur*, 271.
11. Johann Wolfgang von Goethe and Friedrich Schiller, *Xenien* (1796), ed. E. Schmidt and B. Suphan, Weimar, 1893, 14.
12. Thomas Rohkrämer, *A Single Communal Faith? The German Right from Conservatism to National Socialism*, Oxford, 2007, 64–66.
13. Richard Wagner, *Richard Wagners gesammelte Schriften*, ed. Julius Kapp, Leipzig, n.d, vol. 1, 192.
14. Ibid., vol. 13, 163 f.
15. Ibid., vol. 10, 177.
16. Ibid., vol. 14, 40.
17. Ibid., vol. 13, 166 f.
18. Ibid., vol. 1, 68–70; ibid., vol. 14, 59.
19. Ruth Henry and Walter Mönch, *Richard Wagner und Frankreich*, Bayreuth, 1977.
20. August Julius Langbehn, *Rembrandt als Erzieher. Von einem Deutschen*, 56th edn, Leipzig, 1922, 380.
21. Quoted in Geoffrey Field, *Evangelist of Race. The Germanic Vision of Houston Stewart Chamberlain*, New York, 1871, 34.
22. Winfried Schüler, *Der Bayreuther Kreis. Wagnerkult und Kulturreform im Geiste völkischer Weltanschauung*, Münster, 1971; Gangolf Hübinger (ed.), *Versammlungsort moderner Geister. Der Eugen Diederichs Verlag – Aufbruch ins Jahrhundert der Extreme*, Munich, 1996.
23. Diethart Kerbs and Jürgen Reulecke (eds), *Handbuch der deutschen Reformbewegungen 1880–1933*, Wuppertal, 1998; Kai. Bucholz, Rita Latocha, Hilke Peckmann and Klaus Wolbert (eds), *Die Lebensreform. Entwürfe zur Neugestaltung von Leben und Kunst um 1900*, Darmstadt, 2001. Catherine Repussard and Marc Cluet (eds.), *Lebensreform. Die soziale Dynamik der politischen Ohnmacht*, Tübingen, 2013.
24. Ferdinand Tönnies, *Community and Civil Society*, ed. Jose Harris, Cambridge, 2001.
25. Ludwig Klages, 'Mensch und Erde', in Ludwig Klages, *Sämtliche Werke*, vol. 3, Bonn, 1974, 614–36, here 620. See more generally Rohkrämer, *Eine andere Moderne?*, chapter 11.
26. Ludwig Klages, *Der Geist als Widersacher der Seele*, in Ludwig Klages, *Sämtliche Werke*, vols 1 and 2, Bonn, 1966 and 1969, 748.
27. Rohkrämer, *Eine andere Moderne?*, chapter 5. Competitors criticized his company, AEG, however, for its allegedly American or Jewish business practices. See Alois Riedler, *Emil Rathenau und das Werden der Großwirtschaft*, Berlin, 1916.

28. Friedrich Nietzsche, *The Gay Science. With a Prelude in Rhymes and an Appendix of Songs*, transl. with commentary by Walter Kaufmann, New York, 1974, 326.
29. Quoted in Andrei S. Markovits, *Amerika, dich haßt sich's besser. Antiamerikanismus und Antisemitismus in Europa*, Hamburg, 2008, 84.
30. Friedrich Nietzsche, *Twilight of the Idols*, trans. Walter Kaufmann, New York, 1954, 46 (italics in the original).
31. Wagner, *Richard Wagners gesammelte Schriften*, vol. 13, 9 f.
32. Uwe Puscher, *Die völkische Bewegung im wilhelminischen Kaiserreich. Sprache – Rasse – Religion*, Darmstadt, 2001.
33. While Klages mostly criticized Judaism as an ideology, his introduction to the work of Alfred Schuler is one of the worst anti-Semitic tracts. Ludwig Klages, 'Einführung des Herausgebers', in Alfred Schuler, *Fragmente und Vorträge. Aus dem Nachlaß*, ed. Ludwig Klages, Leipzig, 1940, 1–119.
34. Cincinnatus (Josef Lettenbauer), *Der Krieg der Worte*, Stuttgart, 1916.
35. Reprinted in Klaus Böhme (ed.), *Aufrufe und Reden. Deutsche Professoren im Ersten Weltkrieg*, Stuttgart, 1975, 49.
36. Quoted in Friedrich Lenger, *Werner Sombart 1863–1941. Eine Biographie*, Munich, 1994, 139.
37. Werner Sombart, *Händler und Helden. Patriotische Besinnungen*, Munich, 1915.
38. Thomas Mann, 'Gedanken im Krieg', in Thomas Mann, *Essays*, vol. 1, ed. Hermann Kurzke and Stephan Stachorskil, Frankfurt/Main, 1993, 188.
39. Friedrich Meinecke, *Die deutsche Erhebung von 1914. Vorträge und Aufsätze*, Stuttgart, 1914, 29.
40. Johann Plenge, *1789 und 1914. Die symbolischen Jahre in der Geschichte des politischen Denkens*, Berlin, 1916.
41. Barbara Beßlich, *Wege in den 'Kulturkrieg'. Zivilisationskritik in Deutschland 1890–1914*, Darmstadt, 2000.
42. Vejas Gabriel Liulevicius, *War Land on the Eastern Front. Culture, National Identity and German Occupation in World War I*, Cambridge, 2000.
43. Carl Schmitt, *Gespräch über die Macht und den Zugang zum Machthaber*, Stuttgart, 2008, 88. See more generally Carl Schmitt, *Der Begriff des Politischen. Text von 1932 mit einem Vorwort und drei Corollarien*, Berlin, 1987.
44. Oswald Spengler, *Der Untergang des Abendlandes. Umrisse einer Morphologie der Weltgeschichte*, 2 vols, Munich, 1918 and 1922; Oswald Spengler, *The Decline of the West*, transl. Charles Francis Atkinson, New York, 1926–1928.
45. Thomas Rohkrämer, 'Fighting Nihilism through Promoting a New Faith. Heidegger within the Debates of his Time', in Bogdan Costea, Kostas Amiridis and Paul Hemming (eds), *The Movement of Nihilism. Heidegger's Thinking after Nietzsche*, London, 2011, 39–53, here 49–50.
46. Axel Schildt, *Zwischen Abendland und Amerika. Studien zur westdeutschen Ideenlandschaft der 50er Jahre*, Munich, 1999.
47. Arthur Moeller van den Bruck, *Das Recht der jungen Völker*, Munich, 1919.
48. Arthur Moeller van den Bruck, *Das dritte Reich*, Berlin, 1923; Oswald Spengler, *Preussentum und Sozialismus*, Munich, 1919.
49. In this vein, Carl Schmitt famously stated: 'Whoever says humanity, wants to deceive'. Carl Schmitt, *Positionen und Begriffe. Im Kampf mit Weimar – Genf – Versailles 1923–1939*, Berlin, 1994, 162.
50. Moeller van den Bruck, *Das dritte Reich*, 35.
51. Alf Lüdtke (ed.), *Amerikanisierung. Traum und Alptraum im Deutschland des 20. Jahrhunderts*, Stuttgart, 1996; Rohkrämer, *Eine andere Moderne?*, 252–60.

52. Carl Schmitt, *The Crisis of Parliamentary Democracy*, Cambridge, Mass, 1988 (first published 1923).
53. Ernst Jünger, *Das Abenteuerliche Herz. Aufzeichnungen bei Tag und Nacht*, Berlin, 1929, 189.
54. Martin Heidegger, *Being and Time*, London, 1962 (first published 1927), chapter 5, division 2.
55. Martin Heidegger, 'The Self-Assertion of the German University', reprinted in Richard Wolin (ed.), *The Heidegger Controversy*, New York, 1991, 29–39, here 38.
56. Michael Wildt, 'Die Ungleichheit des Volkes. "Volksgemeinschaft" in der politischen Kommunikation der Weimarer Republik', in Frank Bajohr and Michael Wildt (eds), *Volksgemeinschaft. Neue Forschungen zur Gesellschaft des Nationalsozialismus*, Frankfurt/Main, 2009, 24–40.

Chapter 13

NO PLACE FOR 'THE WEST'
National Socialism and the 'Defence of Europe'

Philipp Gassert

Anti-'Westernism' was a prominent feature of First World War debates, when German intellectuals pitted the 'ideas of 1914' against the 'ideas of 1789'.[1] However, though this way of thinking lingered on during the early Weimar years, it lost its significance from the mid 1920s. After Nazi rule was established in 1933, it was anti-Bolshevism that became the guiding political idea shaping right-wing thought on Western nations such as Britain, France, the Netherlands and the United States. Moreover, like many German nationalists, the Nazis preferred to speak of 'Europe', which needed to be defended spiritually and militarily against 'Eastern' Bolshevism and Americanism. 'Europe', of course, was essentially different from the abstract idea of a West that during the First World War had come to include non-European 'white' nations. At first a means of anti-Soviet propaganda, the Nazi idea of Europe increasingly acquired anti-American undertones, especially after the fall of France in 1940.

To be sure, the German Right sometimes spoke of 'Western democracies'. In the racialized worldview of National Socialist ideology, however, 'the West' tended to mean the global hegemony of the 'white nations'. This excluded the 'Asiatic' Soviet Union but, during the interwar period, did take in the United States – at least until Nazi propaganda during the 1930s began to make out that a 'Jewish element' was gaining dominance there. In this way of thinking, Germany was as much a part of 'the West' as were Britain and France – although, sometimes France was excluded from the 'white West' for being too 'Africanized', along with the other 'coloured' southern European nations.[2] Thus, the Nazi idea of the West largely accorded with the projections imperialists imposed on the globe in the nineteenth century, when, despite European colonial rivalries, the world was envisaged as divided between 'Europe' and 'the rest'. From this point of view, the peoples of Europe had a common goal in fighting back all kinds of 'yellow and brown perils', and also 'the American menace'.[3]

This is not to say that the odd anti-Western quotation cannot be tracked down during the period in question. Authors like the cultural anthropologist Wilhelm E. Mühlmann – to give but one example – referred to the political ideals of the 'Western' world and described them as contrasting sharply with the right of ethnic self-determination upheld by the German *Volk*;[4] but these individual instances do not invalidate the overall argument, especially when dealing with a heterogeneous phenomenon like National Socialism. An in-depth analysis of the literature of the Nazi period and the final years of the Weimar Republic would probably demonstrate that key terms like *Abendland* (occident), *Demokratie*, *Kapitalismus*, *Plutokratie*, *Europa*, *Großraum*, *Lebensraum* and *Sowjetrussland* were much more current than was *Westen*. In an intellectual world shaped by Social Darwinism, race was the prime organizational factor in international relations. This is why the concept of *Westraum* – a term referring to the western border regions of Germany – was not really one around which ideological oppositions could form. As an ethnographic term, *Westraum* was important for the German hegemonic reordering of European spaces during the Second World War; yet it did not really signify an ideological division between Germany and 'the West' and was not the ground for political struggles.[5]

The argument above stands in stark contrast to what is held to be true in a prominent current of historical scholarship. Fritz Stern has argued that 'National Socialism was the triumph of anti-Westernism'. According to Stern, the Third Reich was 'a demonstrative turning away from the West'.[6] In a similar fashion, Heinrich August Winkler has devoted hundreds of pages to the argument that National Socialism was the epitome of anti-'Westernism' in Germany.[7] While these scholarly statements may make sense from an early twenty-first-century viewpoint, they do not do justice to the historical discourse of the 1930s. To think of National Socialism as an anti-'Western' ideology is to ignore how it was commonly seen during the period itself. There can be no doubt that Nazi Germany turned against the liberal-democratic values represented by the French and American revolutions, according to which the normative concept of the West is commonly defined. Democratic rule was abolished; basic civil rights were trampled underfoot; the regime's political and racial enemies were incarcerated and killed; whole ethnic groups were singled out for extermination. Yet this National Socialist anti-liberalism was seldom thought of as a turning against 'the West' and no such sentiment was expressed with any special vehemence. Yes, an opposition to the 'ideas of 1789' figured prominently enough in Nazi ideological parlance,[8] but the 'National Revolution' of 1933 was primarily geared to a turning against 'the East'. The National Socialist *Volksgemeinschaft* ('people's community') saw itself locked in an ideological struggle against Bolshevism and against the Weimar constitutional order, which was understood equally as an outgrowth of Marxism.

The first part of this chapter will explore briefly how 'the West' was marginalized in certain parts of German right-wing discourse during the 1920s. The second part will focus on Adolf Hitler's thinking. While this may come across as an old-fashioned 'Hitler-centric' approach, the leader of the National Socialist Party can hardly be ignored when attempting to understand how Nazi worldviews developed. While there were competing concepts among the intellectual and political grandees of Nazi Germany, Hitler's ideas mostly won out. The third and final part of the chapter will contextualize Hitler's thinking within the ideological and propagandistic conflicts of the Second World War. The chapter will conclude with a brief comment on the return of German anti-'Westernism' during the first post-war decade.

The Abandonment of Anti-Westernism

The relative absence of the idea of the West from significant strands of German right-wing thought in the years between 1925 and 1945 may come as a surprise after the enormous investment in anti-Western thought that had taken place during the First World War.[9] In 1918, in *Betrachtungen eines Unpolitischen*, Thomas Mann had famously proposed that German political culture and 'Western' democracy could not be reconciled. In a similar vein, leading intellectuals at the time of the First World War – among others, the theologian Ernst Troeltsch, the historian Friedrich Meinecke, the economist Werner Sombart and the sociologist Alfred Weber – had blasted 'Western' individualism and liberalism for their inherent weaknesses. It was, they maintained, Germany's mission to overcome bourgeois class society to achieve a more just, less atomized social order. During the early years of the Weimar Republic, while some, like Troeltsch, came round to republicanism and were willing to highlight the commonalities between German and 'Western'

European culture,[10] radical right-wing intellectuals such as Arthur Moeller van den Bruck continued to dwell on Germany's anti-'Western' mission.[11]

As the decade wore on, however, the idea of a cohesive West became less convincing, even though anti-liberalism and anti-democratic thinking continued to attract many right-wing intellectuals.[12] Cracks appeared in the former Western camp. Politically, not much remained of the grand alliance of the First World War: Britain felt uneasy about the Versailles settlement; the United States opted for a political disentanglement from Europe; France stood alone. The former Allied powers and their associates were deeply divided over the question of how to deal with Germany. Therefore from the mid 1920s, Germans could not find much that a sociopolitical concept of the West could be pinned on. The 1928 edition of *Meyers Lexikon* defined the term *Westen* in a purely geographical and directional sense, as opposed to *Süden*, *Norden* and *Osten*. According to the same encyclopaedia a 'Westerner' was an inhabitant of the west or the southwest regions of the United States.[13] Thus, when Adolf Hitler and his followers were developing and testing their ideas, the ground was not fertile for either 'Western' or anti-'Western' strands to the new German ideology. 'The West' had been a useful concept during the First World War but when tensions among the victorious powers mounted, its plausibility diminished.

Moreover, the 'roaring twenties' were the heyday of the debate over Americanism. Writers made much of the 'American menace' to Europe and little of any 'Western menace' to Germany. With the products of Henry Ford's assembly lines conquering the world, Hollywood fighting for access to film markets everywhere, African-American jazz competing with European high culture and the 'American way of life' threatening to undermine traditional societies, the presence of the U.S.A. loomed as large over France and Britain as it did over Germany.[14] Adolf Halfeld's book *Amerika und der Amerikanismus*, the bible of German anti-Americanism, was subtitled 'critical observations of a German and European'.[15] America was the 'menace in the West'.

The idea of a cohesive West was further undermined by political and intellectual developments in the United States. There, the country's entry into the First World War came under attack from isolationist-minded conservatives as well as from progressives, who believed that the U.S.A.'s international predicament had been brought about by the selfishness of mercantile interests. The term 'dollar diplomacy' was popularized by the American political scientists Scott Nearing and Joseph Freeman, who saw U.S. expansionism in the Caribbean and Pacific as purely economically motivated. Their controversial book came out in 1925 and was immediately translated into German. Although the argument was of an economic determinist variety akin to Marxist analysis, the book was well received among sections of the German Right. The eminent geographer and geopolitician Karl Haushofer, the teacher of Hitler's deputy Rudolf Heß, contributed a preface to the German edition, in which he called for a 'united Europe' as the only way to resist the grasp of the *Kraken* (octopus) that U.S. 'imperialist capital' represented.[16] Haushofer's endorsement of this need to resist *Dollardiplomatie* foreshadowed ideas of the German hegemonic reordering of 'Europe' that would come during the Second World War.

Indicatively, Alfred Rosenberg, chief ideologue of the National Socialists, was highly critical of any talk of a 'Western spirit'. What people called 'the West', he argued, was a mixture of a degenerate 'Frenchness' and the 'Jewish democratic idea', which had found its political expression in contemporary parliamentarianism. 'One should not talk in the abstract about the rule of a so-called "West" but more specifically about a Jewish-French system of thought.' It was this decadence, according to Rosenberg, that was now threatening England, too, and for some time even Italy.[17]

Hitler and the 'Decline of the West'

The few instances in which Hitler talked about 'the West' in an ideological sense occurred mostly during the first half of the 1920s, when anti-'Western' sentiments were still widespread among the German Right. Apart from that, Hitler had quite a positive view of U.S. immigration and racial policies. He was well aware of the eugenics programmes of several of the American federal states and cited them as examples for Germany.[18] During the 1920s, he sometimes referred to a common Jewish element connecting the United States, France and Britain. In 1925, for example, he blasted 'the big bankers from London, Paris, and New York'. This was a reference to a Jewish financial elite that had not only conspired to bring about the First World War but was also trying to retain dominance in the 1920s by working on the monetary settlement following the outcome of the war.[19] When Hitler claimed that 'Western democracy, on the one hand, and Russian Bolshevism, on the other [create] the form within which today's Jewish *Weltanschauung* finds its expression', he was indeed using the term 'Western democracy' as an ideological marker.[20] The crucial context, however, was anti-Semitic. The Soviet system was linked to Western democracy through racial and anti-Semitic bonds. National Socialism was opposed to liberal democratic as well as illiberal communist rule, because they were both means of supposed 'Jewish world domination'.

As is well known, Hitler had developed a relatively fixed vision of foreign policy by the mid-1920s. Ultimately he aimed to work toward the eastward expansion of Germany's *Lebensraum* (its living space) at the expense of Poland and the Soviet Union.[21] For this purpose, he wanted to secure a pact with liberal-democratic Great Britain and Fascist Italy. This is why he was willing to leave the Southern Tyrol to the Italians and renounce Germany's claims to its former colonies in Africa. Working with Britain and Italy, he believed, Germany could wage war against France and the Soviet Union, thereby averting a situation like that in the First World War, when Germany had to deal with the three great European powers simultaneously. From the mid 1920s onwards he highlighted the ruptures between the former First World War allies. He repeatedly pointed to a growing naval and trade rivalry between the two democratic sister nations, Great Britain and the United States. Throughout the 1920s and 1930s he searched for clues to demonstrate the growth of an Anglo-American antagonism: one such was the London Naval Conference of 1930.[22] In his unpublished *Second Book* (1928) Hitler famously called for a German-British alliance. Britain might have won the war in 1918, but it did so at great cost: for that country now, the American giant posed an enormous challenge to its empire and was becoming the kind of rival Wilhelmine Germany had been before 1914.[23]

In Hitler's strategic thinking, it was only a matter of time before the rise of the United States would lead the reliably liberal British nation to side with anti-liberal Germany. Here 'West' was ranged against 'West', and the British 'West' would come to side with Germany. Hitler's remarks on the 'Western' American 'colossus' expressed his privileging of geopolitics and economic prowess over ideological affinity as indications for the course of international relations. Although he had mixed feelings toward the United States, Hitler believed that America was the best example anywhere of a large territorial expanse that could be the model for his future pan-Germanic empire.[24] Gloatingly, he observed the commonalties between the rising British-American antagonism and the German-British rivalry prior to the First World War. He maintained that Great Britain would find 'the gigantic American colossus of a nation state, with its enormous riches from a virginal Earth' more difficult to deal with than imperial Germany had ever been.[25]

Hitler's speeches of the 1920s were shaped by the 'America craze' of the 1920s, when Fordism and cultural Americanization became an obsession in Europe. After the onset of the Great Depression, he lost interest in the United States. Yet he would continue to elaborate on the coming British-American antagonism throughout his time in office as Reich Chancellor. Even after the signing of the Atlantic Charter in 1941 and after the United States had been attacked by Japan and entered the war against Germany, he continued to deplore the missed opportunity a British-German alliance would have presented. When, in late 1941, the fall of Singapore looked a distinct possibility, he did not wholeheartedly celebrate the impending victory of Germany's ally, Japan. Rather, he saw it as an ominous sign of the decline of 'the West', by which he meant Europe and its empires. In a similar fashion he lamented the loss of Dutch rule in the East Indies. As he had predicted time and time again, another fratricidal war in Europe could wipe white domination off the East Asian map; and in the long run, Japan might even conquer Australia.[26] The one country that had had every reason not to wage war had been Britain. All it needed to retain control of its empire was to keep a strong defensive navy and air force free for their protective tasks.[27] This is not to say that Hitler did not welcome the Japanese entry into the war for pragmatic reasons. 'A millstone', he said, 'has fallen off my neck'. Yet, at the same time, he lamented the fall of East Asia, because it was 'a loss for the white race'.[28]

Race was the central divider, even though Hitler wholeheartedly cooperated with the non-'white' Japanese as part of a strategic forward defence meant to deter the United States. How little Hitler believed that 'Western democracy' was a common denominator of the Anglo-American alliance is shown in some rather surprising remarks he made about the U.S. constitution. In early 1942 he reflected that Nazi Germany's political system was somewhat similar to that of the United States, whose president combined the offices of head of state and chief of government. The pre-1914 *Kaiserreich*, on the other hand, had tended towards the British parliamentary model, where the king was the titular head of the nation but did not exercise great political powers.[29] What Hitler admired in Britain, however, was the system of an 'absolute state church'.[30] While these commentaries demonstrate a rather shallow knowledge of the domestic political orders in Britain and the U.S., they do make clear that Hitler did not think of National Socialism as categorically different from 'Western' political systems.

Along with many of his intellectual fellow travellers, Hitler tended to think of the world of international relations in Social Darwinist and racial terms as well as in terms of *Lebensraum* and geographical expansion. Especially during the Second World War, he used the watchword 'Europe', which militarily, economically and to some extent politically had become a temporary unit, albeit under a ruthless German hegemony. In terms of culture and race, this 'Europe' would include Britain. To Hitler's great and continued regret, this Germanic island nation – especially now that it was under the leadership of Winston Churchill – continued to oppose his plans of creating a new European order strong enough to purge 'Jewish Bolshevism' from the earth, keep the 'American menace' at bay and preserve white rule in Asia and Africa. In his thinking 'Europe' and 'race' were far more important than any concept of the West; and for this reason he hardly talked of 'Western democracy' in any consistent or meaningful way. For Hitler, 'the West' seemed to have lost its significance already during the second half of the 1920s. The concept was never systematically resurrected in German propaganda during the Second World War. So the situation was markedly different from that of the First World War, when German intellectuals had striven to define German political culture as something that was almost genetically anti-'Western'.

'Europe' in Nazi Propaganda

Against this backdrop of an overall move away from ideas of an anti-'Western' German mission – prevalent at the time of the First World War but actively abandoned by the Nazi Party – it is not surprising that the concept of an antagonistic West was not wholeheartedly endorsed after 1933. For a brief moment in 1933 itself, however, it seemed as though Nazi Germany faced the united opposition of the former 'Western nations'. The boycott of Jewish shops in Germany on 1 April 1933 provoked outrage in British, French and U.S. newspapers. This action served to highlight the ideological differences between Nazi Germany and 'the West'.[31] Even so, there was a pronounced tendency in German propaganda to stress commonalities when it came to the economic policies of Nazi Germany and New Deal America. In their approaches for overcoming the Great Depression both Hitler and Roosevelt appeared to be following a worldwide trend towards 'state socialism'. A few days after Roosevelt's inauguration in early March 1933, the Nazi Party newspaper *Völkischer Beobachter*, for example, surprised its readers with a headline in the business section that read: 'Roosevelt's adaptation of National Socialist reasoning'. The headline was inspired by what was described as Roosevelt's 'fight against Wall Street financiers', a struggle that 'in several respects' resembled 'the German national movement against international financial capital'.[32]

Several days later, a story appeared about 'Roosevelt's fight against speculation', in which parallels were drawn between Hoover's unsuccessful policy and 'the preceding German events'. The article referred to the Americanism debate, arguing that there was a direct connection between the 'proverbial prosperity' of the 1920s, the 'drive toward an exaggerated rationalization and mechanization of the economy' and the onset of the Great Depression. The failed attempts in Brüning's Germany and Hoover's U.S.A. to save 'a highly developed, capitalist economic order' were held to show 'that this system is not suitable to maintain a healthy economy, let alone to be the basis of a global economy'. National Socialist policy and the New Deal had both supposedly broken with these liberal free-market traditions and would now direct economic development down new pathways. 'As in Germany', wrote the *Deutsche Wirtschaftszeitung*, the U.S.A. did not limit itself merely 'to undertaking individual measures to rebuild a healthy, well-balanced economic base; what is occurring instead is a major effort to confront the crisis'.[33]

The anti-liberalism and anti-capitalism that National Socialism stood for was thus portrayed as not at all unique to 1930s Germany. From the Nazi point of view, this new state socialism represented a broad international trend encompassing many countries of 'the West'. Although it soon became obvious that Roosevelt was not travelling along the same economic pathway as Hitler, and though various American political groups were fiercely critical of Nazi racial policies and the infringement of civil liberties in Germany, Nazi propaganda did not, by and large, elaborate on any commonalities among the former Western allies that Germany did not share. Rather, it stressed common interests between itself and the former Western powers. Moreover, during most of the 1930s, the Nazis tried to play up anti-Bolshevism as a common theme among all European nations. A good example was to be seen in Germany's pavilion at the Paris World Exposition in 1937. The display demonstrated the achievements of the 'new social order' in Germany and the technological advances that Germany had seen under Nazi rule. Here, developments in Germany were even paraded as an example to other Western nations. Moreover, anti-Bolshevism was stressed while anti-Westernism was toned down. The German and Soviet pavilions, which were erected in prominent positions opposite each other at the entry to the Paris Exposition grounds, represented physically the most important ideological dividing line of the 1930s. As an icon of 'architectural anti-Bolshevism', Albert Speer's building reminded all Europeans that Moscow threatened 'European civilization'. This argument would later become a central element of German propaganda in France after the beginning of the Occupation in 1940.[34]

A spatial distancing of 'Europe' from both the U.S.A. and the Soviet Union became a standard propaganda ploy during the Second World War. In a notorious speech to the German Reichstag on 28 April 1939, Hitler theatrically pronounced a 'European Monroe Doctrine' that 'prohibited the intervention of powers foreign to the region': it was to apply to Europe and 'by all means to the territory of the Greater German Reich'.[35] This 'European Monroe Doctrine' was envisioned as bringing in a renaissance of the American tradition of hemispheric isolation, which was contrasted with 'British universalism'.[36] In this context, authors like Adolf Halfeld interpreted '1776' and the American War of Independence as the initial steps in a long progression of anti-imperialist revolutions now culminating in Germany's European war effort.[37]

It is not necessary here to discuss the many misunderstandings and errors that took the 'European Monroe Doctrine' to its short-lived but stellar career in Nazi propaganda. The idea had been floating around in the 1920s and 1930s and had even occasionally been used against Woodrow Wilson. In taking up the idea, Hitler had once again been influenced by Karl Haushofer and other geographers, who conceived of international relations along geopolitical and (to a certain extent) ethnic lines.[38] Among the German population, the proclamation of a 'European Monroe Doctrine' fell on fertile soil. According to reports of popular opinion, the German public received it 'with vigorous approval as an intrinsically clear and distinct, moderately stated and overall self-confident rejection of American interference in European relations'.[39] Carl Schmitt believed at the time that it would have to become clear 'which side the other Anglo-Saxon power, the United States of America, will join; whether it will decide for the original, genuine, continental *Großraum*-concept of the Monroe Doctrine or whether it wants to enter an alliance or even a fusion with the wealth and tradition of British universalism'.[40]

The 'European Monroe Doctrine' was one way of playing up differences between Britain, France and the United States. It lost its importance as an offensive element in Nazi thought and propaganda after the U.S. entry into the Second World War. The doctrine was then degraded to one among many arguments in the rhetorical arsenal of Nazi propagandists that sounded increasingly shallow as the war progressed, though it continued to be discussed in certain serious academic circles and Nazi publications. Moreover, the dominating anti-Bolshevist theme of the doctrine was placed on the back burner from 1939 to 1941 out of tactical considerations necessitated by the German-Soviet Non-aggression Pact. Anti-Bolshevism was revived with a vengeance, however, after June 1941 and became the new basis for agitation in favour of a 'Europe for the Europeans'. Towards the close of the war, when Germany had long lost all options it had had in 1941/42 to shape Europe's fate, some recollections of the 'European Monroe Doctrine' appeared again here and there. A listener wrote to the *Großdeutsche Rundfunk* in September 1944, saying that it should be explained to the Americans 'that we Germans are fighting for the creation of the United States of Europe in order to eradicate war within Europe in the future'.[41]

Conclusion

Most of the Nazis and their intellectual fellow travellers had no conception of the West as a cohesive political and ideological entity. Some referred to it in passing; others ignored 'the West' altogether; yet others went to great lengths to underscore the differences among the former 'Western powers' of the First World War. This relative neglect of anti-'Westernism' as an instrument of Nazi propaganda need not come as a surprise if the Nazi view of history is taken seriously. 'Race' and *Lebensraum* were the core National Socialist concepts according to which European societies were to be reordered. Simply calling the Nazis 'anti-Western' fails to give their murderous racial ideology its correct place in history. Compared to anti-Semitism, anti-Bolshevism and belief in a 'Jewish world conspiracy', 'the West' did not offer a sufficiently challenging enemy image to support the Nazi view of world history. When it seemed opportune, National Socialist politicians and ideologues would even stress commonalities between German and U.S. racial policies, or they would point to the common goals that Britain and Germany shared, as the two Germanic sister nations. Many Nazi ideologues, including Hitler, thought highly of the British Empire but lamented that Churchill was bringing it down – to the detriment of the 'white race' in general.

Against this backdrop of the declining intellectual power of the anti-'Western' argument in Germany from the mid 1920s to the mid 1930s, the post-1945 era looks like a period when both pro- and anti-'Western' thought underwent a reconstruction. To some extent, the return of liberal democracy to Germany also meant the return of anti-'Westernism', which was now restored to its traditional place within Germany's political culture. There were now three Western zones of occupation run by the key members of the grand alliance of the First World War. With a powerful bloc of 'Western nations', under the leadership of the United States, working towards a reordering of Europe that would leave the old world divided, some conservative and right-wing intellectuals may well have been prompted to recall intellectual conflicts at the time of the First World War. However, many conservatives made their peace with 'the West'. Under the leadership of Konrad Adenauer, they now saw the best hope for (West) Germany's future prospects as lying within a strong Western alliance. Even those 'occidentalists' who remained sceptical about the cultural, political and economic influence of the United States and who hated 'Americanization' often shared positive notions of a conservative and democratic European 'West' with their peers in France, Italy and Spain. Whereas, during the First World War, 'the West' had served as a negative foil, giving Germans an identity in opposition to it, the concept was now turned into a force for cohesion among members of the West German and European Right.[42]

Notes

1. See Anselm Doering-Manteuffel, *Wie westlich sind die Deutschen? Amerikanisierung und Westernisierung im 20. Jahrhundert*, Göttingen, 1999, 21.
2. Alfred Rosenberg, *Der Mythus des 20. Jahrhunderts. Eine Wertung der seelisch-geistigen Gestaltenkämpfe unserer Zeit*, 23rd/24th edn, Munich, 1934 (first published 1930), 640–43.
3. Heinz Gollwitzer, *Europabild und Europagedanke. Beiträge zur deutschen Geistesgeschichte des 18. und 19. Jahrhunderts*, Munich, 1964 (first published 1951), 328–32.
4. Walter E. Mühlmann, *Krieg und Frieden. Ein Leitfaden der politischen Ethnologie*, Heidelberg, 1940, 212.
5. Thomas Müller, *Imaginierter Westen. Das Konzept des 'deutschen Westraums' im völkischen Diskurs zwischen Politischer Romantik und Nationalsozialismus*, Bielefeld, 2009, 356–60.
6. Fritz Stern, *Der Westen im 20. Jahrhundert. Selbstzerstörung, Wiederaufbau, Gefährdungen der Gegenwart*, Göttingen, 2008, 23.
7. Heinrich August Winkler, *Der lange Weg nach Westen*, 2 vols, Munich, 2000; Heinrich August Winkler, *Geschichte des Westens*, vol. 2: *Die Zeit der Weltkriege 1914–1945*, Munich, 2011.
8. See Philipp Gassert, *Amerika im Dritten Reich. Ideologie, Propaganda und Volksmeinung 1933–1945*, Stuttgart, 1997, 14–15.
9. For a summary on this and on the following see Johann Baptist Müller, *Deutschland und der Westen*, Berlin, 1989, 28–40.
10. Ernst Troeltsch, *Naturrecht und Humanität in der Weltpolitik*, Berlin, 1923.
11. See Fritz Stern, *Kulturpessimismus als politische Gefahr. Eine Analyse nationaler Ideologien in Deutschland*, Bern, 1963; and most recently André Schlüter, *Moeller van den Bruck. Leben und Werk*, Cologne et al., 2010; and Volker Weiß, *Moderne Antimoderne. Arthur Moeller van den Bruck und der Wandel des Konservatismus*, Paderborn et al., 2012. See also Thomas Rohkrämer's chapter in this volume.
12. Kurt Sontheimer, *Antidemokratisches Denken in der Weimarer Republik. Die politischen Ideen des deutschen Nationalismus zwischen 1918 und 1933*, Munich, 1962.
13. *Meyers Lexikon*, 7th edn, Leipzig, 1930, vol. 12, 3010.
14. Egbert Klautke, *Unbegrenzte Möglichkeiten. 'Amerikanisierung' in Deutschland und Frankreich, 1900–1933*, Stuttgart, 2003.
15. Adolf Halfeld, *Amerika und der Amerikanismus. Kritische Betrachtungen eines Deutschen und Europäers*, Jena, 1927. The book starts out with a transatlantic boat passage. After landing at Portsmouth, one of Halfeld's fellow travellers, a British-educated Indian engineer, exclaims: 'I am glad to come back to a civilized country'. According to Halfeld this means Europe (p. 4).

16. Scott Nearing and Joseph Freeman, *Dollar-Diplomatie. Eine Studie über amerikanischen Imperialismus*, transl. Paul Fohr, foreword by Karl Haushofer, Berlin, 1927 (English original 1925). A second edition was published in 1943, ed. by Friedrich Schönemann.
17. Rosenberg, *Der Mythus des 20. Jahrhunderts*, 643; see also Alfred Rosenberg, *Der Zukunftsweg einer deutschen Außenpolitik*, Munich, 1927, 85.
18. Detlef Junker, 'The Continuity of Ambivalence. German Views of America', in David E. Barclay and Elisabeth Glaser-Schmidt (eds), *Transatlantic Images and Perceptions. Germany and America Since 1776*, New York, 1997, 243–64.
19. Adolf Hitler, *Reden, Schriften, Anordnungen. Februar 1925 bis Januar 1933*, vol. 1, Munich, 1992, 192–93 (28 October 1925).
20. Hitler, *Reden, Schriften, Anordnungen* 1, 153 (17 September 1925).
21. The development of Hitler's foreign policy ideas has been the focus of enormous scholarly attention; still unsurpassed is Eberhard Jäckel, *Hitlers Weltanschauung. Entwurf einer Herrschaft*, revised edn, Stuttgart, 1991.
22. See Hitler, *Reden, Schriften, Anordnungen* 3.1, 203 (3 November 1928); ibid., 43 (29 January 1930).
23. Adolf Hitler, *Hitler's Secret Book*, introduced by Telford Taylor, New York, 1962.
24. See Gassert, *Amerika im Dritten Reich*, 90–92.
25. Hitler, *Reden, Schriften, Anordnungen* 1, 292 (12 February 1926). On British-American antagonism see also Hitler, *Reden, Schriften, Anordnungen* 3.2, 306–308 (27 July 1929).
26. Adolf Hitler, *Monologe im Führerhauptquartier 1941–1944*, ed. by Werner Jochmann, Hamburg, 1980, 156 (18 December 1941).
27. Ibid., 168 (3/4 January 1942).
28. Ibid., 179 (5 January 1942). See also Gerwin Strobl, *The Germanic Isle. Nazi Perceptions of Britain*, Cambridge, 2000, 202–209.
29. Hitler, *Monologe*, 272–73 (8 February 1941).
30. Ibid., 150 (13 December 1941).
31. Gassert, *Amerika im Dritten Reich*, 199–203.
32. *Völkischer Beobachter* 70/71, 11–12 March 1933; 'Roosevelts Kampf gegen Wallstreet', *Völkischer Beobachter* 72, 13 March 1933.
33. 'Wirtschaftliche Gleichschaltung in U.S.A.', *Deutsche Wirtschaftszeitung* 27, 6 July 1933.
34. See Holger Skor, *'Brücken über den Rhein'. Frankreich in der Wahrnehmung und Propaganda des Dritten Reiches 1933–1939*, Essen, 2011, 346–50.
35. Adolf Hitler, *Reden und Proklamationen 1932–1945*, vol. 3, ed. Max Domarus, Wiesbaden, 1973, 1173.
36. Carl Schmitt, *Völkerrechtliche Großraumordnung mit Interventionsverbot für raumfremde Mächte. Ein Beitrag zum Reichsbegriff im Völkerrecht*, 3rd edn, Berlin, 1941 (first published 1940). For a detailed discussion see Lothar Gruchmann, *Nationalsozialistische Großraumordnung. Die Konstruktion einer 'deutschen Monroe-Doktrin'*, Stuttgart, 1962, 20–27.
37. Adolf Halfeld, *Deutschland und die Westmächte*, Jena, 1940, 160. Halfeld further elaborates on the differences between the U.S. and Britain as 'estranged brothers' in Adolf Halfeld, *England*, 2nd edn, Jena, 1935 (first published 1933).
38. There were at least two conflicting approaches among German geopoliticians. See Müller, *Imaginierter Westen*, 360–67.
39. Heinz Boberach (ed.), *Meldungen aus dem Reich 1938–1945. Die geheimen Lageberichte des Sicherheitsdienstes der SS*, vol. 4, Herrsching, 1984 (first published 1965), 1279 (20

June 1940). It should be pointed out, however, that these public opinion surveys, while opening up windows on popular opinion, need to be read with care. They were part of the political agenda of the SS *Sicherheitsdienst* (SD) and cannot be compared to modern-day public opinion sampling.

40. Carl Schmitt, 'Die Raumrevolution. Durch den totalen Krieg zum totalen Frieden', *Das Reich* 19, 29 September 1940.
41. Propaganda proposal of one Heinrich Nolzen from Höxter to Hans Fritzsche, *Leiter Rundfunk* of the Reich Propaganda Ministry, 9 September 1944, Bundesarchiv Berlin, R 55/532/211 f.
42. See Martina Steber's chapter in this volume.

Chapter 14

'THE WEST', TOCQUEVILLE AND WEST GERMAN CONSERVATISM FROM THE 1950S TO THE 1970S

Martina Steber

When Hans Maier was appointed Professor of Political Science at the Ludwig-Maximilians-University in Munich in 1962, he introduced himself to his Munich audience by reminding them of the fateful history of the notion 'Germany and the West'. It had culminated in an ideological opposition between the 'ideas of 1914' and those of '1789' and had left behind the debris of two world wars. Now, due to the German connection with 'the West' born of 'reason and exigency', the German 'fanfare', Maier stated, had finally turned into a *'recte'*. According to Maier, however, the ideological conflicts of the world wars were lingering on in the political sciences. With a concentration on the nineteenth century, in which the differing strands were most distinct, the older German *Staatslehre* had slipped out of focus – indeed, it had been pushed aside deliberately. It was in this *Staatslehre*, Maier argued, that the German tradition of political thought and the Western tradition had their common ground. German thought was – this was Maier's main thesis – rooted in a common European tradition of political theory, which had only become submerged and been partly destroyed in the nineteenth century. Historically, Germany was an intrinsic part of 'the West', and its integration into the contemporary 'West' did not have to imply a denial of national traditions. The contrary was the case.[1] This was a powerful message for the Munich audience of the early 1960s.

'Germany and the West' was indeed a high-profile notion in the first three decades of the Federal Republic of Germany (FRG), and this was especially true among West German conservatives. Although, in the 1950s, the political option of aligning with the 'Western' bloc powers was accepted by the majority of politicians in the Union parties, as well as by conservative intellectuals, the actual appropriation of the liberal democratic model associated with 'the West' was, in ideological terms, anything but unequivocal. The debate mirrored the plurality of West German intellectual and political conservatism, which drew from different strands of political thought and from a diversity of party political roots.[2] In the post-war years the concept of 'the West' posed a serious challenge to conservative intellectuals. At its core it demanded a positive stance towards liberal democracy, particularly as developed in the Anglo-American and French traditions, and it also implied a positive acknowledgement of the U.S.-American tradition of politics and political thought. In opposition to this, widespread conservative thinking about the '*Abendland*' in the 1950s encouraged the cultivation of Eurocentric, anti-American and anti-Bolshevist conceptions, which were more in line with the anti-democratic notions of the 1920s than with the liberal demands of the day.[3] It is, however, indicative that when, from the late 1950s onwards, the '*abendländisch*' hopes lost their persuasive power, the concept of the West moved to the centre of the conservative rapprochement with liberal democracy. Essentially, the political realities of the Cold War, together with opposition to the Soviet Bloc and to 'Bolshevism' associated with 'the East', prompted the majority of German conservative politicians and intellectuals to accept, with varying degrees of enthusiasm, the demands and categories of a U.S.-led 'West'.[4]

The Present Discovered in the Past: Tocqueville and 'the West'

At the heart of West German conservatives' attempts to understand and come to terms with 'the West' was a French political theorist of the nineteenth century: Alexis de Tocqueville (1805–1859). From the late 1940s the West German public witnessed an explosion of interest in Tocqueville's works, above all in his *Democracy in America*, its two volumes first published in 1835 and 1840 respectively. Tocqueville could be encountered virtually everywhere: in learned journals, newspaper feuilletons, intellectual magazines, philosophical and sociological treatises, Ph.D. dissertations and of course new editions of his books.[5] The reception of his works sums up the conservative discourse over 'the West' in a nutshell: it reveals the plurality of West German conservatism, and it vividly shows the convoluted path it took from the mere acceptance of liberal democracy to a confident defence of the institutionalized democracy of the FRG, which was faced by demands for ongoing democratization in the late 1960s and 1970s.

So far, this powerful line of reception, which indeed took up nineteenth-century notions of 'the West' but transformed and updated them within the framework set by the Cold War, has been largely overlooked; it is even assumed that Tocqueville was entirely forgotten.[6] Above all, his prophecy of an East–West dichotomy at the end of the first of book of *Democracy in America*, his prophecy of the global conflict between the future superpowers of Russia (pictured as a society governed by blank authority and servitude) and the United States (presented as the incarnation of freedom)[7] fascinated many people in the 1950s and 1960s, who saw their own present described in a book dating from the 1830s. 'After the experiences of the last century,' Eberhard Kessel reflected in 1956, 'we approach Tocqueville's writings with different eyes. The period since his death has by and large proved his perspectives. One now starts to experience the problems firsthand which he indeed had illustrated … back then'.[8] Carl J. Burckhardt, one of the most important conservative Tocqueville interpreters of the time, was certainly right in his observation that the French philosopher's texts had become 'a sensation for wide circles' of West German society.[9]

Tocqueville's basic aim had been to analyse the democratic experiment in the United States. He was convinced that the development of equality and freedom would be an unstoppable historical process, intended by God and sooner or later affecting all nations on the globe. Democracy was 'inescapable',[10] an idea that appealed immensely to the reluctant West German conservative democrats of the 1950s. Basically, the theme of a fundamental tension between freedom and equality lay at the heart of the conservatives' reading of Tocqueville. The images Tocqueville painted of 'America' in general and of U.S. democracy in particular were understood as incarnations of 'the West', on the one hand, and as eternally valid on the other.[11] In conservatives' perceptions, Tocqueville provided a way of understanding the basics of 'Western' democracy and society; and the fact that his real interest lay in the question of how a democratic society, rather than the state, was organized and how it functioned gave further resonance to his ideas. The inevitability which the French aristocrat ascribed to the development of democracy provided a means of explaining the German ideological defeat and break in tradition, and saved people from having to enquire too deeply into the actual causes. His rather sober acceptance of democracy also offered a role model to German conservatives, who were reluctant to embrace this 'Western' import. For Hans-Joachim Schoeps, Tocqueville figured as the lonely individual who understood that 'the Christian *Abendland*' had come to its end – an end that could only be mourned, while the new, the era of 'the West', had to be acquiesced in.[12] Hence, Schoeps's contemporaries were clearly aware of the semantic shift from '*Abendland*' to 'the West' and the intellectual consequences this entailed.[13]

For conservatives, Tocqueville's depiction of democracy offered enough evidence to support a sceptical stance towards the prospect of too much freedom and equality. This was especially so because the French philosopher described the 'Eastern' despotic autocracy as a possible final outcome of democracy – a notion very much in line with contemporary theories of totalitarianism. It allowed the ubiquitous anti-communism of the time to be fused with ideas of the West, and the Nazi regime to be integrated into models that saw the totalitarian 'barbarism' of the twentieth century as emanating from the secularism, utopianism and egalitarianism associated with 'modernity'.[14] Tocqueville's ambivalent anthropology struck an equally appealing chord, as did his recipes for containing the 'excesses' of democracy: he praised institutions, hinted at the need for shared values and a common morality, pointed to the importance of tradition and religion, stressed the relevance of self-government and civic participation, lauded federalism, warned against centralization and bureaucratization, and reminded his readers of the individual's responsibility for the whole community. In short, the West German conservatives believed that in Tocqueville's writings they had found a congenial programme for the problems of their own age – which did not go unnoticed in the German Democratic Republic (GDR).[15]

Moreover, the conservative appropriation of the concept of the West via the reception of Tocqueville's works not only took place at a discursive level but also opened doors to the intellectual community of the contemporary 'West', and particularly to the liberal-conservative discourse on democracy. In fact, this discourse was shaped by European-American entanglements with Jewish emigrants from Nazi Germany who participated in the formation of a new interpretation of Tocqueville in the U.S. in the 1930s, which was then taken up in West Germany from the early 1950s.[16] The two most important figures in this regard were the two socialist émigré scholars Albert Salomon and Jacob Peter Mayer. The first had put together a selection of Tocqueville's writings in German in 1935, which was published in Switzerland shortly before he left for the U.S. He built the first scholarly articles he wrote in English upon them.[17] The latter had escaped to the U.K. in 1936, and published his Tocqueville interpretation there in 1939, entitling it *The Prophet of the Mass Age*. It appeared in German in 1954 and set the tone for the conservative interpretation of Tocqueville in the 1950s.[18] Mayer dedicated his life to editing Tocqueville's works and to researching his political thought; he was convinced that Tocqueville had become his 'contemporary'.[19] The intellectual and personal entanglements in Tocqueville interpretation went a step further, however, as will be shown later: former emigrants who had encountered Tocqueville's work in the U.S. took it back to West Germany and introduced it to the intellectual debate of the early FRG. From the 1960s West German conservatives could link their enthusiasm for Tocqueville with the emerging Tocquevillean theme of U.S. neoconservative thought.[20] Also in Europe, two of the leading (liberal-)conservatives of the time, Raymond Aron in France and Michael Oakeshott in Britain, could share an appreciation of Tocqueville with their German counterparts.[21]

West German Shades of Tocqueville: the French Philosopher in Conservative Discursive Arenas

As recounted above, the reception of Tocqueville's works reflects the West German conservatives' stance towards liberal democracy from the late 1940s to the 1970s and their reconciliation with it. Although it was one single discourse, stretching over some thirty years, discussion of Tocqueville's ideas was characterized by fundamental shifts. Not only did it provide the younger generation of conservatives of the late 1960s and 1970s with an important platform to distinguish them from earlier strands of conservative thought, it also gave them a means of finding answers to the challenges from the Left. Five different discursive arenas can be identified, each specifically bound to a certain interpretation and time. Altogether, the emphasis shifted from an appreciation of the 'prophet of the mass age' to an acknowledgement of Tocqueville's warning against the dangers of an untamed democratization process.

The first to remind the German public after the war of Tocqueville's analysis of the U.S.A. was none other than Carl Schmitt, and he triggered a further reception of Tocqueville in the circles of technocratic conservatism. By highlighting the East–West prophecy, by recognizing Tocqueville, the prophet, as a defeated man who accepted his defeat, and by hinting that the course of history must inevitably lead towards democracy, Schmitt set the parameters for further interpretation.[22] The theorist of the Nazi regime was clearly drawing parallels with his own situation. The image of Tocqueville as a lonely voice in the desert who was proved right in the end – the defeated, not the victor, writing history – became a standard feature in the self-perceptions of men like Ernst Forsthoff, Arnold Gehlen and Hans Freyer.[23] What became more important, however, was their constant reference to the French theorist to support their criticism of the expanding welfare state and of consumer society, developments they exclusively ascribed to the idea of equality. Thus, paradoxically, the traditional anti-Americanism of the German Right was played out via the reception of a theoretician of democracy, whose reputation was international and whose ideas were developed from the U.S. example.[24] The Schmitt school's Tocqueville interpretation essentially focused on four arguments. Individuals, they held, would lose their freedom and power in the welfare state due to the bureaucratization, institutionalization and centralization that accompanied the state's attempt to create equality. Equality was gained, the argument went, but freedom was lost; and by losing their freedom, individuals would become estranged from themselves.[25] Secondly, they stressed, the trend towards individualization would eventually lead to atomization and the death of all social life, just as the French philosopher had observed. Thirdly, the consumer society with its materialist worldview would distract citizens from exerting their rights and liberties; it would level them down intellectually, and eventually lead to the loss of personality in a streamlined, centralized society.[26] Did Tocqueville, Gehlen asked his readers, 'with his dreadful words "controlled, mild and peaceful servitude" that could "establish itself even in the shadow of a consumer dictatorship" perhaps not even mean anything political, but a consumer dictatorship, which gives the impression of freedom?' And Gehlen also found answers in Tocqueville: small communities, ancient institutions and 'intimate groups'.[27] Finally, the Schmitt school referred to Tocqueville in the framework of a fourth and slightly different argument. Here it was his interpretation of revolution that attracted their attention. In 1959, taking as a starting point Tocqueville's idea that the French revolution had set the pattern for modern revolutions and would hence repeat itself again and again, Hanno Kesting developed the notion of a long-lasting European 'civil war'. This was a war between two incompatible philosophies of history, stemming from the nineteenth century, that, since 1917, had widened into a worldwide conflict between the U.S. and the U.S.S.R. and which dominated the present times.[28]

These arguments were omnipresent in a second discursive arena of the 1950s: the more popularized cultural-critical conservative literature, which had put Tocqueville high on a pedestal. There, the French philosopher became the key witness to the 'dangers that impended on the democratic development'[29] and his works a mine for quotations in the discussion on safeguards to counter these dangers. Authors like Carl J. Burckhardt, Hans-Joachim Schoeps, Hans Zbinden and Wilhelm Röpke used Tocqueville to underline their critique of 'mass society' and the loss of individuality and freedom it would necessarily involve.[30] Their writings are variations on a theme that had been set by Jacob Peter Mayer's Tocqueville interpretation in the late 1930s, and which had deeply influenced David Riesman's argument presented in *The Lonely Crowd* of 1950, which was published in German in 1956, introduced by Helmut Schelsky.[31] The authority of Tocqueville was further invoked in the context of a cultural-philosophical, economic critique of the welfare state, as advanced by Wilhelm Röpke, who warned of a state *dirigisme* that would not only impede the free market, but hinder individuals' exertion of freedom and force them down into the conformity of mass society.[32] This argument was often combined with a warning about technological progress triggering rationalization and state planning and, again, wresting freedom from the individual and degrading people to being mere objects.[33]

In its scepticism towards the 'masses' in a consumerist society, the cultural critique of the Right met with that of the Left,[34] and the cultural critiques of both political wings also met in their reverence for Tocqueville. This is not altogether surprising, bearing in mind the socialist roots of Salomon's and Mayer's Tocqueville interpretations of the 1930s. Mayer's Tocqueville-inspired descriptions of contemporary society in the 1950s and early 1960s did not really differ from their conservative counterparts.[35] Indicative of a Left-liberal departure from this tradition, however, was Kurt Sontheimer's debate on 'conformity' in contemporary industrial society, which he published in the *Frankfurter Allgemeine Zeitung* in 1957. There, though admittedly he agreed with the conservatives' diagnosis of contemporary mass society, he diverged from their interpretation by stressing both the potentials for autonomy left to the individual (despite all constraints) and the potentials for democracy itself.[36]

The third group to embrace Tocqueville's theories from the mid 1950s onwards consisted of prominent conservatives who had experienced life in the United States as exiles from Nazi Germany. After their return, they saw it as their duty to help build up the young West German democracy. In particular, they wanted to introduce an appreciation of American life, history and, especially, democracy to their fellow countrymen. It was no coincidence that they adopted Tocqueville as their guide: when they discovered his account of their country of exile, mediated among others by fellow émigrés, they could draw on their own experiences. Golo Mann called him one of the 'dearest of my historicizing, sociologizing, philosophizing and memorializing friends'.[37] Even though they saw themselves as advocates of democracy, they embraced Tocqueville's warnings of democracy's dangers. Golo Mann praised the model of 'freedom in the framework of order'.[38] In the French philosopher he found a historical and moral approach to the realities of life combined in an ideal way, which he himself aspired to as a historian and public intellectual.[39]

Siegfried Landshut, who edited a collection of Tocqueville's works in German in 1954, accentuated the dangers of the equality postulate, the state of a society dominated by the 'common man' which would result in the 'ubiquitous force of the state' and the 'administrative regulation of all human activities'.[40] Landshut was equally struck by the nineteenth-century analysis of a society of equals, which he described as a mass consumer society with a strong tendency towards individualism on the one hand and loss of individuality on the other, both developments being intrinsically intertwined. He believed the pursuit of equality would inevitably give omnipotent power to an almighty, centralized government apparatus. Landshut therefore advocated the strengthening of all forms of individual freedom, responsibility, sociability and morality. He was following in the footsteps of Tocqueville, whom he portrayed as a conservative sceptic who, in a 'last, desperate attempt', accepted 'the world as it is and as it was about to become'.[41] Without doubt, Tocqueville represented a tradition of 'Western' political thought in Landshut's eyes, though Landshut did not interpret his acceptance of democracy as a particularly French development. Instead, with Tocqueville's theory of the inevitable advance of democracy in mind – a notion that profoundly relativized the historical significance of the French Revolution – it was possible for him to conceive of democracy as rooted in the tradition of the '*Abendland*' to which Germany belonged. Democracy, Landshut maintained, in an essential claim that distinguished his Tocqueville interpretation from that of the Schmitt school, was not 'un-German' at all, nor was Germany's place in 'the West' unhistorical. The reverse was the case.[42] For Arnold Bergstraesser, whose work in the 1950s was pivotal in the construction of a community of 'the West' based on historically shared, universal values,[43] it was obvious that the Frenchman had anticipated the theories of mass society as laid out by David Riesman. Yet, he also stressed the 'great American efforts' to overcome the dangers of democracy. Again 'liberal institutions', 'decentralization', 'the nourishment of a communal spirit' and 'the doctrine of well-understood interest' were listed and marked as powerful 'counterpoints'.[44]

Bergstraesser and other former exiles to the U.S. recognized in Tocqueville the founding father of the art of political science in a democratic society.[45] His claim that 'a completely new world requires a new political science' became a standard phrase. It summed up the former emigrants' deep conviction that political education was crucial in order to build up West German democracy. Further, it reflected the elitist self-understanding of these men, for which they could again find backing in Tocqueville's works, a fact that also helped account for the Tocqueville veneration found in the circles of conservative cultural critique.[46] As early as 1954 it attracted A.J.P. Taylor's pungent and striking sneer.[47] Through the lens of America, therefore, these men reflected on the development of the FRG. They viewed the new state with approval, and indeed they thought of the profound change in West Germany after 1945 as its final return into the community of 'the West'.

These interpretative patterns, prevalent amongst the West German public, were taken up by the Christian Democratic Union (CDU) politician, Minister President of Baden-Württemberg and later Chancellor, Kurt Georg Kiesinger, who liked to depict himself as an intellectual trapped as a politician.[48] His love for Alexis de Tocqueville became almost legendary, and journalists repeatedly alluded to the politician 'always carrying the French philosopher in his knapsack'. Kiesinger did actually take Tocqueville's account as the manual for his politics. When asked by *Der Spiegel* in 1967 whether fixation on Tocqueville might not be obstructive to the business of contemporary everyday politics, the then chancellor of the grand coalition forcefully rejected this accusation, stating that the French philosopher had already said the necessary words regarding the difficulties of political life.[49] However, the Tocqueville Kiesinger presented to the public bore technocratic conservative traits. Kiesinger explicitly reverted to Hans Freyer's critique of mass consumerism and the welfare state, which in itself drew inspiration from Tocqueville, and, in cultural-critical mode, he recognized Helmut Schelsky's 'levelled-down middle-class society' in the French philosopher's depiction of a democratic society.[50] Moreover, Kiesinger evoked another stereotypical element of the Tocqueville interpretation prevalent in the early FRG, and particularly in the former exiles' texts: the confrontation between Karl Marx and Alexis de Tocqueville as contemporary interpreters of the social problems of industrial society. Of course, this corresponded with the East–West opposition of the time[51] and, needless to say, Tocqueville's analysis was seen as the 'right' one. 'When faced with Tocqueville's impartial judgment, his unclouded view of the reality of mankind', Marx's 'chiliasm', Kiesinger stated, could only appear 'inhibited and distorted'.[52] The politician also drew on the conservative interpretation of revolution, with which Tocqueville had become associated, seeing it as a steady and inevitable process towards increased equality and freedom – a revolution that had to be accepted. Strong institutions, a dedicated elite and bourgeois morality were the antidotes the CDU politician found in Tocqueville.

Kiesinger's enthusiasm for Tocqueville found its way into the party, so that in 1963 Bruno Heck, who was then *Bundesminister für Familie und Jugend* and later the general secretary of the CDU, developed his analysis of the future of Europe from Tocqueville's East–West prognosis. It gave him the intellectual means to trace the roots of the Cold War back to Europe, and essentially to 'Europeanize' both the United States and the Soviet Union. Heck saw the relationship between freedom and order as lying at the heart of all contemporary problems, challenging 'the West' and 'the East' alike.[53] Again Tocqueville can be glimpsed in the background to this idea – that is his notion of the steady advance of equality and freedom as universal traits. In the heyday of the Atlanticist-Gaullist debate, however, Heck's emphasis on the European roots of the 'West' and the European heritage incorporated in the United States – and all of this through the eyes of a French philosopher – was certainly intended to bridge the gap between the two opposing camps among the Union parties.[54]

Hans Maier did not mention Tocqueville in his inaugural lecture, though for him, too, the French political philosopher provided much food for thought. Maier's appreciation of this was especially evident in his works on Catholicism and democracy. In Tocqueville he found great inspiration not only on the question of compatibility between the Catholic faith and democracy, but even more on the high relevance of Catholicism for a stable and contained democracy in 'the West'.[55] With regard to the importance ascribed to political science, Maier stated in his autobiography, 'Tocqueville was our man' anyway.[56] Maier's reception of Tocqueville was in line with that of a fifth group of West German conservatives, who were often influenced by the former émigré scholars discussed above. From the mid 1960s, and especially from 1968/69, Tocqueville again became a focus of interest. Yet, what the new liberal conservatives discovered in Tocqueville differed fundamentally from what their predecessors had discussed. They were not so much interested in the 'dangers of equality' or of the consumer society, and they did not delve into cultural critique; rather they discussed with reference to Tocqueville the principle of freedom and how it could be maintained in an egalitarian society. This shift from equality to freedom did not come out of the blue, however, but was initialized by Otto Vossler's Tocqueville study of 1966.[57]

The young conservative intellectuals of the late 1960s and early 1970s were particularly challenged by the student movement and by the Left-liberal reforms and attendant ideas of 'democratization' as a genuine principle for ordering social life. Wilhelm Hennis, in particular, harked back to Tocqueville when he warned of the destructive forces of 'democratization'.[58] He stressed the need to uphold a distinction between the public and the private as a fundamental principle of 'Western' political thought; and he underlined the corrosive consequences of the individual's 'emancipation' taken in its sense of mere liberation. Instead, he highlighted the need for humanity, compassion and social responsibility, as well as for a common value system. Hennis emphasized that the key topic, the thread running through Tocqueville's works, was not the opposition between equality and freedom, as a generation of interpreters had thought, but the opposition between freedom and compassion.[59] His reluctance to characterize Tocqueville as a liberal, even a 'Liberal of a new kind' (the French philosopher's own self-perception) revealed a great deal about Hennis's own convictions.[60] In the French aristocrat, whose grandfather was Chateaubriand, one of the most eminent figures of modern French conservatism, the German conservatives of the late 1960s and 1970s, who were attempting to merge liberal and conservative thought, recognized a precursor.

It was in this context that Tocqueville became attractive again. With the help of Edmund Burke and Tocqueville – the two of them increasingly discussed in one breath[61] – Christian von Krockow defined his model of *Konservatismus der Freiheitswahrung*,[62] Constantin von Barloewen advocated localism as a counterweight to centralization[63] and Rudolf von Thadden found inspiration for his theory of institutions.[64] Even those intellectuals who sought to 'reconstruct conservatism' in a way based on the German tradition of conservative thought linked their arguments to Tocquevillean themes. Gerd-Klaus Kaltenbrunner, for example, found particular importance in Tocqueville's discussion of the opposition between liberal and despotic democracy and, like him, warned about the rapid retreat of liberal fundamentals and institutions, a retreat which Kaltenbrunner obviously perceived as a contemporary threat to 'the West',[65] while Caspar von Schrenck-Notzing elevated Tocqueville into his gallery of conservative masterminds.[66]

It was therefore no coincidence that the 1970s and early 1980s witnessed attempts by the Left to establish an alternative version of Tocqueville.[67] Imanuel Geiss emphasized Tocqueville's interpretation of revolution, thereby drawing on Franz Schnabel's reverence for the French political philosopher and harking back to an earlier attempt to counter the conservative reception,[68] and Michael Hereth interpreted the French philosopher in 1980 as searching for a 'sensible order' that 'corresponded to the freedom and worthiness of every human being'.[69]

The reception of Tocqueville mirrors the appropriation of democracy by West German conservatism under the flexible roof provided by the concept of the West. By the 1960s at the latest, the great majority of West German conservatives had not only reconciled themselves to the 'Western' import but wholeheartedly embraced democracy – so much so that when there were demands for more democratization from the Left, they felt 'Western' democracy was being fundamentally challenged. They saw it as their duty to defend not only this 'Western' democracy but, as Wilhelm Hennis put it, the whole 'Western tradition of political thought', to which Germany seemed to be integrally bound.[70] The development of conservatism in the FRG was thus characterized by a profound engagement with German, European and U.S.-American traditions of political thought. The multidimensional appropriation and steady reevaluation and reconstruction of the concept of the West were part and parcel of this process; and these drew heavily on nineteenth-century notions of the West.

Notes

1. Hans Maier, *Ältere deutsche Staatslehre und westliche politische Tradition. Münchner Antrittsvorlesung*, Tübingen, 1966.
2. See Axel Schildt, *Konservatismus in Deutschland. Von den Anfängen im 18. Jahrhundert bis zur Gegenwart*, Munich, 1998.
3. Axel Schildt, *Zwischen Abendland und Amerika. Studien zur westdeutschen Ideenlandschaft der 50er Jahre*, Munich, 1999; Vanessa Conze, *Das Europa der Deutschen. Ideen von Europa in Deutschland zwischen Reichstradition und Westorientierung (1920–1970)*, Munich, 2005; Christian Bailey, 'The Continuities of West German History. Conceptions of Europe, Democracy and the West in Interwar and Postwar Germany', *Geschichte und Gesellschaft* 36 (2010), 567–96.
4. For the continuation of '*abendländisch*' ideas see Vanessa Conze, 'Abendland gegen Amerika! "Europa" als antiamerikanisches Konzept im westeuropäischen Konservatismus (1950–1970). Das CEDI und die Idee des "Abendlandes"', in Jan C. Behrends, Árpád von Klimó and Patrice G. Poutrus (eds), *Antiamerikanismus im 20. Jahrhundert. Studien zu Ost- und Westeuropa*, Bonn, 2005, 204–24.
5. Alexis de Tocqueville, *Das Zeitalter der Gleichheit. Eine Auswahl aus dem Gesamtwerk*, ed. Siegfried Landshut, Stuttgart, 1954; Alexis de Tocqueville, *Werke und Briefe*, ed. Jacob Peter Mayer with Theodor Eschenburg and Hans Zbinden, vol. 1, Stuttgart, 1959. For a contemporary overview see Eberhard Kessel, 'Das Tocqueville-Problem. Eine Auseinandersetzung mit der neuesten Literatur', *Jahrbuch für Amerikastudien* 1 (1956), 168–76. For Ph.D. dissertations see Bernhard Fabian, *Alexis de Tocquevilles Amerikabild. Genetische Untersuchungen über Zusammenhänge mit der zeitgenössischen, insbesondere der englischen Amerika-Interpretation*, Heidelberg, 1957; and Eckhart G. Franz, *Das Amerikabild der deutschen Revolution von 1848/49. Zum Problem der Übertragung gewachsener Verfassungsformen*, Heidelberg, 1958.
6. See for instance Karlfriedrich Herb and Oliver Hidalgo, *Alexis de Tocqueville*, Frankfurt/Main, 2005, 159.
7. See Alexis de Tocqueville, *Democracy in America and Two Essays on America*, trans. Gerald E. Bevan with an introduction and notes by Isaac Kramnick, London et al., 2003, 484–85.
8. Kessel, 'Das Tocqueville-Problem', 170. See also, as an example, Paul Rohrbach, 'Am Rande bemerkt', *Frankfurter Allgemeine Zeitung*, 9 October 1951.
9. Carl J. Burckhardt, 'Alexis de Tocqueville', *Merkur* 8/10 (1954), 901–12, here 903; Carl J. Burckhardt, 'Alexis de Tocqueville', in Carl J. Burckhardt, *Bildnisse*, Frankfurt/Main, 1958, 89–125.
10. Dietrich Gerhard, 'Alexis de Tocqueville und die Vereinigten Staaten von heute', in Karl Erich Born (ed.), *Historische Forschungen und Probleme. Festschrift für Peter Rassow*, Wiesbaden, 1961, 342–57, here 344.

11. See ibid.
12. Hans-Joachim Schoeps, *Was ist der Mensch? Philosophische Anthropologie als Geistesgeschichte der neuesten Zeit*, Göttingen et al., 1960, 28.
13. On Konrad Adenauer, see Hélène Miard-Delacroix, 'Der Westen als Hort. Diskursanalytischer Beitrag zur Deutung des Begriffs "Westen" in den Reden Konrad Adenauers zu Beginn der 1950er Jahre', in Klaus Hildebrand, Udo Wengst and Andreas Wirsching (eds), *Geschichtswissenschaft und Zeiterkenntnis. Von der Aufklärung bis zur Gegenwart. Festschrift für Horst Möller*, Munich, 2008, 397–407.
14. See Jean Solchany, 'Vom Antimodernismus zum Antitotalitarismus. Konservative Interpretationen des Nationalsozialismus in Deutschland 1945–1949', *Vierteljahrshefte für Zeitgeschichte* 44 (1996), 373–94.
15. Gerhard Lozek and Horst Syrbe, *Geschichtsschreibung contra Geschichte. Über die antinationale Geschichtskonzeption führender westdeutscher Historiker*, (East) Berlin, 1964, 100–102.
16. For the influence of socialist, Jewish intellectuals from Central Europe, see Matthew Mancini, *Alexis de Tocqueville and American Intellectuals. From His Times to Ours*, Lanham, 2006, 187–94.
17. Alexis de Tocqueville, *Autorität und Freiheit. Schriften, Reden und Briefe*, chosen and introduced by Albert Salomon, Zürich et al., 1935; Albert Salomon, 'Tocqueville: Moralist and Sociologist', *Social Research* 2 (1935), 405–27; Albert Salomon, 'Tocqueville's Philosophy of Freedom', *The Review of Politics* 1 (1939), 400–431. For Salomon see Carl Mayer, 'In Memoriam Albert Salomon', in Peter Gostmann and Peter Wagner (eds), *Albert Salomon Werke*, vol. 1: *Biographische Materialien und Schriften, 1921–1933*, Wiesbaden, 2008, 59–73; and Norman Birnbaum, 'Albert Salomon – Zeuge und Beispiel', in Gostmann and Wagner (eds), *Albert Salomon Werke* 1, 75–80.
18. Jacob Peter Mayer, *Prophet of the Mass Age. A Study of Alexis de Tocqueville*, London, 1939 (German edition: *Alexis de Tocqueville. Prophet des Massenzeitalters*, Stuttgart, 1954). For Mayer see M.R.D. Foot, 'Obituary: Professor J.-P. Mayer', *The Independent*, 21 December 1992; and Mancini, *Alexis de Tocqueville and American Intellectuals*, 188–92.
19. Jacob Peter Mayer, 'Tocqueville heute', in Mayer/Zbinden/Eschenburg (eds), *Tocqueville, Über die Demokratie*, xi–xvi, here xiii. See also Jacob Peter Mayer, 'Tocqueville heute', *Der Monat* 11/121 (1958), 46–49; and Jacob Peter Mayer, 'Alexis de Tocqueville. Nach hundert Jahren', *Archiv für Sozialgeschichte* 1 (1961), 9–17. For Mayer's Tocqueville editions see, among others, Alexis de Tocqueville, *Oeuvres complètes*, ed. André Jardin and Jacob Peter Mayer, Paris, 1952; and Alexis de Tocqueville, *Democracy in America*, ed. Max Lerner and Jacob Peter Mayer, New York, 1966.
20. See Mancini, *Alexis de Tocqueville and American Intellectuals*, 187–220; and Matthew Mancini, 'Too Many Tocquevilles. The Fable of Tocqueville's American Reception', *Journal of the History of Ideas* 69/2 (2008), 245–68.
21. See Matthias Oppermann, *Raymond Aron und Deutschland. Die Verteidigung der Freiheit und das Problem des Totalitarismus*, Ostfildern, 2008, 277; Raymond Aron, 'Alexis de Tocqueville und Karl Marx', in Raymond Aron, *Über die Freiheiten. Essay*, Stuttgart, 1981, 13–45; and Paul Franco, *Michael Oakeshott. An Introduction*, New Haven and London, 2004.
22. Carl Schmitt, 'Historiographia in Nuce. Alexis de Tocqueville', in Carl Schmitt, *Ex Captivitate Salus. Erfahrungen der Zeit 1945/47*, Cologne, 1950, 25–33. See Reinhard Mehring, *Carl Schmitt. Aufstieg und Fall. Eine Biographie*, Munich, 2009, 445–48.
23. See Dirk van Laak, *Gespräche in der Sicherheit des Schweigens. Carl Schmitt in der politischen Geistesgeschichte der frühen Bundesrepublik*, Berlin, 1993, 103–104.

24. See Gesine Schwan, *Antikommunismus und Antiamerikanismus in Deutschland. Kontinuität und Wandel nach 1945*, Baden-Baden, 1999; and Christoph Hendrik Müller, *West Germans against the West. Anti-Americanism in Media and Public Opinion in the Federal Republic of Germany, 1949–1968*, New York et al., 2010. For a comparable group see Marcus M. Payk, 'Ideologische Distanz, sachliche Nähe. Die USA und die Positionswechsel konservativer Publizisten aus dem "Tat"-Kreis in der Bundesrepublik bis zur Mitte der 1960er Jahre', in Behrends et al. (eds), *Antiamerikanismus*, 225–49.
25. See Hans Freyer, 'Das soziale Ganze und die Freiheit des Einzelnen unter den Bedingungen des industriellen Zeitalters', *Historische Zeitschrift* 183/1 (1957), 97–115, here 102–103; and Hans Freyer, *Theorie des gegenwärtigen Zeitalters*, Stuttgart, 1956, 161–65.
26. See esp. Arnold Gehlen, *Die Seele im technischen Zeitalter und andere sozialpsychologische, soziologische und kulturanalytische Schriften, 1957/1972* (*Arnold Gehlen Gesamtausgabe*, vol. 6, ed. Karl-Siegbert Rehberg), Frankfurt/Main, 2004, 1–140, esp. 80–83.
27. Ibid., 82–83.
28. Hanno Kesting, *Geschichtsphilosophie und Weltbürgerkrieg. Deutungen der Geschichte von der Französischen Revolution bis zum Ost-West-Konflikt*, Heidelberg, 1959, xi.
29. Burckhardt, 'Alexis de Tocqueville' (1954), 912.
30. See for example Schoeps, *Was ist der Mensch?*; Burckhardt, 'Alexis de Tocqueville' (1954 and 1959); Curt Hohoff, 'Tocqueville und das Wesen der Revolution', *Hochland* 47 (1954/55), 586–88; Hans Zbinden, *Der bedrohte Mensch. Zur sozialen und seelischen Situation unserer Zeit*, Bern and Munich, 1959; Hermann J. Meyer, *Die Technisierung der Welt. Herkunft, Wesen und Gefahren*, Tübingen, 1961, esp. 280–87; Wilhelm Röpke, 'Die Massengesellschaft und ihre Probleme', in Albert Hunold (ed.), *Masse und Demokratie*, Erlenbach and Stuttgart, 1957, 13–38; or Wilhelm Röpke, *Jenseits von Angebot und Nachfrage*, Erlenbach et al., 1958, 95–96. For this discourse, figuring prominently in the West German public arena of the 1950s, see Paul Nolte, *Die Ordnung der deutschen Gesellschaft. Selbstentwurf und Selbstbeschreibung im 20. Jahrhundert*, Munich, 2000, 303–14.
31. David Riesman, *Die einsame Masse. Eine Untersuchung der Wandlungen des amerikanischen Charakters*, Darmstadt, 1956.
32. See Röpke, 'Die Massengesellschaft und ihre Probleme', 26–31; Röpke, *Jenseits von Angebot und Nachfrage*, 211–33; and Wilhelm Röpke, 'Alte und neue Fronten der Wirtschaftspolitik', *Frankfurter Allgemeine Zeitung*, 24 October 1957.
33. See for example Meyer, *Die Technisierung der Welt*.
34. See Andreas Wirsching, 'Konsum statt Arbeit? Zum Wandel von Individualität in der modernen Massengesellschaft', *Vierteljahrshefte für Zeitgeschichte* 2 (2009), 171–99, here 173–79.
35. See the works cited in footnotes 18 and 19; a further example is Henry Jacoby, *Die Bürokratisierung der Welt. Ein Beitrag zur Problemgeschichte*, Neuwied and Berlin, 1969.
36. Kurt Sontheimer, 'Die Welt der vielen Gleichen', *Frankfurter Allgemeine Zeitung*, 16 February 1957.
37. Golo Mann, *Erinnerungen und Gedanken. Eine Jugend in Deutschland*, Frankfurt/Main, 1986, 194.
38. Golo Mann, 'Tocqueville und das Amerika von heute' (1959), in Golo Mann, *Geschichte und Geschichten*, Frankfurt/Main, 1962, 343–64, here 364.
39. See Jeroen Koch, *Golo Mann und die deutsche Geschichte. Eine intellektuelle Biographie*, Paderborn et al., 1998; Tilman Lahme, *Golo Mann. Biographie*, 2nd ed., Frankfurt am Main, 2009.

40. Siegfried Landshut, 'Einleitung', in Alexis de Tocqueville, *Das Zeitalter der Gleichheit. Auswahl aus Werken und Briefen*, 2nd revised edn, transl. and ed. Siegfried Landshut, Cologne and Opladen, 1967, ix–xxxii, here xv; Rainer Nicolaysen, *Siegfried Landshut. Die Wiederentdeckung der Politik. Eine Biographie*, Frankfurt am Main, 1997, 388–397.
41. Landshut, 'Einleitung', xxix.
42. See also Siegfried Landshut, 'Der Prophet des Massenzeitalters', *Die Zeit*, 17 April 1959.
43. See Alfons Söllner, 'Normative Westernization? The Impact of Rémigrés on the Foundation of Political Thought in Post-War Germany', in Jan-Werner Müller (ed.), *German Ideologies since 1945. Studies in the Political Thought and Culture of the Bonn Republic*, New York et al., 2003, 40–60.
44. Arnold Bergstraesser, 'Macht und moderne Demokratie. Alexis de Tocqueville', in Arnold Bergstraesser, *Die Macht als Mythos und Wirklichkeit. Eine Untersuchung*, Freiburg im Breisgau, 1965, 47–68, here 62.
45. See ibid., 58.
46. See Röpke, 'Die Massengesellschaft und ihre Probleme'. For the discourse on elites see Morten Reitmayer, *Elite. Sozialgeschichte einer politisch-gesellschaftlichen Idee in der frühen Bundesrepublik*, Munich, 2009.
47. A.J.P. Taylor, 'Die Masse als Schreckgespenst. Zur Neuauflage von Tocquevilles "Démocratie en Amérique"', *Der Monat*, 7/73 (1954), 66–68.
48. For Kiesinger see Philipp Gassert, *Kurt Georg Kiesinger, 1904–1988. Kanzler zwischen den Zeiten*, Munich, 2006.
49. 'Wenn ich länger Kanzler war?', *Der Spiegel*, 11 September 1967.
50. Kurt Georg Kiesinger, 'Alexis de Tocqueville. Vortrag am 3. Dezember 1960 in Karlsruhe', in Kurt Georg Kiesinger, *Stationen. 1949–1969*, Tübingen, 1969, 109–24.
51. See ibid., 116–17. On this theme see Kessel, 'Das Tocqueville-Problem', 173–74.
52. Kiesinger, 'Alexis de Tocqueville', 117.
53. See Bruno Heck, 'Hat Europa noch eine Zukunft?' (1963), in Bruno Heck, *Auf festem Grund. Aufsätze und Reden*, Stuttgart, 1977, 257–67.
54. For the controversy see Tim Geiger, *Atlantiker gegen Gaullisten. Außenpolitischer Konflikt und innerparteilicher Machtkampf in der CDU/CSU, 1958–1969*, Munich, 2008; and Ronald J. Granieri, *The Ambivalent Alliance. Konrad Adenauer, the CDU/CSU, and the West, 1949–1966*, New York et al., 2003.
55. See Hans Maier, *Revolution und Kirche. Studien zur Frühgeschichte der christlichen Demokratie, 1789–1850*, Freiburg im Breisgau, 1959.
56. Hans Maier, *Böse Jahre, gute Jahre. Ein Leben 1931 ff.*, Munich, 2011, 132; Hans Maier, 'Tocqueville als Advokat der politischen Wissenschaft', *Frankfurter Allgemeine Zeitung*, 26 May 1965.
57. Otto Vossler, *Tocqueville*, Wiesbaden, 1966; Otto Vossler, *Alexis de Tocqueville. Freiheit und Gleichheit*, Frankfurt/Main, 1973; and see Dolf Sternberger's review: 'Die Kontinuität der Freiheit', *Frankfurter Allgemeine Zeitung*, 6 October 1973.
58. Wilhelm Hennis, 'Demokratisierung. Zur Problematik eines Begriffs' (1970), in Wilhelm Hennis, *Die missverstandene Demokratie*, Freiburg im Breisgau, 1973, 26–51. For Hennis see Stephan Schlak, *Wilhelm Hennis. Szenen einer Ideengeschichte der Bundesrepublik*, München, 2008.
59. Wilhelm Hennis, 'Tocquevilles "Neue Politische Wissenschaft"', in Justin Stagl (ed.), *Aspekte der Kultursoziologie. Aufsätze zur Soziologie, Philosophie, Anthropologie und Geschichte der Kultur. Festschrift für Mohammed Rassem*, Berlin, 1982, 385–407, here 386.

60. Hennis, 'Tocquevilles "Neue Politische Wissenschaft"', 401.
61. This connection was also established in the neoconservative reception in the U.S. See Mancini, *Alexis de Tocqueville and American Intellectuals*, 191.
62. 'Conservatism of the maintenance of freedom'; Christian von Krockow, *Herrschaft und Freiheit. Politische Grundpositionen der bürgerlichen Gesellschaft*, Stuttgart, 1977, 140. See further, Christian von Krockow, *Reform als politisches Prinzip*, Munich, 1976.
63. Constantin von Barloewen, *Gleichheit und Freiheit. Alexis de Tocqueville in Amerika. Seine Darstellung des Verhältnisses von zentralstaatlicher Lenkung und lokaler Eigenverantwortung, untersucht am historischen Beispiel Pennsylvanias*, Munich, 1978.
64. Rudolf von Thadden, 'Die Zerstörung der Institutionen durch Gleichgültigkeit', *Frankfurter Allgemeine Zeitung*, 13 October 1976. See also Rudolf von Thadden, 'Geschichte als Prozess bei Alexis de Tocqueville', in Karl-Georg Faber and Christian Meier (eds), *Historische Prozesse*, Munich, 1978, 143–56.
65. See Gerd-Klaus Kaltenbrunner, 'Alexis de Tocqueville. Der Konservative als Liberaler', in Gerd-Klaus Kaltenbrunner, *Der schwierige Konservatismus. Definitionen – Theorien – Porträts*, Herford and Berlin, 1975, 223–28.
66. See Klaus Hornung, 'Alexis de Tocqueville (1805–1859)', in Caspar von Schrenck-Notzing (ed.), *Konservative Köpfe. Von Machiavelli bis Solschenizyn*, Munich, 1978, 63–74.
67. Jürgen Habermas's rejection of Tocqueville's concept of the public sphere was certainly an important reason for the lack of attention from the Left; see Jürgen Habermas, *Strukturwandel der Öffentlichkeit. Untersuchungen zu einer Kategorie der bürgerlichen Gesellschaft*, Neuwied, 1962, 145–57.
68. See Imanuel Geiss (ed.), *Tocqueville und das Zeitalter der Revolution*, Munich, 1972; and Imanuel Geiss, 'Tocqueville und Karl Marx. Eine vergleichende Analyse anlässlich des 100. Todestages von Alexis de Tocqueville', *Die Neue Gesellschaft* 6/3 (1959), 237–40. For Schnabel see Thomas Hertfelder, *Franz Schnabel und die deutsche Geschichtswissenschaft. Geschichtsschreibung zwischen Historismus und Kulturkritik, 1910–1945*, vol. 1, Göttingen, 1998, 412–16.
69. Michael Hereth, *Alexis de Tocqueville. Die Gefährdung der Freiheit in der Demokratie*, Stuttgart, 1979, 15; Michael Hereth, 'Die Gleichheit als Gegner der Freiheit?', *Aus Politik und Zeitgeschichte* B 31/80 (1980), 34–41.
70. See Hennis, 'Demokratisierung', 37. Hennis, interestingly, did not distinguish between the concepts of *Abendland* and 'the West'.

Part 5

SOCIALISTS BETWEEN 'EAST' AND 'WEST'

Chapter 15

'THE WEST' AS A PARADOX IN GERMAN SOCIAL DEMOCRATIC THOUGHT
Britain as Counterfoil and Model, 1871–1945

Stefan Berger

What did 'the West' mean to German Social Democrats in the nineteenth century and the first half of the twentieth? A full-scale exploration of the conceptual history of 'the West' in Social Democratic political thought has yet to be written, but this article will argue that for most Social Democrats 'the West' – implying a bloc upholding a unified set of ideas and social practices – was not at first a concept carrying a lot of weight. Yet, even though the discursive construction of 'the West' was not fully developed in their thought before 1945, many Social Democrats had long identified certain key states in Western Europe as prime examples of economic and political modernity. The main ones singled out were Britain and France, and they were often contrasted with the states in Eastern Europe – especially with Russia, which was a byword for economic backwardness and political autocracy. In this sense, Social Democratic understandings of 'the West' were in line with the temporalization and politicization of the concept that developed from the early nineteenth century onwards, starting off an identification of 'the West' with the future while its mirror opposite, 'the East', became associated with stunted states of development.[1] In 1902, Karl Kautsky suggested that Europe's revolutionary centre might move from 'west' to 'east', with the Slavs playing a major role as the gravediggers of capitalism,[2] but such inversions of the more traditional equations of 'the West' with progress and 'the East' with reaction were rare. From about 1900, the Social Democrats increasingly looked outside Europe to the United States, to discern the most modern forms of capitalism and their political and cultural superstructures. They linked what they saw with their perceptions of economic and political developments in Germany.

In line with the strong nationalization of politics and social systems that intensified in Europe during the second half of the nineteenth century, German Social Democrats concentrated, first and foremost, on national politics and developments within the German nation (after 1871, the German nation state). But this is not to say that they did not look elsewhere when seeking to determine the direction in which German social democracy was to develop. It was 'the West' in its most prominent national incarnations – Britain, France and the United States – that was most drawn on to inform discussions surrounding the ideological self-understanding of German social democracy in the period under review.

The present chapter can only present a very selective survey of the evidence. It zones in on the perceptions German Social Democrats had of Britain,[3] and attempts to assess how far these perceptions shaped their ideological self-understanding. Britain, and, later on, the United States, presented a paradox to them: these countries were experiencing the most advanced forms of capitalism, yet their labour movements were weak. According to Marxist theory, the most advanced capitalist countries should produce the most self-conscious working classes, which, through militant organization, would lead the struggle against capitalism. The scene in 'the West' was not like this. How could this puzzle be explained? Coming to terms with this paradox was a central theme in developments from the late nineteenth century to the 1950s.

Social Democracy and 'the West' before the First World War

In 1890, the Social Democrats in Germany adopted the Erfurt Programme which committed the party to Marxism. The Programme did not make a spatial distinction between East and West. Instead it proclaimed: 'The interests of the working class are the same in all countries with capitalist modes of production.' And it continued: 'Hence the liberation of the working class is a work in which all workers of all cultural nations [*Kulturländer*] are equally engaged.'[4] The vague reference to 'cultural' or developed nations is noteworthy. It presupposes the existence of less 'cultured' nations and, perhaps, those not 'cultured' at all. In their attempts to establish a 'scientific socialism', Karl Marx and Friedrich Engels had been very clear in identifying the countries of 'the West', and especially

Britain, as the most advanced capitalist regions. One could perhaps be forgiven for thinking of them as also the most 'cultured'. In contrast to 'Eastern' countries, characterized by backwardness and an 'Asiatic mode of production', Britain and the advanced capitalist countries of 'the West' led the way on the historical trajectory that, according to Marxist theory, all societies had to travel sooner or later. Hence, for many Marxists, 'Western' nation states became the *locus* from which to gauge the future development of capitalism everywhere.[5]

Marx, of course, drew on the work of English economists like Adam Smith and David Ricardo in his economic analyses, and he relied heavily on the French Romantic historians for his history. Early German socialists also took a particular interest in the political development of Western nation states. Thus there was considerable interest in the English Chartist movement, which many German Social Democrats saw primarily as a proletarian movement for the emancipation of working people. Karl Marx had close relations with Ernest Jones, the Chartists' champion, and although neither he nor Engels played a central role in Chartist politics, they believed they saw in Chartism signs of a strong working-class consciousness which, they hoped, would eventually overthrow capitalism.[6] Ferdinand Lassalle consciously modelled himself on the Chartist orator Feargus O'Connor, even if his strategy for political mobilization was ultimately very different. The Chartists had been very loosely organized and when, ultimately, they failed, Lassalle drew the conclusion that only a highly organized political party with strong structures could be capable of bringing about political change.[7]

It was not only British political developments that fired the imagination of German Social Democrats. Many looked admiringly to the revolutionary traditions of France, in which they saw premonitions of the coming proletarian revolution. In 1871 August Bebel argued before the German Reichstag that the Paris Commune was an expression of the desire of workers everywhere for social revolution and the abolition of capitalism. Paris and the revolutionary Jacobin traditions of France, he claimed, were leading the way towards global working-class emancipation.[8]

Such revolutionary rhetoric was used by Otto von Bismarck to vilify German Social Democrats as 'enemies of the Reich'. In 1878 he succeeded in passing his Anti-Socialist Laws through the Reichstag, banning the Social Democrats from organizing, campaigning and publishing. Persecution under these laws drove many thousands of them into exile and many went west. Their encounters with Western nation states led to varying reactions, but in general what they saw reinforced their impression of the Western nation states as being the most progressive societies in both economic and political terms. For some, like

Eduard Bernstein, the time abroad was a transformative experience. Bernstein, who had vehemently opposed Bismarck's government, was in exile for more than twenty years, and he settled in London. His very wide circle of British friends included Marxists from the Social Democratic Federation (SDF), ethical socialists from the Independent Labour Party (ILP), Fabians, and many who were close to the radical wing of the Liberal Party. It is no exaggeration to say that Bernstein learnt to endorse the parliamentary system during his time in Britain. Deeply impressed with what he saw of Lib-Labism, the Liberal-Labour approach to social policy and the piecemeal reforms it achieved, he adapted his Marxism to fit the liberal-democratic framework he encountered in Britain.[9] Socialism, he concluded on the basis of his English experience, was achievable through a mixture of democratic franchise and true parliamentary government.[10]

In the writings of Social Democratic revisionists, the model for the future of capitalism, and for the politics to deal with it, lay in 'the West'. The liberal-democratic political framework that had developed there was seen as the best structure under which to work for socialism. The paradox at the heart of Britain, the country where capitalism was most advanced in all nineteenth-century Europe, could only be solved, they argued, by endorsing parliamentary politics, and this was an example to follow. Conclusions drawn from observing Western nation states thus pushed sections of the German Social Democrats away from revolution and towards an endorsement of liberal democracy from the early twentieth century onwards.

Orthodox Marxists, however, continued to criticize the insularity they saw in British socialism and its lack of unity[11] – the latter criticism applying just as well to socialist-leaning groups in the United States. These Marxists welcomed with enthusiasm all signs of more radical action in Britain,[12] for they still believed that it was from the most advanced capitalist countries that the revolution overthrowing capitalism would inevitably come. Even more than their revisionist rivals, the Marxists were troubled by the paradox that the most advanced capitalist states (Britain and the U.S.) had not produced strong, class-conscious labour movements.

Social Democracy and 'the West' between War and Exile

Having been branded 'fellows without a fatherland' for years, many Social Democrats rejoiced at the possibility of becoming part and parcel of a 'national community' in the crisis of August 1914. Some, like

Lothar Erdmann, who had mingled with the Fabians, even claimed that they had learnt how to combine socialism and nationalism in England. Intrigued by the mixture of social concern and national commitment that he encountered in the 'national efficiency' campaign when staying in Britain in 1912/13, he was struck by the strong identification of sections of British socialism with the British nation – and this was something he subsequently tried to bring into German socialism.[13]

Yet the outbreak of war in August 1914 was to show that there could be a slippery slope from positive identification with the German nation to nationalism. In line with the traditional Social Democrat perception that the most advanced economic and political societies lay to the west of Germany and all backwardness to the east, the initial fire of patriotic Social Democrats was concentrated on Russia. Many held Russia responsible for the outbreak of the war: they believed German culture had to be defended against Russian barbarism – and that Social Democrats should join in the defence. However, some German Social Democrats went further as the war progressed, and combined the traditional 'perfidious Albion' stereotype of Britain (prevalent in Germany) with notions of a specific 'Anglo-Saxon' capitalist greed that had to be defeated by German socialism. Thus the influential German Social Democratic Party (SPD) politicians Eduard David and Albert Südekum supported the government throughout the war in all its highly expansionist and annexationist war aims.[14] Max Cohen-Reuß, a Social Democratic deputy in the Reichstag, vociferously supported economic warfare against England in order to destroy what he perceived to be the pernicious economic greed emanating from Britain.[15] The idea that the advanced capitalist 'Anglo-Saxon' nations, Britain and the United States, were using the First World War to ensure the defeat of their most dangerous rival – Germany – and establish their long-term global dominance was frequently expressed amongst the more nationalistic Social Democrats.[16]

The German Social Democrats did not all succumb to anti-British feelings. In fact there were some notable voices against wartime German nationalism, especially that of Eduard Bernstein. Bernstein had already watched the growing Anglo-German rivalry before the First World War with increasing anxiety. He sought to counter it with his pen, writing both in German and in English.[17] He remained consistent in his opposition to the war after 1914, and this alienated him from many of his former revisionist allies and took him, for a brief time, into the Independent Social Democratic Party (USPD), where he rubbed shoulders with radical leftists like Clara Zetkin, Karl Liebknecht, Rosa Luxemburg and Franz Mehring. On balance, the USPD could be better relied on to denounce the wave of nationalism that swept over Germany during the war, taking so many Social Democrats with it, and to uphold the internationalism that had characterized German social democracy before 1914.[18]

It was a sign of the enduring strength of socialist internationalism that, at the end of hostilities, immediate attempts were made to resurrect the Socialist International.[19] British socialists led attempts to overcome the international isolation of fellow socialists in Germany and to reintegrate the German Social Democrats into the International.[20] Throughout the early years of the Weimar Republic, the Labour Party was committed to helping the Social Democrats in their struggle to stabilize the new political system and help Germany come to terms with the social, political and economic consequences of a devastating peace treaty.[21]

Not only were relations between the British and the German Social Democratic Parties remarkably good in the interwar period, but the Social Democrats in the young republic began to take an increasingly positive view of the British Labour Party and the way British politics worked. So what had been restricted to the revisionist wing of the SPD before 1914 now became more mainstream. Seeking to justify their coalition politics in the Weimar Republic, many German Social Democrats pointed to the British Labour Party as a model of a responsible socialist party in government (in 1924 and then again between 1929 and 1931). They commended its pragmatism and its orientation towards implementing specific reform policies.[22] While there were Social Democrats, such as those associated with the *Sozialistische Monatshefte*, who looked towards France as a key alliance partner for Germany and a political model,[23] the majority, especially those with an interest in foreign policy, were all more favourably disposed towards Britain and the British Labour Party. In the bitter intra-party conflict over 'coalitionism' in Germany, the successes of the Labour Party in Britain offered a justification against those inside the SPD who would not accept coalition politics. However, when in 1931 Ramsay MacDonald, Philip Snowden and a handful of Labour leaders entered into a national government with Conservatives and Liberals and the move was seen as a massive 'betrayal' of socialism, this was immediately picked up by critics of coalitionism within the SPD to point to the dangers of cosy arrangements between party leaders and 'bourgeois' politicians. Overall, the divisions within the SPD on how they viewed British parliamentary democracy continued to mirror the divisions between Left and Right. The difference was that, after 1918, the reformist Right had become the mainstream, while the Marxist Left had become a minority.

There was now growing hostility in mainstream social democracy to the communist Soviet Union and to home-grown communist movements. This also encouraged looking over to 'the West' – to the parliamentary and presidential democracies of Britain and France. The Social Democrats' anti-Bolshevism was built on a long-established perception of Russia as an economically backward and politically repressive regime. The Bolsheviks were portrayed as a group continuing this tradition and perverting the message of socialism. It was not the dictatorship of the proletariat the Social Democrats championed as an effective means to further the progress of socialism, but parliamentary democracy. Just as the British Labour Party, before 1931, had seemed to be transforming British politics and society, so the SPD hoped it could achieve a similar transformation in Germany as time went on. Close cooperation between the SPD, the British Labour Party and the French Section Française de l'Internationale Ouvrière (SFIO) after 1923 cemented this 'Western' orientation.[24]

If Britain had been the model of the most advanced capitalist development for nineteenth-century German Social Democrats, this role was increasingly taken over by the U.S. in the twentieth century. One of the main theoreticians of social democracy in the interwar period, Rudolf Hilferding, formulated his theory of 'organized capitalism' very much with developments in the U.S. in mind. In the U.S. he observed a great acceleration in cartelization and in various mechanisms for rationalizing production. In Hilferding's view, the U.S. showed that competitive capitalism was increasingly being replaced by organized capitalism and planned production. In other words, developments in the most advanced capitalist society in the world demonstrated that capitalism was moving towards a socialist planned economy by its own logic.[25]

If, for many Social Democrats, the U.S. and Britain showed the way as far as capitalist development and socialist politics were concerned, the Soviet Union served frequently as a negative counterfoil to these 'Western' developments. Though a handful of socialist intellectuals were fascinated by the Bolsheviks and their revolution and the party's left wing tended to insist on allowing the Soviet Union its own path to socialism, the party's mainstream was more likely to denounce Soviet communism. Julius Kaliski, who wrote in the *Sozialistische Monatshefte*, described the Bolsheviks as 'marauders of the revolution' and, like Gustav Mayer, equated 'Russian' and 'barbarian' in his assessment of developments. A 'socialism *asiaticus*' (Eugen Großmann), a 'despotic socialism' (Otto Bauer) and a 'military despotism' (Karl Kautsky) could not be a model for democratic socialism.[26] Social Democrats such as Rudolf Hilferding, Eduard Bernstein and Otto Bauer argued that, while violent revolution had been possible in the backward 'agrarian East', Germany belonged to the progressive 'industrial West'.[27]

Social Democrats in Exile: Personal Experiences of 'the West'

Instead of achieving an advance towards democratic socialism, however, the Left was, of course, defeated by the National Socialists in the 1930s, and many members of the SPD had, once again, to go into exile. The good relationship between many leading Social Democrats and Labour Party figures abroad helped ensure that support networks were in place in Britain, although it was never easy for exiles to establish themselves in a foreign country. Despite the difficulties of daily life, they were impressed by what they saw and experienced of democracy in Britain and the United States. It convinced many of them of the need for a democratic political framework to be established in Germany once Hitler and the National Socialists had been overthrown.

Fritz Heine belonged to the reformists in the SPD who had already looked to Britain for inspiration in the 1920s. On behalf of his party's national executive (as head of the SPD's first Campaigning and Intelligence Department), he had observed the British election campaign in 1929, and had tried to learn lessons on electioneering and self-presentation for the German Social Democrats. In exile, Heine worked closely with Richard Crossman, assistant editor of the *New Statesman* between 1938 and 1942, who also headed the Psychological Warfare Division of the British Government during the war. Crossman employed Heine as an intelligence analyst, and he was involved in interrogating German prisoners of war in Africa. Both Heine and Crossman were to become highly influential post-war politicians: Heine in the German Social Democrats, Crossman in the British Labour Party. They were well acquainted with each other's party lines and well disposed towards them.[28]

Curt Geyer and Friedrich Stampfer (both of whom had an editing role in *Vorwärts*) and Rudolf Hilferding, too, developed similar ideas of an alliance of 'Western' democracies as a bulwark against all forms of totalitarianism, including National Socialism and Soviet communism. They hoped that, after the victory over National Socialism, they would see Germany moving into line with these 'Western' democracies. Liberalism, freedom, pluralism – these were the solid foundations on which democratic regimes were to flourish. These socialists' praise for 'Western' democracies was accompanied by an equal condemnation of the Soviet Union, which they perceived as another terror state, bringing shame to humanity and to socialism. While they could go along with a tactical alliance between the 'Western' democracies and the Soviet Union in order to defeat Nazism, they were adamant that the model for a future democratic Germany lay with the democratic pattern of 'the West'. During their time in exile, various German socialist groups coalesced around a similar belief: 'Western' democratic values were the most effective bulwark against totalitarianism from both Left and Right.[29]

It therefore comes as no surprise that, when the German socialists tried to explain the victory of the Nazis in their country, they referred to a deviation Germany had made from the 'Western' path to modernity. For example, in 1936 Richard Löwenthal, the Left-socialist leader of the resistance group New Beginning (*Neu Beginnen*) and for most of his exile based in London, argued that 'the basic peculiarity of the German development up to 1918 was the contradiction between the speed and quality of industrial development and the backwardness of political rule: the most developed industrial country of Europe was ruled by semi-absolutist forms'. It was due to the peculiarities present at the foundation of the Reich that 'German national consciousness had a different character from those of the great nations of the West'. Whereas in 'the West' the national idea became associated with ideas of freedom, in Germany it was infused with notions of power; whereas the 'Western states' had their great democratic revolutions, the upheavals of 1918 had failed to provide such a foundational moment for Germany. Hence it was the deficits of Germany vis-à-vis 'the West' that, in large measure, explained the success of Hitler's followers in Germany.[30]

Fritz Heine and Richard Löwenthal were not the only influential socialists who spent the war years in Britain. In December 1940, the national executive of the Social Democratic Party in Exile (Sopade) moved its headquarters from Prague to London, and this brought Erich Ollenhauer, Hans Vogel and other prominent Social Democrats there.[31] Later, in 1952, Ollenhauer stepped into the position of party chairman of the SPD, following the death of Kurt Schumacher, and many of the London exiles played important roles in the post-war SPD. Many had encountered in Britain what they perceived as a functioning parliamentary democracy that could be adopted as a framework to achieve socialist objectives. Many were impressed too by the ability of the U.S.A., Britain and France to withstand and defeat fascist and right-wing challenges to democracy in their own countries.[32] It is for these reasons that the mental map of the Social Democrats was significantly transformed during the years of exile and, when they were faced with the emerging spatial logic of the Cold War, which crystallized in 1946–1948, those who returned to their home country were confirmed in their conclusion that Germany had to become part of 'the West'.[33]

Conclusion

For much of the period under discussion, the German Social Democrats were troubled by a major paradox they found at the heart of the 'Western' democracies. On the one hand, these democracies were seen as a blueprint for the future of all regions in which capitalism was developing – and hence they provided a window onto Germany's own future. On the other hand, the continuing weakness of socialist labour movements in some of the most advanced 'Western' countries, notably Britain and the U.S., prompted the question: how was capitalism going to be transformed? The revolutionary traditions of France offered one perspective – it was an event like the Paris Commune, Bebel had told the Reichstag, that would be the fate of all capitalist states – but no hint of revolution had occurred in Britain and the U.S.

With the strong nationalization of labour movements everywhere,[34] coupled with the organizational successes and self-declared ideological supremacy of Marxist socialism, many Social Democrats were content to see in 'Western' democracies the future economic development of capitalism and to convince themselves that their own strength would bring about the downfall of capitalism in Germany – and that they would be the first to achieve this. It was a notion sometimes shared by groups on the Left outside Germany. After all, the SPD was the dominant force in the Second International before 1914,[35] and even when the Bolsheviks were successful in overthrowing capitalism in Russia, it was thought that revolution in a less 'backward' country was needed. Throughout the early 1920s, many socialists hoped for revolution in Germany and argued that, without it, the world revolution could not be successful.

In the end, however, the 'Western' nation states not only provided the blueprint for expected global economic developments, but increasingly served as political models. The politics of negotiation influenced by 'Western' labour movements appealed especially to reformist Social Democrats intent on abandoning the 'revolutionary *attentism*'[36] that characterized Imperial German social democracy: they wanted to enter a more constructive engagement with genuine political processes. The political perceptions German Social Democrats had of 'Western' countries were shaped in a major way by their recurring experiences of exile. During the period when Bismarck's Anti-Socialist Laws were in force in the 1880s and then again during the Third Reich, leading Social Democrats left Germany to live in 'Western' countries and their experiences had important repercussions on their perception of the 'Western' states and their ideological worldviews. Thus the parliamentary and presidential democracies of the 'West' came to represent fitting political frameworks for the realization of socialism through the ballot box.

Arguably, the revisionism debate that pushed German social democracy towards a hesitant endorsement of forms of evolutionary socialism had its origins in Eduard Bernstein's exile in Britain. Similarly, the ideas for transforming the SPD into a catch-all party that culminated in the Bad Godesberg programme of 1959 were deeply influenced by what Social Democratic politicians had seen of the British and U.S. political systems during their exile years. The political 'Westernization' of German social democracy came fully into its own only after the Second World War.

Notes

1. Riccardo Bavaj, '"The West". A Conceptual Exploration', *European History Online* (EGO), published by the Institute of European History (IEG), Mainz 2011, online: http://www.ieg-ego.eu/bavajr-2011-en, URN: urn:nbn:de:0159-2011112107 (accessed 15 March 2012).
2. For Kautsky's statement see Denis Sdvižkov's chapter in this volume.
3. Stefan Berger, *The British Labour Party and the German Social Democrats, 1900–1931. A Comparison*, Oxford, 1994.
4. 'Programm der Sozialdemokratischen Partei Deutschlands beschlossen auf dem Parteitag in Erfurt 1891', in Dieter Dowe and Kurt Klotzbach (eds), *Programmatische Dokumente der deutschen Sozialdemokratie*, Berlin, 1984, 187–92, here 189.
5. Shlomo Avineri, *The Social and Political Thought of Karl Marx*, Cambridge, 1970.
6. John Charlton, *The Chartists. The First National Workers' Movement*, London, 1999, 87 ff.
7. Christiane Eisenberg, 'Chartismus und Allgemeiner Deutscher Arbeiterverein. Die Entstehung der politischen Arbeiterbewegung in England und Deutschland', in Arno Herzig and Günter Trautmann (eds), *'Der kühnen Bahn nun folgen wir …'. Ursprünge, Erfolge und Grenzen der Arbeiterbewegung in England und Deutschland*, 2 vols, Hamburg, 1989, vol. 1, 151–70.
8. *Stenographische Berichte über die Verhandlungen des Deutschen Reichstages, 1. Legislaturperiode, Sitzung vom 25. Mai 1871*, vol. 2, 921. See also Beatrix W. Bouvier, *Französische Revolution und deutsche Arbeiterbewegung. Die Rezeption des revolutionären Frankreich in der deutschen sozialistischen Arbeiterbewegung von den 1830er Jahren bis 1905*, Bonn, 1982.
9. See Manfred B. Steger, *The Quest for Evolutionary Socialism. Eduard Bernstein and Social Democracy*, Cambridge, 1997, 66–71.
10. See Eduard Bernstein, *Die Voraussetzungen des Sozialismus und die Aufgaben der Sozialdemokratie*, Stuttgart, 1899, 195.
11. See Gerhard A. Ritter, 'Die britische Arbeiterbewegung und die deutsche Sozialdemokratie, 1900–1923', in Gerhard A. Ritter and Peter Wende (eds), *Rivalität und Partnerschaft. Studien zu den deutsch-britischen Beziehungen im 19. und 20. Jahrhundert*, Paderborn, 1999, 95.
12. See, for example, Clara Zetkin's article on the 1912 miners' strike in *Die Gleichheit*, 1 April 1912, 209 f.

13. See Ilse Fischer, *Versöhnung von Nation und Sozialismus? Lothar Erdmann (1888–1939). Biographie und Auszüge aus den Tagebüchern*, Bonn, 2004.
14. Max Bloch, *Albert Südekum (1871–1944). Ein deutscher Sozialdemokrat zwischen Kaiserreich und Diktatur*, Düsseldorf, 2009; *Das Kriegstagebuch des Reichstagsabgeordneten Eduard David, 1914–1918*, ed. by Susanne Miller, Düsseldorf, 1966.
15. Max Cohen-Reuß, 'England und Rußland', *Die Glocke* 2/2 (1916): 5–9.
16. See Matthew Stibbe, *German Anglophobia and the Great War, 1914–1918*, Cambridge, 2001, 156 f.
17. Eduard Bernstein, *Die englische Gefahr und das deutsche Volk*, Berlin, 1911. See also Bernstein's pre-war articles for the Liberal newspaper *The Nation*. In a different way, one of his arch-rivals from the revisionism debate, the party leader August Bebel, also sought to contribute towards the prevention of conflict by warning the British foreign office in a series of secret communications about the dangers of Prussian militarism. See R.J. Crampton, 'August Bebel and the British Foreign Office', *History* 58 (1973), 218–32.
18. Robert F. Wheeler, *The Independent Social Democratic Party and the Internationals: an Examination of Socialist Internationalism in Germany 1915–1913*, Ph.D. thesis, University of Pittsburgh, 1970. See also Robert F. Wheeler, *USPD und Internationale. Sozialistischer Internationalismus in der Zeit der Revolution*, Frankfurt/Main, 1975.
19. On the importance of socialist internationalism in the twentieth century see Talbot Imlay, *Practising Internationalism. European Socialists and International Politics, 1918–1960*, Oxford, forthcoming, 2015.
20. Julius Braunthal, *History of the International, 1914–1943*, New York, 1967.
21. Wolfgang Krieger, *Labour Party und Weimarer Republik. Ein Beitrag zur Außenpolitik der britischen Arbeiterbewegung zwischen Programmatik und Parteitaktik 1918–1924*, Bonn, 1978.
22. See, for example, Egon Wertheimer, *Portrait of the Labour Party*, London, 1929, xi; or Egon Wertheimer, 'Sozialismus für unsere Generation', *Die Gesellschaft* 3 (1926), 444–57.
23. On the so-called 'continental socialists' (*Kontinentalsozialisten*), see Stefan Feucht, *Die Haltung der sozialdemokratischen Partei Deutschlands zur Außenpolitik während der Weimarer Republik (1918–1933)*, Frankfurt/Main, 1998.
24. See Jürgen Zarusky, *Die deutschen Sozialdemokraten und das sowjetische Modell. Ideologische Auseinandersetzung und außenpolitische Konzeptionen 1917–1933*, Munich, 1992, 182–84.
25. See F. Peter Wagner, *Rudolf Hilferding. Theory and Politics of Democratic Socialism*, New Brunswick, 1993; for the general context see Stefan Berger, *Social Democracy and the Working Class in Nineteenth and Twentieth Century Germany*, London, 2000, 124–29. See also Mary Nolan, *Visions of Modernity. American Business and the Modernization of Germany*, Oxford, 1994.
26. All quotations are from Gerd Koenen, 'Überprüfungen an einem "Nexus". Der Bolschewismus und die deutschen Intellektuellen nach Revolution und Weltkrieg 1917–1924', *Tel Aviver Jahrbuch für deutsche Geschichte* 24 (1995), 359–91, here 363. See also Donal O'Sullivan, *Furcht und Faszination. Deutsche und britische Rußlandbilder 1921–1933*, Cologne, 1996, 267–75; Jürgen Zarusky, 'Vom Zarismus zum Bolschewismus. Die deutsche Sozialdemokratie und der "asiatische Despotismus"', in Gerd Koenen and Lev Kopelev (eds), *Deutschland und die russische Revolution 1917–1924*, Munich, 1998, 99–133; Kai-Uwe Merz, *Das Schreckbild. Deutschland und der Bolschewismus 1917–1921*, Frankfurt/Main, 1995; Uli Schöler, '*Despotischer Sozialismus*' oder '*Staatssklaverei*'? *Die theoretische Verarbeitung der*

sowjetrussischen Entwicklung in der Sozialdemokratie Deutschlands und Österreichs (1917–1929), Münster, 1990; and Peter Lösche, *Der Bolschewismus im Urteil der deutschen Sozialdemokratie 1903–1920*, Berlin, 1967.

27. See especially Otto Bauer, *Bolschewismus oder Sozialdemokratie?*, Vienna, 1920, 71; Eduard Bernstein, *Die deutsche Revolution von 1918/19. Geschichte der Entstehung und der ersten Amtsperiode der deutschen Republik*, Bonn, 1998 (first published Berlin, 1921), 237, 268 f. For Rudolf Hilferding see Heinrich August Winkler, 'Demokratie oder Bürgerkrieg. Die russische Oktoberrevolution als Problem der deutschen Sozialdemokraten und der französischen Sozialisten', *Vierteljahrshefte für Zeitgeschichte* 47 (1999), 1–23, here 10.
28. See Stefan Appelius, *Heine. Die SPD und der lange Weg zur Macht*, Essen, 1999.
29. For an early indication of how right-wing and left-wing totalitarianisms were juxtaposed in ideas of Western democracy see Richard Löwenthal, 'Historische Voraussetzungen des deutschen Nationalsozialismus' (1936), in Richard Löwenthal, *Faschismus – Bolschewismus – Totalitarismus*, ed. by Mike Schmeitzner, Göttingen, 2009, 112–32, esp. 119 f. See also Rainer Behring, 'Option für den Westen. Rudolf Hilferding, Curt Geyer und der antitotalitäre Konsens', in Mike Schmeitzner (ed.), *Totalitarismuskritik von links. Deutsche Diskurse im 20. Jahrhundert*, Göttingen, 2007, 135–60; and Udo Vorholt, *Die Sowjetunion im Urteil des sozialdemokratischen Exils 1933–1945. Eine Studie des Exilparteivorstandes der SPD, des Internationalen Sozialistischen Kampfbundes, der Sozialistischen Arbeiterpartei und der Gruppe Neu Beginnen*, Frankfurt/Main, 1991.
30. Löwenthal, 'Historische Voraussetzungen des deutschen Nationalsozialismus', 113, 119.
31. See Anthony Glees, *Exile Politics during the Second World War. The German Social Democrats in Britain*, Oxford, 1982.
32. See Gerd-Rainer Horn, *European Socialists Respond to Fascism. Ideology, Activism and Contingency in the 1930s*, Oxford, 1996.
33. See Julia Angster, *Konsenskapitalismus und Sozialdemokratie. Die Westernisierung von SPD und DGB*, Munich, 2003. See also Rainer Behring, *Demokratische Außenpolitik für Deutschland. Die außenpolitischen Vorstellungen deutscher Sozialdemokraten im Exil, 1933–1945*, Düsseldorf, 1999.
34. See Marcel van der Linden, 'The National Integration of European Working Classes (1871–1914)', *International Review of Social History* 33 (1988), 285–311.
35. See J. P. Nettl, 'The German Social Democratic Party 1880–1914 as a Political Model', *Past & Present* 30 (1965), 65–95.
36. Dieter Groh, *Negative Integration und revolutionärer Attentismus. Die deutsche Sozialdemokratie am Vorabend des ersten Weltkrieges*, Frankfurt/Main, 1974.

Chapter 16

BRIDGE OVER TROUBLED WATER
German Left-Wing Intellectuals between 'East' and 'West',
1945–1949

Dominik Geppert

Bridges and bridge-building are popular metaphors, and not only with American pop singers like Paul Simon and Art Garfunkel. Very rarely, however, have these metaphors been used so widely as among left-wing intellectuals in Germany between 1945 and 1949. These years marked the heyday of idealistic visions of putting democratic socialism into practice and building a new society on the debris of the Third Reich.[1] The intellectual bridge-builders who are the subject of this chapter were part of what was later called the 'homeless Left'. They belonged to the Left because they adhered to Marxist socialism in one form or another, and they were homeless because they felt estranged from the Labour movement in both its organized forms: communism and Social Democracy.[2] The metaphorical bridge the 'homeless Left' had in mind was a connection between East and West, with Germany and/or Europe serving as a kind of vaguely defined mediator (the forward slash indicating that the terms 'Germany' and 'Europe' were sometimes used synonymously). The images of the West the left-wing intellectuals evoked as part of their bridge-building project are interesting not because they became the guiding ideas of the post-war era in Germany (they did not) but because they represent a path not taken, or rather a bridge not crossed.

In order to gain a first impression of what the bridge-building of the 'homeless Left' was about, one could hardly choose a better starting point than Hans Werner Richter. He was a writer and ex-communist in his late thirties when he returned from a prisoner-of-war camp in the United States and, from 1946, earned a living as the editor of *Der Ruf*. This Munich-based magazine boasted that it was the 'voice of the young generation'.[3] In October 1946, *Der Ruf* published an essay by Richter entitled 'Germany – Bridge between East and West'. After the collapse of the Third Reich, Richter argued, the young generation in Germany faced both a challenge and an opportunity:

> It has got the socialism of the East and the democracy of the West. ... It has to start where those two orders meet. It has to democratize socialism and socialize democracy. In this way, the young German generation can build the bridge that leads from West to East and from East to West. This will be the bridge to the future of Europe.[4]

Richter's essay was a typical example of the political discourse German left-wing intellectuals engaged in over their country's future. The notion that defeated Germany had a new role as spiritual mediator between 'East' and 'West' was widely voiced in *Der Ruf* and similar journals, such as the *Frankfurter Hefte*, edited by Eugen Kogon and Walter Dirks, two Catholics with socialist leanings.[5] In his aptly named magazine *Ost und West*, which was published in East Berlin from 1947 to 1949, Alfred Kantorowicz emphasized the spiritual dimension of Germany's new mission which was a consequence of the country's military defeat.[6] Germany was – and would be for some time – an object rather than a subject of world history, Kantorowicz explained. 'If we speak of bridge-building', he stated, 'we do not think of political mediation or even the balancing and equilibrating of power groups but of spiritual bridge-building'.[7]

Periodicals such as *Der Ruf*, *Frankfurter Hefte* or *Ost und West* were amongst the most important vehicles of political debate in Germany between the end of the war and the currency reform of 1948. They steadily sold several tens of thousands of copies per issue. This was mainly because, at that time, the book market was still in ruins and a shortage of paper meant that daily newspapers could not yet compete with magazines that were published on a fortnightly or monthly basis and were thus much cheaper to produce. Moreover, the intellectual drought of the Nazi years had resulted in a widely shared need to catch up on uncensored political exchange, and this further contributed to the blossoming of sophisticated political-cultural journals in the second half of the 1940s. As regards their aims and visions, the left-wing intellectuals pinned their hopes on the notion of a democratic and socialist Europe, which could overcome the excesses of both nationalism and capitalism without committing the mistakes of communist dictatorship. They demanded a radical break with the past, and did not confine this to the remnants of National Socialism. Capitalism and liberal democracy had to go too because, allegedly, they had made fascist dictatorship possible. The social force to bring this revolution about was the young generation that had grown up during the Nazi dictatorship, a group that had had its fill of totalitarian dictatorship and was untainted by sympathies with capitalism and liberalism – political forces it had never known.[8]

Using *Der Ruf*, *Ost und West* and the *Frankfurter Hefte* as examples, this chapter will sketch answers to three sets of questions. The first set mainly concerns the years 1945 to 1949. What did Richter, Kantorowicz, Dirks, Kogon and others actually mean when they were writing about 'the West'? What function did it fulfil in their argument? How did they use images of the West to further their political aims? The second set of questions is mainly relevant for the years up to 1945. What were the origins of these images of the West? What kinds of personal experience backed them up? Did the left-wing intellectuals live up to their own demand for a radical break with the past? And were there traces of older images that linked their debates to earlier notions of the West? The final set of questions deals with the years from 1949 to the 1960s, by asking how perceptions changed over time. Did 'the West' grow or shrink geographically? Did it include or exclude the new West German state that was founded in 1949?

What Kind of 'West'?

The key words defining 'the West', as the 'homeless Left' saw it, were 'capitalism' and 'democracy' – as opposed to public ownership and the dictatorship of the proletariat in the East. Linked associations included 'personal freedom', 'liberalism' and 'the rule of law' – as opposed to Eastern notions of 'planning', 'collectivism' and the 'socialist state'.[9] Even before the Cold War turned hot in 1947/48, 'the West', which was delineated by these kinds of characteristics, was almost exclusively identified with capitalism and democracy as practised in the United States of America, in the same way as 'the East' was associated with the communism and state planning of the Soviet Union. The reason for this was that 'the West', just like 'the East', was stereotyped in a negative way, as 'other'. This stereotype contrasted the 'new' superpowers with the 'old' continent, and, seen like this, France and Britain belonged to 'Europe', not to 'the West'.[10]

German left-wing intellectuals associated 'the West' with everything Germany and Europe were not – or at least should not be or should not become. In its current situation, Kantorowicz stated, Germany could schematically adopt neither the American way of life nor the type of socialism that had developed in the Soviet Union.[11] Dirks put it more stridently when he claimed in late 1945: 'We do not want Russian Bolshevism or American mammoth fascism but Europe'.[12] In the West, Kogon agreed, human beings were reduced to spenders and consumers (*Kaufkraftträger*). In the East, they were tools and victims of Bolshevist totalitarianism.[13]

To emphasize the contrast between 'us' in Europe and 'them' beyond Europe's borders in East and West, left-wing intellectuals stressed similarities between the U.S.A. and the U.S.S.R. Americans and Russians inhabited whole continents, Kogon wrote in January 1947, and they were accustomed to thinking in wide-ranging categories ('*sie denken weiträumig*'). As ethnic melting pots, both the U.S.S.R. and the U.S. were young nations, not old ones. Both of them had rich natural resources, which made their economies extremely powerful. In different ways, both Americans and Russians believed in the progress of civilization. For them, technology and material wealth were essential ingredients of life. Both of them were inclined to simplify complex problems and overestimate the value of organization. Both had a tendency towards mechanistic and hasty solutions: 'They believe they can "fix" anything' (*Alles glauben sie 'machen' zu können*).[14]

The intended purpose of this kind of stereotyping was evident enough. It conveyed the impression that, even though Europe was not as big, powerful or energetic any more as the new superpowers in East and West, it was still spiritually superior: old but experienced, materially poor but intellectually and historically rich; overcrowded and divided into different nations but culturally prolific because of its diversity. The question was how Germany and Europe could learn from past mistakes and turn their rich heritage into future strength.

On the face of it, *Ost und West* suggested the most moderate solution. In the programmatic editorial of the first issue of his new magazine, Kantorowicz distanced himself from the notion that Germany in her present state could claim a role as an active broker: 'We are not immediately thinking of exporting German intellectual life over these bridges, which will lead backwards and forwards, but about importing those intellectual goods which have been denied to us since 1933'.[15]

The aim was to catch up with others rather than teach them. In retrospect, however, Kantorowicz claimed to have pursued the more ambitious intention of reestablishing Germany's traditional role of 'spiritually mediating between East and West', which, in his view, was predetermined by 'geopolitical necessities'.[16] Translated into a political programme, this amounted to somewhat vaguely formulated demands to abolish the concentration of economic and political power, abrogate social privileges, realize social justice and individual independence, and follow humane, ethical principles in politics.[17]

Der Ruf propagated a more energetic and positive role for Germany. By absorbing the socialist ideology of 'the East' and the democratic ideology of 'the West', Richter claimed, Germany would be able to combine them on a higher level. The result would be what Richter referred to somewhat vaguely as 'socialist democracy' – a form of government supposedly in tune with the nation's true nature and current development.[18] According to the editors of *Der Ruf*, Westernizing Soviet communism meant liberating it from Bolshevist dogmatism and, at the same time, reconciling it with the idea of freedom. This was what Richter and his co-editor Alfred Andersch called 'socialist humanism'. Kogon's and Dirks's concept of Europe as a 'Third Force' similarly sought a middle way between Soviet Bolshevism and North American capitalism. Kogon and Dirks described Richter's and Andersch's 'socialist humanism', as 'socialism from Christian responsibility' (*Sozialismus aus christlicher Verantwortung*).[19] The difference was hardly noticeable as both *Der Ruf* and the *Frankfurter Hefte* remained rather vague about the specific political and economic implications of their visions.

The most important distinction concerned the notion of Europe. To Richter's and Andersch's eyes 'Europe' amounted to not much more than the expectation that the socialist nations of the future would cease to be hostile towards each other and live in perpetual peace.[20] How their idea of a unified, neutralized and independent Germany between 'East' and 'West' could be reconciled with the interests and apprehensions of its neighbours remained unclear. Dirks, on the other hand, was sharply critical of any plans to neutralize Germany. He considered 'neutralism' another word for nationalism which he believed to be the root cause of Europe's problems. Instead, Dirks proclaimed 'the end of the sovereign nation state' and asserted that the European nations had become too small to trade on their own account. He demanded a European confederation in which Germany, Britain, France and others would pool their natural resources and methodically organize their common workforce. Only European collective planning would open the door to the new epoch of 'realized socialism'.[21] The Marxist inspiration of Dirks's philosophy of history is unmistakable. Just as newly developed means of production had promoted Germany's unification as a nation state in the nineteenth century, they pushed political unification one step further towards a European solution in the middle of the twentieth century.[22]

Ideological and Biographical Origins of the Imagined 'West'

To locate the roots of these images of the West one needs to examine individual biographical experiences as well as the more general ideological traditions that helped individuals interpret their experiences.[23] Although Dirks, Kogon, Richter and Andersch often posed as exponents of the young generation, none of them actually belonged to the 'generation of 45' which they thought was destined to lead their country and their continent into a better future. They had all grown up before the Nazis came to power. Kantorowicz was born in 1899, Dirks in 1901, Kogon in 1903, Richter in 1908 and Andersch in 1914. As an age cohort they were part of the so-called 'war youth' generation of the First World War and did not belong to the Hitler Youth generation, born in the 1920s, which has recently been so widely discussed under the label of the 'forty-fivers'.[24] This meant they had undergone their politically formative period during the interwar years, rather than under Hitler. Their traumatic experience was the fall of the Weimar Republic and not the Second World War, which Andersch and Richter survived as soldiers in the *Wehrmacht*, Kantorowicz in exile in the United States, Kogon in the Buchenwald concentration camp and Dirks, as editor of the *Frankfurter Zeitung*, in 'inner emigration'. What plagued them more than anything else after 1945 was the question of why the Weimar Republic had been allowed to collapse.[25]

Alfred Kantorowicz, who had the most intimate personal knowledge of the U.S., came from a conservative Berlin family of Jewish origin. In the Weimar Republic he worked as a journalist for several Left-liberal dailies and weeklies. In 1931, however, he joined the Communist Party – mainly because it seemed to offer the most resolute answer to the world economic crisis and the rise of National Socialism. After the Nazis had come to power, Kantorowicz was forced into exile – first to France, and later, after fighting on the Republican side in the Spanish Civil War, to the United States. There, he lived with his wife from 1941 to 1946 working for the American radio station CBS (the Columbia Broadcasting System), intercepting and analysing enemy broadcasts.[26]

Judging by his newspaper articles, the image he formed of the U.S. during this time was highly ambivalent. On the one hand, he defended what many Germans denounced as 'Americanization' by pointing to the energy and time that the 'mechanization of life' set free. He praised the magnanimity of his American hosts, their optimism, enterprising spirit, open-mindedness, hospitality and readiness to help others.[27] On the other hand, he characterized the Americans as 'money mad' people who turned everything into a 'business', and sometimes a 'racket'. (The terms 'money mad', 'business' and 'racket' are in English in the German original.) He had genuinely adored Roosevelt and was highly sceptical of his successor, Truman, whom he suspected of giving in to the 'pressure of the reactionary pack in the press, business and congress'.[28] After Kantorowicz had left America and returned to Germany, he initially propagated an evolutionary German way to socialism by returning to an idea he had first developed in 1930. Germany need not, indeed could not, Kantorowicz claimed, repeat the revolutionary experience of France in 1789 or of Russia in 1917.[29] When in the following months the Cold War turned hotter, however, Kantorowicz criticized the U.S. more vehemently. In an article for *Neues Deutschland*, the mouthpiece of the East German Socialist Party SED, he suggested that American friends who needed to escape the 'claws of their gaolers' in America would always be welcome in East Germany.[30]

Hans Werner Richter's and Alfred Andersch's idiosyncratic synthesis of 'Western' humanism and 'Eastern' socialism reflected a similar ambivalence towards the U.S. In their case, however, it was rooted in their experiences as prisoners of war rather than as political exiles. Richter came from a family of fishermen who lived near Bansin on the island of Usedom in the Baltic Sea. His parents were Social Democrats; one brother was a pacifist; and another was a member of the *Spartakusbund*.[31] Andersch's background could not have been more different. His family hailed from Bavaria. The father had joined the Nazi Party as early as 1920.[32] Like Kantorowicz, however, both Richter and Andersch joined the Communist Party in the last years of the Weimar Republic. Andersch renounced communism after the Nazi seizure of power and a brief spell in Dachau concentration camp in 1933. Richter had been expelled from the Communist Party in 1932 because of alleged Trotskyite tendencies. As with Andersch, though, Richter's more important inner break with communism was triggered by Stalin's alliance with Hitler in 1939.[33]

Richter and Andersch became acquainted with the United States as prisoners of war (POWs). From 1944 to 1946, they were detained in several POW camps on American soil. The most important one for their future life was Fort Philip Kearny in Rhode Island. It was there, as part of the U.S.A.'s reeducation programme, that they were selected to contribute to a newspaper produced by German POWs for German POWs. *Der Ruf. Zeitung der deutschen Kriegsgefangenen in USA* was distributed in all POW camps in the U.S., starting with ten thousand copies and reaching a circulation of seventy-five thousand in April 1946. According to an article in the last issue explaining its philosophy, the paper was intended to revitalize true democratic thinking among German POWs and contribute to the rebuilding of 'enduring democracy' in Germany after the defeat of National Socialism. One way of achieving this was to get the German

POWs acquainted with the 'democratic principles and constitutional arrangements of the United States'.[34]

Andersch rather enjoyed his encounter with America. When he was eventually sent home, it is said that he had his backpack crammed full of American contemporary literature (plus, one should add, a copy of Ernst Jünger's *Storms of Steel*). Richter, on the other hand, intensely disliked the U.S. reeducation policy. In his contributions to the American *Ruf*, he had already cautiously criticized the notion of Germany's collective guilt and developed his idea of the country's balancing role between 'East' and 'West'. What was necessary, he wrote in July 1945, was an open view in all directions. The view to the East had to include the view to the West. For it was in the middle, between 'East' and 'West', that Germany's fate lay.[35] In the Munich *Ruf*, which Andersch and Richter edited together after their return from America, Richter further developed this train of thought. In an article entitled 'The Transformation of Socialism – and the Young Generation', he pinned his hopes for a fusion of socialism and liberty on the war experience of his generation. The experience of the mass organization of war and captivity had supposedly forged the soldier into the prototype of the new 'socialist man'. His generation knew, Richter claimed, 'that it can only end its hunger if the economy is organized according to a plan and that, at the same time, it can only find life if the planned economy, this new economic order, does not again take away their freedom'.[36]

Andersch, Richter and Kantorowicz were steeped in Marxist theory. Thus, their concept of Germany as a bridge between 'East' and 'West' owed much to dialectic materialism – with socialist humanism being the synthesis of the Western thesis and Eastern antithesis. At the same time, however, the 'bridge' concept transcended orthodox Marxism. Andersch, for example, stated categorically that Europe's youth would leave the socialist camp if it gained the impression that socialism was synonymous with economic determinism and the denial of human freedom of will.[37]

Dirks and Kogon did not have any first-hand knowledge of either the United States or communism. Dirks's social background was Westphalian Catholicism. In his youth, he had been a member of the Catholic Youth Movement (*Quickborn*) and worked as the secretary of the religious philosopher Romano Guardini. As editor of the *Rhein-Mainische Volkszeitung* from 1924 until 1934, he was an exponent of a left-wing Catholicism that supported the Centre politician Joseph Wirth and his plea for a radical democratic coalition of Christians and Marxist workers. Kogon, on the other hand, had represented an extreme right-wing Austrian Catholicism. A fierce anti-socialist, he was a follower of Franz von Papen and supported ideas of a Christian corporate state. For a while, he postulated an alliance between conservative Catholics and National Socialists. In the end, however, he joined the Catholic opposition against Hitler and, after 1938, was incarcerated in Buchenwald concentration camp for seven years.[38]

Although they came from opposite ends of political Catholicism, Dirks and Kogon shared key aspects of their worldviews such as anti-capitalism, anti-liberalism and anti-parliamentarianism. What is more, their disagreements, with regard to socialism, for instance, faded away with the experience of Nazi dictatorship. In Buchenwald, Kogon cooperated with communists and Social Democrats in the illegal 'self-administration' of the concentration camp prisoners. At the same time, Dirks refined his theory of 'socialism from Christian responsibility' by secretly preparing an agenda of Catholic social reform on behalf of Herder publishers in Freiburg. This was to be published after the expected defeat of the Nazi regime.[39] The bridge-building concept of the *Frankfurter Hefte* thus owed less to Marxism than to notions of Catholic social mediation and the participation in anti-Nazi resistance together with communists and Social Democrats. Due to the editors' lack of personal knowledge of the U.S., America featured rather vaguely and abstractly in their writings – either as the homeland of capitalism or as a possible candidate for a fascist takeover modelled on the German experience of January 1933.[40]

Left-Wing Images of the West after 1948/9

When contextualizing the ways in which the 'homeless Left' perceived 'the West' after the Berlin Airlift and the foundation of the two German states, one needs to bear in mind that, immediately after 1945, left-wing intellectuals had believed they were swimming with the tide of an incoming European socialism. From 1947/8 onwards, however, they found themselves swimming against the tide of the times, which were now characterized by an intensified confrontation between the U.S. and the Soviet Union, and the division of Europe into Western and Eastern blocs. The year 1949 witnessed the establishment of two German states: a communist dictatorship in the East was confronted by a Federal Republic that exhibited all the characteristics of 'the West' the 'homeless Left' abhorred. This West German state was a capitalist parliamentarian democracy dominated by more or less the same parties and led by the same politicians that in the eyes of men like Kantorowicz, Richter or Kogon had been responsible for the collapse of the Weimar Republic. This is what Dirks, in his most famous essay, described as the 'restorative character of the epoch' – an expression quickly taken up by most other left-wing intellectuals.[41]

In the suspicious atmosphere of the Cold War, left-wing intellectuals were increasingly confronted with the question of which side they were on. This was a question they could not answer if they wanted to remain true to their concept of a bridge between 'East' and 'West'. It is no accident therefore that neither *Der Ruf* nor *Ost und West* survived the foundation of the two German states. The trouble for *Ost und West* began when the idea of a 'special German path to socialism' fell out of favour with the Soviet and SED leadership. In 1949, it was discontinued. *Der Ruf* was shut down in the same year, after having transferred its editorial office from Munich to Mannheim. Richter and Andersch, however, had already left in the spring of 1947, having clashed with the U.S. Information Control Division in Germany. (Andersch, incidentally, signed on with Dirks's and Kogon's *Frankfurter Hefte* for a short period after April 1947.)[42]

This is not the place to analyse in detail the political activities and ideological developments of the 'homeless Left' after the decisive caesura of 1948/9.[43] Instead, this chapter seeks to sketch four modes of reaction to the worldwide sea change just outlined. The reactions were: denial, compromise, exile and, finally, opposition.

The first mode of reaction was denial that such a sea change had taken place at all. There are traces of this in Kogon's and Dirks's writings in the *Frankfurter Hefte* throughout the years 1947 to 1950. They put 'the West', 'Western Europe' and 'West Germany' in inverted commas to indicate that these terms did not represent reality but merely a picture distorted by fear, ill will and ideology.[44] After the foundation of the two German states, however, this way of thinking was increasingly difficult to uphold. Accordingly, the inverted commas gradually disappeared. The Federal Republic of Germany (FRG) was now regarded as part of the Western camp. In this respect, 'the West' did indeed grow geographically. It was no longer confined to the U.S. but also included Britain, France, the Bonn Republic and other member states of NATO.

The second mode of reaction was compromise. Kantorowicz, for instance, was willing to compromise by subjecting himself to the SED party line and denouncing 'the West'. In 1949, in an open letter to a fictitious student in Göttingen, he explained that Western 'liberty' was only available as patches of 'liberties' designed to satisfy the specific needs, lusts and addictions of the powerful and the requirements of 'free enterprise' (which he put in English in the original). This 'liberty', Kantorowicz asserted, included 'the "freedom" to enrich oneself through the physical work of other human beings, to wage war to conquer new markets and oppress other peoples, the "freedom" to gamble on the stock exchange, to buy public opinion, to lie, to agitate to outlaw Jews, negroes, communists'.[45]

For this kind of rabble-rousing Kantorowicz was rewarded with a chair of German literature at the Humboldt University in East Berlin in 1954. In a more subtle and humane way, Kogon and Dirks also compromised by adapting their commitment for a socialist Europe to the changing circumstances of liberal capitalist integration after 1950. Dirks even went so far as to endorse German remilitarization, so long as it remained within the framework of the supranational European army envisaged by the Pleven Plan. Only when the European Defence Community failed in 1954 did Dirks revert to his former pacifist position of opposing German rearmament in any form.[46]

The third mode of reaction was exile. This could be metaphorical exile, as in the case of Richter, who, in 1947, founded the literary discussion circle Group 47 – a step that has been interpreted as an 'escape into literature' due to his despair over the political restoration in West Germany.[47] Richter always denied this and claimed that he had remained true to his political convictions, merely moving from the direct short-term actions of a journalist to more long-term, indirect forms of political commitment via literature. It can hardly be denied, though, that Richter's political activities in the early 1950s seem rather low key when compared to those in the years 1946–47 when he edited *Der Ruf* or, indeed, to those in the 1960s when he conspicuously politicized Group 47.[48] Andersch chose a different kind of exile. Although he initially took part in Group 47, he later withdrew from most political and literary activities in West Germany, judging Adenauer's 'chancellor democracy' to be an only slightly improved version of authoritarian fascism, comparable to that in Franco's Spain and Salazar's Portugal. As soon as he could afford it, after publishing his bestselling novel *Sansibar*, he left Germany, explicitly describing his move as 'going into exile'. One might speculate whether this was a belated overcompensation for his failing to leave Germany during the Third Reich.[49] When Andersch left the Bonn Republic in 1957, Kantorowicz also left 'his' part of Germany, the GDR. He justified this decision by pointing to the oppressive cultural policies of the Ulbricht regime that gagged any independent intellectual activity and had been transformed, in Kantorowicz's words, into a new form of 'fascism and barbarism by apparatchiks'.[50] Whereas Kantorowicz went to Hamburg, Andersch moved to neutral Switzerland, thereby combining the pleasantness of living in the Ticino with a confirmation of his refusal to accept the rigid antagonisms of the Cold War.

Outright political opposition only became an attractive mode of reaction for the 'homeless Left' towards the end of the 1950s, when the East–West tension eased and Adenauer's government ran into increasing difficulties. In 1956/7, Richter organized the Grünwald Circle to protest against German rearmament and what he regarded as the continuing and ever growing influence of ex-Nazis in West Germany. Thereafter, he briefly took part in the extraparliamentary opposition to nuclear weapons, at one stage even becoming chairman of the European Federation against Nuclear Armament.[51] He stuck to his ideas about humanist socialism as a superior alternative to what he called the 'Adenauer state'. In the 1960s, at least partly overcoming his dislike of parties and parliamentary politics, he even campaigned for Willy Brandt as the Social Democratic Party candidate for the chancellorship. In the last resort, however, Richter did not expect that humanist socialism could be achieved in an evolutionary way in 'the West', but only in a revolutionary way in 'the East'.[52] At any rate, this is what his enthusiastic reactions to the Hungarian uprising in 1956[53] and the Prague Spring in 1968[54] indicate. Richter's continuing devotion to the idea of the revolution can be interpreted as a sign of how persistently Marxist conceptions of historical change survived in the thinking of the 'homeless Left' and how attractive the notion of *ex oriente lux* still was, even if it meant revolution against Bolshevism.[55]

Conclusion

When looking at the 'bridge' concept held by the 'homeless Left', one cannot isolate 'the West' from 'the East'. The two points of the compass need to be seen in combination as a joint means of emphasizing the (potentially) positive features of Germany and of Europe through contrasting perspectives. 'East' and 'West' served to justify the notion of German exceptionalism in the face both of the catastrophe of the Third Reich and of the overwhelming political, economic, ideological and military might of the new superpowers. The bridge was necessary, it could be said, just because the water beneath it was troubled, not calm. But, by maintaining a sense of German exceptionalism, the thinking of the left-wing intellectuals failed to represent the radical break with the past they themselves had called for. On the contrary, it was Adenauer's policy of integration into 'the West', so vehemently opposed by men like Richter, Andersch, Dirks, Kogon and Kantorowicz, that proved to be the real caesura in German images of the West.

Notes

1. See Alexander Gallus, *Die Neutralisten. Verfechter eines vereinten Deutschland zwischen Ost und West 1945–1990*, Düsseldorf, 2001, esp. 94–108; and Dominik Geppert and Udo Wengst (eds), *Neutralität – Chance oder Chimäre? Konzepte eines Dritten Weges für Deutschland und die Welt 1945–1990*, Munich, 2005.
2. The term was used for the purpose of self-characterization by left-wing intellectuals both in the Weimar Republic and in the early post-war period; see for instance Dominik Geppert, 'Von der Staatsskepsis zum parteipolitischen Engagement. Hans Werner Richter, die Gruppe 47 und die deutsche Politik', in Dominik Geppert and Jens Hacke (eds), *Streit um den Staat. Intellektuelle Debatten in der Bundesrepublik, 1960–1980*, Göttingen, 2008, 46–68, esp. 62.
3. Jerome Vaillant, *Der Ruf. Unabhängige Blätter der Jungen Generation (1945–1949). Eine Zeitschrift zwischen Illusion und Anpassung*, Munich et al., 1978.
4. Hans Werner Richter, 'Deutschland – Brücke zwischen Ost und West', *Der Ruf* 4 (1946), 1–2.
5. For Dirks see Ulrich Bröckling, 'Der "Dritte Weg" und die "Dritte Kraft". Zur Konzeption eines sozialistischen Europas in der Nachkriegspublizistik von Walter Dirks', in Joachim Köhler and Damian van Mehlis (eds), *Siegerin in Trümmern. Die Rolle der katholischen Kirche in der deutschen Nachkriegsgesellschaft*, Stuttgart, 1998, 70–84.
6. Barbara Baerns, *Ost und West – eine Zeitschrift zwischen den Fronten. Zur politischen Funktion einer literarischen Zeitschrift in der Besatzungszeit (1945–1949)*, Münster, 1968.
7. Alfred Kantorowicz, 'Einführung', *Ost und West* 1 (1947), 3–8, here 4.
8. Dominik Geppert, 'Hans Werner Richter, die Gruppe 47 und die "Stunde Null"', in Alexander Gallus and Axel Schildt (eds), *Rückblickend in die Zukunft. Politische Öffentlichkeit und intellektuelle Positionen in Deutschland um 1950 und um 1930*, Göttingen, 2011, 203–20, here 216–17.
9. See Richter, 'Deutschland – Brücke zwischen Ost und West', 47.
10. See Michel Grunewald and Hans Manfred Bock (eds), *Der Europadiskurs in den deutschen Zeitschriften (1945–1955)*, Bern, 2001; and Vanessa Conze, *Das Europa der Deutschen. Ideen von Europa in Deutschland zwischen Reichstradition und Westorientierung (1920–1970)*, Munich, 2006.
11. Kantorowicz, 'Einführung', 7–8.
12. Quoted in Gallus, *Die Neutralisten*, 94.
13. Eugen Kogon, 'Über die Situation' (1947), in Eugen Kogon, *Die restaurative Republik. Zur Geschichte der Bundesrepublik Deutschland* (Gesammelte Schriften, vol. 3), Weinheim and Berlin, 1996, 23–48, here 36.
14. Ibid., 32.
15. Reprinted in Alfred Kantorowicz, *Vom moralischen Gewinn der Niederlage*, Berlin, 1949, 344–51, here 346.
16. Alfred Kantorowicz in 1965, quoted in Baerns, *Ost und West*, 74.
17. Baerns, *Ost und West*, 141–42.
18. Richter, 'Deutschland – Brücke zwischen Ost und West', 1.
19. Walter Dirks, 'Thesen zu einer "Sozialistischen Einheitspartei"' (1945), in Walter Dirks, *Sozialismus oder Restauration*, Zurich, 1987, 33–36; Kogon, 'Über die Situation'.
20. Alfred Andersch, 'Das junge Europa formt sein Gesicht' (1946), in Hans A. Neunzig (ed.), *Der Ruf. Unabhängige Blätter der jungen Generation*, Munich, 1976, 19–25;

Hans Werner Richter, 'Churchill und die europäische Einheit', (1947), in Neunzig (ed.), *Der Ruf*, 256–62.
21. Walter Dirks, 'Die zweite Republik' (1946), in Dirks, *Sozialismus oder Restauration*, 40–59, here 48–49.
22. See Bröckling, 'Der "Dritte Weg" und die "Dritte Kraft"', 73.
23. Interpretative designs like these are usually discussed as generations. See Ulrike Jureit, *Generationenforschung*, Göttingen, 2006; and Björn Bohnenkamp, Till Manning and Eva-Maria Silies (eds), *Generation als Erzählung. Neue Perspektiven auf ein kulturelles Deutungsmuster*, Göttingen, 2009.
24. See A. Dirk Moses, 'The Forty-Fivers. A Generation between Fascism and Democracy', *German Politics and Society* 17 (1999), 94–126; and A. Dirk Moses, *German Intellectuals and the Nazi Past*, Cambridge, 2007.
25. For wider implications see Sebastian Ullrich, *Der Weimar-Komplex. Das Scheitern der ersten deutschen Demokratie und die politische Kultur der frühen Bundesrepublik 1945–1959*, Göttingen, 2009.
26. See Wolfgang Gruner, '*Ein Schicksal, das ich mit sehr vielen anderen geteilt habe*'. *Alfred Kantorowicz – sein Leben und seine Zeit von 1899 bis 1935*, Kassel, 2006.
27. Kantorowicz, *Vom moralischen Gewinn der Niederlage*, 205–48.
28. Alfred Kantorowicz, 'Abschied von America' (1946), in Kantorowicz, *Vom moralischen Gewinn der Niederlage*, 334–36.
29. Kantorowicz, 'Einführung', 3–4.
30. Alfred Kantorowicz, 'Im Namen der Freiheit', (1948), in Kantorowicz, *Vom moralischen Gewinn der Niederlage*, 328–33.
31. For Richter's own account of his youth see Hans Werner Richter, *Spuren im Sand. Roman einer Jugend*, Vienna, 1953.
32. Stephan Reinhardt, *Alfred Andersch. Eine Biographie*, Zurich, 1996.
33. Geppert, 'Hans Werner Richter, die Gruppe 47 und die "Stunde Null"', 214–16.
34. Quoted in Heinz Ludwig Arnold, *Die Gruppe 47*, Reinbek bei Hamburg, 2004, 17.
35. Quoted in Erich Embacher, *Hans Werner Richter. Zum literarischen Werk und zum politisch-publizierten Wirken einer engagierten deutschen Schriftstellers*, Frankfurt/Main, 1985, 281.
36. Hans Werner Richter, 'Die Wandlung des Sozialismus – und die junge Generation', (1946), in Neunzig (ed.), *Der Ruf*, 134–39, here 138.
37. Alfred Andersch, 'Das junge Europa formt sein Gesicht'.
38. For Kogon's and Dirks's Weimar roots see Karl Prümm, *Walter Dirks und Eugen Kogon als katholische Publizisten der Weimarer Republik*, Heidelberg, 1984.
39. Walter Dirks, 'Vorwort', in Dirks, *Sozialismus oder Restauration*, 5–10; Gottfried Erb, 'Vorwort', in Kogon, *Die restaurative Republik*, 7–14.
40. Walter Dirks, 'Ein falsches Europa', (1948), in Dirks, *Sozialismus oder Restauration*, 221–42, here 232–42.
41. Walter Dirks, 'Der restaurative Charakter der Epoche', (1950), in Dirks, *Sozialismus oder Restauration*, 326–48.
42. See Arnold, *Die Gruppe 47*, 26–31; and Baerns, *Ost und West*, 85–90.
43. See Friedrich Kießling, *Die undeutschen Deutschen. Eine ideengeschichtliche Archäologie der alten Bundesrepublik*, Paderborn, 2012.
44. See Dirks, *Sozialismus oder Restauration*, 210–348; and Kogon, *Die restaurative Republik*, 48–82.
45. Alfred Kantorowicz, 'Suchende Jugend' (1949), quoted in Baerns, *Ost und West*, 65.
46. Walter Dirks, '*Sagen, was ist*'. *Politische Publizistik, 1950–1968*, Zürich, 1988.

47. See for instance Friedhelm Kröll, *Gruppe 47*, Stuttgart, 1979, 22–23; or Herbert Lehnert, 'Die Gruppe 47. Ihre Anfänge und ihre Gründungsmitglieder', in Manfred Durzak (ed.), *Die deutsche Literatur der Gegenwart. Aspekte und Tendenzen*, 3rd edn, Stuttgart, 1976, 37. Differing voices are Helmut Peitsch and Hartmut Reith, 'Keine "innere Emigration" in die "Gefilde" der Literatur. Die literarisch-politische Publizistik der "Gruppe 47" zwischen 1947 und 1949', in Jost Hermand, Helmut Peitsch and Klaus R. Scherpe (eds), *Nachkriegsliteratur in Westdeutschland*, vol. 2, Berlin, 1983, 129–61.
48. See Geppert, 'Von der Staatsskepsis zum parteipolitischen Engagement'.
49. This, at least, was Richter's interpretation of Andersch's behaviour: see Hans Werner Richter, 'Einmal durch eine belebte Gasse gehen und nicht erkannt werden: Alfred Andersch', in Hans Werner Richter, *Im Etablissement der Schmetterlinge. 21 Portraits aus der Gruppe 47*, Munich and Vienna, 2004, 29–43, here 37. Recently, there has been some controversy about Andersch's behaviour during the Third Reich caused by the writer W.G. Sebald: 'Der Schriftsteller Alfred Andersch', in W.G. Sebald, *Luftkrieg und Literatur. Mit einem Essay zu Alfred Andersch*, Munich, 1999, 121–60.
50. Quoted in Baerns, *Ost und West*, 68.
51. Dominik Geppert, '"Kreuzwegqual zwischen Politik und Literatur". Der Umbruch Ende der 1950er Jahre als Zäsur in der Geschichte der Gruppe 47', in Alexander Gallus and Werner Müller (eds), *Sonde 1957. Ein Jahr als symbolische Zäsur für Wandlungsprozesse im geteilten Deutschland*, Berlin, 2010, 343–62.
52. See Geppert, 'Hans Werner Richter, die Gruppe 47 und die "Stunde Null"'.
53. Hans Werner Richter to Otto Richter, 29 November 1956, in Sabine Cofalla (ed.), *Hans Werner Richter. Briefe*, Munich and Vienna, 1997, 239–40, here 239; Hans Werner Richter, 'Der Petöfi-Kreis. Die ungarischen Schriftsteller und die Revolution in der sozialistischen Gesellschaft', *Die Kultur* 73 (1956), 4–5.
54. Hans Werner Richter to Reinhard Lettau, 31 March 1968, in Cofalla (ed.), *Hans Werner Richter*, 662–63, here 663.
55. See Hans Werner Richter, *Mittendrin. Die Tagebücher 1966–1972*, ed. Dominik Geppert and Nina Schnutz, Munich, 2012.

Chapter 17

ANTIPATHY AND ATTRACTION TO THE WEST AND WESTERN CONSUMERISM IN THE GERMAN DEMOCRATIC REPUBLIC

Katherine Pence

During the Cold War, East Germans referred to their neighbour across the border simply as 'the West'. They spoke of 'West packages', 'West TV', 'West chocolate' and 'West money'.[1] This shorthand for anything emanating from the Federal Republic of Germany (FRG) demonstrated how large 'the West' loomed in the imaginations of those relegated to Germany's eastern half, the German Democratic Republic (GDR).

East Germany's relationship to the West was deeply schizophrenic. The GDR was the westernmost state in the Eastern Bloc, yet it was abruptly severed from its Western affiliation through the vicissitudes of Cold War political division. Not only did the GDR break with 'the West', but in an effort to define itself as the true heir to the German nation rather than the FRG, the new state drew on Soviet/Russian alternative narratives of progress and emphasized negative aspects of the West as a concept. To legitimize this new identity, the GDR state and the Socialist Unity Party (SED) expended much energy spreading messages about the ills of retrograde Western culture and materialism. Yet the East German masses and even the Party elites ardently desired Western products and orchestrated complex and often illegal means to obtain them. This central conflict between antipathy and attraction to the West animated East German identities. No wonder, then, that East Germany officially accused Western influences of sabotaging its project of building a unified socialist country.

In fact, it was not just the influence of the West, but the conflicted relationship East Germans had to it that served to undermine and sabotage East German socialism, creating fissures in socialist society right up to its collapse in 1989.

The major breaking point between East and West came with the dual currency reforms in 1948, the subsequent Berlin Blockade and Airlift, and the political division of the nation a year later. East and West Germany then battled each other for state legitimacy both domestically and globally. Under Christian Democratic leadership in the 1950s and 1960s, FRG state policy refused to acknowledge the GDR as a legitimate state. Rather, FRG politicians portrayed the GDR as a totalitarian Soviet colony formed without popular consent.[2] West Germans referred to the GDR as 'the so-called GDR', 'the Soviet Occupation Zone' or simply 'the Zone'. Starting in 1955, the FRG campaigned to isolate the GDR diplomatically through its Hallstein Doctrine, which mandated that no state could simultaneously establish diplomatic relations with both the FRG and the GDR. This strategy straitjacketed the GDR's foreign relations, restricting them largely to the socialist world and some non-aligned states.[3]

East Germany countered the FRG's offensive by casting the Bonn government as one promoting a continuation of Nazi personnel and ideology. East German politician Albert Norden's *Brown Book* of 1965 listed Nazi wartime criminals still employed within the FRG government.[4] East German media popularized the image of Nazi continuities among the 'Bonn big-shots' (*Bonner Bonzen*).[5] The GDR officially claimed, by contrast, that its own anti-fascist roots and break with capitalism automatically eradicated the bases for Nazism.[6]

The GDR opposed the FRG's Hallstein Doctrine through a show of anti-imperialist solidarity with decolonizing and 'developing' countries.[7] East Germany defined FRG interactions with Africa or Asia as oppressive, self-serving 'neo-colonialism' or 'neo-imperialism', implying continuities with nineteenth-century imperialism and Nazi aggression.[8] East German Committees for Solidarity with Africa and Asia propagated this message abroad and at home, where school curricula featured lessons on 'Bonn's neo-colonialism'.[9] Most damning was the condemnation of West Germany's close trading ties with the South African apartheid regime. In addition, the GDR linked the racism inherent in Western imperialism to a general racism that was becoming increasingly recognized because of the African-American Civil Rights Movement.

A corollary to the neo-imperialist label was condemnation of Western militarism. Soviet bloc regimes associated communism with peace. By contrast, the West's rearmament and integration into NATO by 1955 and the stationing of U.S. nuclear weapons in West Germany undergirded a deep critique of Western capitalism as integrally militaristic. Moreover, the GDR reviled the West's popular culture, such as that found in American westerns and gangster films, as symbolic of a harmful Western attraction to violence.[10] These accusations became critical to the GDR's argument that the West was more corrupt, oppressive and retrograde than the progressive, socialist East.

Condemnation of the West also dovetailed with criticism of Americanization as 'mass industrial non-culture'.[11] The Marshall Plan linked West Germany culturally, economically and politically with the United States within the Cold War concept of Atlanticism.[12] Whereas West Germans, and indeed Western Europeans, had long viewed Americans as uncultured lemmings of mass society, the Atlantic Alliance helped dispel such stereotypes.[13] The Marshall Plan brought West Germany more tightly into the U.S.'s orbit to make it a bulwark against communism. Some scholars have also associated this Americanization with the Westernization and 'recivilization' of West Germany.[14] The GDR, however, kept alive the antipathy towards American 'non-culture', thereby offering an alternative account of West German history, stressing fascist continuities bolstered, rather than broken, by the alliance with the U.S. Soviet military administrators in Germany, such as Andrei Zhdanov, foregrounded the superiority of Soviet culture over American 'decadence', 'degeneration' and 'cosmopolitanism'.[15] The GDR Information Office's 1950 brochure called *Ami [American] Go Home!* branded Americans as 'sharks' and highlighted their problems of poverty, racism and militarism. It condemned the U.S. exploitation of West Germany, ostensibly underpinning fascist ideology there through the leadership of Chancellor Adenauer, one of 'Truman's brown marionettes'.[16] Thus, West Germany was seen as a conduit for transmitting destructive American culture into East Germany. This Atlanticist alliance fuelled claims that the 'class enemy' was attempting to injure East Germany by attracting the population to 'the so-called American lifestyle'.[17]

The question of lifestyle became paramount during the Economic Miracle, as the two German states competed for their citizens' political allegiance, perhaps most visibly in the effort to provide a superior material culture. East German socialism focused on work and the equitable provision of its population's needs as more critical than the identification of GDR society as a consumer culture. Ina Merkel posits a theory of 'the self-understanding of the GDR, which never sought to become a Western-style consumer society but rather saw itself as embarking on the path toward a more civilized, humane "culture society" (*Kulturgesellschaft*)'.[18] The SED leadership held fast to pre-war Marxist ideologies that were deeply sceptical of commodity fetishism, material status symbols, fashion and consumer acquisitiveness in general.[19] However, the juxtaposition of this societal model with an increasingly consumption-focused West Germany sabotaged GDR efforts to eschew consumerism. The permeable East–West border kept the GDR from turning a deaf ear to consumer needs and desires, since the 'Golden West' so often dazzled East Germans. As a result the GDR worked to develop satisfying material conditions for its worker-consumers as an alternative to the West's more profit-driven consumer landscape. Consumerism was a tough battlefield, however. As Milena Veenis argues, the GDR's gap between promises of consumer fulfilment and the reality of material deficits within the socialist system led to popular fantasies of the West and its consumer world as a more attractive site of fulfilment than the socialist state. Spurred by consumer desires, fascination with the West became an integral part of East Germans' identities.[20]

'Golden West' or 'Fool's Gold'?

The 'Golden West' was a pervasive and problematic myth facing the GDR. It lured East Germans into making contrasts between the living standards in the two halves of Germany and to long for the unattainable across the border. A spectacular return of basic commodities to shop windows accompanied West Germany's 1948 currency reform, since Ludwig Erhard freed food, clothing and shoes from rationing and encouraged hoarding by shopkeepers prior to the reform. The East German media decried this Western 'shop-window politics', insisting that most cash-poor West Germans could only gaze longingly at the goods inside the windows.[21] Still, the conspicuously more abundant and increasingly attractive merchandise in West Germany profoundly influenced the East Germans' impressions of the West.

The East–West split also fuelled black market smuggling. Smugglers, grouped with other so-called 'parasites' and 'speculators' reviled across the Soviet bloc, became official scapegoats for domestic problems. The types of goods traded on the black market reflected disparities between the two systems. Western shoppers went east to buy subsidized staples, such as bread or eggs. West Berliners also spent money on services, which, unlike goods, did not entail a risk of police confiscation at the border. The journalist Curt Riess described these shopping patterns in the 1950s: 'The West Berlin women got their hair done, a manicure, their teeth fixed, outfits made out of fabric they brought with them, and their shoes soled. For many, this didn't even suffice, and they had to ride to the East to buy the cheaper bread there.'[22] Functionaries of the GDR worried that

Westerners would 'buy out' the GDR. The SED feared that West Berlin 'agents and other criminal offenders' were smuggling in propaganda and trashy literature.[23] The Western shoppers also inflamed resentment and stereotypes of privileged Westerners driving in 'slick western cars', displaying 'haughtiness'.[24] Border-crossing shopping trips put material distinctions at the core of East–West friction.

Into the 1950s, GDR leaders increasingly worried about border crossing in the other direction – from East to West. As the FRG economy boomed and the GDR faced economic crisis in 1952 and an uprising in 1953, the GDR increased its border policing. Increasingly, the West became a Mecca for prized commodities, such as tropical agricultural products – bananas, oranges, coffee and chocolate – all in short supply in East Germany.[25] In the 1950s, fashionable Western crepe-soled shoes exemplified a frequently smuggled commodity, signifying divergent standards of living under the two regimes.[26] Police and customs officials in the GDR vigilantly tried to confiscate these Western-style items and other commodities and to imprison or fine smugglers.[27] But still East Germans sought Western versions of products, which they often believed to be superior.[28]

The flow of goods across the border gave Western brands a constant presence in the socialist state, but access to these goods depended on individuals' cultivation of informal networks of exchange, including barter, smuggling, the black market and gifts from Western friends and relatives. Due to their scarcity and the extraordinary efforts made to obtain them, Western brand names took on iconic status in the GDR as 'unrivalled cultural capital'.[29] Some East Germans would proudly display empty Western shampoo bottles in their bathrooms.[30] East German citizens were divided amongst themselves according to whether they possessed Western currency and goods, the very status symbols the SED hoped to erase from GDR consciousness.

Even more potentially deleterious to the SED was the influence of the Western media. East Germans visited Western border cinemas offering special deals for GDR viewers to see Hollywood westerns or gangster films or films promoted by the FRG government. Reportedly twenty-six thousand East Berliners per day frequented these cinemas in 1956 and 1957 alone.[31] Western radio and television streaming into the GDR allowed East Germans to 'stray Westward' without physically leaving home.[32] Western music fans listened to the Armed Forces Network (AFN) or the Radio in the American Sector (RIAS) from West Berlin. Campaigns tried to dissuade East Germans from listening to these so-called 'NATO stations'.[33] Officials in the GDR presented the Western media as 'the voice of the political opposition' which was 'antithetical to our life interests, our desires, and our politics'.[34] Nonetheless, as Dorothee Wierling puts it, 'the attempt to prevent or limit Western music consumption through personal pledges, bans, controls, pronunciations and sanctions completely failed. Young East Germans increasingly listened to, viewed and recorded the West German "Deutschlandfunk", Radio Luxemburg, and the West German TV show Beat-Club'.[35] Access to Western news and entertainment might have helped stabilize the GDR by disabusing East Germans of illusions about the West rather than attracting them to it, and access to Western television programmes might have served as a ventilator for pent-up desires for Western-style leisure. However, the SED blamed Western media for 'sabotaging' the GDR.[36]

The damage to the East from border traffic in black-market goods and from the Western media paled in comparison to the flight of GDR citizens to the West, a phenomenon caused by a variety of domestic factors, but exacerbated by the persistent gaze Westward. From 1945 to the time of the erection of the Berlin Wall in August 1961, an estimated 3.5 million people (out of approximately 18 million in East Germany) left for the West.[37] The SED frequently blamed this exodus on Western sabotage hindering 'the development of socialist consciousness in the transition period from capitalism to socialism'. Officials worried that, alongside economic difficulties, 'hostile propaganda from the West influence[s] our people' to flee.[38]

The Battle for Youth

The younger generation was most likely to flee the GDR. The GDR's ultimate inability to capture the hearts of this generation – the future of socialism – frustrated the regime. The SED used its mass organizations, the Young Pioneers and the Free German Youth (FDJ), socialist education and workplace youth brigades to mould socialist youngsters. However, as post-war teenagers came of age, many looked Westward for cultural influences. Thus, the SED increased surveillance, marginalization and even arrests of youths who exhibited the so-called 'asocial' behaviours associated with Western decadence and materialism.

The post-war generation developed new 'teenage' popular cultures centred on Western music and fashion. They took to jeans, radios and records of Anglo-American bands, especially Elvis in the 1950s, the Beatles in the 1960s and punk music in the 1980s.[39] The attraction of German youth to jazz, boogie-woogie, rock and roll and punk caused anxiety and outrage amongst the older generations, who associated these

Americanized music-influenced subcultures with degeneracy. After 1955 West Germany normalized these cultures whereas East Germany continued to condemn such symbols of Westernization and Americanization.[40]

Young people in the GDR strove to attain 'authentic' Western mass-produced products. However, limited access to them meant that GDR youths had to create homemade copies of fashions seen in the West German teen magazine *Bravo* or in catalogues.[41] The vibrant 'second economy' provided ample material for constructing personal styles, including those associated with American 'hooliganism'.[42]

In the early 1950s Western jazz fans' clothing – ankle-length trousers and striped socks – came to be coded as 'asocial' signs of Americanization and effeminacy.[43] Later in the decade, the youth subculture that aroused the greatest concern in both East and West was that of the *Halbstarken*, young toughs or male rowdies similar to British Teddy Boys, who wore blue jeans, leather jackets and 'ducktail' hairstyles, rode motorcycles and followed rock and roll music. They infamously staged riots in the late 1950s. As Kaspar Maase argues, the *Halbstarken* played a role in eventually ushering in acceptance of new forms of popular culture in the West.[44] The GDR used the riots, however, to inflame fears within West Germany of 'American-led Western self-destruction'.[45]

Nonetheless, there were *Halbstarken* in the GDR too. The East German DEFA studio's neo-realist film *Berlin – Ecke Schönhauser* of 1957 depicted a gang of these West-oriented ruffians. The West provided a perfect leitmotif for explaining the so-called degeneracy of these youths. The attraction of the film's characters to the West led them to tragic outcomes – teenage pregnancy for the girl and imprisonment and death for the boys. Thus the film clearly portrayed the West as a source of risk and trauma for wayward youth.[46] The GDR press echoed this sensationalist panic about Western influence on youths, recounting, for example, tales of women who strayed to the West only to be roped into prostitution.[47]

The GDR regime closely monitored youth activity for Western influences, such as cults around Elvis or the Beatles. In January 1961 during FDJ elections at a factory for agricultural machines in Leipzig, a security officer reported to the SED that, with 'Western trashy literature, several youths congregated in a so-called "Presley-Club". A youth named Jäger duplicated a number of Presley photos ... . Members of this club often travel to West Berlin. In the steel casting department a number of workers watch Western Zone television and corresponding ideological effects are evident'.[48] In the 1960s Beatlemania supplanted the cult of Elvis Presley. The East German authorities now looked for 'Beats', wearing long 'mushroom' (*Pilzkopf*) shag haircuts and flared trousers. Like the 1950s jazz fans, these 'youth[s] were called "outsiders, loiterers or beatniks", and their way of "dancing apart" (to rock-and-roll) or playing guitar was denounced as the expression of undisciplined, effeminate, out-of-control bodies'.[49]

This kind of surveillance and repression of youths was oddly mixed with increasing tolerance of rock and roll and youth fashions, as stated emblematically in the 1963 Youth Communiqué. To connect with youth audiences, a GDR pop music radio station, DT64, began broadcasting in 1964. Western music could be played if 60 per cent of the content came from socialist countries. In 1965 the FDJ even called for a battle of amateur bands, many of which had been practising in cellars in an underground 'Beat' scene.[50] However, when the SED cancelled the contest, because too many bands had English names or seemed to be otherwise Western-influenced, 2,500 people protested in Leipzig and 267 demonstrators were arrested.[51] Recognizing, in the wake of this conflict, that Western symbols had become a catalyst for generational rebellion against Eastern authorities, the SED reversed its earlier liberality toward youth, and the State Secret Police (Stasi) accelerated surveillance of nonconformist behaviour.[52] This surveillance increased in the 1970s and 1980s as a number of GDR youth subcultures developed, including blues fans, environmentalists and punks. After initial uneasy tolerance, by 1983 punks in particular faced repression and imprisonment. Although punks were themselves critical of Western values, the Stasi perceived them as yet another sign of evidence of Western cultural imperialism threatening socialist identity politics.[53]

Overtaking the West

The SED's wavering stance toward Beat music and punks exemplified the complicated dance of approach and avoidance (*Annäherung und Abgrenzung*) the regime performed in relation to the West. Officially, the GDR shunned the West as a decadent and corrupting influence. However, both state and Party policies and practices fostered a constant gaze over the border and attraction to Western commodities. The GDR defined its own modernizing trajectory as part of the Marxist plot of history, in which communism's destiny was to supplant capitalism as a higher stage of modernity.[54] Paradoxically, however, GDR planners and politicians still used the West as a measuring stick against which to judge GDR achievements, a narrative Achilles heel for Soviet states. Jeffrey Kopstein has suggested that, 'in setting up capitalist modernity as the yardstick against which it measured itself, rather than defining a "yardstick" of its own, communism was doomed to live in capitalism's shadow'.[55]

Efforts to usher in communism's triumph compared Eastern and Western levels of productivity. Party chair Walter Ulbricht followed the Soviets' lead in his 1958 declaration of the 'Main Economic Task', claiming that by 1961 the GDR would 'catch up and overtake' West Germany in per capita consumption amongst its 'working population'.[56] This declaration reflects both the concern that GDR living standards lagged behind those of the FRG and an optimism concerning socialism's potential, fostered by recent economic successes, such as an end to rationing, and technological triumphs, such as the Soviet launch of *Sputnik*. However, the terms of measurement themselves may have owed much to Western models. As Victoria de Grazia has shown, one of the influences of the 'American empire' on Europe was the spread of a focus on measuring and raising the population's 'standard of living'.[57]

This Westward orientation was also reflected in efforts of designers and producers to meet the 'world-class standard' (*Weltniveau*) of quality and style. Greg Castillo has described how GDR designers and functionaries initially rejected Western modernist International Style as bourgeois degeneracy, formalism and kitsch and promoted Stalinist neo-classicism and functionalism as an alternative. However, by the 1960s GDR designers also embraced modernist aesthetics, recast as an affordable form of socialist functionalism.[58] In another example, the GDR clothing industry strove to create 'socialist fashion' while also sending designers to Paris and giving boutiques French names.[59] Plastic products, touted as cutting-edge achievements in socialist consumer culture, were lent legitimacy at the annual Leipzig Trade Fair by the claim that they reflected the *Weltniveau* of new synthetics.[60] In 1962 the GDR Ministry of Finance exploited the idea that products meeting the 'world-class standard' could demand a higher price, when it created a new *Weltniveau* quality mark, 'Q', as justification for raising prices on such goods by 2 per cent.[61] Industrial and trade ministries often monitored Western technological and consumer advances to learn their methods. For example, in 1956 the GDR Ministry for General Machine Construction sent a delegation of women to the Cologne Trade Fair to evaluate refrigerators.[62] The SED promoted household appliances similar to those developing in the West, but tried to reframe this technologization of kitchens as part of a socialist campaign to ease the household burden of working women so they could join the workforce. Thus world-class products were promoted not just as meeting 'Western' criteria. Trade delegates also travelled throughout the socialist world to gather inspiration for new products and designs. Still, the West often remained the implicit standard-bearer for quality and consumer modernity.

GDR officials also played into the desire for Western products by enabling their purchase within GDR territory. The primary means of purchasing Western brands within the GDR was in the *Intershops*, established in the 1950s and expanded in 1962. Initially, like their counterparts in other socialist countries, the *Intershops* aimed to offer Western goods to Western tourists for Western money, thereby providing the regime with much-needed hard currency. East Germans would make Sunday afternoon pilgrimages to the *Intershops* to stare at forbidden goods, as if they were in a foreign country.[63]

When Erich Honecker came to power as SED General Secretary in 1971, he opened the *Intershops*' doors to East Germans: from 1974 it was no longer illegal for them to possess Western currency. This innovation in retail strategy 'encouraged an orientation toward the West' and 'offered East Germans the very same social fantasies that the SED officially condemned as commodity fetishism'.[64] East Germans fondly associated the *Intershops* with high quality and fashionable goods and with a particular smell emanating from the Irish Spring and Lux soaps, Poison perfume, Jacobs Krönung coffee and various kinds of chocolate.[65] Even so, limited access to Western currency made only select East Germans able to purchase the *Intershop* commodities. The *Intershops*' presence within the GDR consumer landscape disrupted the ideological goal of socialist egalitarianism by turning Western goods into prized rarities and signifiers of high status. The *Intershops* also underpinned social distinctions created through the cherished access to Western currency. It was not least through the *Intershops* that, as Daphne Berdahl has argued, 'commodity fetishism was an integral part of daily life in "actually existing socialism"'.[66] The *Intershops* became the Trojan Horse of Western materialism, helping to undermine the logic of socialist ideology within the GDR.

The West in Eastern Crises

The GDR's complex relationship with the West grew acute during moments of crisis for the SED regime. The first major crisis came in 1953, following worsening shortages and rising production quotas.[67] On 17 June, after angry construction workers left the sites where they were working on East Berlin's Stalin-Allee, three hundred thousand demonstrators nationwide joined them to demand that prices be lowered in the *Handelsorganisation* (Retail Trading Association) by 40 per cent, and that there be a reduction in production quotas and an end to SED authority. Soviet tanks and GDR police stopped the protest, killing twelve demonstrators.

Officials in the GDR quickly blamed Western saboteurs for inciting a so-called 'Western-sponsored "fascist putsch" against the GDR'.[68] The SED propaganda depicted the demonstrators of 17 June as isolated, overtly Americanized rowdies influenced by Western 'provocateurs' or 'bandits'. The Party organ, *Neues Deutschland*, described the typical provocateur: 'Texas shirt with cowboy [a T-shirt with a cowboy printed on it], Texas tie with a picture of nude women, Texas haircut, a criminal's face – these are the knights of the "Christian West", the typical representatives of the American way of life'.[69]

The *Volkspolizei* monitored closely whether the population internalized this type of language and argumentation. The political section of the police even read letters written by wounded officers to their family members after the uprising. The resulting report expressed satisfaction that thirteen out of nineteen letters described the Berlin situation 'correctly', in language consistent with SED understandings of Western and American influence. For example, K. Böhme from Köthendorf/Burgstädt wrote in a letter, presumably to his wife:

> My dear, we survived some difficult hours on 17 June, but the main thing is that the provocateurs, who were mostly West Berlin fascists and criminals, were rebuffed. Lapsing into murderousness, robbery, plunder, and a destructive mania, these brutes [*Unmenschen*] tore through the streets of Berlin. Dear Buttchen, I can tell you that one witnessed American non-culture [*Unkultur*], expressed through the gangster methods of teenage boys in high-water trousers, striped socks, and Texas shirts.[70]

On the other hand, the SED also blamed the radio station RIAS for inciting many East Berliners to revolt. Although RIAS did spread word of the unrest, Eastern propaganda wrongly located the uprising's origins exclusively as coming from outside the GDR, thereby diverting attention from the internal sources of dissatisfaction precipitating the event.[71] The 17 June uprising loomed over the GDR's subsequent history like a warning of the effects of Western influence.

The inability to resolve this problematic relationship with the West, and particularly with West Berlin, precipitated the next crisis: the erection of the Berlin Wall in 1961. Ulbricht sought a solution to the mass exodus of East German citizens, which had increased after his renewal of the push to collectivize farms and repress private enterprises in 1958. Shortages became acute once again in the early 1960s. The SED blamed the West for these problems. The SED described the Berlin Wall, built on 13 August, as an 'anti-fascist protection wall', so as to emphasize its role not in prevention of flight from the country, but as a means to staunch the flow of harmful influences into the GDR from the bourgeois, militaristic, retrograde West. Preventing Western smugglers from buying up cheap, subsidized goods in the GDR was one of the major justifications for the wall.[72]

After twenty-eight more years of relative stability, the fall of the Berlin Wall in 1989 and the subsequent reunification of Germany seemed in part to be the ultimate result of Western sabotage of the socialist republic. Causes of the surprising turn of events of the *Wende* have been debated elsewhere, and it is clear that this was an indigenous East German movement rather than something incited by Western agents, as the SED had suspected about the 1953 uprising. Even so, the influence of the West was certainly an undercurrent of the event, particularly since the population called initially for a more openly democratic version of socialism based partly on Western models.

Once the Berlin Wall fell, the other major source of Western 'sabotage' became spectacularly prominent: this was consumerism. With one hundred Western Deutschmarks in 'welcome money', East German citizens streamed across the border, eager to buy Western products they had long been eyeing on Western television, coveting in the GDR's *Intershop* stores or hoping Western relatives would send them in gift packages – jeans, stereos, cigarettes and tropical fruit. One cigarette brand called 'West' even played into Easterners' consumer longings with the advertising slogan 'Test the West' seen in the 1990s on ubiquitous billboards alongside images of awkward, dowdy or elderly people being offered a smoke by trendy, fashionable, young counterparts. The message of these ads was clear: Western products offered a route from so-called Eastern backwardness towards presumed Western modernity. This eagerness to 'test the West' and its commodities seemed to suggest that the fall of the Wall was a 'consumer revolution' that the West had won with its products.[73] It appeared that the people's attraction to the West was ultimately powerful enough to topple the communist regime.

However, only a few years into the 1990s, a new trend challenged this narrative of celebrated Western triumph. Former GDR citizens began exhibiting signs of *Ostalgie* or 'Eastern nostalgia'.[74] They returned proudly to East German brands, some of which were now produced by private enterprises, such as Florena hand cream, F6 cigarettes, Spee detergent and Rotkäppchen sparkling wine. This reversal betrayed a new reorientation in attitudes about the West among those living in the 'new federal states' (or 'Eastern Germany') within the reunified republic.

Ostalgie had much to do with disillusionment with the 'consumer wonderland' of the 'golden West' and with a sense that Westerners looked down on their 'poorer' Eastern neighbours. Western Germans targeted Easterners as 'dumb *Ossis*' in part because of their naivety about consumer choices. The *Ossis* in turn felt humiliated by their own lack of knowledge about the capitalist consumer economy. Western suspicion of ostensible Eastern German authoritarian impulses or reactionary xenophobia tied into these doubts about their democratic potential as commensurate with their inability to navigate the choices within the new marketplace. In this sense, ineptitude in dealing with the capitalist consumer world made Easterners feel like outsiders within their own country. Eastern Germans developed the stereotype of the *Besserwessi*, the obnoxious Westerner who always thought he/she knew better. *Ostalgie* was not nostalgia for the GDR regime, but perhaps a way for Eastern Germans to remember how they had once been the core citizenry of their defunct state, equipped with knowledge and skills for living in that difficult consumer world that had given them a sense of being savvy, resourceful customers rather than 'dumb *Ossis*'. By robbing Eastern Germans of this sense of expertise and pride in a common culture and by literally robbing many of them of their livelihoods, the West performed the final act of 'sabotage' against the GDR, even after the regime was defunct.[75]

Thus, in reunified Germany, Eastern Germans' image of the West continued to be haunted by the shadow of the GDR's conflicted relationship to it. On the one hand, Easterners had been willingly subsumed by the West and eagerly participated in a Western consumer culture and liberal democracy. On the other hand, a continuing 'wall in the head' and sense of not belonging in their own country made integration with the West tense and uneasy. Many of these barriers have faded in subsequent decades since 1989. Still, the dissatisfaction of Eastern Germans over their merger with their Western neighbours raises questions about triumphant narratives of reunified Germany's final 'arrival' in a liberal, progressive version of 'the West'. This unease with reunification may have been the final legacy of East Germany's fraught position between the 'East' and the 'West' – one that outlived the GDR.

Notes

1. Stefan Wolle, 'Allmacht und Ohnmacht in der Diktatur. Das SED-System auf dem Weg in den Zusammenbruch', in Hans-Hermann Hertle and Stefan Wolle (eds), *Damals in der DDR: Der Alltag im Arbeiter- und Bauernstadt*, Munich, 2006, 331–32.
2. Corey Ross, *The East German Dictatorship. Problems and Perspectives in the Interpretation of the GDR*, London, 2002, 152.
3. William Glenn Gray, *Germany's Cold War. The Global Campaign to Isolate East Germany, 1949–1969*, Chapel Hill, 2003.

4. Albert Norden, *Braunbuch. Kriegs- und Naziverbrecher in der Bundesrepublik und in Berlin (West)*, (East) Berlin, 1965.
5. Fred Lufer (ed.), 'Bonner Panoptikum', *Taschen-Eulenspiegel* 5 (1959).
6. Antonia Grunenberg, *Antifaschismus. Ein deutscher Mythos*, Hamburg, 1993.
7. Hans Siegfried Lamm and Siegfried Kupper, *DDR und Dritte Welt*, Munich and Vienna, 1976.
8. Rüdiger Korff, 'Der Stellenwert der Entwicklungspolitik in der Bundesrepublik Deutschland', in Hans-Jörg Bücking (ed.), *Entwicklungspolitische Zusammenarbeit in der Bundesrepublik Deutschland und der DDR*, Berlin, 1998, 42.
9. Bundesarchiv Potsdam (BAP) DZ8 7358, Solidaritätskomitee der DDR Afrika, Berlin, 28 March 1961, Einschätzung des 2. Betreuerlehrganges – Afrika – an der Zentralschule in Bantikow.
10. Uta Poiger, *Jazz, Rock, and Rebels. Cold War Politics and American Culture in a Divided Germany*, Berkeley, 2000, 55.
11. Gerlinde Irmscher, 'Der Westen im Ost-Alltag', in Neue Gesellschaft für Bildende Kunst (ed.), *Wunderwirtschaft. DDR-Konsumkultur in den 60er Jahren*, Cologne, 1996, 185.
12. Greg Castillo, 'East as True West. Redeeming Bourgeois Culture, from Socialist Realism to Ostalgie', *Kritika* 9/4 (2008), 747–68.
13. Richard Kuisel, *Seducing the French. The Dilemma of Americanization*, Berkeley, 1993.
14. Konrad H. Jarausch, *After Hitler. Recivilizing Germans, 1945–1995*, Oxford, 2006, 103–29; Heinrich August Winkler, *Germany. The Long Road West*, 2 vols, Oxford, 2006–2007.
15. Poiger, *Jazz, Rock, and Rebels*, 45.
16. Amt für Information der Regierung der Deutschen Demokratischen Republik (ed.), 'Ami Go Home! Warum die Amis heimgehen sollen', *Die Wahrheit dem Volke* 7 (1950), (East) Berlin, 27.
17. Ina Merkel, 'Consumer Culture in the GDR, or How the Struggle for Antimodernity Was Lost on the Battleground of Consumer Culture', in Susan Strasser, Charles McGovern and Matthias Judt (eds), *Getting and Spending. European and American Consumer Societies in the Twentieth Century*, Cambridge, 1998, 285.
18. Ina Merkel, 'Alternative Rationalities, Strange Dreams, Absurd Utopias. On Socialist Advertising and Market Research', in Katherine Pence and Paul Betts (eds), *Socialist Modern. Everyday East German Politics and Culture*, Ann Arbor, 2008, 327.
19. Eric Weitz, *Creating German Communism, 1890–1990. From Popular Protests to Socialist State*, Princeton, 1997.
20. Milena Veenis, *Material Fantasies. Expectations of the Western Consumer World among East Germans*, Amsterdam, 2012.
21. *Neues Deutschland*, 13 October 1948, 4; *Neues Deutschland*, 8 October 1948, 3.
22. Curt Riess, *Berlin Berlin 1945–1953*, Berlin, 1953, 175.
23. BAP DO-1/11-955, Berlin, 28 September 1954, Verkehr zwischen den Westsektoren und dem demokratischen Sektor von Groß-Berlin, 4, 19.
24. Edith Sheffer, *Burned Bridge. How East and West Germans Made the Iron Curtain*, Oxford, 2011, 227.
25. André Steiner, *The Plans that Failed. An Economic History of the GDR*, London, 2010, 186.
26. Maria Sack, 'Damenschuhe und Cowboystiefel. Schwarz als Modefarbe der Wintersaison – Kreppsohlen noch immer beliebt', *Der Tagesspiegel*, 8 October 1950, 4; Susan Reid, 'Cold War in the Kitchen. Gender and the De-Stalinization of Consumer Taste in the Soviet Union under Khrushchev', *Slavic Review* 61/2 (2002), 230.

27. BAP DO-1/11-758, Bl. 91, 29 October 1955, An die BDVP–Abteilung VE und U, Betr: Illegale Einfuhr von Schuhen aus Westberlin durch Bürger der DDR. Signed, Leiter der Untersuchungsabt. Pabst, VP-Kommandeur und Stellv. Leiter der HA/VE Rodis, 1.
28. Charlotte Brinkmann, 'Bananen mit Ketchup. Eßkultur: Beobachtungen in einer markt- und einer planwirtschaftlich orientierten Gesellschaft', in Wolfgang Kaschuba (ed.), *Blick-Wechsel Ost-West. Beobachtungen zur Alltagskultur in Ost- und Westdeutschland*, Tübingen, 1992, 91.
29. Paul Betts, 'The Twilight of the Idols. East German Memory and Material Culture', *The Journal of Modern History* 72 (2000), 741.
30. Merkel, 'Consumer Culture in the GDR', 284.
31. Poiger, *Jazz, Rock, and Rebels*, 85.
32. Stefan Wolle, *Die heile Welt der Diktatur. Alltag und Herrschaft in der DDR 1971–1989*, Berlin, 1998, 69.
33. Ibid., 209.
34. Werner Lamberz in 1977, quoted in Dorothee Wierling, 'Youth as Internal Enemy. Conflicts in the Education Dictatorship of the 1960s', in Pence and Betts (eds), *Socialist Modern*, 164.
35. Ibid.
36. Ibid., 71. See also Wolle, 'Allmacht und Ohnmacht', 336.
37. Corey Ross, 'Before the Wall. East Germans, Communist Authority, and the Mass Exodus to the West', *The Historical Journal* 45 (2002), 459; Patrick Major, *Behind the Berlin Wall. East Germany and the Frontiers of Power*, Oxford, 2010, 56.
38. BAP DY 30 IV2/6.10/68, SED ZK, Abt. Handel, Versorgung, und Außenhandel, Berlin, 11 October 1957, Ministerium für Außenhandel und Innerdeutschen Handel, Kaderabteilung, Analyse der Republikfluchten.
39. Jeff Hayton, 'Härte gegen Punk. Popular Music, Western Media, and State Response in the German Democratic Republic', *German History* 31 (2013), 523–49.
40. Poiger, *Jazz, Rock, and Rebels*.
41. Irmscher, 'Der Westen im Ost-Alltag', 190–91.
42. Wierling, 'Youth as Internal Enemy', 157–82.
43. Poiger, *Jazz, Rock, and Rebels*, 63.
44. Kaspar Maase, 'Establishing Cultural Democracy. Youth, "Americanization", and the Irresistible Rise of Popular Culture', in Hannah Schissler (ed.), *The Miracle Years. A Cultural History of West Germany, 1949–1968*, Princeton, 2001, 429.
45. Poiger, *Jazz, Rock, and Rebels*, 84.
46. Joshua Feinstein, *The Triumph of the Ordinary. Depictions of Daily Life in the East German Cinema, 1949–1989*, Chapel Hill, 2002, 45–77.
47. *Neue Berliner Illustrierte* 44 (1959), 10.
48. BAB DY 30 IV 2/12/113, Bl. 11, Berlin, 25 January 1961, Otto Walter an das Zentralkomitee der SED, Abteilung für Sicherheitsfragen, Genossen Renkwitz.
49. Wierling, 'Youth as Internal Enemy', 165. See also Michael Rauhut, *Schalmei und Lederjacke. Udo Lindenberg, BAP, Underground. Rock und Politik in der DDR der achtziger Jahre*, Erfurt, 1996.
50. Mark Fenemore, *Sex, Thugs and Rock 'n' Roll. Teenage Rebels in Cold-War East Germany*, London, 2009, 169.
51. Wierling, 'Youth as Internal Enemy', 162–63.
52. Fenemore, *Sex, Thugs and Rock 'n' Roll*, 201.
53. Jeff Hayton, *Culture from the Slums. Punk Rock, Authenticity and Alternative Culture in East and West Germany*, Ph.D. Thesis, University of Illinois, 2013, chapter 7.

54. Odd Arne Westad, *The Global Cold War. Third World Interventions and the Making of our Times*, Cambridge, 2005, 40.
55. Jeffrey Kopstein, *The Politics of Economic Decline in East Germany, 1945–1989*, Chapel Hill, 1997, 196. See also the discussion in Katherine Pence and Paul Betts, 'Introduction', in Pence and Betts (eds), *Socialist Modern*, 19.
56. André Steiner, *Plans that Failed. An Economic History of the GDR, 1945–1989*, New York, 2010, 90 ff.
57. Victoria de Grazia, *Irresistible Empire. America's Advance through Twentieth-Century Europe*, Cambridge, Mass, 2005, 75–129.
58. Greg Castillo, *Cold War on the Home Front. The Soft Power of Midcentury Design*, Minneapolis, 2010.
59. Judd Stitziel, *Fashioning Socialism. Clothing, Politics, and Consumer Culture in East Germany*, Oxford, 2005, 64, 127.
60. Eli Rubin, *Synthetic Socialism. Plastics and Dictatorship in the German Democratic Republic*, Chapel Hill, 2008, 157.
61. André Steiner, *Die DDR-Wirtschaftsreform der sechziger Jahre. Konflikt zwischen Effizienz- und Machtkalkül*, Berlin, 1999, 380.
62. Katherine Pence, '"A World in Miniature". The Leipzig Trade Fairs in the 1950s and East German Consumer Citizenship', in David F. Crew (ed.), *Consuming Germany in the Cold War. Consumption and National Identity in East and West Germany*, Oxford, 2003, 21–50, here 36.
63. Katrin Böske, 'Abwesend Anwesende. Eine kleine Geschichte des Intershops', in Neue Gesellschaft für Bildende Kunst (ed.), *Wunderwirtschaft*, 219.
64. Jonathan Zatlin, *The Currency of Socialism. Money and Political Culture in East Germany*, Cambridge, 2007, 244.
65. Böske, 'Abwesend Anwesende', 221.
66. Daphne Berdahl, *Where the World Ended. Re-unification and Identity in the German Borderland*, Berkeley, 1999, 105.
67. Torsten Diedrich, *Der 17. Juni 1953 in der DDR. Bewaffnete Gewalt gegen das Volk*, Berlin, 1991; Hubertus Knabe, *17. Juni 1953. Ein deutscher Aufstand*, Munich, 2003.
68. Gary Bruce, 'The Prelude to Nationwide Surveillance in East Germany. Stasi Operations and Threat Perceptions, 1945–1953', *Journal of Cold War Studies* 5/2 (2003), 28.
69. 'So sieht die faschistische Brut der Adenauer, Ollenhauer, Kaiser und Reuter aus!', *Neues Deuschland*, 21 June 1953, reprinted in Poiger, *Jazz, Rock, and Rebels*, 62.
70. BAP DO1/11-45, Bl. 93, Berlin, 20 June 1953, Polit-Abteilung, Einschätzung der Briefe von verletzten Genossen an ihre Angehörigen, Koch.
71. Jonathan Sperber, '17 June 1953. Revisiting a German Revolution', *German History* 22 (2004), 628.
72. Andreas Glaeser, *Divided in Unity. Identity, Germany, and the Berlin Police*, Chicago, 2000, 264.
73. Konrad H. Jarausch and Michael Geyer, *Shattered Past. Reconstructing German Histories*, Princeton, 2003, 270.
74. Betts, 'The Twilight of the Idols', 731–65; Daphne Berdahl, '(N)ostalgie for the Present. Memory, Longing and East German Things', *Ethnos* 64/2 (1999), 192–211; Rosemarie Mielke and Stefanie Eifler, *Stereotype über Ost- und Westdeutsche in Ost und West. Wer hat die höhere Mauer im Kopf?* Bielefeld, 1993; Rainer Gries, 'Der Geschmack der Heimat: Bausteine zu einer Mentalitätsgeschichte der Ostprodukte nach der Wende', *Deutschland Archiv* 27 (1994), 1041–59.
75. Veenis, *Material Fantasies*, chapter 7.

Selected Bibliography

Adamovsky, Ezequiel, 'Euro-Orientalism and the Making of the Concept of Eastern Europe in France, 1810–1880', *Journal of Modern History* 77 (2005), 591–628.

Adamovsky, Ezequiel, *Euro-Orientalism. Liberal Ideology and the Image of Russia in France (c. 1740–1880)*, Oxford, 2006.

Allardyce, Gilbert, 'The Rise and Fall of the Western Civilization Course', *American Historical Review* 87 (1982), 695–725.

Anderson, Jeffrey, G. John Ikenberry and Thomas Risse (eds), *The End of the West? Crisis and Change in the Atlantic Order*, Ithaca and London, 2008.

Angster, Julia, *Konsenskapitalismus und Sozialdemokratie. Die Westernisierung von SPD und DGB*, Munich, 2003.

Aydin, Cemil, 'Beyond Civilization. Pan-Islamism, Pan-Asianism and the Revolt against the West', *Journal of Modern European History* 4/2 (2006), 204–22.

Aydin, Cemil, *The Politics of Anti-Westernism in Asia. Visions of World Order in Pan-Islamic and Pan-Asian Thought*, New York, 2007.

Baerns, Barbara, *Ost und West – eine Zeitschrift zwischen den Fronten. Zur politischen Funktion einer literarischen Zeitschrift in der Besatzungszeit (1945–1949)*, Münster, 1968.

Bailey, Christian, 'The Continuities of West German History. Conceptions of Europe, Democracy and the West in Interwar and Postwar Germany', *Geschichte und Gesellschaft* 36 (2010), 567–96.

Bailey, Christian, *Between Yesterday and Tomorrow. German Visions of Europe, 1926–1950*, New York and Oxford, 2013.

Baritz, Loren, 'The Idea of the West', *American Historical Review* 66 (1961), 618–40.

Barraclough, Geoffrey, 'Europa, Amerika und Russland in Vorstellung und Denken des 19. Jahrhunderts', *Historische Zeitschrift* 203 (1966), 280–315.
Barth, Boris and Jürgen Osterhammel (eds), *Zivilisierungsmissionen. Imperiale Weltverbesserung seit dem 18. Jahrhundert*, Konstanz, 2005.
Bassin, Mark, 'Russia between Europe and Asia. The Ideological Construction of Geographical Space', *Slavic Review* 50/1 (1991), 1–17.
Bavaj, Riccardo, '"Western Civilization" and the Acceleration of Time. Richard Löwenthal's Reflections on a Crisis of "the West" in the Aftermath of the Student Revolt of "1968"', *Themenportal Europäische Geschichte* (2010), online: http://www.europa.clio-online.de/2010/Article=434.
Bavaj, Riccardo, '"The West". A Conceptual Exploration', *Europäische Geschichte Online* (2011), online: http://www.ieg-ego.eu/bavajr-2011-en.
Bennett, James C., *The Anglosphere Challenge. Why the English-Speaking Nations Will Lead the Way in the Twenty-First Century*, Lanham, 2004.
Berg, Manfred and Philipp Gassert (eds), *Deutschland und die USA in der Internationalen Geschichte des 20. Jahrhunderts. Festschrift für Detlef Junker*, Stuttgart, 2004.
Berger, Stefan, 'Rising Like a Phoenix... The Renaissance of National History Writing in Germany and Britain since the 1980s', in Stefan Berger and Chris Lorenz (eds), *Nationalizing the Past. Historians as Nation Builders in Modern Europe*, Basingstoke, 2010, 426–51.
Berghahn, Volker R., *America and the Intellectual Cold Wars in Europe*, Princeton and Oxford, 2001.
Beßlich, Barbara, *Wege in den 'Kulturkrieg'. Zivilisationskritik in Deutschland 1890–1914*, Darmstadt, 2000.
Biermann, Harald, *Ideologie statt Realpolitik. Kleindeutsche Liberale und auswärtige Politik vor der Reichsgründung*, Düsseldorf, 2006.
Bonnett, Alastair, *The Idea of the West. Culture, Politics and History*, Basingstoke and New York, 2004.
Browning, Christopher S. and Marko Lehti (eds), *The Struggle for the West. A Divided and Contested Legacy*, London and New York, 2010.
Bruendel, Steffen, *Volksgemeinschaft oder Volksstaat. Die 'Ideen von 1914' und die Neuordnung Deutschlands im Ersten Weltkrieg*, Berlin, 2003.
Carrier, James G. (ed.), *Occidentalism. Images of the West*, Oxford, 1995.
Coker, Christopher, *Twilight of the West*, Boulder, 1998.
Coker, Christopher, *Rebooting the West. The US, Europe and the Future of the Western Alliance*, Abingdon, 2009.
Conrad, Sebastian and Dominic Sachsenmaier (eds), *Competing Visions of World Order. Global Moments and Movements, 1880s–1930s*, Basingstoke, 2007.

Conter, Claude D., *Jenseits der Nation – Das vergessene Europa des 19. Jahrhunderts. Die Geschichte der Inszenierung und Visionen Europas in Literatur, Geschichte und Politik*, Bielefeld, 2004.
Conze, Vanessa, *Das Europa der Deutschen. Ideen von Europa in Deutschland zwischen Reichstradition und Westorientierung (1920–1970)*, Munich, 2005.
Di Fabio, Udo, *Die Kultur der Freiheit*, Munich, 2005.
Doering-Manteuffel, Anselm, *Wie westlich sind die Deutschen? Amerikanisierung und Westernisierung im 20. Jahrhundert*, Göttingen, 1999.
Doering-Manteuffel, Anselm, 'Internationale Geschichte als Systemgeschichte. Strukturen und Handlungsmuster im europäischen Staatensystem des 19. und 20. Jahrhunderts', in Wilfried Loth and Jürgen Osterhammel (eds), *Internationale Geschichte. Themen – Ergebnisse – Aussichten*, Munich, 2000, 93–115.
Doering-Manteuffel, Anselm, 'Eine politische Nationalgeschichte für die Berliner Republik. Überlegungen zu Heinrich August Winklers "Der lange Weg nach Westen"', *Geschichte und Gesellschaft* 27 (2001), 446–62.
Doering-Manteuffel, Anselm, 'Amerikanisierung und Westernisierung', *Docupedia-Zeitgeschichte* (2011), online: http://docupedia.de/zg/Amerikanisierung_und_Westernisierung.
Duchesne, Ricardo, *The Uniqueness of Western Civilization*, Leiden, 2011.
Europäische Schlüsselwörter. Wortvergleichende und wortgeschichtliche Studien, vol 3: Kultur und Zivilisation, ed. by Sprachwissenschaftliches Colloquium (Bonn), Munich, 1967.
Fabian, Bernhard, *Alexis de Tocquevilles Amerikabild. Genetische Untersuchungen über Zusammenhänge mit der zeitgenössischen, insbesondere der englischen Amerika-Interpretation*, Heidelberg, 1957.
Federici, Silvia (ed.), *Enduring Western Civilization. The Construction of the Concept of Western Civilization and its 'Others'*, Westport, 1995.
Ferguson, Niall, *Civilization. The Six Killer Apps of Western Power*, London, 2012 (first published in 2011 with the subtitle *The West and the Rest*).
Fisch, Jörg, 'Zivilisation, Kultur', in Otto Brunner, Werner Conze and Reinhart Koselleck (eds), *Geschichtliche Grundbegriffe. Historisches Lexikon zur politisch-sozialen Sprache in Deutschland*, vol 7, Stuttgart, 1992, 679–774.
Fischer, Jürgen, *Oriens – Occidens – Europa. Begriff und Gedanke 'Europa' in der späten Antike und im frühen Mittelalter*, Wiesbaden, 1957.
Fischer-Tiné, Harald, '"Deep Occidentalism"? Europa und "der Westen" in der Wahrnehmung hinduistischer Intellektueller und Reformer ca. 1890–1930', *Journal of Modern European History* 4/2 (2006), 171–203.

Fraenkel, Ernst, *Deutschland und die westlichen Demokratien*, ed. Alexander von Brünneck, Frankfurt/Main, 1991 (first published 1964).

Fry, Greg and Jacinta O'Hagan (eds), *Contending Images of World Politics*, Basingstoke et al., 2000.

Gassert, Philipp, 'Die Bundesrepublik, Europa und der Westen', in Jörg Baberowski, Eckart Conze, Philipp Gassert and Martin Sabrow, *Geschichte ist immer Gegenwart. Vier Thesen zur Zeitgeschichte*, Stuttgart and Munich, 2001, 67–89.

Gassner, Florian, *Germany versus Russia. A Social History of the Divide between East and West*, Ph.D. thesis, Vancouver, 2012.

GoGwilt, Christopher, *The Invention of the West. Joseph Conrad and the Double-Mapping of Europe and Empire*, Stanford, 1995.

Goldammer, Kurt, *Der Mythus von Ost und West. Eine kultur- und religionsgeschichtliche Betrachtung*, Munich and Basel, 1962.

Gollwitzer, Heinz, *Europabild und Europagedanke. Beiträge zur deutschen Geistesgeschichte des 18. und 19. Jahrhunderts*, Munich, 1964 (first published 1951).

Gollwitzer, Heinz, *Geschichte des weltpolitischen Denkens*, 2 vols, Göttingen, 1972/82.

Gress, David, *From Plato to NATO. The Idea of the West and its Opponents*, New York, 1998.

Groh, Dieter, *Russland und das Selbstverständnis Europas. Ein Beitrag zur europäischen Geistesgeschichte*, Neuwied, 1961 (republished as *Russland im Blick Europas. 300 Jahre historische Perspektiven*, Frankfurt/Main, 1988).

Hall, Stuart, 'The West and the Rest. Discourse and Power', in Stuart Hall and Bram Gieben (eds), *Formations of Modernity*, Oxford, 1992, 275–320.

Hammen, Oscar J., 'Free Europe versus Russia, 1830–1854', *American Slavic and East European Review* 11/1 (1952), 27–41.

Heller, Kathleen M., *The Dawning of the West. On the Genesis of a Concept*, Ph.D. thesis, Cincinnati, 2006.

Hempfer, Klaus W. and Alexander Schwan (eds), *Grundlagen der politischen Kultur des Westens. Ringvorlesung an der Freien Universität Berlin*, Berlin and New York, 1987.

Herman, Arthur, *The Idea of Decline in Western History*, New York, 1997.

Hildebrand, Klaus, 'Der Westen. Betrachtungen über einen uneindeutigen Begriff', in Dieter Hein, Klaus Hildebrand and Andreas Schulz (eds), *Historie und Leben. Der Historiker als Wissenschaftler und Zeitgenosse*, Munich, 2006, 595–603.

Hochgeschwender, Michael, *Freiheit in der Offensive? Der Kongress für kulturelle Freiheit und die Deutschen*, Munich, 1998.

Hochgeschwender, Michael, 'Was ist der Westen? Zur Ideengeschichte eines politischen Konstrukts', *Historisch-Politische Mitteilungen* 11 (2004), 1–30.
Hühn, Helmut, 'Westen; Okzident, I', in *Historisches Wörterbuch der Philosophie*, vol. 12, Darmstadt, 2004, col. 661–68.
Hühn, Helmut, 'Die Entgegensetzung von "Osten" und "Westen", "Orient" und "Okzident" als begriffsgeschichtliche Herausforderung', in Ernst Müller (ed.), *Begriffsgeschichte im Umbruch? (Archiv für Begriffsgeschichte, Sonderheft 4)*, Hamburg, 2005, 59–67.
Ifversen, Jan, 'Who Are the Westerners?', *International Politics* 45 (2008), 236–53.
Jackson, Patrick Thaddeus, '"Civilization" on Trial', *Millennium. Journal of International Studies* 28 (1999), 141–53.
Jackson, Patrick Thaddeus, *Civilizing the Enemy. German Reconstruction and the Invention of the West*, Ann Arbor, 2006.
Kagan, Robert, *Paradise and Power. America and Europe in the New World Order*, revised edn, London, 2004 (first published 2003).
Kirby, Dianne, 'Divinely Sanctioned. The Anglo-American Cold War Alliance and the Defence of Western Civilization and Christianity, 1945–48', *Journal of Contemporary History* 35 (2000), 385–412.
Klein, Bradley S., 'How the West Was One. Representational Politics of NATO', *International Studies Quarterly* 34 (1990), 311–25.
Koenen, Gerd, *Der Russland-Komplex. Die Deutschen und der Osten, 1900–1945*, Munich, 2005.
Lemberg, Hans, 'Zur Entstehung des Osteuropabegriffs im 19. Jahrhundert. Vom "Norden" zum "Osten" Europas', *Jahrbücher für Geschichte Osteuropas* 33/1 (1985), 48–91.
Lewis, Martin W. and Kären E. Wigen, *The Myth of Continents. A Critique of Metageography*, Berkeley, 1997.
Liulevicius, Vejas Gabriel, *The German Myth of the East. 1800 to the Present*, Oxford, 2009.
Llanque, Marcus, *Demokratisches Denken im Krieg. Die deutsche Debatte im Ersten Weltkrieg*, Berlin, 2000.
Lorenz, Dagmar and Ingrid Spörk (eds), *Konzept Osteuropa. Der 'Osten' als Konstrukt der Fremd- und Eigenbestimmung in deutschsprachigen Texten des 19. und 20. Jahrhunderts*, Würzburg, 2011.
Marchand, Suzanne L., *German Orientalism in the Age of Empire. Religion, Race, and Scholarship*, Cambridge, 2009.
Mariano, Marco (ed.), *Defining the Atlantic Community. Culture, Intellectuals, and Policies in the Mid-Twentieth Century*, London and New York, 2010.

Marquand, David, *The End of the West. The Once and Future Europe*, Princeton and Oxford, 2011.
Maxwell, Alexander (ed.), *The East–West Discourse. Symbolic Geography and its Consequences*, Oxford et al., 2011.
McGetchin, Douglas T., *Indology, Indomania, Orientalism. Ancient India's Rebirth in Modern Germany*, Madison, 2009.
Meyer, Manfred, *Freiheit und Macht. Studien zum Nationalismus süddeutscher, insbesondere badischer Liberaler 1830–1848*, Frankfurt/Main et al., 1994.
Miliopoulos, Lazaros, *Atlantische Zivilisation und transatlantisches Verhältnis. Politische Idee und Wirklichkeit*, Wiesbaden, 2007.
Morris, Ian, *Why the West Rules – for Now*, London, 2010.
Müller, Johann Baptist, *Deutschland und der Westen*, Berlin, 1989.
Neitzel, Sönke, *Weltmacht oder Untergang. Die Weltreichslehre im Zeitalter des Imperialismus*, Paderborn et al., 2000.
Neumann, Iver B., *Russia and the Idea of Europe. A Study in Identity and International Relations*, London and New York, 1996.
Neumann, Iver B., *Uses of the Other. 'The East' in European Identity Formation*, Minneapolis, 1999.
Nolte, Paul, 'Jenseits des Westens? Überlegungen zu einer Zeitgeschichte der Demokratie', *Vierteljahrshefte für Zeitgeschichte* 61 (2013), 275–302.
O'Hagan, Jacinta, *Conceptualizing the West in International Relations. From Spengler to Said*, Basingstoke and New York, 2002.
Osterhammel, Jürgen (ed.), *Geschichtswissenschaft jenseits des Nationalstaats. Studien zu Beziehungsgeschichte und Zivilisationsvergleich*, Göttingen, 2001.
Osterhammel, Jürgen, *Die Verwandlung der Welt. Eine Geschichte des 19. Jahrhunderts*, Munich, 2009.
Osterhammel, Jürgen, 'Fremdbeschreibungen. Spuren von "Okzidentalismus" vor 1930', in Lutz Raphael (ed.), *Theorien und Experimente der Moderne. Europas Gesellschaften im 20. Jahrhundert*, Cologne, 2012, 287–311.
Paddock, Troy R.E., *Creating the Russian Peril. Education, the Public Sphere, and National Identity in Imperial Germany, 1890–1914*, Rochester NY, 2010.
Patterson, Thomas C., *Inventing Western Civilization*, New York, 1997.
Péteri, György (ed.), *Imagining the West in Eastern Europe and the Soviet Union*, Pittsburgh, 2010.
Schenk, Frithjof Benjamin, 'Mental Maps. Die Konstruktion von geographischen Räumen in Europa seit der Aufklärung', *Geschichte und Gesellschaft* 28/3 (2002), 493–514.

Schildt, Axel, *Zwischen Abendland und Amerika. Studien zur westdeutschen Ideenlandschaft der 50er Jahre*, Munich, 1999.
Schildt, Axel, 'Westlich, demokratisch. Deutschland und die westlichen Demokratien im 20. Jahrhundert', in Anselm Doering-Manteuffel (ed.), *Strukturmerkmale der deutschen Geschichte des 20. Jahrhunderts*, Munich, 2006, 225–39.
Schulin, Ernst, *Die weltgeschichtliche Erfassung des Orients bei Hegel und Ranke*, Göttingen, 1958.
Schulte Nordholt, Jan Willem, *The Myth of the West. America as the Last Empire*, Grand Rapids, 1995.
Schulze Wessel, Martin, 'Westen; Okzident, II: Russland', in *Historisches Wörterbuch der Philosophie*, vol. 12, Darmstadt, 2004, col. 668–72.
Segal, Daniel A., '"Western Civ" and the Staging of History in American Higher Education', *American Historical Review* 105 (2000), 770–805.
Struck, Bernhard, *Nicht West – nicht Ost. Frankreich und Polen in der Wahrnehmung deutscher Reisender zwischen 1750 und 1850*, Göttingen, 2006.
Thum, Gregor (ed.), *Traumland Osten. Deutsche Bilder vom östlichen Europa im 20. Jahrhundert*, Göttingen, 2006.
Tolz, Vera, 'The West', in William J. Leatherbarrow and Derek Offord (eds), *A History of Russian Thought*, Cambridge, 2010, 197–216.
Vogel, Barbara, '"Option gegen den Westen". Anfänge eines politischen Schlüsselworts zwischen Revolution und "Neuer Ära" in Preußen', in Dagmar Bussiek and Simona Göbel (eds), *Kultur, Politik und Öffentlichkeit. Festschrift für Jens Flemming*, Kassel, 2009, 134–55.
Walter, Stephan, *Demokratisches Denken zwischen Marx und Hegel. Die politische Philosophie Arnold Ruges. Eine Geschichte der Demokratie in Deutschland*, Düsseldorf, 1995.
Weiß, Volker, 'Dostojewskijs Dämonen. Thomas Mann, Dmitri Mereschkowski und Arthur Moeller van den Bruck im Kampf gegen "den Westen"', in Heiko Kauffmann, Helmut Kellershohn and Jobst Paul (eds), *Völkische Bande. Dekadenz und Wiedergeburt – Analysen rechter Ideologie*, Münster, 2005, 90–122.
Weiß, Volker, *Moderne Antimoderne. Arthur Moeller van den Bruck und der Wandel des Konservatismus*, Paderborn et al., 2012.
Winkler, Heinrich August, *Der lange Weg nach Westen*, 2 vols, Munich, 2000 (In English: *Germany. The Long Road West*, 2 vols, Oxford, 2006–2007).
Winkler, Heinrich August, *Deutschland, Europa und der Westen. Versuch einer Ortsbestimmung*, Bonn, 2004.
Winkler, Heinrich August, 'Was heißt westliche Wertegemeinschaft?', in Heinrich August Winkler, *Auf ewig in Hitlers Schatten? Anmerkungen zur deutschen Geschichte*, Munich, 2007, 180–201.

Winkler, Heinrich August, *Geschichte des Westens*, 3 vols, Munich, 2009–2014.
Wolff, Larry, *Inventing Eastern Europe. The Map of Civilization on the Mind of the Enlightenment*, Stanford, 1994.

Contributors

Riccardo Bavaj is Lecturer in Modern European History at the University of St Andrews. From 2009 to 2012 he was a Feodor Lynen Research Fellow of the Alexander von Humboldt Foundation. His research focuses on the intellectual and spatial history of twentieth-century Germany and is currently concerned with a project on academics and transatlantic liberalism in the Cold War era. His publications include *Die Ambivalenz der Moderne im Nationalsozialismus* (2003), '"The West". A Conceptual Exploration', *European History Online* (2011) and *Intellektuelle im Kalten Krieg* (ed. with Dominik Geppert, theme issue of *Geschichte in Wissenschaft und Unterricht* 3/4, 2014).

Martina Steber is Research Fellow at the Institut für Zeitgeschichte München-Berlin. From 2007 to 2012 she was based at the German Historical Institute London, in 2012/13 as a Junior Fellow at the Historisches Kolleg. Her research focuses on German and British political history, the history of Nazism and the history of conservatism. Her publications include *Ethnische Gewissheiten. Die Ordnung des Regionalen im bayerischen Schwaben vom Kaiserreich bis zum NS-Regime* (2010) and *Visions of Community in Nazi Germany. Social Engineering and Private Lives* (ed. with Bernhard Gotto, 2014).

Stefan Berger is Professor of Social History at Ruhr-Universität Bochum, where he is also Director of the Institute for Social Movements and Executive Chair of the Foundation Library of the Ruhr. He previously taught at the Universities of Glamorgan and Manchester. His research focuses on comparative European history, especially labour history, the history of social movements, the history of historiography, the history of nationalism and national identity and British-German relations. His publications include *The Past as History. National History Writing in Modern Europe* (with Christoph Conrad, 2014) and *Friendly Enemies. Britain and the GDR, 1949–1990* (with Norman LaPorte, 2010).

Anselm Doering-Manteuffel is Professor of Modern History and Head of the Department of Contemporary History at the University of Tübingen. He is an expert in twentieth-century German history and is especially concerned with the social history of ideas. His most recent publications include 'Die deutsche Geschichte in den Zeitbögen des 20. Jahrhunderts', *Vierteljahrshefte für Zeitgeschichte* 62/3 (2014), *Das doppelte Leben. Generationenerfahrungen im Jahrhundert der Extreme* (2013) and *Nach dem Boom. Perspektiven auf die Zeitgeschichte seit 1970* (with Lutz Raphael, ³2012).

Philipp Gassert is Professor of Contemporary History at the University of Mannheim. He previously taught at the University of Heidelberg, the University of Pennsylvania and Augsburg University. In 2008–2009 he served as Deputy Director of the German Historical Institute Washington. His research focuses on transatlantic and international history as well as German contemporary history. His publications include *Amerika im Dritten Reich. Ideologie, Propaganda und Volksmeinung 1933–1945* (1997), *Kurt Georg Kiesinger, 1904–1988. Kanzler zwischen den Zeiten* (2006) and *Coping with the Nazi Past. West German Debates on Nazism and Generational Conflict, 1955–1975* (ed. with Alan E. Steinweis, 2006).

Dominik Geppert is Professor of Modern History at the Rheinische Friedrich-Wilhelms-Universität Bonn. He previously was a Research Fellow at the German Historical Institute London and a Heisenberg Fellow of the Deutsche Forschungsgemeinschaft. His main fields of research include international history and intellectual history of the nineteenth and twentieth centuries as well as British and German contemporary history. His most recent publications include *Die Ära Adenauer* (³2012), *Pressekriege. Öffentlichkeit und Diplomatie in den deutsch-britischen Beziehungen, 1896–1912* (2007), *Hans Werner Richter. Mittendrin. Tagebücher 1966–1972* (ed., 2012) and *Ein Europa, das es nicht gibt. Die fatale Sprengkraft des Euro* (2013).

Austin Harrington is Reader in Sociology at the University of Leeds. He has completed a monograph on Weimar sources in German cosmopolitan social thought and the idea of the West (forthcoming with Cambridge University Press). His publications also include *Art and Social Theory.*

Sociological Arguments in Aesthetics (2004), *Hermeneutic Dialogue and Social Science. A Critique of Gadamer and Habermas* (2001), *Modern Social Theory. An Introduction* (ed., 2005) and the *Routledge Encyclopedia of Social Theory* (ed. with Barbara L. Marshall and Hans-Peter Müller, 2006).

Mark Hewitson is Senior Lecturer in German History and Politics at University College London. His research interests include the history of nationalism, nineteenth- and early twentieth-century constitutional, political, military and diplomatic history, the history of European integration and historical theory. His publications include *National Identity and Political Thought in Germany* (2000), *Germany and the Causes of the First World War* (2004), *Nationalism in Germany, 1848–1866* (2010) and *History and Causality* (2014). He has co-edited *What Is a Nation? Europe, 1789–1914* (with Timothy Baycroft, 2006), and *Europe in Crisis. Intellectuals and the European Idea, 1917–1957* (with Matthew D'Auria, 2012).

Marcus Llanque is Professor of Political Theory at Augsburg University. He is co-editor of the journal *Zeitschrift für Politische Theorie*. His research interests concern the genealogy of democratic thinking and he is currently working on a theory of political collectivity. Recent publications include *Souveräne Demokratie und soziale Homogenität. Das politische Denken Hermann Hellers* (ed., 2010), *Geschichte der politischen Ideen. Von der Antike bis zur Gegenwart* (2012) and 'Der Begriff des Volkes bei Rousseau zwischen Mitgliedschaft und Zugehörigkeit' in Oliver Hidalgo (ed.), *Der lange Schatten des Contrat social* (2013).

Douglas T. McGetchin is Associate Professor of History at Florida Atlantic University. His research focuses on connections between Europe and South Asia in the nineteenth and twentieth centuries. He received a Fulbright–Nehru Scholar grant to conduct research in Kolkata, India in 2013–14. His publications include *Indology, Indomania, Orientalism. Ancient India's Rebirth in Modern Germany* (2009), *Sanskrit and 'Orientalism'. Indology and Comparative Linguistics in Germany, 1750–1958* (ed. with Peter K. J. Park and Damodar SarDesai, 2004) and *Transcultural Encounters between Germany and India. Kindred Spirits in the Nineteenth and Twentieth Centuries* (ed. with Joanne Miyang Cho and Eric Kurlander, 2013).

Frank Lorenz Müller is Professor of Modern History and has taught at the University of St Andrews since 2002. His main research interests concern the political and cultural history of nineteenth-century Europe (mainly Germany and Britain). He has published *Britain and the German Question.*

Perceptions of Nationalism and Political Reform, 1830–1863 (2002), *Die Revolution von 1848/49* (⁴2012) and – most recently – *Der 99-Tage-Kaiser. Friedrich III. von Preußen* (2013). He currently leads an AHRC-funded project on royal heirs across nineteenth-century Europe.

Katherine Pence is Associate Professor and Chair of History as well as Director of Women's Studies at Baruch College, CUNY. Her research focuses on Cold War consumer culture in East and West Germany, women and gender, and Germany's connections with decolonizing Africa in the 1960s. She has held an SSRC grant and a Conant Fellowship at Harvard. Her publications include *Socialist Modern. East German Everyday Culture and Politics* (ed. with Paul Betts, 2008) and 'Grounds for Discontent? Coffee from the Black Market to the *Kaffeeklatsch* in the GDR' in Paulina Bren and Mary Neuburger (eds), *Communism Unwrapped. Consumption in Cold War Eastern Europe* (2012).

Thomas Rohkrämer is Reader in Modern European History at the University of Lancaster. His research focuses on German history, especially the history of political cultures and mentalities from 1871 to 1945. He is currently engaged in projects on the history of the *Lebensreformbewegung* and on hero cults in German history. His most recent publications include *A Single Communal Faith? The German Right from Conservatism to National Socialism* (2007) and *Die fatale Attraktion des Nationalsozialismus. Über die Popularität eines Unrechtregimes* (2013).

Benjamin Schröder is currently completing his dissertation on electioneering practices in interwar Britain and Germany, funded by the Johannes-Rau-Gesellschaft. Between 2011 and 2014 he worked as a Research Associate at Humboldt-Universität zu Berlin. He is interested in European cultural and political history in the nineteenth and early twentieth centuries. His publications include *Wahlen in der transatlantischen Moderne* (ed. with Claudia Gatzka and Hedwig Richter, 2013).

Denis Sdvižkov is Research Fellow at the German Historical Institute Moscow. His research focuses on Russian and European social history of the eighteenth and nineteenth centuries, the history of concepts and new military history. His publications include *'Poniatie o Rossii'. K istoricheskoi semantike imperskogo perioda ['The Concept of Russia'. On the Historical Semantics of the Imperial Period]* (ed. with Alexei Miller and Ingrid Schierle, 2012) and *Das Zeitalter der Intelligenz. Zur vergleichenden Geschichte der Gebildeten in Europa bis zum Ersten Weltkrieg* (2006).

Bernhard Struck is Reader in Modern History and Director of the Centre for Transnational History at the University of St Andrews. His research focuses on issues of space, the history of travel and cartography as well as transnational history during the eighteenth and nineteenth centuries. He is the author of *Nicht West – nicht Ost. Frankreich und Polen in der Wahrnehmung deutscher Reisender, 1750–1850* (2006) and *Revolution, Krieg und Verflechtung. Deutsch-Französische Geschichte 1789–1815* (with Claire Gantet, 2008).

Stefan Vogt is Research Fellow at the Martin Buber Chair for Jewish Thought and Philosophy at Goethe-Universität Frankfurt am Main. He worked at the University of Amsterdam, New York University and Ben-Gurion University of the Negev. His research focuses on the history of European nationalism, German-Jewish history, and the history of colonialism. His publications include *Nationaler Sozialismus und Soziale Demokratie. Die sozialdemokratische Junge Rechte 1918–1945* (2006) and several articles on the history of nationalist ideas in the German socialist movement and the history of German Zionism.

INDEX

Aachen, 139, 146
Abendland (see also Occident), 4, 7, 9, 20–21, 23, 55, 102, 119, 143, 186, 188, 210, 217, 231, 233, 237
Adelung, Christian, 46
Adenauer, Konrad, 22, 226, 272–273, 279
Adriatic, 65
Africa, 21, 223, 256, 278
    Africanized, 217
    South Africa, 63, 278
Agnoli, Johannes, 193
Alexander I, Tsar, 143
Alexandria, 115
Alldeutscher Verband, 62
Allgemeine Zeitung des Judenthums, 128
Alsace, 47
America (see United States of America)
Andersch, Alfred, 266–269, 271–273
Angermann, Eric, 154–155
Anti-Communism, 6, 87, 193, 233
    Anti-Bolshevism, 86, 216, 224–226, 231, 255
Anti-Semitism, 15, 60, 63, 87, 125, 127, 129, 131–132, 152, 171, 208, 220, 226
    Boycott of 1933, 223
Anti-Westernism, 18, 20–21, 23, 87, 89, 91, 105–106, 193, 217–218, 224, 226
Arabia, 10, 113
Archenholz, Johann Wilhelm von, 48
Archiv für Sozialwissenschaft und Sozialpolitik, 59
Arendt, Hannah, 184
Aristocracy, 9, 158, 160–161, 172, 232, 240
Aron, Raymond, 234
Aryan, 61, 113–114, 116–120
Aschheim, Steven, 124, 126
Asia, 8–10, 22, 61, 63, 99–101, 104, 111–112, 114–116, 118–120, 143, 147, 174, 176, 178, 216, 223, 251, 255, 278
    Central Asia, 104, 118
    East Asian, 222
    Eurasia, 120, 168
    South Asia, 118
    South East Asia, 63
Asiatic Society of Bengal, 112
Assimilation, 125, 129, 131, 133
Athens, 178
Atlantic, 3, 5–6, 48, 51, 64, 82, 167, 169, 172, 177, 179, 222, 239, 279
Auschwitz, 185
Australia, 63, 222
Austria, viii, 50, 55, 63, 76, 85, 103, 143, 146, 154, 172, 176, 269
    Habsburg monarchy, 46, 62, 85, 172, 176

Bad Godesberg, 259
Baden, 146
Baden-Württemberg, 238
Baghdad, 63
Balkans, 64–65
Baltic, 45–46, 50, 62, 65, 104, 268
Bar Kochba, 129
barbarism, barbarians, 8, 43, 50, 83, 98, 127–128, 142–143, 146, 148, 233, 253, 272
Barloewen, Constantin von, 240
Bauer, Otto, 255
Bavaria, 268
Bayreuth, 206
Bebel, August, 62, 251, 258
Beckerath, Hermann von, 147–148
Belgium, 71, 83, 139, 141, 144–146, 148, 158
Belinskiĭ, Vissarion, 99
Berdahl, Daphne, 286
Bergstraesser, Arnold, 237
Berlin City Council, 152, 156
Berlin, 2–3, 42, 44, 56–57, 59, 63, 72, 77, 89, 99–100, 103, 117–118, 130, 132, 142, 147, 152, 155–156, 183, 185, 192, 267, 270, 278, 282–283, 287–288
    East Berlin, 263, 272, 281, 286–287
    West Berlin, 89, 185–186, 191–193, 280–281, 283, 287

Bernhardi, Friedrich von, 62, 65
Bernstein, Eduard, 252-253, 255, 259
Bethmann Hollweg, Theobald von, 75, 78
Bildung, 42, 46, 203-204
Birnbaum, Nathan, 129-131
Bismarck, Otto von, 16, 76, 152, 156, 251-252, 258
Blackstone, Sir William, 161
Blavatsky, Madame, 119
Blum, Robert, 141
Bluntschli, Johann Caspar, 161
Bockum-Dolffs, Florens von, 156
Bohemia, 45-46, 65
Bolshevism, 5, 87, 171-172, 216, 218, 220, 223, 231, 265-266, 273
Bonn, 2, 117, 147, 271-272, 278
Börne, Ludwig, 41
Bornhak, Conrad, 154, 157
Bote aus Westen/Westbote, 143-145
Bracher, Karl Dietrich, 2, 190-191
Brandt, Willy, 273
Brater, Karl, 161
Brenner, David, 129
Breslau, 101
Britain/United Kingdom viii, 2-3, 5-8, 13, 16-17, 20-23, 44-47, 49-50, 55, 58-60, 64-65, 70-71, 73-76, 81-87, 89-91, 100, 112, 117-118, 131, 139, 141, 144-146, 148, 152-155, 157-164, 167-169, 171, 177, 184, 186-187, 193, 201-212, 216-226, 233-234, 249-259, 264, 266-267, 271, 283-284
   Anglophilia, 13, 154
   Anglophobia, 176
   Anglo-Saxon, 15, 77, 82, 177-178, 188, 225, 253
   British Empire, dominions, 55, 58, 70, 226
Brüggemann, Karl Heinrich, 143
Brüggen, Ernst von der, 104
Brüning, Heinrich, 224
Bryce, James, 74
Buber, Martin, 129-132
Buchenwald, 267, 270
Budapest, 45
Buddha, 117-119
Bülow, Bernhard von, 64
Burckhardt, Carl J., 232, 235
Burgess, John, 75
Burke, Edmund, 240
Büsching, Anton Friedrich, 42
Byzantine Empire, 101, 176

Cambridge University, 116
capitalism, 1, 5, 20, 22, 24, 58-60, 65, 88, 90-91, 175, 203, 209, 224, 249-252, 255, 258, 263-264, 266, 270, 278-279, 282, 284
Caribbean, 219
Cassirer, Ernst, 170, 173-174
Castillo, Greg, 285
Catholicism, 14, 48, 64, 114, 141, 156, 170, 172, 176, 179, 210, 239, 263, 269-270
Caucasus, 116-117
Centralverein deutscher Staatsbürger jüdischen Glaubens, 127
Centralverein für das Wohl der arbeitenden Klassen, 152
Chaadaev, Pëtr, 10
Chamberlain, Houston Stewart, 61, 204, 206, 208
Chamisso, Adelbert von, 10
Charlemagne, 173
Chateaubriand, François-René de, 240
Chicago, 185, 207
China, 3, 6, 63, 73, 112, 119
Christian Democratic Union (*Christlich-Demokratische Union*, CDU), 238, 278
Christianity, Christian, 1, 4, 9, 13-14, 23, 46, 58, 62-63, 99, 101, 114, 169, 172, 174-176, 179, 208, 210, 233, 266, 269-270, 287
Churchill, Winston, 44, 223, 226
citizenship, 56, 185, 192, 203
civil law, 186
civil liberties, 12, 224
civilization (see also Western civilization), 1-8, 10-11, 15-20, 25, 43-45, 59-60, 62, 65, 69, 71, 84-85, 98-99, 101, 105, 116-117, 131, 141, 147, 168-170, 172-176, 204-206, 209-212, 224, 265, 279
Cohen-Reuß, Max, 253
Cold War, viii, 3, 6, 22-23, 25, 44-45, 90, 184, 188, 192, 231-232, 238, 257, 264, 268, 271-272, 277, 279
Cologne, 146, 285
colonialism, 3, 6, 16, 63, 111, 117-118, 120, 124, 126, 128, 143, 217, 278
common law, 186
communal faith, 206-208
communism, 3, 5, 22, 44, 87, 90-91, 142, 177, 221, 254-256, 262-264, 266-270, 272, 278-279, 284-285, 288
Communist Party of Germany (*Kommunistische Partei Deutschlands*, KPD), 177, 267-268
Comte, Auguste, 177
conceptual history, 7, 25, 184, 249
Condorcet, Marie Jean Antoine Nicolas Caritat, Marquis de, 48
Congress for Cultural Freedom, 6, 90

Conrad, Sebastian, 57
consensus capitalism, 5, 90-91
conservatism, 4, 8, 13-14, 18, 20, 23, 62,
    64-65, 72, 76, 103-106, 139-140,
    153-154, 168-169, 172, 175, 179, 193,
    201-203, 211, 219, 226, 230-241, 254,
    267, 270
constitutionalism, 8, 9, 12, 17, 20, 85,
    139-141, 144, 147, 152-157, 163-164,
    169-170, 184, 189, 202, 218, 269
    constitutional history, 43, 153, 184,
        189
consumer society, 89, 235, 237, 239, 279
    consumerism, 1, 19, 236, 238, 280, 288
Continental Europe, 82, 153, 186, 189
Coudenhove-Kalergi, Richard Nikolaus Graf
    von, 172
Courier, 145
Creuzer, Friedrich, 114
    Creuzer *Streit* (Creuzer controversy), 114
Crick, Bernard, 184
Crimea, viii, ix, 10, 13-15, 19, 62, 100-102,
    106, 141
    Crimean War, ix, 10, 13-15, 19, 100-
        102, 106, 141
crisis, viii, 78, 163, 192, 206, 224, 252, 267,
    281, 286-287
    of liberalism, 81, 86
    of the West, 24-25, 169, 178
Crossman, Richard, 256
cultural criticism, 14, 60, 65, 105, 133,
    201-212, 235-239
Curtius, Ernst Robert, 170, 174

Dachau, 268
Dahlmann, Friedrich Christoph, 154
Dahrendorf, Ralf, 2
Danilevskiĭ, Nikolaĭ, 11, 101, 175
Danzig, 48
Darwin, Charles, 16, 21, 217, 222
David, Eduard, 253
David-Fox, Michael, 5
Dehn, Paul, 60
Delbrück, Hans, 72
democracy (see also Western democracy), 1,
    4-5, 8-9, 11, 17, 20-21, 23-24, 44,
    59, 64, 69-79, 83, 85-91, 103, 105,
    125, 141-142, 147, 153, 155-156, 160,
    164, 167, 169-170, 179, 183-193, 202,
    207-209, 211-212, 216-223, 226-227,
    231-240, 249-259, 262-264, 266,
    268-270, 272-273, 277-278, 288-289
democratization, 7, 59, 74-76, 78, 169, 191,
    193, 232, 234, 239-240
Descartes, René, 207
Deutsche Volkszeitung, 63

Dewey, John, 75, 85
Di Fabio, Udo, 2
Dicey, Albert Vernon, 73-74
Diderot, Denis, 48
Diederichs, Eugen, 206
Diezel, Gustav, 13
Dirks, Walter, 263-267, 269-273
Dmitriev Mikhail, 99
Dmitriev, Ivan, 99
Dostoevskiĭ, Fëdor, 18, 103, 105, 175
Dresden, 41, 48
Dubos, Jean-Baptiste, 46

East Indies, 222
East, viii, ix, 5, 8-15, 17-20, 22-23, 25, 41-
    47, 49-51, 56, 61-65, 90-91, 98-106,
    111-112, 114-120, 124-132, 140-148,
    170-172, 175-179, 188-190, 192,
    210-211, 216, 218, 231-234, 238-239,
    249-251, 255, 262-266, 268-271, 273,
    277-285, 287-289
    East Central Europe, 5, 10, 42
    Eastern Europe, 10, 43-45, 97, 100-
        103, 106, 124, 126-127, 129, 145,
        185, 249
Ebert, Friedrich, 170
Edward V, 82
egalitarianism (see also equality), 233, 239,
    286
Egypt, 179
Eisleben, 156
Eisner, Kurt, 59
emigration, émigrés, 62, 81, 88, 145,
    184-185, 190, 192, 233-234, 236-237,
    239, 267
Empire, 9, 16, 50, 56, 76, 91, 102-103, 160,
    164, 172, 177, 204, 221-222, 285
    British Empire (see also Britain)
    German Empire, 63, 75, 77, 97,
        102-103, 126, 167, 207
    Russian Empire, 63, 85, 103, 106
Encounter, 90
Engels, Friedrich, 62, 105, 250-251
England (see Britain)
equality, 59, 82, 133, 176, 232-233, 235,
    237-240
Erdmann, Lothar, 253
Erfurt, 250
Erhard, Ludwig, 280
ethnography, 19, 48
Europe, 3, 5-6, 8-15, 18-22, 42-51, 55,
    57-65, 69, 71-73, 75, 77, 79, 81-86,
    90-91, 97-106, 111-120, 124, 126-
    129, 139-148, 153-154, 157-158, 161,
    164, 167-179, 185-187, 189, 206-207,
    209-211, 216-217, 219-227, 230,

233-235, 238-239, 241, 249-250, 252, 257, 262-266, 269-273, 279, 285
Eurocentrism, 58
'European Monroe Doctrine', 224-225
European Union, EU, viii, 25
exceptionalism, 4-5, 19-21, 273
exile, 22, 41, 50, 145, 184, 190, 236-238, 251, 256-259, 267-268, 271-272

Fadeev, Rostislav, 101-102
Fallmerayer, Jakob Philipp, 13, 101
Ferguson, Niall, 3
Feyerabend, Carl, 48
Fichte, Johann Gottlieb, 131
Fischer, Fritz, 91
Flake, Otto, 73
Fontane, Theodor, 104
Ford, Henry, 219, 221
Forster, Georg, 48, 112
Forsthoff, Ernst, 192, 234
Fox, Charles James, 164
Fraenkel, Ernst, 2, 23, 183-194
France, viii, 5, 7-8, 11-14, 17, 21, 23, 41-42, 44-50, 55-56, 58-60, 62, 64-65, 70-71, 73-74, 81-84, 86-87, 89-91, 98, 100, 103, 106, 112, 125, 131, 139, 141-148, 153-155, 157-158, 162-164, 167-171, 174, 177, 186-187, 201-208, 210, 212, 216-221, 223-225, 227, 231-240, 249-251, 254-255, 257-258, 264, 266-268, 271, 285
Francophobia, 13
Franco, Francisco, 272
Frankfurter Allgemeine Zeitung, 236
Frankfurter Hefte, 22, 263-264, 266, 270-271
Frankfurter Zeitung, 103, 267
Franzos, Karl Emil, 63
Free University Berlin, 89, 183, 186, 190, 192-193
freedom, viii, 2, 6, 11-13, 17, 65, 69, 71-72, 76-77, 82-83, 85, 90, 114-115, 139-140, 142, 146, 154, 158, 161, 164, 170, 188, 232-233, 235-240, 256-257, 264, 266, 269, 271
Freeman, Joseph, 219
Freiburg, 270
Freiligrath, Ferdinand, 12
Freistatt, Die, 129
Freyer, Hans, 234, 238
Friedrich Wilhelm IV, crown prince, 147
Fundgruben des Orients, 113

Gagern, Heinrich von, 140
Gandhi, 119
Ganz, Hugo, 103

Gaulle, Charles de, 239
Gehlen, Arnold, 234-235
Geiss, Imanuel, 240
gentry, 157
geography, 1, 7-9, 13, 17, 19, 41-44, 46-50, 58, 69, 84, 97-99, 103, 106, 117, 119-120, 140-142, 145, 147, 153, 175, 188, 219, 222, 264, 271
George III, 160-161
George, Stefan, 60
German College of Politics (*Deutsche Hochschule für Politik*), 170, 186-187
German-Soviet Non-Aggression Pact, 225
Germany
    East Germany (see GDR)
    Federal Republic of Germany (FRG), 4-5, 8, 22-24, 81-82, 85, 88-91, 106, 183-194, 211, 226-227, 230-234, 236-241, 264, 270-273, 277-285
    German colonies, 16, 221
    German Confederation, 57-58, 140
    German Democratic Republic (GDR), 24, 91, 233, 268, 272, 277-289
    Germanic, 11, 13-14, 16, 23, 50, 58-59, 73, 102, 104, 140, 171, 175-176, 178, 205, 207, 221, 223, 226
    Imperial Germany/Kaiserreich, 15, 19, 55, 64-65, 72, 84-85, 88, 91, 221-222
    West Germany (see FRG)
    Wilhelmine Germany, 15-16, 56-59, 61, 64-65, 82, 84, 167, 206, 221
Geyer, Curt, 256
Glogau, 41
Gneist, Rudolf von, 12-13, 152-164
Gnesen, 41
Godkin, Edwin Lawrence, 74
Goebbels, Joseph, 172
Goethe, Johann Wolfgang von, 76, 112-114, 204
GoGwilt, Christopher, 6
Goldmann, Nachum, 131
Gollwitzer, Heinz, 4, 22
Göttingen, 271
Grazia, Victoria de, 285
Great Depression, 90, 221, 223-224
Greece, 58, 62, 112, 114-117, 119, 131, 206-207, 210-211
    Graecophilia, 114
Grimm, Johann Friedrich Carl, 47
Groh, Dieter, 4, 22
Großdeutscher Rundfunk, 225
Großmann, Eugen, 255
Guardini, Romano, 269

Gutzkow, Karl, 41

Habermas, Jürgen, 24
Hafiz, 113
Hahn, Erich, 155
Halem, Gerhard Anton von, 48
Halfeld, Adolf, 219, 225
Hälschner, Hugo, 147
Hamburg, 49, 63, 272
Hammer-Purgstall, Joseph von, 113
Hansemann, David, 139, 145-147
Harnack, Adolf von, 77
Hasbach, Wilhelm, 74
Hatschek, Julius, 154, 160
Haushofer, Karl, 220, 225
Haxthausen, August von, 62
Hay, Stephen, 119
Heck, Bruno, 238-239
Hegel, Georg Friedrich Wilhelm, 8-10, 12, 16, 50, 99-100, 114-116, 120, 131, 177, 202
Heidegger, Martin, 210-211
Heidelberg, 114, 163, 168, 177
Heine, Fritz, 22, 256-257
Heine, Heinrich, 41, 50, 145
Helbig, Karl Gustav, 49
Hennis, Wilhelm, 239-240
Herder, Johann Gottfried, 50, 270
Hereth, Michael, 240
Herodotus, 44
Herzl, Theodor, 128
Heß, Rudolf, 220
Hesse, Hermann, 119
Hilferding, Rudolf, 255-256
Hilfsverein der deutschen Juden, 128
Hintze, Otto, 64, 77
Historikerstreit, 24
history of concepts (see Conceptual history)
Hitler, Adolf, 218-226, 256-257, 267-268, 270
Hobsbawm, Eric, 86
Hobson, John Atkinson, 76
Hoetzsch, Otto, 62, 65
Hofmannsthal, Hugo von, 172
Holland (see Netherlands)
Hollywood, 219, 281
Holy Alliance, 9, 11
Holy Roman Empire, 47, 57
Honecker, Erich, 286
Hoover, John Edgar, 223-224
horizon of expectation, 7, 9, 15, 17, 22, 24-25
Humboldt, Wilhelm von, 50, 115
Hungary, 143, 177, 188, 273
Huntington, Samuel, 3

ideas of 1789, 17, 66, 70-71, 78, 210, 216, 218, 230
ideas of 1914, 4, 17, 19, 70-72, 78, 84, 87-88, 105-106, 187, 210, 216, 230
identity, ix, 3-5, 10, 14-15, 20, 25, 57, 59, 61, 82, 99-100, 116, 124-128, 132-133, 192-193, 204, 210, 212, 227, 277, 284
ideology, viii, ix, 6, 8, 12-18, 21, 24, 64, 69-70, 73-74, 77-78, 81-82, 86-89, 91, 131-132, 140, 142, 191, 208, 210, 212, 216-221, 223-224, 226, 230-232, 250, 258, 266-267, 271, 273, 278-279, 283, 286
ideologization, 7
imperialism, 6, 24, 58, 278, 284
Independent Social Democratic Party of Germany (*Unabhängige Sozialdemokratische Partei Deutschlands*, USPD), 253
India, 6, 10, 111-120
Indologists, 119
industrial society, 90, 236, 238
industrialization, 55, 57-58, 65, 81-83, 86, 126, 146, 148, 175, 177, 202, 207
international relations, 11, 13-16, 19, 217, 221-222, 225
Iron Curtain, 44, 188
Iskra, 105
Italy, 46, 49, 71, 90, 112, 144, 220-221, 227

Jackson, Patrick, 5
Jahrbücher der Geschichte und Staatskunst, 9
Japan, 6, 15, 18, 62-63, 65, 104, 119, 222
Jellinek, Georg, 163
Jerusalem, 179
Jews, Jewish, 15, 60-61, 63, 87, 104, 114, 119, 124-133, 141, 185, 208, 211, 216, 220-221, 223, 226, 233, 267, 272
Jones, Ernest, 251
Jones, Sir William, 112
Jörg, Joseph Edmund, 14
Journal des débats, 145
Jude, Der, 129
Jüdische Rundschau, 130
Jüdischer Verlag, 129
Junge, Franz Erich, 59
Jünger, Ernst, 211, 269

Kaliski, Julius, 255
Kaltenbrunner, Gerd-Klaus, 240
Kant, Immanuel, 48, 76, 82, 207
Kantorowicz, Alfred, 263-265, 267-273
Kaufmann, Erich, 76-77
Kaufmann, Fritz Mordechai, 129

Kautsky, Karl, 105, 249, 255
Kessel, Eberhard, 232
Kessler, Harry Graf, 203
Kesting, Hanno, 235
Khomiakov, Alekseï, 100
Kiesinger, Kurt Georg, 238
Kipling, Rudyard, 118
Kips, J.H. Valckenier, 74
Kjéllen, Rudolf, 74
Klages, Ludwig, 207-208
Kochmann, Wilhelm, 59
Kogon, Eugen, 263-267, 269-273
Kohn, Hans, 130
Kölnische Zeitung, 140, 142-143
Kopstein, Jeffrey, 284
Koselleck, Reinhart, 7, 42-45
Krieger, Leonard, 72, 154
Krockow, Christian von, 240
Kronstadt, 100
Kulturkreis, 18-19, 173, 175

labour movement, 250, 252, 258, 262
Labour Party, 252, 254-256
Lagarde, Paul de, 131, 206, 208
Lamer, Reinhard, 155
Lamprecht, Karl, 58, 60
Landsberg, 41
Landshut, Siegfried, 237
Langbehn, Julius, 204, 206, 208
Lassalle, Ferdinand, 251
Lassen, Christian, 117, 120
Latinate, 169-170, 176
Lebensraum (living space), 217, 221-222, 226
Lederer, Emil, 59
left, 12, 22, 24, 61, 64, 76, 87, 90, 147, 156, 168, 172, 179, 183, 193-194, 234, 236, 239-240, 253-258, 262-265, 267, 269-271, 273
Leipzig, 41, 283-285
Lemberg/Lviv, 48
Lenau, Nikolaus, 10
Lenin, Vladimir, 105
liberalism, liberal, liberty, 3-5, 8-16, 18, 21-24, 50, 64, 74, 76, 81-87, 89-91, 103-105, 125, 127-129, 131-133, 139-140, 142-143, 145-148, 153-156, 158, 161, 164, 167-169, 171-175, 177-179, 183, 190-194, 203, 217-221, 224, 226, 231-234, 236-237, 239-240, 252, 254, 256, 264, 267, 272, 289
  anti-liberalism, 18, 88-91, 193, 218-219, 221, 224, 270
  consensus liberalism, 5, 24, 90-91
  liberalization, 23-24
  liberal movement, 139, 146

Liebknecht, Karl, 253
Life Reform Movement, 207
Lloyd George, David, 71
Locke, John, 82, 84, 171
London, ix, 46, 56, 81, 152, 157, 177, 220-221, 252, 257
Lorraine, 47
Low, Sidney, 73, 163
Lowell, Abbot Lawrence, 73
Löwenthal, Richard, 2, 22, 193-194, 257
Lübbe, Hermann, 187
Ludwig-Maximilians-University Munich, 230
Lukács, Georg, 177-178
Luther, Martin, 174, 179
Luxemburg, Rosa, 253

MacDonald, Ramsay, 254
Macpherson, James, 98
Maier, Charles, 56
Maier, Hans, 230, 239
Maizière, Lothar de, 25
Manchuria, 63
Mann, Golo, 236
Mann, Thomas, 17-18, 105, 175, 209-210, 218
Marcuse, Herbert, 193
Marx, Karl, 9, 21, 24, 72, 177-178, 211-212, 218, 220, 238, 250-252, 254, 258, 262, 266, 269-270, 273, 279, 284
Masaryk, Tomáš, 188
mass society, 73, 209, 235-237, 279
materialism, 19, 58-60, 105, 119, 131, 178-179, 203-204, 208-209, 235, 269, 277, 282, 286
Mayer, Gustav, 255
Mayer, Jacob Peter, 233-234, 236
mechanization, 207, 224, 267
Mehring, Franz, 253
Meinecke, Friedrich, 65, 77, 210, 218
Mensching, Gustav, 119
mental mapping, mental map, viii, 1, 4, 7-11, 13, 15, 97-99, 101-102, 106, 141, 143, 147, 191, 257
Merkel, Ina, 279
Meseritz, Ludwig von, 9
Metternich, Klemens von, 50
Mevissen, Gustav, 147
Meyer, Manfred, 147
middle class society, 238
militarism, 1, 70-72, 75-78, 83-84, 103, 105, 113, 146, 186, 209-210, 216, 222, 255, 263, 272-273, 278-279, 288
Mill, John Stuart, 177
Mitteleuropa, 19-20, 172

modernity, 7-8, 18, 20-21, 24, 42-43, 45-46, 51, 58, 60, 69, 71-73, 77, 79, 81, 83, 85-88, 90, 100, 112-115, 118, 125, 127, 146, 153-154, 157, 163, 167, 169, 173-175, 177, 179, 183, 186, 201-202, 205-209, 233, 235, 240, 249-250, 257, 284-285, 288
    modernization, 60, 78, 82, 126, 177, 201-202, 206, 209
    modernization theory, 85, 194
Moeller van den Bruck, Arthur, 18, 105, 172, 211, 219
Mohl, Robert von, 163
monarchy, 46, 62, 83, 85-86, 91, 139-140, 148, 160, 202
Monat, Der, 90
Monroe, James, 224-225
Montesquieu, Charles de, 46, 82, 153, 171
Moravia, 65
Moscow, 45, 65, 175, 177-178, 224
Mühlmann, Wilhelm E., 217
Müller, Adam, 202
Müller, Friedrich Max, 116-117, 120
Munich, 230, 263, 269, 271
Mussolini, Benito, 172
Mutzenbecher, Johann Daniel, 49

Napoleon, ix, 8, 24, 50, 58, 98
    Napoleonic, 106, 113, 146, 202, 204
Nation, The, 74
nation state, 15-16, 55-57, 64, 83, 85, 91, 126, 147-148, 156, 169, 179, 204, 221, 250-252, 258, 266
    national self-determination, 86, 173
nationalism, ix, 4, 6, 11-13, 16, 18-19, 41, 47, 49, 56-59, 64-65, 84, 86, 88, 98-99, 101, 103-105, 112-113, 126-128, 130-133, 155-156, 160, 164, 167-174, 176, 183, 192-193, 202, 204-211, 216, 223, 230, 250, 252-254, 256-258, 263, 266
national socialism, 21-22, 81, 86-87, 91, 172, 211, 216-218, 220, 222-224, 226, 256, 264, 267-268, 270
    Nazi propaganda, 216, 224-226
NATO, 1, 5, 25, 190, 271, 278, 281
    Atlantic Community, 3, 5-6
natural law, 170-171, 187, 189
Naumann, Friedrich, 172
Nearing, Scott, 219
neo-pluralism, 23, 189, 191
neo-romanticism, 129-130
Netherlands, 46-47, 65, 74, 141, 216, 222
Neue Rundschau, 59
Neues Deutschland, 268, 287

New Deal, 88, 90-91, 187, 223-224
New York Evening Post, 74
New York, 74, 157, 185, 220
Nicholas I, Tsar, 11, 139
Nietzsche, Friedrich, 18, 83, 119, 207
Norden, Albert, 278
Novalis/Georg Philipp Friedrich Freiherr von Hardenberg, 113

O'Connor, Feargus, 251
Oakeshott, Michael, 234
Occident (see also *Abendland*), 7, 20-21, 42-44, 58, 61, 111-113, 117, 119-120, 128, 130, 143, 169, 176, 186, 188-190, 210, 217
    Occidental schism, 186, 190
    Occidentalism, 6, 226
Office for Strategic Services (OSS), 88
Oldenberg, Hermann, 117-118, 120
Ollenhauer, Erich, 22, 257
Oppenheimer, Franz, 127-128
Orient, 6-8, 10, 13, 42-45, 63, 101, 111-120, 124, 127-128, 130, 143, 176
    Orientalism, 6, 10, 13, 45, 101, 111-120
Orthodox Church, 14, 63, 98, 100-101, 176-177, 252, 269
Ost und West, 22, 129-130, 263-265, 271
Ostjude, 15, 125, 129, 131
Otto, Rudolf, 119
Ottoman Empire, viii, 55, 63, 85, 143

Pacific, 63, 219
Palestine, 128
Palmer, William, 100
pan-Slavism, 11, 15, 18, 61, 101, 104, 176
Papen, Franz von, 269
Paris, 41, 46, 56, 99, 158, 175, 185, 205, 207, 220, 224, 251, 258
    Paris World Exposition 1937, 224
parliamentarianism, 1, 12, 20, 24, 70, 72-73, 77-78, 85, 87-89, 91, 139, 148, 154-156, 158-161, 163-164, 169, 193, 211-212, 220, 222, 252, 254-255, 257-258, 270, 273
Parsons, Talcott, 20
Penka, Karl, 117
Persia, 113, 117
Peter the Great, 97
Pflanze, Otto, 154
Platen, August Graf von, 10
Plenge, Johann, 210
pluralism, 23-24, 89, 164, 170, 176, 189, 191, 193, 256

Poland, 41–42, 45–50, 61, 102, 104, 139, 142–145, 188, 221
Polenz, Wilhelm von, 60
Polevoï, Nikolaï, 99
political culture, 4–6, 22–24, 69–70, 72, 77, 87–88, 91, 183–185, 189–192, 218, 223, 226
political language, 7–8, 16, 21–22, 43, 51, 187
political science, 89, 157, 183, 191, 230, 237, 239
politicization, 7, 13, 99, 106, 249
Pomerania, 156
Portugal, 144, 272
Posen, 41, 61
Prague, 129–130, 257, 273
Preuß, Hugo, 75, 154
Preuves, 90
progress, viii, 3, 7–13, 15–16, 21–22, 24, 43, 45, 76, 82–86, 88, 102–103, 115, 139–143, 146–148, 154, 163, 168, 175, 179, 192–193, 219, 236, 249, 251, 255, 265, 277, 279, 289
Protestantism, 14, 20, 25, 48, 77, 82, 114, 141, 144, 155, 168, 174, 203
Provence, 47
Prussia, viii, 12–13, 41, 50, 60–61, 72, 77–78, 98, 100, 104, 113–115, 139–140, 143, 145–147, 152–158, 161, 163–164, 202, 204, 211
Prussian Council of State (*Staatsrat*), 152, 156
Prussian *Landtag*, 152, 156

racism, race, racialization (see also Social Darwinism), 6, 14–16, 19, 21, 278–279
Ranke, Leopold von, 174, 191
Rathenau, Walther, 207
Redlich, Josef, 154–155
Reichstag, 152, 224, 251
Reims, 83
Rembrandt/Rembrandt Harmenszoon van Rijn, 206
remigration, rémigrés, 22–23, 81, 183, 192
revolution, viii, 6, 9–11, 13, 18, 21, 62, 65, 85, 87–88, 103, 105, 118, 147–148, 153, 157–158, 168, 172, 178, 184, 187, 202–204, 208, 225, 235, 238, 240, 249, 251–252, 257, 273, 288
　1789 (French Revolution), 11, 13, 48, 125, 153, 174, 202, 206, 210, 217, 235, 237, 251, 258, 268
　1830, 10, 12, 139
　1848/49, 13, 61, 82, 100, 139–141, 156
　1917 (Russian Revolution), 62, 177, 179, 255, 268
　1933, 87, 218, 264
　1989, 24, 44, 91, 278, 288–289

Rhineland, 12, 91, 139–140, 145–147, 177, 185
Rhode Island, 268
Ricardo, David, 251
Richter, Hans Werner, 263–273
Riehl, Wilhelm Heinrich, 205
Riesman, David, 236–237
Riess, Curt, 280
Riga, 45
Rohan, Karl Anton Prinz, 172
Rohrbach, Paul, 65
Rohrer, Joseph, 48
Roman Empire, 11, 13–16, 23, 49–50, 58, 62, 73, 102–103, 106, 112–116, 153, 173–178, 205
Romania, 127
romanticism, 10, 58, 72, 97–99, 104, 106, 111–114, 120, 179, 187, 193, 202, 251
Rome, 46, 56, 175, 178
Roosevelt, Franklin Delano, 187, 223–224, 268
Röpke, Wilhelm, 235–236
Rosenberg, Alfred, 220
Rousseau, Jean-Jacques, 48, 171, 191
Rückert, Friedrich, 113
Rückert, Heinrich, 101
Ruf, Der, 22, 263–264, 266, 268, 271–272
Ruge, Arnold, 12
Rühe, Volker, 25
rule of law, 1, 8, 12, 17, 25, 146, 264
Russia, viii, 5, 8–15, 17–19, 41, 45–46, 48–50, 55–56, 61–63, 65, 76, 85, 97–106, 116, 127, 141, 143, 145–146, 148, 168, 170, 175–177, 179, 220, 232, 249, 253, 255, 258, 265, 268, 277
Russophobia, 5, 12, 101
Rzewuski, Baron, 113

Said, Edward, 6, 45
Saint Petersburg, 46, 48, 56, 62, 104
Saint-Simon, Henri de, 177
Salazar, António de Oliveira, 272
Salm-Reifferscheid-Dyck, Prince Joseph of, 140
Salomon, Albert, 233, 236
Sanskrit, 111–113, 115, 117
Sardinia, viii
Sattelzeit (saddle period), 7, 11, 25, 41–44, 46–47, 49, 51
Saxony, 49, 141
Scandinavia, 48, 50, 65, 87
Scheler, Max, 168, 170, 174, 176–178
Schelling, Friedrich Wilhelm Joseph, 101, 202
Schelsky, Helmut, 236, 238
Schiemann, Theodor, 62, 65

Schiller, Friedrich von, 204
Schlegel, August Wilhelm von, 117, 120
Schlegel, Friedrich von, 13, 112, 114, 117, 203
Schlesinger, Georg, 59
Schlözer, August Ludwig, 42
Schmitt, Carl, 191-193, 210, 225, 234-235, 237
    Schmitt school, 235, 237
Schnabel, Franz, 240
Schoeps, Hans-Joachim, 233, 235
Scholz, August, 104
Schopenhauer, Arthur, 118
Schrenck-Notzing, Caspar von, 240
Schumacher, Kurt, 257
Schwan, Alexander, 2
Seckel, Emil, 154
self-government, 58, 74, 155, 158-163, 233
Sering, Max, 77
Seume, Johann Gottfried, 48
Siberia, 63
Siebenpfeiffer, Philipp Jakob, 143-144
Silesia, 41
Simmel, Georg, 170, 174, 178
Simplicissimus, 61
Singapore, 222
Skobelev, General Mikhail, 104
Slavic, Slavs, 11, 13-16, 50, 61-63, 99, 101-103, 105, 141, 143, 176, 189, 210, 249
    Slavic world, 13, 189
Smith, Adam, 251
Smith, Munroe, 155, 157
Snowden, Philip, 254
social Darwinism, 16, 21, 217, 222
social democracy, 21, 59, 64, 74, 87, 90, 105, 156, 249-259, 262, 268, 270
    Social Democratic Party of Germany (*Sozialdemokratische Partei Deutschlands*, SPD), 89-90, 249, 253-254, 257, 259, 273
socialism, 4, 22-24, 62, 72-73, 78, 87-88, 90, 171, 177-178, 183, 211-212, 223-224, 233, 236, 251-259, 262-266, 268-273, 277-282, 284-286, 288
    Socialist Unity Party of Germany (*Sozialistische Einheitspartei Deutschlands*, SED), 277-288
society, 23-24, 58, 62, 72-73, 85, 87-90, 112, 116, 125-130, 133, 146, 157-161, 163-164, 171, 179, 183, 193, 202, 209-212, 218, 232, 235-239, 255, 262, 278-279
Söllner, Alfons, 184
Solov'ev, Sergeĭ, 102
Solov'ev, Vladimir, 101
Sombart, Werner, 60, 209, 218

Sonderweg (special path), 1-2, 4, 24, 85, 190, 193-194
Sontheimer, Kurt, 2, 190-191, 236
Southern Tyrol, 221
Soviet Union/U.S.S.R., 3, 5, 22, 81, 87, 91, 177-178, 188, 216, 220-221, 224-225, 235, 239, 254-256, 264-266, 270-271, 277-280, 284-286
space, 1, 4, 7-11, 18-19, 21, 23, 42-49, 51, 56, 65, 97-99, 101, 106, 115, 141, 174, 184, 188, 191, 194, 206, 217, 221, 224, 250, 257
    spatial turn, 7, 44
    spatialization, 8, 184, 194
Spain, 49, 144, 227, 267, 272
Spann, Othmar, 172
Spazier, Richard Otto, 41-43, 47, 49, 50
Spencer, Herbert, 177
Spengler, Oswald, 21, 58, 119, 210-211
Staatslehre, 230
Stael, Madame de, 98
Stalin, Joseph, 81, 268, 285-286
Stampfer, Friedrich, 256
Stedmann, Karl, 147
Steffen, Gustav, 74
Steinmetz, Willibald, 7
Stern, Fritz, 217
Strauss, David Friedrich, 114
student activism/1968, 24, 193-194, 239, 273
Südekum, Albert, 253
Suhr, Otto, 185
Suhr, Susanne, 185
Sweden, 49, 74
Switzerland, 46, 49, 233, 272
Sybel, Heinrich von, 146

Tacitus, 45, 48-49
Tagore, Rabindranath, 119
Taylor, A.J.P., 238
Taylor, Frederick W., 59
    Taylorism, 59
technology, 58-59, 82, 84, 86, 118, 126, 204, 207, 224, 236, 265, 285
Tempo Presente, 90
temporalization, 7, 9, 11-12, 17, 249
Thadden, Rudolf von, 240
Ticino, 272
TimeSpace, 7, 11
Times, The, 152
Tiutchev, Fëdor, 100-101
Tocqueville, Alexis de, 9, 23, 74, 230-240
Tönnies, Ferdinand, 169, 207
totalitarianism, 24, 142, 189, 194, 233, 256-257, 264-265, 278
Toynbee, Arnold, 3

transnationalism, ix, 6, 19, 23, 56, 153, 192-193
travel, 1, 9-10, 41-50, 63, 87, 99, 119, 145, 157, 178, 208, 222, 224, 226, 251, 283, 285
    travelogues, 10, 42, 45, 47-48, 50
Treaty of Versailles, 20, 81, 167
Treitschke, Heinrich von, 57, 72
Trier, 177
Troeltsch, Ernst, 23, 77, 168, 170-171, 173-174, 178-179, 187, 218
Trotsky, Leon, 268
Truman, Harry S., 268, 279
Tübingen, 5, 184
Turfan, 118
Turgenev, Aleksandr, 98
Turkey, 63, 103, 143

Ulbricht, Walter, 272, 285, 287
United States of America, viii, 1, 3, 5-6, 8-14, 16-17, 19, 21-24, 48, 55, 58-60, 63, 65, 71, 73-77, 81-82, 84-91, 115, 126, 142, 154-155, 164, 167-169, 171-172, 177-179, 184-187, 189-190, 192-193, 201-203, 206-208, 211-212, 216-217, 219-227, 231-237, 239, 241, 250, 252-253, 255-259, 262-271, 278-279, 281, 283, 287
    African-American, 219, 278
    American Revolution, 13, 48, 217
    American War of Independence, 225
    Americanism, 60, 86-87, 193, 216, 223
    Anglo-American, 6, 60, 86-87, 90-91, 188-190, 221-222, 231, 282
    Anti-Americanism, 60, 186, 190, 216, 219, 231, 235
    British-American, 221-222
    European-American, 81, 187, 233
University of Berlin, now Humboldt University, 72, 152, 156
University of Heidelberg, Institute for Social and Legal Sciences, 168
University of Leuven, 83
Usedom, 268

Veblen, Thorstein, 85, 88
Veenis, Milena, 280
Verein für Socialpolitik, 152
Vestnik Evropy, 103
Victoria, Queen, 163, 285
Vienna, 15, 49, 56, 113, 141
Villiers, Brougham, 74
Vogel, Hans, 257
Völkisch, 88-89, 130, 132, 208
Volksgemeinschaft, 4, 212, 218
Volksstaat, 4, 75

Vormärz, 12-13, 41, 141-142, 148, 154
Voss, Johann, 114
Vossler, Otto, 239

Wagner, Adolf, 57
Wagner, Richard, 205-206, 208
Waldersee, General Alfred von, 63
Warburg, Otto, 128
Warsaw, 42, 45-46, 48
Washington, D.C., 81, 88, 185
Weber, Alfred, 168, 175, 177-178, 218
Weber, Max, 2, 20, 56, 65, 78-79, 168
Weber, Werner, 192
Weimar Republic, 20-21, 23, 72, 87, 119, 132, 167-168, 170, 174, 183, 189-190, 194, 201, 211-212, 216-218, 254, 267-268, 270
Welcker, Carl, 154
welfare state, 72, 77, 235-236, 238
Welt, Die, 127
Weltreichslehre, 16
Weltsch, Robert, 130, 133
Westbindung, 22
Westermanns illustrierte deutsche Monatshefte, 104
Western
    civilization, 3-6, 16, 25, 84-85, 169, 173, 178, 209, 211
    democracy, 4, 17, 20, 23-24, 69, 73, 75-78, 183-184, 186-193, 216, 218, 220, 222-223, 232, 240, 256-258
    hemisphere, 184, 189
    world, 25, 55, 103, 115, 189, 211, 217
Westernization, 5-6, 8, 10, 17, 22-24, 81-82, 85, 89, 104, 106, 126, 183-184, 193, 259, 279, 283
Westphalia, 269
Weyl, Walter E., 74
Whalen, Hugh, 155
Widmann, Christian Adolf Friedrich, 13
Wierling, Dorothee, 282
Wilhelm II (see also Germany, Imperial Germany, Wilhelmine Germany), 84
Wilson, Woodrow, 21, 75-76, 85-86, 168, 171-173, 209, 225
Winckelmann, Johann, 114
Winkler, Heinrich August, 2-3, 183, 194, 217
Winz, Leo, 129
Wirsing, Giselher, 172
Wirth, Joseph, 269
Wolff, Larry, 43-45
working class, 88, 159, 162, 211, 250-251
World War
    First World War, 4-5, 16-22, 56, 58, 61-62, 69, 71, 74-75, 81-88, 91, 98, 105, 111, 118-120, 131, 167, 170,

172, 176, 178, 185, 201–202, 204, 209–212, 216, 218–223, 226–227, 253, 267
Second World War, 4, 15, 21, 87, 118, 188, 217–218, 220, 222–225, 259, 267
Wupper valley, 146

Zbinden, Hans, 235
Zedler, Johann Heinrich, 46
Zehrer, Hans, 172
Zetkin, Clara, 253
Zhdanov, Andrei, 279
Ziegler, Leopold, 204
Zionism, 124–125, 127–133